ARBITRATION CONCERNING THE SOUTH CHINA SEA

Contemporary Issues in the South China Sea

Series Editors: Shicun Wu, National Institute for South China Sea Studies, China; Keyuan Zou, University of Central Lancashire, UK

The South China Sea involves a wide array of complex issues covering sovereignty over islands and reefs, maritime delimitation, maritime security, cooperation against piracy and terrorism, resource development and environmental protection, all of which require extensive research. The area's importance largely results from one-third of the world's shipping transiting through its waters and that it is believed to hold huge oil and gas reserves beneath its seabed. Several countries have made competing territorial claims over the South China Sea with such disputes being regarded as Asia's most potentially dangerous source of conflict. This series seeks to provide thoughtful consideration of these issues from a variety of interdisciplinary perspectives. It provides an opportunity for early career researchers as well as established scholars to publish theoretically informed monographs and edited volumes that engage with key issues in this region.

Also in the series

UN Convention on the Law of the Sea and the South China Sea
Edited by Shicun Wu, Mark Valencia and Nong Hong

Non-Traditional Security Issues and the South China Sea
Shaping a New Framework for Cooperation
Edited by Shicun Wu and Keyuan Zou

Major Law and Policy Issues in the South China Sea
European and American Perspectives
Edited by Yann-huei Song and Keyuan Zou

Arbitration Concerning the South China Sea

Philippines versus China

EDITED BY

SHICUN WU

National Institute for the South China Sea Studies, China

AND

KEYUAN ZOU

Lancashire Law School of the University of Central Lancashire (UCLan), UK

Routledge
Taylor & Francis Group
LONDON AND NEW YORK

First published 2016 by Ashgate Publishing

Published 2016 by Routledge
2 Park Square, Milton Park, Abingdon, Oxon OX14 4RN
711 Third Avenue, New York, NY 10017, USA

First issued in paperback 2017

Routledge is an imprint of the Taylor & Francis Group, an informa business

British Library Cataloguing in Publication Data
A catalogue record for this book is available from the British Library

The Library of Congress has cataloged the printed edition as follows:

Wu, Shicun, editor / Zou, Keyuan, editor.
Arbitration concerning the South China Sea: Philippines versus China / edited by Shicun Wu and Keyuan Zou.
pages cm. – Contemporary issues in the south china sea
Includes bibliographical references and index.
ISBN 9781472459602 (hardback)
1. South China Sea–International status. 2. Arbitration (International law)
3. Maritime boundaries–China. 4. Maritime boundaries–Philippines.
5. Pacific settlement of international disputes. 6. China–Foreign relations–Philippines.
7. Philippines–Foreign relations–China.

KZA1692.A73 2016
341.4'480916472–dc23

ISBN 13: 978-1-138-30919-7 (pbk)
ISBN 13: 978-1-4724-5960-2 (hbk)

Contents

List of Editors and Contributors

Editors:

Shicun Wu, PhD in History, is President of the National Institute for South China Sea Studies, and Deputy Director of the National Collaborative Center of South China Sea Studies, Nanjing University. Dr Wu's research interests cover the history and geography of the South China Sea, maritime delimitation, maritime economy, international relations and regional security strategy. His main single-authored books include *Solving Disputes for Regional Cooperation and Development in the South China Sea: A Chinese perspective* (Cambridge: Woodhead Publishing, 2013), *A Study on the South China Sea Disputes* (Hainan: Hainan Publishing House, 2005) and *The Origin and Development of the Nansha Disputes* (Brighton: Ocean Press, 1999). His main edited books include: *Recent Developments in the South China Sea Dispute: The Prospect of a Joint Development Regime* (Abingdon: Routledge, 2014), *Securing the Safety of Navigation in East Asia: Legal and Political Dimensions* (Cambridge: Woodhead Publishing, 2013), *Maritime Security in the South China Sea* (Farnham: Ashgate, 2009), *Selective Studies on World Famous Island Economic Bodies* (Beijing: World Knowledge, 2006) and *Collection of Documents Relating to South China Sea Issues* (Hainan: Hainan Publishing House, 2001). Dr Wu has published widely in academic journals and been the subject of frequent media interviews as a senior commentator on South China Sea issues.

Keyuan Zou is Harris Professor of International Law at the Lancashire Law School of the University of Central Lancashire (UCLan), United Kingdom. He specializes in international law, in particular law of the sea and international environmental law. Before joining UCLan, he worked in Dalhousie University (Canada), Peking University (China), University of Hannover (Germany) and National University of Singapore. He has published over 60 refereed English papers in 30 international refereed journals. His recent books include *China-ASEAN Relations and International Law* (single-authored, 2009), *International Law in East Asia* (co-eds, 2011), *Securing the Safety of Navigation in East Asia* (co-eds, 2013), *Major Law and Policy Issues in the South China Sea* (co-eds, 2014) and *Non-Traditional Security Issues and the South China Sea* (co- eds, 2014). He is member of Editorial Boards of the *International Journal of Marine and Coastal Law*, *Ocean Development and International Law*, *Journal of International Wildlife Law and Policy*, *Copenhagen Journal of Asian Studies*, *Journal of Territorial and Maritime Studies*, and *Chinese Journal of International Law*, as well as member of the Advisory Board of the *Global Journal of Comparative Law*, *Korean Journal of Comparative and International Law* and *China Oceans Law Review*.

Assistant Editor:

Nong Hong is Director of the Research Center for Oceans Law and Policy at the National Institute for South China Sea Studies (NISCSS). Dr Hong received her PhD in international law and international relations from the University of Alberta, Canada and held a Postdoctoral Fellowship in its China Institute. She was ITLOS-Nippon Fellow for International Dispute Settlement (2008–2009), and Visiting Fellow at the Center of Oceans Law and Policy, University of Virginia (2009) and at the Max Planck Institute for Comparative Public Law and International Law (2007). She is also a research fellow with China Institute, University of Alberta. Her research takes an interdisciplinary approach to examining international relations and international law, with focus on International Relations and Comparative Politics in general; ocean governance in East Asia; law of the sea; international security, particularly non-traditional security; and international dispute settlement and conflict resolution. Her most recent publications include *UNCLOS and Ocean Dispute Settlement: Law and Politics in the South China Sea* (Abingdon and New York: Routledge, 2012); *Recent Developments in the South China Sea Dispute*, co-edited with Wu Shicun (Abingdon and New York: Routledge, 2014); *Maritime Security Issues in the South China Sea and the Arctic: Sharpened Competition or Collaboration?*, co-edited with Gordon Houlden (Beijing: China Democracy and Legal System Publishing House, 2012); "Beyond oil and gas: alternative fields and models of joint management", in Wu Shicun and Nong Hong (eds), *Recent Developments in the South China Sea Dispute: the Prospect of a Joint Development Regime* (London and New York: Ashgate, 2014), pp. 241–56; Nong Hong, "China's Newly Formed Coast Guard and its Implication for Regional Maritime Disputes", *Ocean Yearbook*, Vol. 28, (2013), pp. 611–30; 'The Energy Factor in the Arctic Dispute: a Pathway to Conflict or Cooperation?' in the *Journal of World Energy Law & Business* (Oxford: Oxford Journal, January 2012).

Contributors:

Sam Bateman retired from the RAN as a Commodore and is now a Professorial Research Fellow at the Australian National Centre for Ocean Resources and Security (ANCORS) at the University of Wollongong in Australia, and an Adviser to the Maritime Security Programme at the S. Rajaratnam School of International Studies (RSIS) at the Nanyang Technological University in Singapore. His naval service included four ship commands ranging from a patrol boat to guided-missile destroyer. He has written extensively on defence and maritime issues in Australia, the Asia-Pacific and Indian Ocean, and was awarded his PhD from the University of NSW in 2001 for a dissertation on "The Strategic and Political Aspects of the Law of the Sea in East Asian Seas". He is widely recognized as a regional maritime security expert and regularly provides comments for Australian and international media. His current research interests include regional maritime security, piracy and maritime terrorism, oceans policy, the strategic and political implications of the Law of the Sea, and maritime cooperation and confidence-building. Recent co-authored publications include several reports for the Australian Strategic Policy Institute (ASPI): 'Staying the Course: Australia and Maritime Security in the South Pacific' (2011), 'Calming troubled waters – Global and regional strategies for countering piracy' (2012), and 'Terms of engagement – Australia's regional defence diplomacy' (2013), as well as the Policy Paper ASEAN and the Indian Ocean (2011) for RSIS. Recent co-edited publications include *Maritime Challenges and Priorities in Asia – Implications for regional security* (Abingdon: Routledge, 2012), and *Southeast Asia and the Rise of Chinese and Indian Naval Power: Between rising naval powers* (Abingdon: Routledge, 2010).

Robert Beckman heads the ocean law and policy programme as well as being Director of the Centre for International Law, a university-wide research centre at the National University of Singapore (NUS) which was established in 2009. Professor Beckman is also an Associate Professor at the NUS Faculty of Law, where he has taught for more than 35 years. He currently teaches Ocean Law & Policy in Asia and International Regulation of Shipping. Professor Beckman lectures in the summer programme at the Rhodes Academy of Oceans Law & Policy in Rhodes, Greece. He is an expert on the issues of law of the sea in Southeast Asia, including piracy, maritime security, the South China Sea and the Straits of Malacca and Singapore. His latest publications include: "The UN Convention on the Law of the Sea and the Maritime Disputes in the South China Sea", *American Journal of International Law*, Vol. 107, (2013), pp. 142–63; Robert C. Beckman and Clive H. Schofield, "Defining EEZ Claims from Islands: A Potential South China Sea Change", *The International Journal of Marine and Coastal Law*, Vol. 29, (2014), pp. 193–243.

Leonardo Bernard is a research fellow at the Centre for International Law, National University of Singapore (NUS), Singapore. Leo completed his LLB at the University of Indonesia and his LLM on International and Comparative Law at NUS. He also has a diploma from the Rhodes Academy of Ocean Law and Policy which he completed in July 2011 and from the International Foundation of the Law of the Sea Summer Academy which he completed in August 2012. His research interests include law of the sea, ASEAN, dispute resolution, South China Sea, maritime boundaries disputes and general public international law.

Anthony Carty is the Sir Y.K. Pao Chair of Public Law at Hong Kong University since 2009. His specialism is international law, with a particular interest in history. He has published extensively on the use of national archival sources as evidence of state practice in international law. In particular with Richard Smith he co-authored

Sir Gerald Fitzmaurice and the World Crisis, A Legal Adviser in the Foreign Office 1932–1945, published with Kluwer Law International in 2000. He has published further articles about the significance of archives for international law questions, such as "The Practice of International Law" in *Handbook of International Law*, edited by David Armstrong (Abingdon: Routledge, 2009), pp. 81–100; "Distance and Contemporaneity in Exploring the Practice of States: The British Archives in Relation to the 1957 Oman and Muscat Incident", in *Time, History and International Law*, edited by Mathew Craven, Malgosia Fitzmaurice, Maria Vogiatzi, and M. Nijhoff (Leiden: Brill, 2007), pp. 231–45; "The Corfu Channel Case and the Missing Admiralty Orders", *The Law and Practice of International Courts and Tribunals*, Vol. 3 (2004), pp. 1–35; "The Japanese Seizure of Korea from the Perspective of the United Kingdom National Archive, 1904–1910", in *Asian Yearbook of International Law*, Vol. 10:1 (2002/2003). Forthcoming is a major study of the place of unequal treaties in international law, a comparative study of Irish and Chinese experience of the British Empire: A. Carty and X. Zhang, "Unequal to Equal Treaty: Between the Anglo-Irish Treaty 1921 and the Belfast Agreement (Good Friday Agreement) 1998 – a Chinese Perspective", accepted for publication in the *Irish Yearbook of International Law*, Vol. 7 (2013). A theoretical exposition of the place of archives within the sources of international law is presented in "Doctrine versus State Practice in International Law" in *Oxford Handbook of the History of International Law*, edited by A. Peters and B. Fassbender, (Oxford: Oxford University Press, 2012), pp. 972–96. Carty was awarded a 2 million HK$ Research Grant by the Hong Kong RGC in 2012 to research "The Role of International Law in the Collapse of the Qing Dynasty and Its Consequences for Today".

Michael Sheng-ti Gau has degrees of LLB (Taiwan University), LLM (Cambridge), LLM (London), and PhD (Leiden), all specialized in public international law. He teaches at the Institute of Law of the Sea in Taiwan Ocean University. Professor Gau has been legal advisor for and commissioned by Ministry of the Interior, Fishery Agency of Council of Agriculture, Ministry of Economics, Ministry of Health, and Ministry of Foreign Affairs on numerous research projects on law of the sea legal issues, negotiations in Regional Fisheries Management Organizations like ICCAT, SPRFMO and WCPFC, as well as WTO fishery subsidies negotiations, and Taiwan's participation in IGOs like ICAO, OIE, WHO, etc. For the past six years, Professor Gau has been focusing on outer continental shelf, CLCS and the South China Sea legal issues, with publications of quite a few articles in *Ocean Development and International Law*, *Chinese Journal of International Law*, *Journal of East Asia and International Law*, etc. Professor Gau is Administrator for the Taiwan Regional Round of the Philip C. Jessup International Law Moot Court Competition since 2000.

Jiang Li is an LLM candidate in international law at the Guanghua Law School of Zhejiang University, China. He earned his LLB at Harbin Institute of Technology.

Xinchang Liu is a PhD candidate in the international law of the sea at the Guanghua Law School of Zhejiang University, China. She obtained her LLB from the East China University of Political Science and Law in 2012; and a visiting scholar at the University of Iowa, United States, 2014–2015. Her main research interests are in the South China Sea and Antarctic environmental protection.

Ted McDorman is a Professor in the Faculty of Law at the University of Victoria in Victoria, British Columbia, Canada. Before joining the University of Victoria in 1985, Professor McDorman was at Dalhousie University in Halifax, Nova Scotia with the Dalhousie Oceans Studies Programme (DOSP). For almost 20 years (1984–2002), Professor McDorman was involved with the Southeast Asian Ocean Law, Policy and Management Programme (SEAPOL) centered in Bangkok, Thailand and through this project had the opportunity to study and write about numerous Southeast Asian ocean law and policy issues. From 2002–2004 and again from 2011–2013, Professor McDorman was "academic-in-residence" in the Legal Affairs Branch of the Canadian Department of Foreign Affairs and International Trade where he was involved in a number of Arctic, law of the sea and environmental matters and represented Canada at several international forums. Professor McDorman has over 120 publications in the areas of ocean law and policy, international trade law and comparative constitutional law. Since 2000, he has been the editor-in-chief of *Ocean Development and International Law*.

Donald R. Rothwell is Professor of International Law, and Deputy Dean at the ANU College of Law, Australian National University where he has taught since July 2006. His research has a specific focus on law of the sea, law of the polar regions, and implementation of international law within Australia as reflected in over 180 articles, book chapters and notes in international and Australian publications. Rothwell has authored, co-authored or edited 19 books including most recently Erik J. Molenaar, Alex G. Oude Elferink, and Donald R. Rothwell (eds), *The Law of the Sea and the Polar Regions: Interactions between Global and Regional Regimes* (Leiden: MartinusNijhoff, 2013), and *Law of the Sea* (Cheltenham: Edward Elgar, 2013). Major career works include *The International Law of the Sea* (Oxford: Hart, 2010) with Tim Stephens, and *The Polar Regions and the Development of International Law* (Cambridge: Cambridge University Press, 1996). Rothwell is also coordinating editor of the *Oxford Handbook on the Law of the Sea* (forthcoming, 2015) and co-editor of the *Australian Year Book of International Law*. Since 2012 he has been Rapporteur of the International Law Association (ILA) Committee on 'Baselines under the International Law of the Sea'. He has taught a range of courses including Law of the Sea, International Dispute Resolution, International Law and Use of Armed Force, International Humanitarian Law, Military Operations Law, and Public International Law. Rothwell was previously Challis Professor of International Law and Director of the Sydney Centre for International and Global Law, University of Sydney (2004–2006), where he had taught since 1988. He has acted as a consultant or been a member of expert groups for UNEP, UNDP, IUCN, the Australian Government, and acted as advisor to the International Fund for Animal Welfare (IFAW). In 2012 Rothwell was appointed an inaugural ANU Public Policy Fellow. He is a regular media commentator on international law issues and has written over 90 opinion comments, including for all of the major daily newspapers in Australia and ABC Online 'The Drum'. His media interviews have included ABC TV 7.30, ABC Radio 'AM' and 'PM', ABC Radio National 'Breakfast', ABC News 24, Al Jazerra (TV), BBC World (TV), and the Voice of America.

Yann-huei Song is currently a research fellow at the Institute of European and American Studies, Academia Sinica, Taipei, Taiwan. He is also an adjunct professor at the Institute of the Law of the Sea, National Taiwan Ocean University and the Institute of Marine Affairs, National Sun Yat-sen University in Taiwan.Professor Song received his PhD in International Relations from Kent State University, Ohio; LLM and JSD from the School of Law (Boalt Hall), University of California, Berkeley, the United States. He has broad academic interests covering ocean law and policy studies, international fisheries law, international environmental law, maritime security, and sovereignty and maritime disputes in the East and South China Seas. He has been actively participating in the Informal Workshop on Managing Potential Conflicts in the South China Sea (the SCS Workshop) that is organized by the government of the Republic of Indonesia. Professor Song is a member of the editorial boards of *Ocean Development and International Law* and *Chinese (Taiwan) Yearbook of International Law and Affairs*. He has frequently been asked to provide advisory opinions by a number of government agencies in Taiwan on the policy issues related to the East and South China Seas and the international law of the sea.

Kuan-Hsiung Wang obtained his PhD degree in International Law from University of Bristol, United Kingdom in 1997. He is a Professor at the Graduate Institute of Political Science, Taiwan Normal University and is also an adjunct professor of international law at Chinese Culture University. Dr Wang studies marine issues concerning the international law of the sea. From 2000 to 2008, he severed as Deputy Secretary-General of the Chinese Society of International Law. Currently, he is one of the members of the board of directors of the Chinese Society of International Law as well as the Institute of Marine Affairs and Policy. He is a member of the Committee on International Law on Sustainable Development (2004–2012), Committee on the Role of International Law in Sustainable Natural Resource Management for Development (2012–present), International Law Association in London. In the field of academic services, Dr Wang also serves as the editor of *Chinese (Taiwan) Yearbook of International Law and Affairs* (English version), *Chinese (Taiwan) Review of International and Transnational Law* (Chinese version), and the *Korean Journal of International and Comparative Law*. Being a teacher of international law and international relations, Dr Wang's teaching and research fields are mainly on public international law, law of the sea,

South China Sea issues, and marine policy. He won the 2007 Canadian Studies Scholarship and accordingly he paid a research visit to Dalhousie University in the summer of 2007. Dr Wang publishes his research work in reputable academic journals, such as *Ocean Development and International Law*, and *Pacific Review*. In 2002, he published a book under the title *Disputes in the South China Sea and Fisheries Joint Cooperation* (in Chinese), which touches upon the issues of maritime disputes and joint development.

Qiang Ye is Assistant Research Fellow at the National Institute for South China Sea Studies (NISCSS), China. He joined the NISCSS in 2013. He received LLB degree from Capital University of Economics and Business (CUEB) in 2008 and a Master of Law degree from Tsinghua University in 2013. His research interests focus on: 1) international disputes settlement, inter alia, boundary and maritime disputes settlement; 2) international adjudication and arbitration; and 3) legal thought and philosophy. His most recent publications include "On the Legal Basis of the Advisory Jurisdiction of ITLOS as a Full Court", *Peking University International and Comparative Law Review*, Vol. 10 (2013), pp. 81–112; "A Study on the Advisory Proceedings before the ITLOS as a Full Court", *China Oceans Law Review*, No. 1 (2014), pp. 1–58; and "China's 'Nine-Dash Line' Claim: US Misunderstands", *RSIS Commentary*, CO15011, 14 January 2015 (co-authored).

Jun Zhao is a Professor at Guanghua Law School, Zhejiang University. He currently serves as the head of the Research Institute of International law, Zhejiang University. He earned his JD at Cornell Law School, LLM at Harvard Law School, and LLB at Zhejiang University. Before joining Guanghua Law School, he was a visiting scholar at Harvard Law School, East Asian Legal Studies. He also worked as a lawyer at Mintz Levin Cohn Ferris Glovsky and Popeo P.C. and Kirkland & Ellis International LLP. He has published widely on international law and comparative law in top academic journals. He is a Director of the Chinese Society of International Law. He also serves as an Executive Director of International Law Section, Law Society of Zhejiang Province.

PART I
Introduction

Chapter 1
Philippines v. China Arbitration Case Concerning the South China Sea: An Introduction

Shicun Wu and Keyuan Zou

Introduction

On 22 January 2013, the Republic of the Philippines instituted arbitral proceedings against the People's Republic of China (PRC) under the United Nations Convention on the Law of the Sea (UNCLOS) with regard to disputes between the two countries in the South China Sea (South China Sea Arbitration). On 19 February 2013, the PRC officially refused to participate in the arbitration. One of the reasons for this refusal is that, according to China, its 2006 Declaration[1] covers the disputes brought by the Philippines and that this case concerns the sovereignty issue, thus preventing the Arbitral Tribunal from asserting its jurisdiction over the case. The Philippines argued otherwise and applied the default rules under Annex VII of the UNCLOS to establish the Arbitral Tribunal. On 25 June 2013, the fifth arbitrator was appointed and the Arbitral Tribunal thus established for the case (the Tribunal).

On 30 March 2014, the Philippines officially presented its Memorial to the Tribunal according to the Rule of Procedure. On 30 March 2014, in response to the submission of the Memorial by the Philippines to the Arbitral Tribunal, Chinese Foreign Ministry spokesman Hong Lei reiterated China's position at a regular press conference that "China does not accept the Philippines' submission of disputes with China in the South China Sea for international arbitration" and urged the Philippines "to comprehensively and effectively implement the consensus repeatedly reaffirmed between the two sides and the DOC, and return to the right track of settling the disputes through bilateral negotiations".[2] On 21 May 2014, China sent a *Note verbale* to the Permanent Court of Arbitration, in

1 For the text of the Chinese Declaration, see <http://www.un.org/Depts/los/convention_agreements/convention_declarations.htm#China after ratification>.

2 Remarks by Foreign Ministry Spokesperson Hong Lei on the Philippines' Submission of a Memorial to the Arbitral Tribunal in Relation to Disputes with China in the South China Sea, Foreign Affairs, 31 March 2014, available at <http://www.fmprc.gov.cn/mfa_eng/xwfw_665399/s2510_665401/2535_665405/t1142356.shtml>.

which it reiterated China's position that it "does not accept the arbitration initiated by the Philippines" and this Note "shall not be regarded as China's acceptance of or participation in the proceedings".[3]

In its Procedural Order No. 2, the Arbitral Tribunal fixed 15 December 2014 as the date for China to submit its Counter-Memorial in response to the Philippines' Memorial. But since China will not participate, there is no need for China to submit a so-called Counter-Memorial. However, China issued a "Position Paper of the Government of the People's Republic of China on the Matter of Jurisdiction in the South China Sea Arbitration Initiated by the Republic of the Philippines" on 7 December 2014,[4] which elaborates the legal basis of China's position that the Arbitral Tribunal has no jurisdiction over the case, and the reasons why China will not participate in the arbitral proceedings.[5] After the deadline of 15 December 2014 passed by, the Arbitral Tribunal issued Procedural Order No. 3 to request the Philippines to file a supplemental written submission addressing, as it considers appropriate, any public statements made by the Chinese government in relation to the dispute until 15 March 2015, and also to request China to provide any comments in response to the supplemental written submission of the Philippines until 16 June 2015.[6] As of the time of writing, the case is still going on.

The South China Sea Arbitration is a landmark case in international law because of the parties involved, the legal questions to be decided and the absence of one of the parties from the arbitral proceedings. It is particularly significant that China, for the first time, be brought to international arbitration concerning maritime entitlement and related legal issues. As revealed in its official statements, the PRC will neither accept nor participate in the arbitration. Nevertheless, despite China's non-appearance, the proceedings of the arbitration can still proceed in accordance with certain rules provided for in the UNCLOS. According to Article 9 of UNCLOS Annex VII, "If one of the parties to the dispute does not appear before the arbitral tribunal or fails to defend its case, the other party may request the tribunal to continue the proceedings and to make its award. Absence of a party or failure of a party to defend its case shall not constitute a bar to the proceedings".[7]

---

3 *Arbitration between the Republic of the Philippines and the People's Republic of China*, Second Press Release, Permanent Court of Arbitration, The Hague, 3 June 2014, available at http://www.pca-cpa.org/showpage.asp?pag_id=1529.

4 "Position Paper of the Government of the People's Republic of China on the Matter of Jurisdiction in the South China Sea Arbitration Initiated by the Republic of the Philippines", available at <http://www.fmprc.gov.cn/mfa_eng/zxxx_662805/t1217147.shtml>.

5 "Remarks by Mr. Xu Hong, Director-General of the Department of Treaty and Law of the Ministry of Foreign Affairs, on the Position Paper of the Government of the People's Republic of China on the Matter of Jurisdiction in the South China Sea Arbitration Initiated by the Republic of the Philippines", available at <http://www.fmprc.gov.cn/mfa_eng/zxxx_662805/t1217150.shtml>. For details, see discussions in Chapter 6 of this book.

6 *Supra* note 3.

7 Text is reprinted in 1833 United Nations Treaty Series 397.

However, the Tribunal, before making its Award, is obligated to satisfy itself not only that it has jurisdiction over the dispute, but also that the claims brought by the Philippines are well-founded in fact and law. Therefore, it is necessary for the Tribunal to look into all the claims and arguments brought forward by the Philippines and all the disputes constituted by the claims in the procedural phases. Meanwhile, the Tribunal also needs to look into all related factors including those from China, though China does not participate in the proceedings.

Structure and Contents

This book brings together chapters contributed from well-known scholars in Asia, Europe and North America, as well as from promising young scholars, addressing the issues arising from the South China Sea Arbitration. It contains five parts, namely: (a) introduction; (b) origins and developments of the South China Sea dispute; (c) dispute resolution procedure, jurisdiction and admissibility; (d) the U-shaped line and geographic features; and (e) law enforcement and regional impact.

In Part II on origins and developments of the South China Sea dispute, there are two chapters. The one contributed by Shicun Wu is from a Chinese perspective and argues that the China–Philippine dispute in the South China Sea is essentially over territorial sovereignty and maritime delimitation. This chapter briefly reviews the history of the China–Philippine territorial dispute over the South China Sea islands, and weaknesses of the Philippines' basis of claims. It also briefly discusses the evolution of China's U-shaped line, and different interpretations of the legal status of the U-shaped line by Chinese scholars. Wu also discusses the different approaches to dispute resolution between China and the Philippines.

Chapter 3 contributed by Anthony Carty points out that the Philippine Memorial invites the criticism that the Arbitration Tribunal is faced with a dispute which is non-justiciable. The chapter reviews in details that evolution of the South China Sea dispute from a historic perspective and demonstrates that the core of the dispute is the different claims to the sovereignty of the geographic features in the South China Sea. Recognizing that international law can have a role to play, Carty argues that the time is not yet appropriate and the issues have not yet been formulated in a sufficiently complex and comprehensive way. He argues that even if there is a law applicable to a dispute and even if a Tribunal has jurisdiction to hear it, it may still be the case that the dispute is not yet ripe for legal resolution.

Part III contains four chapters. Donald Rothwell, in Chapter 8, considers the Article 298 dispute resolution procedures under the UNCLOS, particularly in the context of China's Article 298 Declaration in 2006, and assesses the Annex V conciliation mechanism under the Convention and the track record of conciliation as a means of resolving the law of the sea disputes. Consideration is also given to the exception to conciliation that applies in the case of disputes concerning sovereignty or other rights over continental or insular land territories.

Michael Sheng-ti Gau's chapter on "the Legal Status of Maritime Features in the Sino-Philippine South China Sea Arbitration: Admissibility and Jurisdiction" serves as an informal but professional advice to the Tribunal for reasonably assessing the admissibility and jurisdiction issues underneath the legal arguments of the Philippines as represented by its Memorial with respect to the legal status of the maritime features mentioned. This chapter comes to a conclusion that the submissions of the Philippines in this regard should be considered inadmissible, while the disputes to be constituted by the submissions should be considered beyond the jurisdiction of the Tribunal.

Next is the chapter contributed by Qiang Ye addressing China's Position Paper on the matter of jurisdiction in the South China Sea Arbitration initiated by the Philippines in December 2014. It is China's latest endeavor on the pending arbitration initiated by the Philippines against China's claims and activities in the South China Sea, and becomes China's informal plea that the Arbitral Tribunal does not have jurisdiction over the Philippines v. China Arbitration case. Although the legal status of such an informal plea is not stipulated clearly in the Rules of Procedure adopted for the case, it may be argued that on the basis of the analysis of international judicial and arbitral practice that this kind of diplomatic plea has an equal effect to a Preliminary Objection. Following this reasoning, the Tribunal should bifurcate the proceedings and duly decide on jurisdictional and admissibility issues prior to the ruling on the merits.

Chapter 7 jointly contributed by Jun Zhao and Jiang Li addresses the *Arctic Sunrise* case (The Netherlands v. Russia) and its implications for China. It offers an analysis of the arguments and reasoning in the case and draws attention to a parallel between Russia's behavior in the *Arctic Sunrise* case and the Chinese attitude in the arbitration initiated by the Philippines regarding the South China Sea. After that, in light of the *Arctic Sunrise* case, this chapter probes into China's potential strategy towards the arbitration initiated by the Philippines.

Part IV, with four chapters, touches up some specific issues raised by the Philippines in its Memorial and Statement of Claim such as the U-shaped line (nine-dash line as called by the Philippines) and geographic features in the South China Sea. The first chapter in this part explores the legal implications that would generate from China's U-shaped line. As we know, the U-shaped line in the South China Sea has been challenged in the international community and such a challenge has reached its climax when the Philippines presented China with a Notification and Statement of Claim under Article 287 and Annex VII of the UNCLOS. In its Statement of Claim, the Philippines requests the Annex VII Arbitral Tribunal to adjudge and declare that China's maritime claims based on the U-shaped line are contrary to the LOS Convention and invalid. Against this background, this chapter analyzes the issues concerning the related submissions of the Philippines to see what the consequences would be, to what extent that the line would support China's claims to the South China Sea and whether it generates historic rights in favor of China.

A leading ocean law expert, Ted McDorman, has contributed Chapter 9, which elaborates on historic claims to waters and their intersection with the rights and jurisdiction over resources set out in the UNCLOS. He concludes that there is broad agreement on the elements relevant in evaluating a claim of historic rights to waters and that a state seeking to make such a claim has a significant burden of proof. Moreover, any claim beyond near-shore waters would be exceptional and inconsistent with the history on the law of the sea where, until recently, what existed were narrow bands of national waters along a coast and wide expanses of high seas within which freedoms of high seas were exercised.

The purpose of the chapter contributed by Yann-huei Song is to discuss whether or not the claims made by the Philippines with regard to Scarborough Shoal and the 13 features of the Spratly archipelago, namely, Mischief Reef, Second Thomas Shoal, Subi Reef, Gaven Reef, McKennan Reef, Hughes Reef, Johnson Reef, Cuarteron Reef, Fiery Cross Reef, Itu Aba, Thitu Island, Sin Cowe Island and West York Island, are well founded in fact and law. The chapter provides background on the case filed by the Philippines in January 2013, addresses the commencement of arbitration proceedings, and describes the Chinese response to the Philippines' request for arbitration. Then there is a brief description of geographical facts concerning the 12 features that are specified in the Philippines' Memorial. It discusses the Philippines' claims and arguments relating to the legal status and rights of low-tide elevations (LTEs), rocks, or islands under international law, in particular UNCLOS, and examines law applicable to the claims and arguments made by the Philippines. Finally it explains why the Tribunal should rule that the Philippines' claims are not well founded in fact and law and therefore should be rejected.

Robert Beckman and Leonardo Bernard's chapter addresses the distinctions between islands, rocks and low-tide elevations, as well as reefs, artificial islands, and installations and structures. It argues that under the UNCLOS and general international law the only offshore geographic features that are subject to a claim of sovereignty are those which meet the definition of an island in Article 121 of the UNCLOS. This analysis also sheds light on the issue of who has jurisdiction over low-tide elevations, installations, structures and artificial islands located in the EEZ or on the continental shelf of another coastal state.

The final part – Part V – contains three chapters concerning maritime law enforcement activities in the South China Sea and the potential regional impact of the *Philippines v China* Arbitration case. The first chapter contributed by Dustin Kuan-Hsiung Wang discusses maritime law enforcement concerning fishing activities. The purpose of this chapter is to clarify certain notions on the practices of the UNCLOS, especially when the Philippines initiated the arbitration procedure against China in January 2013. The theoretical background is based on the application of provisional arrangements in UNCLOS Article 74 paragraph 3. States with maritime jurisdiction disputes should seek agreements to reach an equitable solution, but such a solution might not be found easily in many disputed cases where political posturing is diametrically opposed to the spirit of the UNCLOS. In order to resolve the disputes and better utilize resources, a provisional arrangement or a modus vivendi, seems most feasible in the absence of a final resolution.

Also from a legal and political perspective, Nong Hong's chapter discusses and analyzes the complexity of maritime law enforcement in a disputed maritime zone such as in the South China Sea. It argues that the core nature of the claims is actually on law enforcement in a dispute maritime area. Despite the competing claims, the upmost task is to avoid incidents at sea. It seems that there are abundant regulations on the safety of navigation, and the coastal states have also adopted relevant domestic laws and regulations on the safety of navigation. What is missing is confidence building and crisis management, on which the author offers a few recommendations.

One of the claims of the Philippines in the Philippines v. China Arbitration case rests on law enforcement activities at Scarborough Shoal and Second Thomas Shoal. Both China and the Philippines claim sovereignty over these two features. But the Philippines argues that its claims do not involve sovereignty and maritime delimitation, and thus the 2006 Declaration made by China, based on Article 298 of UNCLOS to exclude certain disputes from a third party compulsory settlement mechanism, does not apply. The author, however, argues that, an observation of the history of the bilateral disputes will help the readers have a deeper understanding on the legal merits of the claims, and certainly on the political implication arising therefrom.

The last chapter contributed by Sam Bateman addresses the impact of the Philippines v. China Arbitration case on regional maritime peace and security. Sam Bateman argues that in the short-term and, regardless of whether a traditional or non-traditional view is taken of regional maritime security, the decision by the Philippines to take China to international arbitration over its maritime claims has had a negative impact on regional maritime security. In the long term, should the Philippines succeed in winning some of its case, there may be positive outcomes in terms of clarifying the position with regard to some questions of international law in the South China Sea disputes, but should the Philippines not be successful, nothing will have been achieved.

Prospects and Conclusion

As the Philippines v. China Arbitration case is still pending, we do not know exactly what the result would be. According the Rule of Procedure, the Arbitral Tribunal will determine the further course of the proceedings, including the need for, scope, and scheduling of any other written submissions and hearings, at an appropriate later stage, after seeking the views of the Parties.[8] It is expected that the arbitral hearing will take place soon just after the deadline of 15 June set forth for China's response. It is perceived that without China's participation, the case would close sooner than normal proceedings where two parties are at present.

8 See <http://www.pca-cpa.org/showpage.asp?pag_id=1529>.

One new factor arising in December 2014, in addition to China's Position Paper, is the receipt by the Arbitral Tribunal of the "Statement of the Ministry of Foreign Affairs of Viet Nam for the attention of the Tribunal in the Proceedings between the Republic of the Philippines and the People's Republic of China".[9] As a most vehement claimant to the South China Sea, the Vietnamese Statement has definitely added a new dimension for the Arbitration case and more complexity for the South China Sea disputes as well.

For the purpose of South China Sea studies, the Philippines v. China Arbitration case has provided brand-new ingredients for scholars who are interested in this field to further explore the abyss of the South China Sea disputes and to try to find a solution to the puzzle. Academically, this book serves as a unique intellectual product to be used for continuous studies on the South China Sea issues. Likewise, this book is useful as an enlightening reference for policy and law makers in governments and/or international organizations who are involved in the matters, particularly legal matters, concerning the South China Sea.

Finally, we are obliged to express our gratitude to the contributors to this edited volume. Without their essential contributions, this book project would be a mission impossible. While we acknowledge the efforts made by many of our colleagues, special thanks should go to Dr Nong Hong who coordinated the project with untiring efforts from the very beginning and her contributions are considerable. As an end note, we dedicate this book to our beloved colleagues and friends who care about the South China Sea and have showed continuing interest in the South China Sea studies.

9 See <http://www.pca-cpa.org/showpage.asp?pag_id=1529>.

PART II
Origins and Developments of the South China Sea Disputes

Chapter 2

Competing Claims over the South China Sea Islands and the Way Forward: A Chinese Perspective on the Philippine-China Arbitration Case

Shicun Wu

Introduction

On 22 January 2013, the Philippines initiated arbitral proceedings against China regarding the dispute between the two countries in the South China Sea by presenting the Chinese Embassy in the Philippines a note verbale with Notification and Statement of Claim attached. On 30 March 2014, the Philippines pressed ahead with submitting a memorial to the Permanent Court of Arbitration in The Hague, despite China having rejected its request for the arbitral proceeding from the outset.

China's position towards the Philippines' instituting these arbitral proceedings has been clear and consistent. On 19 February 2013, China formally rejected and returned the Philippines's note verbale together with the Notification and Statement of Claim by a diplomatic note.[1] Although the diplomatic note was not released to the public, China has elaborated and reiterated, via spokesperson and diplomats' statements on various occasions, its positions and reasons for refusing to take part in or accept the arbitration.[2] On 7 December 2014, China's Foreign Ministry released a position paper on the matter of jurisdiction in the South China Sea arbitration, articulating in detail China's legal and political position as well as the legal justification.[3] The position paper elaborated on three main reasons,

1 PCA 'Arbitration between the Philippines and China, Arbitral Tribunal, First Press Release', 27 August 2013, <www.pca-cpa.org> accessed 23 September 2014.

2 See "Documents of the People's Republic of China 1–20", in Stefan Talmon and Bing Bing Jia (eds), *The South China Sea Arbitration: A Chinese Perspective*, Annex I "Selected Documents Relevant to the South China Sea Arbitration" (Portland: Hart Publishing, 2014), pp. 159–75.

3 Ministry of Foreign Affairs of the People's Republic of China "Position Paper of the Government of the People's Republic of China on the Matter of Jurisdiction in the South China Sea Arbitration Initiated by the Republic of the Philippines", 7 December 2014 <http://www.fmprc.gov.cn/mfa_eng/zxxx_662805/t1217147.shtml> accessed 8 December 2014.

concluding that "the Arbitral Tribunal manifestly has no jurisdiction over the present arbitration". The first and foremost reason is that:

> The essence of the subject-matter of the arbitration is the territorial sovereignty over several maritime features in the South China Sea, which is beyond the scope of the Convention and does not concern the interpretation or application of the Convention.[4]

Indeed, although the Philippines did not touch on the territorial issue in the Notification and Statement of Claim, it is impossible to discuss most of its claims without first clarifying Chinese and Philippine sovereignty over the island features in the South China Sea. For example, the majority of the Philippines' claims assume that China has only territorial sovereignty over a few "rocks", such as Chigua Jiao (Johnson Reef), Huayang Jiao (Cuarteron Reef) and Yongshu Jiao (Fiery Cross Reef) in the Nansha Islands (Spratlys),[5] while intentionally ignored the fact that China has claimed sovereignty over the entire Nansha Islands (Spratlys). In order to discuss the territorial claims of the two countries, one must inevitably dig into the history.

An Overview of the South China Sea Dispute

Before focusing on the dispute between China and the Philippines, it is necessary to have an overall understanding of the South China Sea issue. The South China Sea is a semi-enclosed sea, strategically situated as part of several major Sea Lines of Communication (SLOCs) connecting the Pacific and Indian Oceans. It is dotted with numerous island features which fall into four island groups, namely the Nansha Islands (Spratlys) in the far south, the Xisha Islands (Paracels) in the northwest, the Dongsha Islands (Pratas) in northeast, and the Zhongsha Islands (Macclesfield Bank and Scarborough Shoal) to the southeast of Xisha Islands (Paracels). It is blessed with rich fishery resources and is estimated to have several rich hydrocarbon reserves.[6] Under the regime of the exclusive economic zone (EEZ) and the continental shelf of the United Nations Convention on the Law of the Sea (UNCLOS), the individual features in the South China Sea, if qualified as islands, could generate EEZs and continental shelves of their own.

With a number of countries bordering the South China Sea, it is not surprising that a dispute among them would arise of its own accord. Driven by socio-economic and strategic interests, as well as the dynamics between regional and

4 Ibid., para 3.

5 See Republic of the Philippines, Department of Foreign Affairs (DFA), Notification and Statement of Claim, No. 13-0211, 22 January 2013, pp. 12–13, <http://www.dfa.gov.ph/index.php/2013-06-27-21-50-36/unclos/216-sfa-statement-on-the-unclos-arbitral-proceedings-against-china> accessed 22 September 2014.

6 Shicun Wu, *Solving Disputes for Regional Cooperation and Development in the South China Sea: A Chinese Perspective* (Oxford: Chandos Publishing, 2013), pp. 5–8.

extra-regional powers, the dispute has become a complicated and intractable knot. This knot is easier to understand if one divides into three layers. At the core of the knot is the territorial dispute among China (both Chinese mainland and Taiwan), the Philippines, Vietnam, Malaysia and Brunei, the crux of which is the Nansha Islands (Spratlys). Of the five countries, both China and Vietnam claim the entire Nansha Islands (Spratlys), while China has occupied eight features (including Taiping Island controlled by Taiwan) and Vietnam 29 features.[7] The Philippines claims sovereignty over features that were previously claimed by its citizens, the Cloma brothers, in 1956, and has occupied eight of them.[8] Malaysia claims sovereignty over 12 features and has occupied five.[9] Brunei claims sovereignty over the Nantong Jiao (Louisa Reef), but has occupied none.[10] Most of the claimants, including the Philippines, also use national legislation to consolidate their sovereign claims over those island features.[11]

The next layer outside the core is conflicting maritime rights, such as fishing and exploitation of hydrocarbon resources, due to un-delimitated maritime boundary for both EEZ and continental shelf among littoral countries. This layer of conflict also involves Indonesia, plus those five countries mentioned above. It is worth mentioning that Indonesia has just concluded its maritime boundary negotiation with the Philippines in the Celebes Sea, a negotiation which has lasted for decades through twist and turns.[12] China and Vietnam have also started the negotiation on the sea area off the Beibu Gulf (Gulf of Tonkin) after the successful conclusion of a maritime boundary delimitation agreement in the gulf in 2000.[13]

---

7 Shicun Wu, *The Origin and Development of the Nansha Disputes* (南沙争端的由来与发展) (Beijing: Ocean Press, 2009), p. 107.

8 Christopher C. Joyner, *The Spratly Islands dispute in the South China Sea: problems, policies, and prospects for diplomatic accommodation. Investigating Confidence-Building Measures in the Asia-Pacific Region*, [Report No. 28] (Washington: Stimson Center, 1999), pp. 61–2, <http://www.stimson.org/images/uploads/research-pdfs/cbmapspratly.pdf> accessed 8 September 2014.

9 Shicun Wu, *The Origin and Development of the Nansha Disputes* (2009), p. 152.

10 Ted L. McDorman, "The South China Sea islands dispute in the 1990s – a multilateral process and continuing friction" (1993), *International Journal of Marine and Coastal Law*, p. 8, 264; Mark Valencia, Jon M. Van Dyke and Noel A. Ludwig, *Sharing the resources of the South China Sea* (Honolulu: University of Hawaii, 1999), p. 38

11 Shicun Wu, *Solving Disputes for Regional Cooperation and Development in the South China Sea* (2013), p. 153.

12 See "Agreement Between the Government of the Republic of the Philippines and the Government of the Republic of Indonesia Concerning the Delimitation of the Exclusive Economic Zone", 23 May 2014, *Official Gazette*, Department of Foreign Affairs, Government of the Philippines <http://www.gov.ph/2014/05/23/agreement-between-the-government-of-the-republic-of-the-philippines-and-the-government-of-the-republic-indonesia-concerning-the-delimitation-of-the-exclusive-economic-zone-boundary/> accessed 23 December 2014.

13 Ramses Amer and Li Jianwei, "How to Manage China-Vietnam Territorial Disputes" (2013), *China & US Focus*, <http://www.chinausfocus.com/peace-security/how-to-manage-china-vietnam-territorial-disputes/> accessed 23 September 2014.

The third layer of the dispute concerns different interpretations of certain principles and concepts such as "freedom of navigation" and "scientific research", among countries both inside and outside the region. This is also closely related to the dynamics between regional and extra-regional powers, while said extra-regional powers have also greatly contributed to how the South China Sea dispute has arisen and developed through the course of history.

In short, as discussed before, although the Philippines did not touch upon the territorial dispute with China in the Notification and Statement of Claim, the core of the China–Philippine dispute is essentially about the competing territorial claims between the two countries over the Nansha Islands (Spratlys) and Huangyan Island (Scarborough Shoal). In addition, history matters substantially regarding how the China–Philippine territorial dispute over the Nansha Islands (Spratlys) and Huangyan Island (Scarborough Shoal) arose and developed. Thus, to fully comprehend the dispute, a review of the history of dispute between the two countries is indispensable.

A Chronological Review

China was the first country to discover and name the island features in the South China Sea,[14] including the Nansha Islands (Spratlys) and Huangyan Island (Scarborough Shoal). It also exercised continuous administration over those features, despite the succession of different dynasties. Although China's presence in the South China Sea declined while the European colonial powers were expanding in Asia, China never expressed any intention to relinquish sovereignty over those features.[15] Instead, China's claim over the South China Sea islands has been reaffirmed by its fight against foreign encroachment.

As early as 1909, the Chinese government organized expeditions to the South China Sea islands to demonstrate China's sovereignty, being aware that they might be encroached on by foreign naval powers. Led by Admiral Li Zhun, the fleet conducted surveys at Xisha and Nansha Islands (Paracels and Spratlys) and erected flags there.[16]

During the Republic of China (ROC) period, under intensified threat from French and Japanese naval powers, a formal, comprehensive, yet non-military demonstration of China's sovereignty over the South China Sea features seemed more necessary. The "Nine Islands" incident in particular, in which the French

14 Shicun Wu, *Solving Disputes for Regional Cooperation and Development in the South China Sea* (2013), pp. 16–20.

15 Shicun Wu, *The Origin and Development of Nansha Disputes* (南沙争端的起源与发展) (Beijing: China Economic Publishing House, 2010), pp. 15–39.

16 Zhenhua Han, Jinzhi Lin and Fengbin Wu (eds), *A Collection of Historical Materials on the South China Sea Islands* (我国南海诸岛史料汇编) (Beijing: Oriental Press, 1988), pp. 128–30.

colonists gradually occupied 9 of the Nansha Islands (Spratlys) between 1930 and April 1933 and only released the information in July 1933, revealed China's vulnerability in defining and defending borders on the sea. In June 1933, the ROC government appointed the Committee of Reviewing Water and Land Maps to review maps and atlases from private resources. In January 1935, the Committee published the Chinese and English names of 132 insular features in the South China Sea in the first issue of its journal. Those features were divided into Dongsha (Pratas), Xisha (Paracels), Nansha (later renamed Zhongsha, aka. Macclesfield Bank and Scarborough Shoal, of which Huangyan island was one of the features of the island group), and Tuansha islands (later renamed Nansha aka the Spratlys). In April 1935, the Committee published the map of the location of the South China Sea Islands in the second issue of its journal, which charted the southernmost point of the Chinese map at Zengmu Ansha (James Shoal).[17] Those two publications served as important evidence of China's claims over the Huangyan Island (Scarborough Shoal) and Nansha Islands (Spratlys).

The post-World War II recovery of the South China Sea Islands from Japan has further consolidated China's claim over the South China Sea Islands, including the Huangyan Island (Scarborough Shoal) and Nansha Islands (Spratlys). Starting in the 1920s, Japan competed with France for the South China Sea Islands, though most of the effort was conducted quietly by Japanese companies with government backgrounds. During World War II, Japan took the Xisha and Nansha Islands (Paracels and Spratlys) from France and attributed the jurisdiction of the two island groups, together with the Dongsha (Pratas) and Zhongsha Islands (Macclesfield Bank and Scarborough Shoal) to Kaohsiung of Taiwan. After Japan's surrender at the end of World War II, the ROC government recovered the four South China Sea island groups in 1946[18] in accordance with the *Cairo Declaration*[19] and the *Potsdam Proclamation.*[20]

---

17 Stefan Talmon and Bing Bing Jia (eds), *The South China Sea Arbitration*, p. 3.

18 Hungdah Chiu and Choo-Ho Park, "Legal Status of the Paracel and Spratly Islands" (1975), 3 *Ocean Development and International Law*, pp. 1, 12–13.

19 The *Cairo Declaration* states that "It is their purpose that Japan shall be stripped of all the islands in the Pacific which she has seized or occupied since the beginning of the first World War in 1914, and that all the territories Japan has stolen from the Chinese, such as Manchuria, Formosa, and the Pescadores, shall be restored to the Republic of China". See "Conference of President Roosevelt, Generalissimo Chiang Kai-Shek, and Prime Minister Churchill in North Africa, 1 December 1943", United States, Department of State Bulletin, vol. IX, no. 232 (4 December 1943), p. 393 <http://www.ioc.u-tokyo.ac.jp/~worldjpn/documents/texts/docs/19431127.D1E.html> accessed 30 June 2014; since the four island groups in the South China Sea was attached to Taiwan (Formosa), it is in China's recognition that the four South China Sea island groups should be returned to China with Taiwan.

20 The *Potsdam Declaration* states that "(8) The terms of the Cairo Declaration shall be carried out and Japanese sovereignty shall be limited to the islands of Honshu, Hokkaido, Kyushu, Shikoku and such minor islands as we determine". <http://www.upa.pdx.edu/IMS/currentprojects/TAHv3/Content/PDFs/Potsdam_Declaration.pdf> accessed 30 June 2014.

In May 1950, the ROC Government withdrew the garrisons on Yongxing (Woody) Island of the Xisha Islands (Paracels), and Taiping (Itu Aba) of the Nanha Islands (Spratlys), due to losing the civil war. However, neither this withdrawal nor the change in the political situation meant that China had given up the claim over those island groups. From China's perspective, the San Francisco peace treaty and the Sino-Japanese Treaty only further confirmed China's sovereignty. Although the San Francisco peace treaty itself does not specify to which country Japan renounced Nansha Islands (Spratlys) to, the Sino-Japanese Treaty, from China's perspective, was clear that the sovereignty of Nansha Islands (Spratlys) were returned to China.[21] Also, neither the ROC government nor the PRC government was present at the San Francisco peace conference. Thus, article 2(b) and article 2(f) of the San Francisco peace treaty that are related to the sovereignty of the Xisha and Nansha Islands (Paracels and Spratlys) would not affect China's rights. To add more weight to China's argument, in 1951, before the conference was held, Premier Zhou Enlai of the PRC government made it clear in an official statement that China's sovereignty over the Xisha (Paracels), Nansha (Spratlys), Dongsha (Pratas), and Zhongsha (Macclesfield Bank and Scarborough Shoal) would not be affected no matter how the San Francisco peace treaty was drafted.

The Philippines emerged as a competitor for territorial sovereignty and maritime rights in the South China Sea much later. As regarding the dispute over the Nansha Islands (Spratlys), the Philippines recognized the value of the Nansha Islands (Spratlys) in 1930s, but never attempted to challenge China's sovereignty until the late 1950s. Immediately following World War II, the Philippines still recognized China's claim. President Quirino even said at a press conference in 1950 that as long as the ROC held the Spratlys, the Philippines would not press its own claim.[22] 1956 was marked by the Philippines' intensified attempt to occupy the Nansha Islands (Spratlys). On 11 May 1956, Tomas A. Cloma, together with his brother and 40 other fishermen, took "formal" possession of a large area of Spratly islands and announced the establishment of a "Freedomland" (Kalaya'an) for the public.[23] The Philippine government did not unequivocally support this

21 The *Treaty of Peace with Japan*, also known as the *San Francisco Peace Treaty* stated in article 2(f) that "Japan renounces all right, title and claim to the Spratly Islands and to the Paracel Islands", and in article 2(b) that "Japan renounces all right, title and claim to Formosa and the Pescadores" <http://www.taiwandocuments.org/taipei01.htm> accessed 30 June 2014; The *Treaty of Peace between the Republic of China and Japan* stated in article 2 that "It is recognised that under Article 2 of the Treaty of Peace which Japan signed at the city of San Francisco on 8 September 1951 (hereinafter referred to as the San Francisco Treaty), Japan has renounced all right, title, and claim to Taiwan (Formosa) and Penghu (the Pescadores) as well as the Spratly Islands and the Paracel Islands" <http://www.taiwandocuments.org/sanfrancisco01.htm> accessed 30 June 2014.

22 Stein Tønnesson, "The South China Sea in the Age of European Decline" (2006), 40 *Modern Asian Studies*, p. 1, 22.

23 Joseph Morgan and Mark J. Valencia, *Atlas for Marine Policy in Southeast Asia Seas* (Berkeley, CA: University of California Press, 1983), p. 51.

claim at the beginning, but later gradually recognized Cloma's claim. Provoked by the Cloma incident, both Beijing and Taipei were quick to protest the setup of this Philippine "Freedomland", and both reiterated the Chinese claim over the Nansha Islands (Spratlys). Taipei re-established its presence in Taiping (Itu Aba) Island later in 1956, as a gesture to reconfirm its claim to the Nansha Islands (Spratlys).[24]

But, in 1974, the Marcos administration received a document from Cloma transferring all the rights of Thomas Cloma and Associates in this "Freedomland" to the Philippine government. And in 1978, the Philippines issued Presidential Decree No. 1596, proclaiming that the majority of the Nansha Islands (Spratlys), except for Nanwei (Spratly) Island and several others in that immediate vicinity, belonged to the Philippines' Kalayaan island group and declaring that it enjoyed sovereignty over them. The large area claimed in this decree was almost identical to Cloma's claim.[25] At the same time, through five military actions in 1970, 1971, 1978, and 1980, the Philippines invaded the Spratlys. It has since occupied eight islands, cays and reefs, including Mahuan Dao (Nanshan Island), Nanyue Dao (Loaita Island), Zhongye Dao (Thitu Island), Xiyue Dao (West York Island), Beizi Dao (Northeast Cay), Feixin Dao (Flat Island), Shuanghuang Shazhou (Loaita Nan) and Siling Jiao (Commodore Reef).[26]

The Philippines has also made various efforts to consolidate its occupation and control of these eight features of Nansha Islands (Spratlys). Notably, it maintains a continuous military presence. Over years of occupation, the Philippines has constructed lighthouses, radar stations and airport facilities for military outposts, and has stationed troops on most of the features. Secondly, it has made a consistent effort to engage foreign companies in the exploration of oil and gas resources in the disputed area. Thirdly, it has been trying to promote a civilian presence on the disputed features as a way to legitimize its occupation, and to certain extent, deter military moves from other claimant states.[27]

Comparison of Legal Basis of China and the Philippines' Claims

China's territorial claims over the South China Sea features rely on discovery, a long history of continuous uses and administration, as well as international treaty.

24 Stein Tønnesson, "The South China Sea in the Age of European Decline" (2006), pp. 50–51.

25 Rodolfo C. Severino, "ASEAN and the South China Sea" (2010), 6 *Security Challenges*, p. 2, 40.

26 Shicun Wu, *The Origin and Development of the Nansha Disputes* (南沙争端的由来与发展) (Beijing: Ocean Press, 1999), p. 103.

27 Shicun Wu, *Solving Disputes for Regional Cooperation and Development in the South China Sea* (2013), pp. 133–4.

The Philippines, however, based its claims mainly on the three reasons stated in the 1978 decree.[28]

Firstly, " ... much of the above area is part of the continental margin of the Philippine archipelago".

Secondly, " ... these areas do not legally belong to any state or nation but, by reason of history, indispensable need and effective occupation and control established in accordance with international law, such areas must be deemed to belong and be subject to the sovereignty of the Philippines".

Thirdly, " ... while other states have laid claims to some of these areas, their claims have lapsed by abandonment and cannot prevail over that of the Philippines on legal, historical, and equitable grounds".

There are obvious weaknesses in the reasons stated in the decree. First of all, it is illegal for a country to establish sovereignty over maritime features only on the grounds that those features sit on its continental margin or EEZ or that it deems those features indispensible. Secondly, China certainly had not abandoned its claims to the Nansha Islands (Spratlys) by 1978. Instead, as mentioned before, in response to the "Cloma Incident" in 1956, Taipei had regarrisoned Taiping (Itu Aba) Island the same year to demonstrate its claim over the Nansha Islands (Spratlys) and had maintained a presence thereafter. To claim that another states' claim had lapsed by abandonment, when nothing had been abandoned, would make the decree factually flawed. Thirdly, with regard to "effective occupation and control", it is a well-established principle that the illegal use of force does not produce any legal effect in international law. Thus, the military invasions of maritime features of Nansha Islands (Spratlys) by the Philippines from the early 1970s to the late 1980s and its presence since that time does not affect China's territorial sovereignty over those features.

Conclusion

A brief look at the history would show that the Philippines only started make unequivocal claims to features of Nansha Islands (Spratlys) in the late 1970s, while China has claimed sovereignty over the four island groups since long before. The Philippines' claim and occupation of features of Nansha Islands (Spratlys) has always been met with the protests and challenges of China. From China's perspective, China has a better basis of territorial claim over Nansha Islands (Spratlys) than the Philippines. However, China recognizes that the South China Sea issue involves a number of countries that have their respective stakes and interests. It is not easy or realistic to expect the dispute to be resolved in the near future. China always advocates solving the South China Sea dispute through dialogue and negotiation

28 Ferdinand E. Marcos, "Presidential Decree No. 1596" (1978), Chan Robles Virtual Law Library <www.chanrobles.com/presidentialdecrees/presidentialdecreeno1596.html> accessed 30 June 2014.

directly with disputed countries, which is consistent with international law and practice. Yet, to avoid the impasse of territorial dispute, China is also relentlessly promoting "shelving the dispute and seeking joint development".

On 9 August 2014, during the 47th ASEAN Foreign Ministers' Meeting (AMM) held in Nay Pyi Taw, the Philippine Foreign Affairs Secretary Albert F. del Rosario proposed a "triple action plan", which involves immediate, intermediate, and final approaches for solving the South China Sea dispute with China. The immediate action includes a moratorium on "provocative actions"; the intermediate approach is to fully and effectively implement the Declaration on the Conduct of Parties in the South China Sea (DOC) and the expeditious conclusion of the Code of Conduct (COC); and the final approach is to settle disputes through resolution mechanisms in accordance with international law.[29] However, it seems that the Philippines has barely done anything regarding the short-term and mid-term action plan and has jumped directly into the final approach. By doing so the Philippines has closed the door for consultation and negotiation. In response to the Philippines' "triple action plan", Chinese foreign minister Wang Yi further clarified China's position at a press conference after the ASEAN-China Foreign Minsters' Meeting, and called for the "dual track" approach. That is to say, consultations and negotiations by countries directly concerned would be the most effective and viable way to resolve the disputes, a policy which also conforms to international law and common practices and constitutes one of the most important provisions in the DOC. It is the responsibility and obligation of both China and ASEAN to uphold peace and stability in the South China Sea region.[30]

Since it is almost unforeseeable that the arbitration could solve the real problem between China and the Philippines, it would be better if the two countries could move ahead, and not let bilateral relations be trapped in the mire of arbitration. As the position paper of China's Ministry of Foreign Affairs states, "There exists an agreement between China and the Philippines to settle their disputes in the South China Sea through negotiations".[31] Both China and the Philippines are obliged to fulfill their respective commitment and go back to the negotiation table. In addition, the two sides, together with other ASEAN countries, should continue the effort to develop an effective consultation and confidence building mechanism on maritime issues in the South China Sea to create an environment that is conducive to the final settlement of the dispute in the area.

---

29 Department of Foreign Affairs of the Republic of the Philippines, "Philippines Presents Triple Action Plan at 47th ASEAN Foreign Ministers' Meeting in Nay Pyi Taw", 9 August 2014 <http://www.dfa.gov.ph/index.php/2013–06–27–21–50–36/dfa-releases/3789-philippines-presents-triple-action-plan-at-47th-asean-foreign-ministers-meeting-in-nay-pyi-taw> accessed on 16 September 2014.

30 China Daily, "Foreign minister encourages a 'dual-track' approach to sea issue", 11 August 2014 <http://english.gov.cn/news/top_news/2014/08/23/content_281474983028587.htm> accessed 16 September 2014.

31 Ministry of Foreign Affairs of the People's Republic of China, para III.

Chapter 3
The South China Sea Disputes Are Not Yet Justiciable

Anthony Carty

The Issue of Justiciability in International Law

China has declined to accept the jurisdiction of an arbitration tribunal under the 1982 United Nations Convention on the Law of the Sea (UNCLOS) in a dispute with the Philippines. It relies upon the Declaration by the People's Republic of China (PRC) under article 298 UNCLOS (25 August 2006), essentially that it does not accept compulsory adjudication over any question of maritime boundary delimitation, or involving historic bays or titles. China has laid claim for decades, if not centuries, to the Spratly Islands (also the Paracels), on the basis of which it may ground a claim to jurisdiction over a maritime area within a so-called U-Shaped Line which runs close to the coastlines of all South China Sea states. The Philippines claims a continental shelf and exclusive economic zone (EEZ) running broadly from its western archipelago coastlines, 200 miles westward into the South China Sea. This would disregard the significance, if any, of China's claims to the Spratlys. The Philippines also expects the arbitration tribunal to say that the U-Shaped Line is a concept unknown to the UNCLOS. More specifically, it claims that, under its reading of article 121 of the Law of the Sea Convention, islands, such as the Spratlys, are of little legal significance for the purposes of maritime delimitation. In effect the Philippines rewrites article 121 of UNCLOS to apply the terms of article 121(3) to article 121(1) and (2), with devastating consequences for China's territorial and maritime claims, the real substance of the disputes between the two countries.[1]

While these Chinese arguments are almost certainly juridically sound with respect to the jurisdiction of the arbitration tribunal, they do not spare China of a more general criticism. It is failing to observe the principle of the rule of law in

1 See exhaustively on these Philippine claims and their exclusion from adjudication by the Chinese reservation to article 298 of the UNCLOS, see H. Zhang and C. Mi, "Jurisprudential Tenability of the Philippines v China Arbitration on South China Sea Disputes?" in S. Talmon and B. Jia (eds), *The South China Sea Arbitration, a Chinese Perspective* (Oxford, Hart: 2014), pp. 137–58. On the U-Shaped Line see also Z. Gao and B. Jia, "The Nine Dash Line in the South China Sea: History, Status and Implications", *American Journal of International Law* (2013), pp. 98–124.

international society by declining to accept third party adjudication of its disputes with the Philippines. If China is so convinced that its substantive legal arguments and claims against the Philippines are sound, why should it be so unwillingly to allow international legal authority to adjudicate in its favor. To persist in inviting a small country, with whom it appears to have irreconcilable legal views, to persist in endless, fruitless discussions, may appear to be a form of bullying, while also constituting a threat to peace and security of the region, given the continuing unilateral Chinese and Philippine measures to enforce their views in the contested areas.

It is in this context, where China appears to be pushed into a corner in terms of international legal reputation, that it is necessary to explore the most fundamental question, whether the arbitration tribunal is in fact judicially capable, as distinct from jurisdictionally competent, to resolve the legal disagreements between China and the Philippines. China readily and correctly points out that the legal issues are not confined to the UNCLOS. However, this would not be an answer to the proposal to have a special tribunal or the international court of justice adjudicate all legal aspects of the conflict. It is in this wider context that it is worthwhile to explore whether the relevant international law is sufficiently researched and developed to allow of legal determination. This issue is itself not entirely separate from questions about the intellectual openness, subtlety and depth of the international judicial profession, particularly with respect to historical questions.

Justiciability is not an uncontested concept in international law, unlike public law generally. There are many issues, especially concerning foreign affairs and foreign policy, which national courts are not prepared to touch, because it is recognised that they involve so much political assessment and have such serious national security implications, that they are better left to the Executive branch of government. In contrast, international law doctrine, led by Hersch Lauterpacht, has argued that wherever there is an applicable legal rule affecting an issue, then an international court can apply it. It is simply a matter of political will of states and any appeal to such doctrines as vital national security, or a gap in the law, is merely an attempt to avoid the application of the international rule of law. As Lauterpacht puts it:

> The completeness of the rule of law … is an *a priori* assumption of every system of law, not a prescription of positive law. It is impossible, as a matter of *a priori* assumption, to conceive that it is the will of the law that its rule should break down as a result of the refusal to pronounce upon claims.[2]

---

2 Hersch Lauterpacht, *The Function of Law in the International Community* (Oxford: Oxford University Press, 1933), esp. at p. 64. The standing of this book is shown by the fact that it is available in print. There is now available in English translation Serge Sur, *International Law, Power, Security and Justice, Essays on International Law and Relations* (Oxford: Hart, 2010).

This type of strident, dogmatic rhetoric is countered within international law doctrine. There are some who argue that international law is not a complete system of law, such as Jean Combaceau and Serge Sur in France, so that the trick of the Lotus Case[3] – that whatever is not prohibited is permitted – is not a mechanism which can merely serve to create a logically complete system of law. The powerful French positivist doctrine of the nature of international law is that, as the author has already analyzed and synthesized,

> if a state commits itself to a rule it is because it needs a regulated conduct, on the part of others, which it can only have by allowing itself to be regulated … Because of the lack of hierarchy of norms states recognize that no act can be declared invalid objectively, as each state can literally camp on its own position. It can pretend to its own representation of acts and situations and this representation remains subjective as far as any third person is concerned … There is no centralization of legal disposition … Even collective guarantees by states remain an aggregate of subjective, individual representations … The struggle for law as a collection of positive rules has to be seen as a compromise of interests, animated by a power struggle of perceptions and ideologies. The language of universal values has little influence on the politics of states, closed to their own interests, for whom international law is not so much a system of norms as "une partie de chasse".[4]

Another international law theorist, Hans Kelsen, thought that this deficiency could be met with compulsory international adjudication. At the same time he recognized that, in the absence of such compulsory adjudication, the post-1945 prohibition of the use of force to reassert a state's rights, was premature. A legal order, to qualify as such, has to have mechanisms – either judicial, collective, or self-help – to enforce rights. The international legal order does not have such mechanisms and therefore cannot qualify as a complete legal order. This is a very important consideration for China because it has been displaced from its historical positions in the South China Sea from the 1930s by France and later Vietnam and the Philippines.[5]

However, Kelsen's solution – massive law creating authority for judges – can hardly work for as inchoate a community as world society for the reasons given by Roberto Ungar in his theory of adjudication. A judiciary is really an administrative framework for the completion of the details of a legal order so as to apply it to

3 <http://www.icj-cij.org/pcij/serie_A/A_10/30_Lotus_Arret.pdf>.

4 See further Anthony Carty, 'Convergences and Divergences in European International Law Traditions', *European Journal of International Law* (2000) Vol. 11. No. 3, p. 713 at 721. See also for the French doctrine, pp. 720–25 and pp. 726–8.

5 See further Anthony Carty, *Philosophy of International Law* (Edinburgh: Edinburgh University Press, 2007), at pp. 121–2 discussing Hans Kelsen, *Collective Security under International Law* (Washington DC: United States Government Printing Office, 1957).

concrete cases, which raise no serious question of principle. Otherwise the judiciary is going beyond its adjudicatory function as a method of resolving individual disputes and becomes a legislator for the whole of a society or for mankind as a whole. Such judicial conduct will produce a rebellion in a society which does not have a broadly shared consensus with respect to the issues for adjudication.[6]

While these concerns about justiciability permeate all of the arguments presented in this study, one might illustrate in this introduction precisely how the justiciability issue plays out in a central way with respect to the UNCLOS. The purpose of the arbitration brought by the Philippines is to use aspects of the Convention to demonstrate that there is an international legal consensus, based on an interpretation of the UNCOLS, also accepted by China, which applies to the dispute. In this case China's non-participation in the Tribunal's deliberations will not save it from an interpretation of the UNCLOS.

So, if the Tribunal rules, for example, as a matter of interpretation of UNCLOS article 121, that also islands, and not just rocks, which do not usually support habitation economically, cannot generate economic zones and continental shelves, that will defeat almost entirely the Chinese claims in the South China Seas based on ownership of islands. This would be in spite of the fact that the PRC has declined to accept jurisdiction over questions which concern the significance of its historical territorial claims to virtually all the islands in the South China Sea (SCS). It would also be in spite of the fact that China has excluded all questions of delimitation of EEZs and continental shelves (CSs) from compulsory adjudication.[7] It would also be in spite of the fact that China does not in fact possess virtually any of these islands – its hold having been displaced in questionable circumstances[8] – with the consequence that it is severely handicapped in showing what actual use of the islands it might make if it was in possession of them at the present time.

While it may be possible for the Tribunal to argue, logically, that such an effect of its ruling – the absence of any economic significance attaching to the islands in the SCS – is merely an incidental consequence of its universal and therefore abstract ruling about the meaning of article 121 of the UNCLOS, the actual substance of the dispute between China and its SCS neighbors, is that it considers these islands do generate CSs and/or EEZs etc., while its neighbors prefer to

6 Ibid., Carty, *Philosophy of International Law*, at pp. 215–218, discussing Robert Unger's *What Should Legal Analysis Become?* (London: Verso, 1996).

7 As already noted in footnote 1 above, China has made the following reservation to the UNCLOS on 25 August 2006: The Government of the People's Republic of China does not accept any of the procedures provided for in Section 2 of Part XV of the Convention with respect to all the categories of disputes referred to in paragraph 1 (a), (b) and (c) of Article 298 of the Convention. This includes disputes with respect to delimitations of EEZs or CS under articles 74 or 83 or disputes relating to historical bays or titles.

8 See further, Wu Shicun, *Solving Disputes for Regional Cooperation and Development in the South China Sea, A Chinese Perspective* (Oxford: Chandos, 2013), considering comprehensively all the Chinese language literature.

put the islands aside and draw CSs and/or EEZs from their coastlines alone. In other words, the real issue in dispute between China and its neighbors concerns not simply the terms of the UNCLOS – which terms are themselves of doubtful justiciability (see below) – but also whether that Convention is itself an exhaustive standard for the adjudication of the dispute.

Even in the event that the islands are discounted the UNCLOS is not categorical that median lines to determine EEZs should be drawn geologically from baselines along coastlines. These have still to be based on a mutual, i.e. bilateral state consensus that the lines drawn are equitable (UNCLOS articles 74 and 83) – a standard which is not itself justiciable unless both parties agree to leave the adjudication to a Tribunal.

Therefore, it is arguable that, despite the fact that the Tribunal would normally have jurisdiction to interpret authoritatively the meaning of article 121 of the UNCLOS, the juridical policy of non-justiciability would argue against it.

Moving on to individual issues of justiciability, the first most obvious question is whether the Tribunal has enough material before it to form an effective or comprehensive judgment. China (PRC) is actually in possession of only a small part of the Spratly Islands region. So, secondly, a judgment on the supposition that it possessed all of it would be hypothetical. Related to this is the fact that other states having claims or in de facto possession are not parties to the arbitration. These facts may not be a bar to jurisdiction of this Tribunal, but they can be a bar to the desirability of adjudication.

Imperialism as a Disruption of the South China Sea Order

These abstractly formulated considerations are integrally related to the huge historical difficulties about applying any legal standards to the South China Sea Region in the last 150 years. The region was profoundly disturbed by colonial and imperial encounters. China was under constant attack, consequently riven by internal dissension, and until very recently (the 1990s) unable to act effectively on the international stage. Vietnam was locked in an immensely destructive conflict with two Western Powers, France and the United States, from the 1870s to the 1970s. The Philippines and Malaysia did not even exist. During the same time three imperial powers, France, Britain and Japan exercised immense impact in the region and yet now two of these have vanished and are not willing to render any account of their former presence.

The fundamental historical claim of China is that prior to this imperial disruption the South China Sea Islands and their surrounding seas were part of a Chinese domain. Whether China asserted its presence there so as to satisfy the rigors of effective occupation as a primary title to territory[9] is controversial and

9 It came to dominate Western international law doctrine and judicial practice, culminating in the jurisprudence of the late 1920s.

will be considered in the next section. Leaving aside briefly, for this section, the question of the standing of the principle of effectiveness in relation to title to territorial sovereignty based upon occupation, there seems little doubt that the circumstances which would affect the operation of the principle in the SCS are quite unusual. By its nature the law of title to territory by virtue of occupation is historical, being a part of customary international law. It depends upon an observance of state conduct over decades, if not centuries. A huge part of the argument of the Philippines before the Tribunal is that China only occupies a few reefs at present, obviously not viable economically and uninhabitable.[10] However, this argument is presented without any historical context over the last 150 years.

Work has still to be done to begin a comprehensive review of the National Archives of all the countries of the borders of the SCS region. However, some presentation of key findings of the UK (British) and French National Archives will be made, to illustrate both the nature of the imperial disruption and its potential impact upon the territorial claims of Vietnam and the Philippines.

A. The Paracels

The Paracels are not at the moment the subject of arbitration, nor are the Spratlys. The Tribunal is simply asked to rule on the legal significance of possession of islands in the SCS. The Philippines have possession only of some Spratly Islands. However, if Vietnam were to join the litigation, it has claims over the entire islands of the SCS.

The archival record is much more explicit about the intentions of French incursions into the Paracel Islands in the early 1930s, than the Spratlys, but they were clearly part of the same expansionist French strategy. In Britain it was the Admiralty, on behalf of the Royal Navy, that watched most critically the French activities. Following a warning from the British Consul General in Saigon on 13 April 1931 that the French "have intentions on the Paracels", the Admiralty was invited by the Foreign Office to comment.

They provided several memoranda from 21 May until 10 June 1931. The correspondence begins in terms of a warning from the Lords Commissioners of the Admiralty to the Secretary of State for Foreign Affairs, that they have information from a secret source that "the French Government are contemplating proclaiming a protectorate over, or annexing, these (the Paracel) islands". They continued to stress the actual situation in China:

> Although these islands have been regarded as a Chinese possession, as China annexed them on the 6 June 1909 when the Chinese ensign was hoisted on Duncan Island by Admiral Li Tsun who visited them with the gunboats FUPAO

10 In principle the Philippine Memorial to the Tribunal has not been published, but the outlines of its arguments have wide currency.

> and CHIN HAO, if the present Chinese Government falls in the near future, the French may consider it a suitable opportunity for claiming the islands.[11]

The Admiralty therefore recommended that there should be another attempt to encourage the Chinese Government to light the Paracel Islands, i.e. erect lighthouses. There was to have been a 1922 Customs expedition to the Islands. This is a reference to the fact that when in 1922 there were Japanese press reports that the Japanese Foreign Office had intended to annex the Islands, the British had telegrammed their Embassy in Beijing suggesting that "China should be encouraged to assert her sovereignty". This was to be by erecting lights. In addition, it is reported "that the Inspector General had agreed at that time to send a Customs Revenue cruiser on a surveying expedition to Paracels, and that the captain of cruiser would be instructed to be seen by some Japanese vessel".[12] However, this voyage never took place for a variety of reasons, one being that the boat in question was old and that the Paracels were "out of usual beat".

On 1 June 1931 the Admiralty recommended that the Foreign Secretary take the matter up with the French Government, to avoid a *fait accompli.* It suggested that the French were influenced by the fact that a new group of politicians and militarists in Canton had set up in opposition to Chiang Kai Shek's regime in Nanking. They were considered likely to gain some control in the South China.

> This internal dissension, with prospects of renewed civil war, is likely to distract Chinese attention from such relatively minor questions as the ownership of the Paracels.
>
> France has important economic interests in the Southern provinces of China, which march with the Indo-China frontier, and it is possible that French policy may be to support the new regime at Canton, either openly or secretly, by supplying arms etc., as she has done on a large scale in recent civil wars. A minor (secret) quid pro quo for this support might be that the "Southern Government" would not challenge action to be taken by France in annexing the Paracels.[13]

The most exhaustive and categorical statement on the British side, in these records, is a letter from the British Foreign Secretary, Arthur Henderson, to the British Ambassador in Paris, Lord Tyrrell, asking him to approach the French government discretely saying that he hopes there is no truth in the rumour that they intend to occupy the Paracels. The letter recounts that there had been talk that the Japanese were anxious in 1920 to annex the Paracels.

> To forestall this it was suggested to the Chinese Government that they should exert their sovereignty over the group. The Chinese Government proposed to

11 FO 262/ 1790: F 2819/2669/10, 21 May 1931.

12 Telegram to H.M. Minister Nanking no. 90 2 June 1931: FO 262/1790 : 3/285/31.

13 FO 262/1790: F 2971/2669/10 Admiralty 1 June 1931.

> send a gun boat, but apparently, they never actually did so. On 15 September 1922 the Admiralty expressed anxiety lest the Japanese should obtain control of these islands by obtaining a lease of them for a Japanese company. They suggested that HMG "should continue to oppose any party in China which shows a tendency to cede or barter away the sovereignty of the Chinese Republic over her coastwise possessions and islands".[14]

The letter continued to mention the history of the promise of the Chinese Maritime Customs to send a customs cruiser to indicate Chinese sovereignty. Then the Foreign Office stressed that any cession of Chinese territory would be contrary to the Nine-Power Treaty of Washington of 1922 and would be opposed by HMG, whereby China undertook not to cede or lease any of its territory. The letter ends by saying that there was a report from Canton in 1928 that "the Chinese authorities had concluded a survey of the islands and that the Kwantung Government intended to develop the group themselves".[15]

On 6 July 1931, Ambassador Tyrrell in Paris replied to the British Foreign Secretary, Arthur Henderson, of an apparent intention of the French Government to annex the Paracels on the basis of a title going back to 1806 or 1816, of the Emperor of Annan. Tyrrell writes: "The French Government is aware that the Chinese flag was hoisted on Duncan Island in 1909, though I understand that they entered no protest at that time".[16] The French Ministry of Foreign Affairs is reported as saying that the Paracels are largely coral reefs, uninhabitable except for some 20 native fisherman and occasionally Japanese or Chinese guano traders.[17] He reported that the French position is as follows. If the French legal advisers decide that the Emperor of Annan did effectively annex the Paracels in the early nineteenth century, the French Government will address a note to the Chinese Government claiming sovereignty over them. If the claim is disputed arbitration will be proposed.

The French Archive for the same events indicates considerable skepticism both at the political and legal level at the actions then taken by France. The Archive has a retrospective character, concerned in the late 1940s to explain to the French themselves the nature of their entanglements in the SCS.[18] The general political context of this form of compilation of Archive is that after 1945 the French engage in a review of their policy and revisit their original 1930 policy. Vichy France

---

14 FO 262/1790 F 2971/2669/10 Foreign Office 10 June 1931.

15 Ibid.

16 FO 262/1790: F3869/2669/10, 6 July 1931.

17 Ibid.

18 The French Archive's version of these events is in, specifically, the Ministry of Foreign Affaires, Diplomatic Archives Asie-Oceanie 1944–1955 119 QO CHINE Politique extérieure : Iles Paracels. Dossier 215 – (throughout the Archive will simply be cited Dossier with the Number of the Dossier following, and the date of the document). Obviously these archives are in French and the author offers his own translations.

had been on peaceful terms with Imperial Japan until the spring of 1945 and only briefly did the Japanese suspend the French control of Indo-China. After the Japanese surrender, the Nanjing Government moved quickly to occupy some of the Paracels while the French occupied other parts.

Briefly, the wider policy context of the notes in the French Archive is that the French wish to offer to arbitrate the dispute about the Paracels with Nanjing, and in this context, to consider for themselves the strength of their own claim. They appear at this point in time, March 1947, to be indifferent to losing the arbitration, because they are anxious to retain the neutrality of the Nanjing Government in their conflict with Ho Chi Min's Vietnamese insurgents. Arbitration will be simpler than simply abandoning their earlier claims. So they revisit the 1930s discussions.

There is a NOTE FOR THE Secretary General (of the Foreign Ministry)[19] which says (in translation, more or less exact, but with a little summarizing):

> At a time when recent incidents are causing this dispute to pass from the political to the legal level of an arbitration,[20] it is convenient to recall that on the latter level our position has always been considered as rather uncertain.
>
> From their first installation in Indo China until 1930 the French authorities, while all the time aware of the strategic interest of the Paracels, have always abstained from making an act of sovereignty on this archipelago, and (abstained) from indicating to China the rights which Annam had exercised there. In the course of the same period China had, in contrast, proceeded to official acts whose significance (Valeur) one cannot overlook. It is this that in 1909, a Chinese naval mission explored the Paracels, solemnly raised the Chinese flag on the principal islands. Furthermore, in 1921, the Government of "Kouangtoung" published in its Official Journal an ordinance attaching these territories administratively to the Prefecture of Hainan. These initiatives raised no protest from France. The Department then estimated (letter no.719 of 21 August 1921), in agreement with the Governors General of Indo-China) that our efforts should be confined to obtaining the application to the Archipelago of the engagements undertaken by China with regard to the island of Hainan in 1899.[21]
>
> It is in 1931 that a note was addressed, for the first time, to the Chinese Government to claim the rights which we held on behalf of Annam. It seems that these historic

19 E 117-3 (page 18 of Dossier 215) 18 March 1947.

20 This is a reference to a visit to the Chinese occupied Paracel in January 1947 where the French commander is supposed to have asked the Chinese to evacuate and offered to help. The Chinese reacted very angrily and the French claimed that the commander exceeded his orders, which were merely to state the French claim to the Chinese present. The French were always anxious not to disturb the general good relations between Paris and Nanjing.

21 This commitment was not to alienate Hainan, and now the Paracels, to any foreign power.

rights, which besides, in themselves, are not negligible, had been "rediscovered" on the occasion of the request of the Société financière et coloniale française which wished to exploit deposits of phosphates "gisements de phosphetes" on the islands. The reply of the Chinese was to invoke principally arguments of mediocre value (presence of Chinese fishermen, inexact interpretation of the Convention on the Tonkin Chinese frontier). It was easy to respond to these arguments and this there continued an exchange of notes until 1938.[22] ***During this time we were, by the way, helped by favorable political conditions.***[23]

As for the occupation carried out in 1938 by French naval forces, this was effected in agreement with the Chinese government, under a reservation that it would not affect the respective juridical positions of the two countries. It was a matter of barring the way to the Japanese.

On 19 June 1930, M. Basdevant indicated in a consultation: It seems that Annam may have grounds to call itself sovereign of the Paracels. All the same, this opinion can only be formulated with a certain hesitation. Another opinion of the same Jurisconsult of 3 March 1931 notes that " it is rather difficult to say in what sense an arbitral tribunal would pronounce if it was asked to adjudicate on the rights of Annam".

In summary, if the rights of Annam appear more ancient, they have been insufficiently exercised until 1930. Those of China are more recent, but they have been affirmed since the beginning of the century by a series of official acts.

Given the uncertainty of the outcome of an arbitration, the exchange of our rights against territorial advantages on other parts of Indo-China could be envisaged, but the Directorate of Asia does not think there can be an equal bargaining, except for the Spratlys, which are of much less interest. A solution of condominium or partition presents great practical difficulties. In these conditions, an arbitration,

---

22 This is probably a reference to a document dated 16 August 1933, a Note by Mr Charguéraud-Hartmann for the Asia Department, in which he refers to Chinese arguments that the Paracels were part of the territorial sea of Canton etc. This document tries to argue that the Paracels were in 1885 at the time of the Chinese French Peace Treaty over Annam, an integral part of the territory of Annam and that subsequent actions of China from 1909 were a violation of the said Treaty, see Dossier 215, p. 76–7. Such arguments were not accepted or used at a higher level in the French administration. Another relevant background document is a report in 1930 by Vice Admiral Herr to the French Ministry of the Nay that highlights especially the pressure of commercial activity around the Paracels, which he said were driving for some decision to be taken, see Dossier 215, p. 213. This constituted the basis for the reference to pressure coming from a French company wanting to explore phosphate deposits.

23 Author's emphasis.

whatever the indecision about the result, appears to present the best way to get out of the present impasse.

Returning to the 1930s Archive contained in Dossier 215, reference will be made to a summary note of 20 July 1933 E913-9 and the two legal opinions of Basdevant.[24] The 20 July document provides the summary of events up until 1930 upon which the 1947 Note to the Secretary General of the Foreign Ministry relies. The occasion is recent taking possession of the Spratleys and the document refers to the need to summarize a voluminous correspondence for the last 12 years between the Department, the Navy, the Colonies and Peking. The Department of the Colonies has written a long letter dated 18 October 1930, containing its archive, but it is still not easy to prove that Annam continued to exercise sovereignty. From 1909 China proceeded with a real taking possession of the islands. They made no notifications, but there was also no protestation on our part.

The French Government considers that the islands are of strategic interest, but especially, commercial interests of all nationalities have been involved in the islands. There are on the one hand authorizations accorded by the Chinese government (provincial, then central) and on the other hand the desire of the commercial people (commerçants) to have to deal with the French government, and also the desire of Indochina to possess the islands, which are the driving motors of our action. From 1921 to 1931 we accepted the Chinese position, with the proviso of non-alienation to third powers, under the 1897, 1898 Treaties.

The document then quotes the views of Basdevant in the same terms as the Note for the Secretary General. On this point it concludes that our argument is fragile in the case of arbitration. We could reinforce our position "by acts of sovereignty which are discrete and do not provoke controversy". There follows a clear statement of the subsequent French legal, diplomatic strategy outwardly towards China.

On 18 June 1931, after examining all the documents and in the face of the practical risks of French activities on the islands, as indicated by Mr Basdevant, it was decided:

1. To affirm our rights in a diplomatic note to China;
2. In the case of a refusal (by China) to go to arbitration;
3. As a form of retreat position (comme position de repli), argue for the attachment to Hainan, which is inalienable.

Once this position was agreed among the interested Departments a note was sent to the Chinese legation on 4 January 1932. It should have been sent to Peking as well, but unfavorable circumstances prevented this. Nonetheless in March 1932 the Chinese in Canton put up for public procurement rights of exploitation of guano on the Paracel Islands. So the same note was sent there as a form of protest.

24 Beginning at p. 65 of Dossier 215.

The inaccuracies and confusions of the Chinese response have already been noted. There is also mention of the English intervention and a statement that the French said in reply "we believe we have these rights and we are studying ways to make these understood juridically in an amicable way by the Chinese. At the time of our protest (of March 1932) we made a naval expedition to the Paracels to show the flag (des unités navales d'Indochine ont montré notre pavillon aux Paracels). After their response in March 1933 the Chinese also sent an expedition around the Paracels. After this, there was no further activity.

The two legal opinions of Jules Basdevant are hugely important. The Jurisconsult is an academic Professor of International Law, who, while he advises the Foreign Ministry, is not simply an employee. Basdevant played this role from 1930 to 1941, before going on to spend 18 years as a judge of the International Court of Justice, from 1946 till 1964. In that year he was awarded the Legion of Honor by President de Gaulle.[25]

The second opinion of 3 March 1931 is more authoritative than the first of 19 June 1930, being based on more exhaustive information and it will be explained in full. A special package of information was submitted to him on 7 February 1931 from the Asia-Oceanic Department of the Ministry of Foreign Affairs. Basdevant writes:[26]

> These documents appear to establish that at the beginning of the 19th century, the Paracels constituted a dependency of Annam, which at this time effectively exercised its rights on these islands. Since a long time, Annam no longer exercises its authority on these islands. The intention that one could have had to build a lighthouse produced no external manifestation that we can point to. The facts signaled by Mr Lapicque in a brochure in 1929 have not been confirmed in any of the documents made available to me.[27] In these conditions, can one consider that the rights of Annam have been maintained or that they have been tacitly renounced? This is a question of appreciation that an arbitrator could decide one way or the other depending on his state of spirit. Of the two most recent arbitral judgments, the one, THE ISLAND OF PALMAS CASE appears rather more favorable to the annulment of the right of Annam (caducité), the other, the ISLAND OF CLIPPERTON appears more for the maintenance of the right.
>
> The documents confirm the taking of possession of the islands by China in 1909. One sees there also that from that time China has shown through certain authorizations or approvals the right which it claims to have on the islands.

25 <http://en.wikipedia.org/wiki/Jules_Basdevant>.

26 Dossier 215, p. 68, 3 March 1931.

27 The 19 June 1930 opinion gave weight to the documents of Mr Lapicque, that they indicated exercise of sovereignty through activities of the Indo-China Customs in making surveys and oceanographic explorations etc., supposing that these could be proved to have happened, Dossier 215, p. 75.

> There one has facts which would appear of a nature to establish China's right, if it did not come up against a prior right of Annam. One returns then to the question whether the right of Annam subsisted in 1909 …
>
> In these conditions it is really difficult (assez difficile) to say in what sense an arbitral tribunal which was invited would declare on the validity of the rights of Annam. The juridical position of Annam would be fortified if the authority of this Empire on the Paracels was rendered more active and manifested itself by surveillance cruises in the region; it would be also appropriate, by the way, that this activity avoids the form of a taking of possession, it should be presented as an exercise of already pre-existing rights. That, by the way, ought to remain subordinated to an appreciation of the interest which we can have to claim the Paracels in the name of Annam.

B The Spratlys

The context and role of the French and British Archives is more complex. The French began from the stance that they annexed the Spratlys as *terra nullius*, without contestation, but by the 1950s they recognized, particularly in the light of their own legal advice, that their claim to the Spratlys was weak because of failure to exercise effective control. At this point they were reluctant to reassert control because of the presence of the Chinese, Nationalist and PRC. However, they are emphatic that the claims of Vietnam and the Philippines are without foundation in law. At the same time the British note the strength of the French claim through the 1930s to the 1950s, with the caveat that it was very weakly exercised. However, they joined with the French in denying the legality of the Japanese annexation of 1939. As the French claim weakened in the course of the 1950s onwards, the British legal advice, based on the archival resources of the Foreign Office Research Department, conclude that by the 1970s the Chinese claim to the Spratleys had effectively revived. The Vietnamese and Philippine claims had in the meantime been barred by the French, whose withdraw favored China.

Following Philippine independence in 1946 the French Ambassador to China expressed concern to the French Foreign Minister that the Chinese intention to occupy the Spratleys – still known by their Japanese name – Shinangunto – was causing great concern in the Philippines and asked for advice.[28] The French claimed that the Spratleys were *res nullius* when they declared them French in the Journel Officiel on 25 July 1933. There was no reaction from the Philippines, the United States, China or the Netherlands. The British raised questions, and, according to the French, were satisfied with their explanations. Only the Japanese protested. The islands were attached administratively to the province of Balia in Cochina. A little garrison was supposedly put on the islands, but the documentation given

28 French Foreign Ministry Diplomatic Archives Dossier 213, p. 6 E 117-2 Nankin, 5 August 1946.

to the Legal Department does not indicate where or when. Nonetheless, a French detachment seems to have been able to remain on the islands until 1940, alongside the Japanese, after which there is no information. France protested against and would not recognize the Japanese placing of the islands under their jurisdiction on 31 March 1939. The Legal Department did not know whether at that point (September 1946) there were any either French or Indo-Chinese on the islands. The Legal Advice recommended that further details should be provided by the Indo-China authorities and the French Navy, without proceeding to investigations which run the risk of alerting foreign powers.

In order to avoid the situation arising again which arose before, (i.e. the Japanese incursion) the Legal Advice states:

> It is indispensable that our right be reaffirmed in a solemn manner: naval reconnaissance, reestablishment of a garrison, replacement of marks which have disappeared, publication of an official communique etc. This should be done by the Inter-ministerial Committee on Indo-China. It does not need to wait for the Japanese Peace treaty because we have never recognized the Japanese sovereignty. Where other powers contest our position, we can offer arbitration, which should be favourable to us, provided the question is well chosen and the tribunal judiciously chosen.
>
> If China makes a claim it will be very probably be on the basis that the Spratlys were attached to Formosa, which has been restored (restituée á la Chine) to China at the Cairo Conference. For our response it suffices to say that at the time when Formosa was taken from China by Japan, the Spratlys were still *res nullius* and, besides, obviously, the rights of Japan are non-existent.
>
> As for a Philippine claim about which our Consul General warns us, this is not serious, although we should still be in possession of all the historical facts.[29]

There follow messages from the Foreign Ministry to the Ambassador in Nanking and the Consul General in Manila attaching the legal memorandum. In view of the Ambassador's report that the Chinese had declared their intention to occupy the Spratlys, the Ambassador, Jacques Meyrier, was still advised:

> that since China did not contest the French occupation at the time it would be not useful and inopportune for him to take the initiative to engage with the Government of Nankin on a discussion of our sovereignty over the Spratlys. Still, if the matter is raised with you, you can base yourself on the attached document.[30]

29 Ibid., pp. 15–21.

30 Dossier 231, E 117, p. 25, 21 September 1946, Minster of Foreign Affairs to French Ambassador. A similar message is sent to Manila., with respect to Philippine claims. Yet also the Philippines and the US did not contest our rights at our first French occupation,

The French Archive affords information of some interest in terms of French attitudes to the claims of China, Vietnam and the Philippines to the Spratlys. Concerning Vietnam, the French consistently maintained that their initiative to seize the Spratlys was on their own account, and, as will be seen, they maintained this position until the 1970s, with the same caveat that they would not assert it "unnecessarily" to Vietnam, meaning South Vietnam.

There are some incidents preceding a climax in the summer of 1956, which are of historical interest. There was a long deliberation in connection with the request of a Mr Mialhe to exploit phosphates on the Spratlys. A first note for the Secretary General of the Foreign Ministry, dated 5 January 1952 from the Ministry of Overseas Territories states that the PRC claimed these islands as within their frontiers, according to their maps. Nonetheless the Ministry of Overseas Territories proposed either to grant him such a concession or to state to him that the French Government had no objection and that he could undertake this enterprise at his own risk and peril.[31]

There followed an interdepartmental meeting at which it was agreed that the view of the Foreign Ministry was most important as its juridical status was a question for that Ministry. Its representative said that it was not favorable to granting a concession because of the imprecision of the relations of France with China.[32]

Consequently a letter from the Ministry of Foreign Affairs to that of Overseas Territories replied on 17 January 1952, that the granting of a concession to M. Miahle is not opportune at the moment in an overseas territory which is particularly exposed and of which the possession is claimed by several countries, such as China.[33]

This is not to say that to themselves the French gave any credence to either the Chinese or the Philippine claims. For the Chinese (Mainland) it seemed to amount to a historic claim that the South China Sea as such belonged to China. This was reflected in the school maps used in China.[34] This view was highly contestable, and was not accompanied by any claim that China had ever occupied the islands (in modern times). [35] As for the Philippines, it merely claimed that proximity to them gave it title in international law, which was not legally serious.[36]

---

ibid. In a similar tone the Committee for Indochina should encourage action by the Admiral d'Argenlieu, while also asking the U.S. Navy to refrain from encouraging the Philippines to make claims to the Spratlys.

31 Ibid., 117-2, 5 January 1952, p. 86.

32 Ibid., Reunion of 15 January in Ministry of Overseas territories, p. 88.

33 Ibid., 117-2, p. 91.

34 For instance, ibid., 117-2, p. 130 Note of the Direction-General of Political Affairs, 11 July 1955.

35 Ibid., 117-2 Note Ministry Foreign Affairs, Asie-Oceanie 8 September 1953, p. 112.

36 Note 72, p. 131.

Especially important, for an overview, is a memorandum responding to a major naval expedition to the Spratleys from the Republic of China (Taipei) over 13 days in, reported on 16 June 1956 in the *China Post*, including landings and postings of national markers on various islands.[37] Almost simultaneously, on the 18 June 1956, there was a meeting the League of the Civil Servants of the Revolution in the Prefecture of Saigon, with 400 present, where a Vietnamese official made on the 18 June 1956 in which categorical claims were made to both the Spratleys and Paracels, reported by the French Ambassador back to Paris, with a request that France make a clear response.[38]

Following these events, there is the following crucial memorandum from the Minister of Foreign Affairs to the Minister for Overseas French Territories and to the Minister of the Marine, 3 July 1956. It contains extensive reference to legal advice and to indications that the previous legal advice to fortify the French presence on the islands was not followed effectively.[39] The following is a close translation:

> You will have heard of the efforts made by a Philippine subject to lead his government to appropriate certain territory in the archipelago. While the government of the Philippines continues a waiting position (reste dans l'expectative) those of Taipei, Peking and Saigon have publicly claimed exclusive possession of the Spratleys. The government of Hanoi has said nothing.
>
> We have reminded the Philippines that the Spratleys are French, at least since the notice in the Official Journal in 1933. The position has also been made clear to the Nationalist China Chargé d'Affaires in Paris. The government of South Vietnam has been so insistent on its claim, in our view wrong, in the last fifteen days, that it appears difficult not to recall our title to the islands officially, and failure to do so has the danger to weaken in a certain measure our legal position. But such a step can lead to a certain tension in Franco-Vietnamese relations, when we have other more important problems in discussion. Whenever we establish diplomatic relations with Peking this will also be an issue between us. This is the political aspect of the affair.
>
> On the legal level, on the other hand, the Jurisconsult of the Department states that the thesis of French sovereignty over the Spratleys contains, unfortunately, certain weaknesses. Without doubt, against Vietnam, we can validate:

37 Dossier 522, especially 10.234/3 Embassy of France at Taipei, 16 June 1956 to the Minister of Foreign Affairs, Paris p. 322 islands names as Taiping, Nanwei and Hsiyueh were the subject of landings and Nantse, Peitse, Chungnieh, Hungsiu and Nanyeh were the subject of inspections.

38 Ibid., p. 325 Saigon 19 June 1956 Ambassador.

39 Dossier 522, Asie-Oceanie 1944-; Chine 1956–1967 E 10. 23 4/5 p. 330, 3 July 1956.

a) That they were discovered by the French, not the case with the Paracels, Vietnamese since the 18th century;

b) That they were not claimed by Vietnam in 1949, although they figure on French maps;

c) That there was no mention of them in the treaty placing Cochin-China under the authority of the Head of state of Vietnam.

But at the same time

1) If the official possession of the islands by the French government took place in 1933 and was published in the J.O. on 26 July 1933, it appears the islands were never attached by an official decision to a province of Indo-China. In practice they are considered as included administratively in the province of Baria (French Cochina), by virtue of instructions given by the Governor General of Indo-China, in March 1929 "to facilitate possible operations of a company to explore for minerals and study the geological possibilities of the islands".

   The absence of official attachment could, without doubt, constitute an element of refutation of the Vietnamese thesis, but it would be difficult to invoke without weakening our own thesis of French sovereignty on the islands. International law attaches a decisive importance to affirmative, official acts of sovereignty.

2) The argument that one can draw from the absence, in the letter of 19 March 1949 of M. Pignon to Bao Daï, of any mention of the Spratley Islands, is not a proof, and is founded only by arguing a contrario, which, in international law, is not determining.

3) At the San Francisco Conference 7 September 1951 the Vietnam delegate affirmed officially the rights of Vietnam over the Spratleys.

4) The facts of French possession appear to be reduced, since 1949, to two visits of ships, the Commandant Giraud, and in 1955 and the naval escorter, Francis Garnier last January.

On this last point there are plenty of files indicating the true nature of this apparent French activity. For instance there is a telegram from Saigon, dated 17 May 1951, which refers to the 1946 Legal Advice to show presence. It remarks that there was a request from the same Ministry, through the Ministry for Overseas Territories to the Ministry of the Navy, not to send the French Navy in inspection, because it was known that there were Chinese, so that the most that could be eventually envisaged was an aerial reconnaissance. The Chinese Government (Populare) continues to intend to include the whole of the South China Sea (le Mer de Chine Méridionale) in their sphere of influence.[40] As a follow up to this the French Embassy in China (presumably Taipei) registered the existence of a PRC protest against the attempts of French Imperialists to seize the Spratleys in 1933 despite the fact that China's attachment to the islands goes back to the Song Dynasty. The Chinese Government at the time is supposed to have made very strong protest against the incursion into both the Paracels and the Spratleys.[41]

The Minister concludes the same 1956 Memorandum to his colleague in the Ministry of Overseas Territories by asking whether the islands have any practical value to France, given that it no longer has any bases in Vietnam, and given also both the diplomatic aspect and the prospect of an international arbitration.

There follows a very important Note for the Director General of Political Affairs in the French Foreign Ministry, which indicates what steps were taken to make the French position known. The French Government considers the Spratleys French, but recognizes they are claimed by Beijing, Taipei and Saigon, not to mention an individual Philippine. The note states that the Philippine Government and the Chargé d'Affaires of Nationalist China in Paris have had it made clear to them that the Spratleys are under French sovereignty. However, given the insistence of South Vietnam on its rights, France has been minded to inform it also, but given also the fact that, on the juridical level, there are certain weaknesses in France's case, and the likelihood that this issue would have disagreeable consequences for our relations with Vietnam, we wish to know from the Navy and Overseas Territories Ministries how important these islands are after our departure from Vietnam. The same considerations apply also in the event that we reestablish relations with Beijing. This issue will increase our difficulties.[42]

The responses of the two Ministries (Overseas Territories and the Navy) were to affirm that the Spratleys were French territory. The Navy mentioned the additional visit of the "Dumont D'Urville" in July 1956. The absence of territory in Indo-China considerably reduced the interest of the Navy. However, it would be regrettable if the efforts made by the Navy from 1930 to 1956 to maintain and recall French title to the territory would not profit France when it came to negotiations for which there could be some exchange.[43]

Overseas territories had something distinctive to say. It was very important that the Spratleys had not been transferred to Vietnam in 1949. It might appear that the islands have little interest now that France has no footing in Indo-China. However, they are rich in guano deposits and suitable as meteorological station-bases. We should reserve our rights. We should insist on the fundamental point that we do not devolve to Vietnam the title to all the territories which we have in the Far East.

40 Dossier 213, 117-2, p. 76, Saigon 17 May 1951, Hausssaire.
41 Ibid., 117-2, p. 83, 28 August 1951, Chataigneau.
42 Ibid., E1023.4/3 12 July 1956, p. 340.
43 Ibid., E 10.23.h.3 3 August 1956, p. 352.

We should be on guard against the way that Indonesia is behaving with respect to Irian.[44]

A further detail worth elaborating is that there was a visit of a French Navy, already mentioned, "Dumont d'Urvilee" to the Spratleys on 21 July 1956. It was under instruction to make no mark of a French claim but merely to observe. It noticed that some Nationalist Chinese markers had been defaced and removed by the Philippine, Cloma. Chinese signs remained.[45]

There is a note of the Minister of Foreign Affairs to the Ambassador Extraordinary, saying that a naval mission should destroy the Chinese signs and restore the French ones, when they cast anchor before these islands (lorsqu'ils mouillent devants ces iles).[46]

A final document does appear to leave the story very much as the UK National Archive describes it. This is an undated, except that it is probably August 1956 (Note pour the Cabinet of the Minister (of Foreign Affairs)), full of hand written amendments. It states the responses of the Overseas Territories and Navy Ministries to the Foreign Ministry. It adds that the Jurisconsult of the Department considers that "if we have certain juridical titles to the possession of the Spratleys, our file (dossier), in case of international arbitration, still presents certain gaps". It continues:

> It is therefore not entirely excluded that we may be lead, at a date and in conditions not yet determined, to renounce our claims on this archipelago. While we await an eventual regulation of the problem, the attitude of the government ought not to be to make such a renunciation more difficult before its own (national) opinion or before international opinion. It would be also wise not to let this issue weigh heavily on our relations with other governments.
>
> The agitation which has developed with respect to the Spratley Islands in certain foreign countries, since the month of May, renders very desirable, that we conceive, with clarity, the position which we must take. In these conditions there are three possibilities:
>
> 1) Negotiate our rights on the Spratleys with one of the governments which have made claims
> This solution is to be avoided. If we abandon to Vietnam, for example, our rights over the Spratleys, without engaging ourselves subsequently to sustain the Vietnamese claims, one will give us nothing in exchange; and if we contract such an engagement, we will have difficulties with Communist China.

44 Ibid., 4 August Ministry of Overseas territories, p. 354.

45 Ibid., Extraordinary Ambassador Hoppenot, 9 August 1956, p. 357; and Rear Admiral Douguet Report of Visit, Maritime Pacific Force, 6 August 1956, p. 358.

46 Ibid., 22 August 1956, p. 363.

2) Maintain our rights, but with discretion, in reducing as much as possible the number of our actions and public declarations. Such an attitude will not be easy to observe, when one takes into account the agitation of the other claimants.

3) Pretend to consider, contrary to the thesis that we have sustained up until now, that the Spratleys have been transferred implicitly to Vietnam the same time as Cochina.
This option has the advantage of avoiding having to submit to Parliament the cession of the Spratleys.
The Direction for Asie-Oceanie would wish to receive instructions on this subject from the Cabinet of the Minister.[47]

As the UK Archive indicates, until the 1970s this French Department received no instructions!

The final stage in the story, in terms of the archival material so far researched, is the extended survey of the issue of the Spratly Islands by the Legal Advisers and the Research Department concluded in January 1975. It is divided into three parts, an Update of the Memorandum RR 7/2 of 27 January 1972, The Legal Advisers' Minute and the 1972 RR 7/2.[48] RR refers to the Research Department of the Foreign Office, which assembled all the Foreign Office records for perusal by the Legal Advisers. The RR 7/2 is structured in numbered paragraphs which are very frequently cited in the Legal Advisers' Minute. So the Legal Minute has to be read in conjunction with the RR 7/2, while the Update of 1975 appears to conclude the exercise. This comes to about 24 pages of text and is undoubtedly open to various interpretations.

Firstly, the Legal Minute makes a slight criticism of a Law Officers opinion of 29 July 1932 on the strength of the British claim to the Spratleys, which they rejected as too weak in terms of effective exercise of sovereignty. This legal opinion of 1932 was written just before the decision of the PCIJ in the *Legal Status of Eastern Greenland* case. The Court introduced the element of relativity of claims in "thinly populated or unsettled countries".[49] The point the Legal Minute makes is crucial to the style of the legal argument in the Minute which is concerned to juxtapose the relative strength of the different country arguments. The UK claim then based upon granting rights to the Central Borneo Company in 1889 might have prevailed, but much would have depended upon whether there was an alternative

47 Ibid., August 1956 10-23-4-3, pp. 364–6

48 FCO 51/411. The Legal Advisers' Minute is described as "reexamination of claims to sovereignty over the Spratley Islands in a minute of 1 February 1974 from Mrs. Denza to Mr. Chapman in South East Asia Department".

49 Ibid., Legal Advisers' reexamination of claims to sovereignty etc. It is signed by Eileen Denza, but titled so as to suggest that it had been circulated among the legal advisers generally.

claim "or continuous occupation on behalf of China ... ". The Minute quotes the key wording of the Court " ... In many cases the tribunal has been satisfied with very little in the way of actual exercise of sovereign rights, provided that the other State could not make out a superior claim. This is particularly true in the case of claims to sovereignty over areas in thinly populated or unsettled countries ... ".[50]

The structure of the Legal Minute appears to be to defeat the South Vietnamese claim in various stages by showing that the only key claim, apart from China's, is France's. This strategy of legal argument appears then to place France in a position to block the South Vietnamese until 1974 when the Legal Minute was written. North Vietnam can be taken to have admitted the Chinese claim in 1958. The Philippine claim is similarly blocked by virtue of the fact that it relies upon the successful acquisition of title by Japan after 1939 which Japan was then compelled to renounce in favour of no one at the San Francisco Peace Conference. The Legal Minute finally expresses regret at the failure of the Foreign Office up until now to consider the merits of the Chinese claim, speculating as to reasons for this neglect. Given that the Spratlys were never *terra nullius*, that the French continued to be the best claimant against the Chinese until 1971–1974, and given the formal, final abandonment of the British claim, this gave, relatively, the strongest place to the Chinese claim, which goes back comfortably to the nineteenth century at least, and which always contested the French claim.

In the course of considering the British claim, the R.D. RR 7/2 says that the relevant part of the Foreign Office brief for the Japanese Peace Conference in 1951 reads "HMG have a claim to Spratly which has never been formally abandoned; but they are not prepared to contest the French claim to sovereignty which is considered to be good in law".[51] This fact was not admitted to the Americans, when asked, in 1955, but in 1956, in the face of a request to send a UK ship, HMS Dampier, to Spratly to assist the Shell Company of Borneo, it was decided with the concurrence of the Legal Advisers, that HMS Dampier should not hoist the flag, nor even formally visit the island.[52]

However, when the South Vietnamese made their claim in 1971 the British reiterated their own claims from activities in the late nineteenth century, which led to Britain never having acknowledged other claims.[53] However, the main thrust of the Legal Minute was that this was not the case:

> Internally at any rate we had clearly acknowledged the French claim, and we had by acquiescing in it lost any "faint prospect of success" that we had in the

50 Ibid., under the rubric of The United Kingdom.

51 Ibid., RR 7/2 para. 45.

52 Ibid., para. 46.

53 Ibid., para. 47. See further two brief legal minutes by H. Darwin and A. Watts, that Britain should not recognize the Vietnamese claim and say instead that the UK neither abandons its own claims nor recognizes the Vietnamese: FCO 15/1440 FAP 4/2 Darwin to Margetson 19 October 1971; ibid., FAP 4/2, Watts to Gordon, 1 September 1971.

> 1930s in regard to the claim. Moreover we seem to have said to Parliament in 1939, at the time of the Japanese annexation, that the islands belonged to France.[54]

This opens the way to trace the abandonment of the French claim in favor of no one. Firstly, it is noted that the weakness of the Vietnamese claim for the nineteenth century was that occupation was not followed up by "effective administration, exploitation or any other act of sovereignty". Instead:

> The acts relied upon to show effective occupation were later carried on by France. It is quite clear that France was not acting on behalf of Vietnam in carrying out her occupation during the 1930s – and this is underlined by the fact that although France has ceded her rights in respect of the Paracels to Vietnam she has not done this in regard to the Spratley Islands. I therefore do not think that her claim could stand up against a rival claim by France.[55]

This opinion is elaborated at much greater length in R.D. RR 7/2. The French informed the Philippine Department of Foreign Affairs in June 1956 "that France claimed the Spratly Islands by right of occupation in 1932–33". When the subject was discussed again between the British and the French at the Quai d'Orsay in November 1971, the French Sous-Directeur stated "it was unlikely that France would abandon her claim because of the trouble this would cause amongst other claimants".[56] However, the basis of the Legal Minute is:

> At the time of the armed confrontation in the Paracels[57] HMG made informal enquiries of the French as to the status of their claim. The French indicated privately that they considered their own claim to the Spratlys to have lapsed.[58]

This brings one to the Philippines. Apart from arguments about cession (that the Spratleys were part of the Spanish Empire) and contiguity (that they are closest to the Philippines), the main argument considered is that after Japan's defeat the islands became *terra nullius,* and could be made the subject of occupation, which the Philippines have attempted, like the Japanese before them. This supposes Japan acquired title, which is not accepted. It had "only a rather dubious claim":

> The Philippine Government are in a similar position to the Government of Japan in 1939 – they have a claim which might in time, by occupation in the absence

54 Legal Minute, The United Kingdom.
55 Ibid., rubric Vietnam.
56 R.D. RR 7/2.
57 I.e. January 1974.
58 Update memorandum, 21 January 1975, para. 9.

> of protests or challenge by other claimants, transform itself into a valid title. It has not yet done so, and it seems highly unlikely that it will.[59]

The Chinese claim (PRC) is finally favored by a process of elimination of the other claims. On that basis the Legal Minute concludes, ironically, "that China is left cantering past the winning post". According to US sources China's claims date back to the fifteenth century, not merely through maps but because the islands have been visited since time immemorial, annually by Chinese fishermen:

> who have lived on the islands at times for the purpose of fishing in the surrounding waters. Our own Colonial Office List confirms this claim by stating (from 1891) that the islands were visited by Chinese junks for the purpose of collecting turtle.[60]

In 1932 the Foreign Office Legal Advisers refer to an incident on Amboyne Cay in 1879. Two British subjects licensed to extract guano were taking off two cargoes of it when they were attacked by their own Chinese coolies. They shot two of them dead and Mr. Teacher, as British Consul General in Borneo or Governor of Labuan, tried and sentenced the rest at Labuan for this attack. It was queried in Minutes of Colonial Office Papers of 1888–89 what the jurisdiction of Mr. Teacher would have been to try these men for a crime committed in Amboyne Bay, because the papers of 1877–1879 indicate that the islands were beyond the limits of the colony of Labuan.[61] The general point that the Islands were never attached to a Colony may be the tip of the iceberg and ownership of the islands in the minds of the colonial officials needs to be more extensively explored.

In any case, the Legal Minute mentions, how there is no evidence "either that we considered the possibility in the 1870s that the Spratley Islands belonged to China or that China protested our activities. This may well have been due to the fact that we did not regard China at that period as fully as a member of the family of nations".[62] Nonetheless, by the 1930s the Chinese would have had a title, either because they had it before 1877 or because it revived as the British claim was gradually extinguished. They protested, "on all appropriate occasions", the French claims in 1933, the Japanese in 1939, at the Peace Conference in 1951 and recently with the Philippines:

> This would mean that France did not in the 1930s acquire a title by occupation – and there is no doubt that she did not exercise sovereign rights over the islands for long enough to establish a claim by prescription. When Japan relinquished

59 Legal Minute, rubric The Philippines.

60 Legal Minute rubric France and China.

61 CO 273/580/6 W 8753/178/17/1932 Foreign Office to Law Officers of the Crown, para. 8.

62 Legal Minute rubric France and China.

> control of the islands in 1945, Chinese warships were sent to Itu Aba, stone tablets claiming Chinese sovereignty were erected and weather and wireless stations were set up.[63]

While there was little further Chinese activity after 1950, the French, for their part, did not resurrect their activity, which left the Chinese in the lead. The French have made no further assertions in public of their claims since the 1930s and that would leave China "cantering past the winning post".[64]

The Legal Minute concludes that there is no reason to object to any Chinese claim or to any action by China which amounts to exercise of sovereignty over the Spratleys. At the same time in June 1974 the Foreign Secretary advised the Cabinet on treating a British claim as lapsed. Political considerations were that Britain would have no interest to resist a Chinese occupation of the islands. The Chinese claim was the strongest. However, no public indication of preference for the Chinese claim was given.[65]

C. Conclusion to discussion of Imperial Disruption

Quite apart from the difficulties of comparing incomplete Chinese, French, British and other national archives in the region, what the just completed historical narrative illustrates is a further hugely contestable fact about the history of the dispute raised by the Philippines. It is that, after there was known to be a contest about ownership of the Nansha islands, Vietnam and the Philippines have seized many of the islands in the early 1970s against protest from China. Because of the rules post-1945 relating to the use of force, the military occupation of these islands by the Philippines and Vietnam cannot be contested by China. That makes China's physical presence in the region appear weak, to rest somehow on a claim to the South China Sea as such and not to land. While the Philippines and Vietnam may now prefer to separate their maritime zones claims from the islands, that does not stand easily with their fierce struggle to control these islands.

Furthermore, with respect to the same historical narrative, it is important to mention that the Republic of China (Taiwan) occupies, since 1949–50, the largest island in the region, Itu Aba, part of a post-1945 strategy of the Republic of China to exert effective control of all of the Nansha and Xisha islands. This wider policy was frustrated by the Civil War in China and the subsequent partial withdrawal of the Republic of China from the region. Assuming that Itu Aba is an island (a further point of questionable justiciability – see below), it would be enough to generate an EEZ etc. maritime claim which would severely affect the Philippines. However, the Republic of China (Taiwan) has been under severe US pressure not to push diplomatically the significance of its hold over this island in the present

63 Ibid.
64 Ibid.
65 FCO 51/ 411.

dispute. Numerous authoritative reports indicate that the Republic of China is has been pressurized into remaining silent. This is another reason for the Tribunal to regard the adjudication, probably strongly favored by the US, to be operating in a highly politicized context. That context, for reasons of history, severely disadvantages China.[66]

Finally, there is the question whether article 121 of the LSCIII is itself justiciable. The Philippines are asking the Tribunal to declare that the Chinese U Shaped Line is contrary to the LSCIII. While the foundation which China is prepared to provide for this U Shaped Line is not clear, it is possible that it is a function of claiming CS and/or EEZ from the SCS Islands over which it claims sovereignty. If these islands do not generate anything more than at most a territorial sea, this would, presumably strike at the foundation of the Chinese claim. It is submitted that the problems of interpretation arising out of article 121 are too vague and yet too politically important to be left to judges who have essentially a consensual, institutional authority i.e. resting upon the willingness of states to submit to their judgment.

As is generally known, a major part of the Philippine argument is to go against the ordinary meaning of article 121 of the LOSCIII, and to argue that not only rocks but also islands must be able to sustain human habitation and economic life – whatever that itself means – to qualify to generate EEZs etc. The LOSCIII appears to say the contrary, that islands may generate EEZs, while rocks, which are unable to support human habitation or economic life, may not. The Philippines may be trying to argue from supposed wider purposes of the LOSCIII, or in some sense systematically, also by reworking the evidence of the conference preparatory materials. However, once again it is probably the case that the issue is non justiciable.[67] Indeed Dr Yann Huei Song has called for the convening of a review conference in accordance with article 312 of the LOSCIII – which comes to the same as non-justiciability at present.[68]

In any case, underlying these conflicts are wider issues which throw into question the very wisdom of the LOSIII, which attaches so much significance to the principle that claims to the sea and its resources follow from such a vague concept as land. As a matter of both law and politics, a state's territory means a great deal not encompassed by the concept of "land". Claims to historic rights complicate this picture further. A fundamental question in relation to the SCS is the relationship of history to the present. The evolution of "human habitation and economic life" (borrowing the terms of article 121 (3) of the LOSCIII) from, let us say, the fifteenth century to the present is so vastly changed that it is not immediately obvious that criteria for "human habitation or economic life"

66 <http://www.reuters.com/assets/print?aid=USBREA4O0E620140525>.

67 <http://www.un.org/depts/los/convention_agreements/texts/unclos/part8.htm> for the terms of article 121. It says islands have the same CS and/or EEZ as any other land, but that rocks which are not inhabitable or economically viable, do not.

68 <http://chinesejil.oxfordjournals.org/content/9/4/663.full>.

applicable in one century are equally applicable in another. One needs to reflect on how far and in what ways the region of the SCS has changed over the centuries and to what extent these changes should be legally significant.

The Suitability of International Law and International Courts to Determine a Territorial Dispute with an Historical Dimension, Crossing Imperial History Lines

The entire jurisprudence of international law is concerned only with the scenario that former colonial or Western powers are trying to delimit remote boundaries among themselves in circumstances which are not politically volatile. Which of two countries has relatively the better title to a third piece of land in terms of the effective exercise of territorial jurisdiction, a mark of statehood and the only basis of title in modern international law?

The traditional, Western international law of territorial acquisition is indifferent to principles of democracy, self-determination and historical justice. It cannot provide a foundation for the resolution of territorial conflicts except in the context where the States Parties to the conflict decide that the issue is of so little importance to their national interests and identity that they want it ring fenced and disposed of through what is effectively ad hoc arbitration. For instance, it is conceivable that the disputes over islands in the case of Sovereignty over *Pedra Branca/Pulau Puteh*, Middle rocks and South Ledge in a judgment of the ICJ of 23 May 2008, between Malaysia and Singapore, could be resolved because the two states had decided that it was not an issue which should be allowed to affect the overall relations between the two countries. It boiled down to an investigation of the division of responsibilities among colonial districts of the former British Empire, which had control over all of these islands in the past. Given the desire to limit the effect of the dispute, the ICJ would broadly satisfy the parties by having ostensible recourse to colonial administrative history to share out the islands among the two states.[69]

The *Western Sahara Advisory Opinion* is factually closer to the situation in the South China Sea. It is worth mentioning at more length because the whole judgment (technically, opinion) of the Court is taken up with assessing the nature of the display of authority by Morocco and Mauritania over the so-called Western Sahara at the time of the Spanish colonization in the 1880s. Morocco requested the Court (1975, para. 93) to take into account the special structure of the Sherifan state. While the Court did not say that international law required a state to have any particular structure "at the same time, where sovereignty over territory is claimed, the particular structure of a State may be a relevant element in appreciating the reality or otherwise of a display of State activity adduced as evidence of that sovereignty … ". Morocco endeavored to convince the Court that

69 <http://www.icj-cij.org/docket/files/130/14492.pdf>.

it could show displays of "internal" authority by pointing to "the allegiance of Saharan caids to the Sultan … through Tekna caids … the Sultan's authority and influence were exercised on the nomad tribes pasturing in Western Sahara … " (para. 99). The response of the Court to these arguments, and to similar arguments from Mauritania, may usefully be quoted at length:

> 162. The materials and information presented to the Court show the existence, at the time of Spanish colonization, of legal ties of allegiance between the Sultan of Morocco and some of the tribes living in the territory of Western Sahara. They equally show the existence of rights, including some rights relating to the land, which constituted legal ties between the Mauritanian entity, as understood by the Court, and the territory of Western Sahara. On the other hand, the Court's conclusion is that the materials and information presented to it do not establish any tie of territorial sovereignty between the territory of Western Sahara and the Kingdom of Morocco or the Mauritanian entity. Thus the Court has not found legal ties of such a nature as might affect the application of resolution 1514 (XV) in the decolonization of Western Sahara and, in particular, of the principle of self-determination through the free and genuine expression of the will of the peoples of the Territory (cf. paras 54–9 above).[70]

In our context the remarks of Judge Petren in the *Western Sahara Advisory Opinion* seem especially apposite. He posed the question as to whether arguments about applying the principle of self-determination of the peoples to the population of the Spanish Western Sahara in the face of the pre-colonial claims of Morocco and Mauritania to the same territorial space could make sense. An extensive consideration of his comments will give a very full indication of the risks of submitting an East China Sea territorial dispute to the International Court of Justice or other international adjudication.

> … The decolonization of a territory may raise the question of the balance which has to be struck between the right of its population to self-determination and the territorial integrity of one or even of several States. The question may be raised, for example, whether the fact that the territory belonged, at the time of its colonization, to a State which still exists today justifies that State in claiming it on the basis of its territorial integrity. That argument has been put forward, and has been contested. The question of its validity in general and the question of its applicability to Western Sahara are undeniably of a legal character.
>
> *It seems however that questions of this kind are not yet considered ripe for submission to the Court. The reason is doubtless the fact that the wide variety of geographical and other data which must be taken into account in questions of decolonization have not yet allowed of the establishment of a sufficiently*

70 <http://www.icj-cij.org/docket/files/61/6195.pdf>.

> *developed body of rules and practice to cover all the situations which may give rise to problems. In other words, although its guiding principles have emerged, the law of decolonization does not yet constitute a complete body of doctrine and practice. It is thus natural that political forces should be constantly at work rendering more precise and complete the content of that law in specific cases like that of Western Sahara.*[71]

This is the sense of non-justiciabilty for which the present author argues. It is worth considering how well Judge Petren thought the Court had carried out its tasks:

> The Court did not feel the need to seek other information than that submitted to it by the interested States. It did not arrange for experts in Islamic law or in the history of northern Africa to sit with it as assessors, as its Statute would have allowed. It is common knowledge that its internal practice does not provide for the appointment of juges-rapporteurs. It is true that each judge has had to struggle-as far as his knowledge of languages would allow – through the immense literature existing on the questions of African history to which reference was made, and has been able to inform his colleagues of the fruit of his reading. It is nevertheless striking that the Advisory Opinion should be based almost exclusively on the documents and arguments submitted by the interested States, which are accepted or dismissed in the light of an examination of the evidence adduced. One does not find here the margin of uncertainty in which an advisory opinion ought to leave the facts which have neither been proved nor disproved.[72]

Conclusion

This is not to say international law can have no role to play. However, the time is not yet appropriate and the issues have not yet been formulated in a sufficiently complex and comprehensive way.

Firstly, much more thorough research needs to be done in the archives of all the states which have exercised power in the region over the last 150 years to systematize authoritatively a reliable international legal history of the region. The British and the French archives appear to point towards the strength of Chinese historical claims but they are not yet matched with Chinese archival sources. There is obvious scope for a joint Chinese Vietnamese archival inquiry. There is need for much more work on the interaction between the French Indo-China colonial administration and the Vietnamese states after 1945. So much of the Vietnamese claims raise huge difficulties of state succession, not only in relation to France, but also the changing Vietnamese state identity from the early nineteenth century onwards, including the question of the significance of its vassal status in relation to China.

---

71 Italics of the author <http://www.icj-cij.org/docket/files/61/6209.pdf>.
72 <http://www.icj-cij.org/docket/files/61/6209.pdf>.

Authoritative historical judgments need to be drawn by consensus on the significance of the imperialist interventions in the region and the extent it has been disturbed by them. Not merely France and Britain but also Japan were heavily engaged in the SCS region and greatly disturbed it. There were also some German interventions and an American presence during and after World War II, leading up to the San Francisco Peace Conference.

One factor stands out – the French claim to the entire SCS islands, both Xisha and Nansha. The fact that the British watched this very intensely and reported upon it closely, internally and directly to France, is so profoundly disruptive of any possible order in the region precisely because the authority of these two powers has collapsed and vanished and now the both of them want to take no responsibility for the impact of their interventions. They openly declare that they do not want to become involved. So there is a drastic rupture and void of the hegemonic control in the region during the time of Chinese and perhaps Vietnamese eclipse.

Quite apart from the difficulties of comparing incomplete Chinese, British, French and other national archives, another incontestable fact is that since the 1970s Vietnam and the Philippines have been willing to use force to seize most of the Spratley Islands in the South China Seas against protest from China. Because of the rules of international law, post-1945, relating to the use of force, the military occupation of these islands cannot be contested by China. This makes China's physical presence in the region appear weak, resting somehow on the claim to the South China Seas as such and not to land. This situation corresponds fully to the paradigm of international law expounded by Combaceau and Sur, and by Kelsen, in contrast to Lauterpacht. It is to misunderstand the nature of international law as a series of competing, aggressively subjective claims of individual states, to imagine that an international judge can resort, without the consent of the states, to supposedly platonic, general principles of international law to resolve conflicts among the states.

What also of the question of the standing and claims of countries which did not exist during the imperial period? Will historical records show how far the populations of the Philippines, the areas of now Malaysia and the former Dutch East Indies, not to mention other possible candidates, might have evidenced some historical presence in the region.

Obviously, as can be seen from the *Western Sahara Advisory Opinion,* the work has hardly started on the relationship between the concept of historical rights and so-called modern international law on territorial acquisition.

Greater clarity is also necessary on the exact nature of the international legal standards which are supposed to apply to the disputes as to territory ***and their maritime implications***. Do they change with history?

Finally, it has to be decided who has the authority to decide the disputes. Without a consensus on the last question, any appeal to so-called international law standards by one side or the other is merely what has come to be called "lawfare", or war by law. It is arguable that the Philippine arbitration is itself such "lawfare". Calls for China to respect the rule of law and submit to arbitration may also be "lawfare", a form of propaganda which plays on the general impression that there is clearly a LAW to be applied by the Tribunal.

PART III
Dispute Resolution Procedure, Jurisdiction and Admissibility

Chapter 4
Conciliation and Article 298 Dispute Resolution Procedures under the Law of the Sea Convention

Donald R. Rothwell

Introduction

International law has a significant role to play in the multiple disputes that exist throughout the South China Sea. The first relevant area of international law is that dealing with territoriality and the basis under international law that states are able to assert, and have recognised, territorial claims. This area of international law is well developed, and notwithstanding the passing of an era when new lands were being discovered and territorial claims were asserted, international courts are still being called upon to settle a number of contemporary territorial disputes.[1] Some of these disputes concern the direction of a territorial boundary, while others go directly to title over land territory such as islands.[2] The second body of international law of relevance is that associated with the law of the sea. The law of the sea has steadily developed over 400 years, first through customary international law based upon the practice of states and then post-World War II increasingly through the development of new treaties.[3] The Third United Nations Conference on the Law of the Sea ran from 1973–1982 and resulted in agreement being reached upon the 1982 United Nations Convention on the Law of the Sea (LOSC).[4] The LOSC, which entered into force in 1994, remains the dominant international law of the sea instrument that identifies the scope and extent of various maritime zones, provides mechanisms for the delimitation of maritime boundaries, and also for the resolution of international disputes as they relate to the law of the sea.

---

1 See generally Hitoshi Nasu and Donald R. Rothwell, "Re-Evaluating the Role of International Law in Territorial and Maritime Disputes in East Asia", *Asian Journal of International Law* 4 (2014), pp. 55–79.

2 See e.g. *Case Concerning Sovereignty over Pulau Ligitan and Pulau Sipadan* (Indonesia/Malaysia) (2002) *ICJ Reports* 625.

3 Donald R. Rothwell and Tim Stephens, *The International Law of the Sea* (Oxford: Hart, 2010), pp. 1–24.

4 1833 *United Nations Treaty Series* 397.

While international law recognises that 'the land dominates the sea' and accordingly coastal states need to be able to demonstrate their territorial sovereignty in order to be able to assert maritime claims, once territoriality is confirmed then a coastal state enjoys significant entitlements of sovereign rights and jurisdiction over its adjacent maritime domain. While overlapping maritime claims will be subject to an obligation on the part of the coastal states concerned to agree upon maritime boundaries,[5] nevertheless the potential entitlements of a coastal state to be able to enjoy access to living and non-living resources such as fish stocks, and oil and gas, make the confirmation of territoriality and the assertion of appropriate maritime claims a significant sovereign right.

It is in this context that the dispute resolution mechanisms found in Part XV of the LOSC are of particular significance.[6] The LOSC is distinctive amongst multilateral international treaties in that it contains within it compulsory mechanisms for dispute settlement. Every state party to the LOSC is therefore bound to abide by a range of general and specific mechanisms that are designed to bring about the peaceful resolution of international disputes as they relate to the law of the sea. There are some exceptions to the Part XV regime, especially as they relate to matters concerning territorial sovereignty and military operations. There is also a recognition that States Parties may wish to avail themselves of some dispute resolution mechanisms and not others. The consequence of this is that notwithstanding states having made a declaration as to which dispute resolution procedures they have opted out of, there remain in place certain default mechanisms which will always apply.

This chapter will review these issues as they particularly apply with respect to the mechanisms that are available to states under Article 298 of the LOSC with particular reference to the default mechanism of conciliation as a means of dispute resolution. It does so in the context of China's Article 298 declaration and the implications that may have for the outcome of Annex VII Arbitration proceedings commenced by the Philippines against China with respect to certain matters in the South China Sea. This chapter commences with a short review of those proceedings, before turning to consider mechanisms generally under Part XV of the LOSC, Article 298 declarations, and Annex V Conciliation. In conclusion some consideration will be given to the implications of these mechanisms for the Philippines/China South China Sea dispute.

Philippines Annex VII Arbitration Application

The Philippines 2013 initiation of Annex VII arbitration against China over their South China Sea disputes is one of the most significant developments for the law

5 LOSC, Articles 15, 74, 83.

6 See generally Igor V. Karaman, *Dispute Resolution in the Law of the Sea* (Leiden: Martinus Nijhoff, 2012); Natalie Klein, *Dispute Settlement in the UN Convention on the Law of the Sea* (Cambridge: Cambridge University Press, 2005).

of the sea more generally, and the South China Sea more specifically, since the LOSC entered into force in 1994.[7] Given the weight the LOSC places upon dispute resolution and its general significance at the time of the Convention's conclusion, it is clear that emphasis was placed upon not only the general principles of the peaceful settlement of disputes as a cornerstone of the new LOSC law of the sea regime, but also through the new institutional mechanisms established under Part XV to allow for a range of third party dispute settlement options. With this context, it should not be surprising that some states have sought to actively explore those options in the resolution of their law of the sea disputes, especially when the dispute involves states with significant differentials in their political power such as the Philippines and China. For the South China Sea, the Philippines action was also the first formal attempt to utilise third party dispute settlement in order to resolve South China Sea disputes since entry into force of the LOSC, clearly indicating that at least for the Philippines it had concluded that diplomatic options had been exhausted.

The Philippines notification to China, dated 22 January 2013, activated procedures under Article 287 and Annex VII of the LOSC. The Philippines notification and statement of claim provided:

> The Republic of the Philippines brings this arbitration against the People's Republic of China to challenge China's claims to areas of the South China Sea and the underlying seabed as far as 870 nautical miles from the nearest Chinese coast, to which China has no entitlement under the [LOSC] ..., and which, under the Convention, constitute the Philippine's exclusive economic zone and continental shelf.[8]

The Philippines claim gives particular attention to the asserted invalidity under the LOSC of China's "nine dash line". The Philippines contests the validity of this line and any attempts by China to assert sovereignty or sovereign rights over islands and other maritime features found within this area.[9] The Philippines application seeks an Award from the Arbitral Tribunal that:

1. The respective rights and obligations of the parties are governed by the LOSC and that China's claims based on the "nine dash line" are invalid;
2. Determines whether certain maritime features claimed by China and the Philippines are under Article 121 of the LOSC islands, low tide elevations or submerged banks and whether they are capable of generating maritime zones greater than 12 nm;
3. Enables the Philippines to exercise and enjoy rights within its EEZ and continental shelf.[10]

7 Republic of the Philippines, *Notification and Statement of Claim* (22 January 2013).
8 Ibid. para. 1.
9 Ibid. para. 2.
10 Ibid. para. 6.

The Philippines application raises a number of procedural issues that will need to be addressed prior to the Annex VII Arbitral Tribunal determining the claim on the merits. The first relates to China's acceptance of the jurisdiction of the Tribunal to hear and determine the Philippines claim. In 2006 China made a Declaration subsequent to its ratification of the LOSC in which it declared that it did not accept certain compulsory dispute resolution procedures under Part XV, including disputes with respect to "historic bays or titles".[11] This raises issues as to whether elements of China's disputes with the Philippines in the South China Sea would fall within this exception, including what precisely are the historic titles that China asserts in the South China Sea.[12] The second is that on 19 February 2013 China indicated that it would not participate in the proceedings before the Annex VII Tribunal.[13] This position would appear to be based upon China's view that consistent with its Article 298 Declaration the Annex VII Tribunal lacks jurisdiction. On 1 August 2013 China submitted a *note verbale* to the Permanent Court of Arbitration, which is the registry for the proceedings, indicating that "it does not accept the arbitration initiated by the Philippines" and that it will not be participating in the proceedings.[14] Nevertheless, Annex VII of the LOSC contains procedures whereby if one of the parties chooses to not participate in the proceedings, an Arbitral Tribunal can be constituted and proceed to a hearing of the application even in the case of a default appearance.[15] The Tribunal in the case of default of appearance will need to make a determination that it does possess jurisdiction over the dispute but also that the claim is "well founded" in both fact and law.[16]

The Philippines filed its Memorial in this case on 30 March 2014. On 3 June 2014 the Arbitral Tribunal issued its Procedural Order No. 2 in which it fixed 15 December 2014 as the date by which China was to submit its counter-memorial responding to the Philippines Memorial. On 21 May 2014, China submitted a note to the Permanent Court of Arbitration in which it restated the position that it had taken previously that "it does not accept the arbitration initiated by the Philippines".[17]

---

11 China (2006) Declaration made after ratification (25 August 2006) available at <www.un.org/Depts/los/convention_agreements/convention_declarations.htm> (11 October 2013)

12 Z. Gao and B.B. Jia, "The Nine-Dash Line in the South China Sea: History, Status, and Implications" *American Journal of International Law* 107 (2013), p. 98 at 113–15, 121–2; F. Dupuy and P.-M. Dupuy "A Legal Analysis of China's Historic Rights Claim in the South China Sea" *American Journal of International Law* 107 (2013), pp. 124–41.

13 Permanent Court of Arbitration, *The Republic of the Philippines v. The People's Republic of China* (2013).

14 Ibid.

15 LOSC, Annex VII, Articles 3, 9.

16 LOSC, Annex VII, Article 9.

17 Permanent Court of Arbitration, *Press Release: Arbitration between the Republic of the Philippines and the People's Republic of China* (3 June 2014).

Part VX LOSC Dispute Resolution Procedures

As noted above, the LOSC is distinctive because it contains within Part XV compulsory procedures for the settlement of disputes. The law of the sea, alongside the procedures established by the WTO for the settlement of international trade dispute disputes, is therefore one of only two multilateral international treaties that provide for compulsory settlement of disputes. While the framework and mechanisms that are established are in conformity with the general provisions of Article 33 of the Charter of the United Nations and the peaceful settlement of international disputes promoted by the Charter and more generally within the UN system, of which the law of the sea is a part, there is a clear distinction between the mechanisms provided for in in Part XV as follows. Section 1 of Part XV outlines 'General Provisions' which generally reflect Article 33 of the Charter, how these mechanisms may interact with other treaties dealing with law of the sea matters that contain dispute resolution mechanisms, and some specific provisions of a general dispute resolution nature that have application to the LOSC. Section 2 of Part XV, on the other hand, contains 'Compulsory Procedures Entailing Binding Decisions' which as its title suggests establishes the LOSC's distinctive compulsory dispute resolution procedures including new institutional mechanisms. Closely linked to these procedures are 'Limitations and Exceptions to Applicability of Section 2' found in Section 3.

Section 1 of Part XV places emphasis upon the peaceful settlement of international disputes consistent with the Charter of the United Nations,[18] and reaffirms the capacity of states to choose any peaceful means of dispute settlement,[19] thereby reaffirming the capacity of states to not only utilise mechanisms available to them under the LOSC but any other means of their choice to peacefully settle their disputes. Such means may include those that have been provided for under other bilateral, regional or general agreements, or ones that the states have specifically chosen in the context of a particular dispute.[20] In the absence of those alternate mechanisms Part XV creates obligations upon states to exchange views regarding a dispute.[21] There is also direct reference to conciliation procedures and the mechanisms available under Annex V.[22] However, it can be observed under Article 284 that conciliation is a purely voluntary process in which one of the parties will issue an invitation to the other disputing party/parties to agree upon a conciliation procedure and make use of either Annex V conciliation or any other conciliation procedure the parties may agree upon.

Section 2 outlines the default compulsory procedures for dispute settlement that are applicable in the absence of the dispute having been settled under the

18 LOSC, Article 279.
19 LOSC, Article 280.
20 LOSC, Articles 281, 282.
21 LOSC, Article 283.
22 LOSC, Article 284.

general mechanisms provided for in Section 1.[23] Of significance for this chapter is the 'Choice of Procedure' mechanism provided for under Article 287 whereby States Parties to the LOSC are able to elect to choose between referral of a dispute to the International Court of Justice, International Tribunal for the Law of the Sea (ITLOS), Annex VII Arbitration, or Annex VIII Special Arbitration. Other than the International Court of Justice, the latter three bodies are all distinctive to the LOSC. There is a further inbuilt default mechanism provided for in the case of those states that have not made an election as to which procedure they would prefer for the settlement of their disputes, or where the parties to the dispute have not accepted the same procedure. In those instances, arbitration before an Annex VII Tribunal will be adopted unless in the case of where there is incompatibility in choice of the procedures the parties otherwise agree upon another procedure.[24] Notwithstanding the compulsory nature of these mechanisms, the LOSC does anticipate that a dispute may arise as to whether a court or tribunal has jurisdiction to decide a matter and Article 288 (4) anticipates that such matters will be determined by the relevant court or tribunal. Since entry into force of the LOSC there have been occasions where the jurisdiction of ITLOS has been challenged, such as in the 2013 *Arctic Sunrise* case,[25] and also where the jurisdiction of an Annex VII Tribunal has been challenged as occurred in the *Southern Bluefin Tuna* cases.[26] Therefore, notwithstanding the compulsory procedures that have been established under Section 2 it is not unknown for states to contest jurisdiction of a court or tribunal, or to take the view that jurisdiction does not reside with the court or tribunal and to not appear before that body.[27] Ultimately the effect of the Section 2 procedures is that states are given a choice as to which bodies they prefer for the settlement of their disputes, and that in the absence of agreement between disputing states the matter will be determined by an Annex VII Arbitral Tribunal.

---

23 The interaction of Section 1 dispute settlement mechanisms and Section 2 compulsory procedures was briefly considered by the Annex VII Arbitral Tribunal in the *Southern Bluefin Tuna* case (Australia and New Zealand v. Japan) when the Tribunal formed the view that it did not have jurisdiction to consider the claim brought by Australia and New Zealand against Japan because there had been a failure to exhaust procedures under Section 1 as they related to an Article 282 regional agreement – in that instance the Convention on the Conservation of Southern Bluefin Tuna; see *Southern Bluefin Tuna Case* (Australia and New Zealand v. Japan), Award on Jurisdiction and Admissibility (2000) 39 ILM 1359.

24 LOSC, Article 287 (3), (5).

25 The *Arctic Sunrise* case (Kingdom of the Netherlands v. Russian Federation), Provisional Measures (22 November 2013), ITLOS Case No. 22.

26 *Southern Bluefin Tuna Case* (Australia and New Zealand v. Japan), Award on Jurisdiction and Admissibility (2000) 39 ILM 1359.

27 The position of the Russian Federation in the *Arctic Sunrise* case was that they did not accept the jurisdiction of ITLOS to consider provisional measures and accordingly did not appear before the tribunal: The *Arctic Sunrise* case (Kingdom of the Netherlands v. Russian Federation), Provisional Measures (22 November 2013), ITLOS Case No. 22.

Section 3 of Part XV of the LOSC deals with limitations and exceptions to the applicability of Section 2, the effect of which is to place certain constraints upon the way in which the compulsory procedures provided for under Section 2 function. These limitations are divided into two types. The first are those disputes which are excluded from the Section 2 mechanisms and are provided for in Article 297. Generally, these limitations concern disputes that relate to marine scientific research, and decisions made by a state regarding its sovereign rights with respect to the living resources of the exclusive economic zone (EEZ). Importantly for present purposes, Article 297 provides that in these instances settlement of the dispute shall be determined by way of conciliation.[28] The second type of exception is optional and is entirely dependent upon a state lodging a declaration either at the time of signature, ratification, accession or any time thereafter declaring that it does not accept one or more of the procedures provided for under Section 2. The effect of these Article 298 Declarations will be considered below.

Article 298 Declarations

While the LOSC creates a distinctive dispute resolution regime under Part XV, states retain the option of being able to indicate which of the formal third party mechanisms they prefer which they do by way of a declaration. Article 298 Declarations can be made by states with respect to three types of disputes. They are as follows:

a. Disputes with respect to the delimitation of maritime boundaries and the application of Articles 15, 74 and 83 of the LOSC, or disputes involving historic bays or titles;
b. Disputes concerning military activities; and
c. Disputes in respect of which the United Nations Security Council is exercising its functions.

A total of 31 states have lodged declarations in reliance upon Article 298 (1) of the LOSC.[29] The Declaration can relate to any one or more of the procedures provided for under Section 2, such that the state can exempt the dispute from only some of the Section 2 procedures or all of the Section 2 procedures.

28 LOSC, Article 297 (2), (3).

29 Those states are: Angola, Argentina, Australia, Belarus, Canada, Cape Verde, Chile, China, Denmark, Ecuador, Equatorial Guinea, France, Gabon, Ghana, Italy, Mexico, Montenegro, Norway, Palau, Portugal, Republic of Korea, Russian Federation, Saudi Arabia, Slovenia, Spain, Thailand, Trinidad and Tobago, Tunisia, Ukraine, United Kingdom, Uruguay; of which 27 include Article 298 (1)(a) procedures within the scope of their Declaration.

An Article 298 Declaration may raise issues as to its interpretation, and whether the state is able to only issue the Declaration activating the particular optional exception, or whether the terms of the Declaration can include some statement of understanding with respect to the effect of the Declaration. Given the potential ambiguity that may exist with respect to what constitutes 'historic bays or titles', there may be some merit in a state lodging a more expansive Declaration so that it can precisely identify how it interprets those provisions.

Declarations may be withdrawn by the state party, or they may elect to submit a dispute covered by the Declaration to any of the procedures specified in the LOSC.[30] As such there exists a level of flexibility with respect to how a state may seek to modify or withdraw its Article 298 Declaration, or to even elect ad hoc to not be bound by the terms of the Declaration in any particular instance.[31] Likewise, the lodgement of a Declaration does not impact upon proceedings that are pending before a court or tribunal.[32] However, it is important to note that this limitation does not apply with respect to a dispute, but rather only with respect to 'proceedings' that are pending. Article 298 Declarations can therefore have an impact upon an existing dispute which has yet to reach the stage of proceedings before a Section 2 court of tribunal.[33]

Of particular significance to this chapter, Article 298 (1)(a) disputes are not completely excluded from the application of Part XV dispute resolution mechanisms but rather will conditionally be subject to conciliation under Annex V. Three requirements must be met before Annex V conciliation may apply to the resolution of the dispute:

1. That a Declaration has been made relating to the categories of disputes identified in Article 298 (1)(a);
2. That the dispute is one that has arisen subsequent to the entry into force of the LOSC;
3. That no agreement has been reached between the parties "within a reasonable period of time".

Once these requirements are met, then a dispute subject to an Article 298 Declaration albeit exempted from the procedures of Section 2 and accordingly will not other than by way of an exceptional agreement between the parties be determined by a LOSC court or tribunal, becomes subject to conciliation under Annex V. However, when Annex V Conciliation is activated by way of Article 298, a further distinctive set of procedures apply to the conciliation.

30 LOSC, Article 298 (2).

31 Shabtai Rosenne and Louis B. Sohn (eds), *United Nations Convention on the Law of the Sea 1982: A Commentary* Vol V (Dordrecht: Martinus Nijohff, 1989), p. 115 [298.12].

32 LOSC, Article 298 (5).

33 As to the date from which an Article 298 Declaration takes effect, see the discussion in Rosenne and Sohn (eds), *United Nations Convention on the Law of the Sea 1982: A Commentary*, Vol. V, pp. 140–41 [298.44].

Article 298 (1)(a) conciliation procedures can be activated by any of the parties to the dispute. However a further exemption to these procedures applies due to the particular features of a dispute arising with respect to maritime boundaries, historic bays or titles. Here the words of Article 298 (1)(a)(i) need to be quoted in full. They are as follows:

> … any dispute that involves the concurrent consideration of any unsettled dispute concerning sovereignty or other rights over continental or insular land territory shall be excluded from such submission.

In short, this proviso makes clear conciliation procedures can only apply to maritime and not land disputes. [34]

Annex V Conciliation[35]

Procedures associated with conciliation under the LOSC are to be found in Annex V. Two types of conciliation are provided for. The first, referred to in Section 1 of Annex V is voluntary conciliation consistent with Article 284 of the LOSC which is located within the general dispute settlement procedures found in Section 1 of Part XV. The second is found in Section 2 of Annex V, and importantly is titled 'Compulsory Submission to Conciliation Procedure Pursuant to Section 3 of Part XV'. The procedures outlined in Section 2 deal with the particular dynamics of compulsory conciliation, and address the institution of proceedings,[36] failure to reply or to submit to conciliation,[37] and competence of the conciliation commission.[38] In sum, it is made clear that conciliation is a compulsory procedure that can arise under Article 298 (1)(a) and that once commenced the other party to the dispute "shall be obliged to submit to such proceedings". [39] Failure on the part of one of

34 Rosenne and Sohn (eds), *United Nations Convention on the Law of the Sea 1982: A Commentary*, Vol. V, p. 133 [298.31] refer to this category as 'mixed disputes' being "disputes that necessarily involve the concurrent consideration of any unsettled dispute concerning sovereignty or other rights over continental or insular land territory".

35 See generally A.O. Adede, *The System for Settlement of Disputes under the United Nations Convention on the Law of the Sea: A Drafting History and Commentary* (Dordrecht: Martinus Nijhoff, 1987), pp. 202–10; Rosenne and Sohn (eds), *United Nations Convention on the Law of the Sea 1982: A Commentary* Vol V, pp. 309–27.

36 LOSC, Annex V, Article 11.

37 LOSC, Annex V, Article 12.

38 LOSC, Annex V, Article 13.

39 LOSC, Annex V, Article 11 (2); Rosenne and Sohn (eds), *United Nations Convention on the Law of the Sea 1982: A Commentary*, Vol. V, p. 326 [A.V.33] observe that "Through this unilateral institution of proceedings and this obligation to submit to the procedure, a much more thorough system of conciliation than is found in earlier conventions has been created, especially with regard to the obligatory submission of disputes to the conciliation process".

the parties to submit to the proceedings is not a bar to the proceedings,[40] though it is clear in Article 13 that the competence of the conciliation commission may be challenged. Such a challenge could arise on the grounds that as noted above, the dispute arose prior to the entry into force of the LOSC, that a reasonable period of time had not been allowed to pass prior to the commencement of proceedings, or that the dispute was one that concurrently involved consideration of a land dispute.

Other than these distinctive features of Section 2, Annex V, conciliation commenced under Article 298 (1)(a) proceeds under the general conciliation procedures laid down in Articles 2–10 of Annex V.[41] A feature of these procedures is flexibility including the manner in which the procedure to be adopted by the conciliation commission is agreed upon,[42] which extends to whether oral or written submissions are received, and the capacity of the commission to "draw the attention of the parties to any measures which might facilitate an amicable settlement of the dispute".[43] Reaching an amicable settlement is further reinforced in Article 6 of Annex V, which makes clear that the functions of the Commission are to:

> … hear the parties, examine their claims and objections, and make proposals to the parties with a view to reaching an amicable settlement.

The final matter of procedural significance under the Annex V mechanisms is that the conciliation commission is to report within 12 months of its constitution.[44] The report is to be deposited with the Secretary-General of the United Nations who is to transmit the report to the parties.[45]

The general procedures with respect to conciliation are varied in an instance of compulsory conciliation arising under Article 298 (1)(a) once the commission's report has been presented. While Article 7(2) of Annex V makes clear that the report of the commission is not binding upon the parties, Article 298(1)(a)(ii) on the other hand provides that upon presentation of the conciliation report "the parties shall negotiate an agreement on the basis of that report", there by suggesting some level of compulsion on the part of the disputing parties to in good faith engage with the commission report.[46] In the absence of such an agreement being reached,

---

40 LOSC, Annex V, Article 12.

41 LOSC, Annex V, Article 14.

42 LOSC, Annex V, Article 4.

43 LOSC, Annex V, Article 5.

44 LOSC, Annex V, Article 7 (1).

45 LOSC, Annex V, Article 7 (1).

46 Tullio Treves, "What have the United Nations Convention and the International Tribunal for the Law of the Sea to offer as regards Maritime Delimitation Disputes?" in *Maritime Delimitation*, (eds) Rainer Lagoni and Daniel Vignes (Leiden: Martinus Nijhoff, 2006), p. 63, 76 refers to the "pressure" upon the states to settle their dispute arising from these procedures. It is observed that "the pressure on the State that is not ready to follow the recommendations is great". See also Adede, *The System for Settlement of Disputes under the United Nations Convention on the Law of the Sea*, pp. 280–81.

the parties are to mutually submit the dispute[47] to one of the procedures provided for under Part XV, Section 2, unless they agree otherwise.[48]

The consequence of these procedures is that the parties are given every incentive to either endorse the report of the conciliation commission, or to negotiate a settlement of the dispute on the basis of the report. Failure to reach such an agreement will then see the fundamental dispute settlement provisions of Part XV, Section 2 activated with the consequence that the state that originally lodged an Article 298 Declaration so as to exempt a dispute with respect to maritime boundaries, historic bays or titles from Section 2 procedures will eventually be forced to engage in those procedures if it has been unwilling to settle the dispute through Annex V conciliation.

This raises the consideration where conciliation has at face value failed to settle the dispute and Section 2 procedures are now activated as to how the "mutual consent" of the parties could in these circumstances be determined.[49] One view could be that such consent needs to be reached by separate agreement to refer the matter to a Section 2 court or tribunal. This view is taken by Rosenne and Sohn in the *Virginia Commentary* on Article 298. They observed:

> In case no substantive agreement is reached through such negotiations, there is also the further obligation to at least try to reach an agreement to select one of the procedures under Part XV, section 2, or some other procedure for settling the dispute. This agreement must also be negotiated in good faith, but can come into effect only by mutual consent.[50]

Churchill and Lowe commenting on these procedures observe that if the states are unable to reach agreement based on the commission report, "they must agree upon some other procedure for settling the dispute".[51]

A critical procedural issue that arises is how 'mutual consent' is attained, and whether this is consent which is specific to the dispute in question or consent that may previously have been given by the parties. The fact that 'consent' is referred to and not 'agreement' in Article 298 (1)(a)(ii) is significant. As such, it should be possible to refer to where the parties have mutually given their consent to resolve the dispute in either a general or specific context. The better view would therefore

47 LOSC, Article 298 (1)(a)(ii) uses the term 'question', which in context is taken to have the same meaning as 'dispute'.

48 A further exception to these procedures applies in the case of a "sea boundary dispute" where the parties had otherwise reached an arrangement, or via another bilateral or multilateral agreement that was binding upon the parties.

49 See LOSC, Article 298 (1)(a)(ii).

50 Rosenne and Sohn (eds), *United Nations Convention on the Law of the Sea 1982: A Commentary*, Vol. V, p. 134 [298.31].

51 R.R. Churchill and A.V. Lowe, *The law of the sea* 3rd (Manchester: Manchester University Press, 1999), p. 456.

be that in the absence of the parties mutually agreeing between themselves to utilise one of the Part XV, Section 2 courts and tribunals, the default would become arbitration in accordance with Annex VII consistent with the default procedures reflected in Article 287.[52] Here 'mutual consent' could properly be identified through the consent of a state becoming a LOSC party by which that state agrees to become subject to the Part XV procedures with respect to dispute settlement, including the compulsory procedures found in Section 2. Under those procedures, while Article 287 provides for a choice of procedure, in the absence of a state having made a choice by way of a declaration then the default procedure is Annex VII Arbitration.[53] Likewise, if the two disputing states have not accepted the same procedure, then the default once again becomes Annex VII Arbitration. [54]

Conciliation and Law of the Sea Disputes[55]

Crawford has described conciliation as having a "semi-judicial aspect, since the commission of persons empowered has to elucidate the facts, may hear the parties and must make proposals for a settlement, which is normally non-binding".[56] Conciliation as a method of dispute settlement has a history that formally extends throughout the twentieth century into the twenty-first century. Merrills has pinpointed conciliation as a form of recognised dispute settlement extending back to 1920,[57] while the 1928 General Act of Arbitration for the Pacific Settlement of International Disputes is one of the first significant multilateral instruments that directly referred to conciliation.[58] In modern treaty law, the practice of conciliation is often reflected in multilateral instruments as one amongst a number of possible means available to parties to resolve their disputes. Such examples can be found in treaties dealing with general international law, such as the Vienna Convention on the Law of Treaties,[59] or treaties dealing with environmental matters such

52 cf. Rosenne and Sohn (eds), *United Nations Convention on the Law of the Sea 1982: A Commentary*, Vol. V, p. 134 [298.31] who argue that: "If no such agreement can be reached, the only obligation that remains is the one under Part XV, section 1, to proceed expeditiously to an exchange of views regarding the settlement of the dispute by further negotiations or 'other peaceful means'" (article 283, para. 1).

53 LOSC, Article 287 (3).

54 LOSC, Article 287 (5).

55 For a specific analysis of conciliation under the LOSC see Sienho Yee, "Conciliation and the 1982 UN Convention on the Law of the Sea", *Ocean Development and International Law* 44 (2013), pp. 315–34.

56 James Crawford, *Brownlie's Principles of Public International Law* 8th (Oxford: Oxford University Press, 2012), p. 719.

57 J.G. Merrills, *International Dispute Settlement* 5th (Cambridge: Cambridge University Press, 2011), p. 58.

58 [1975] Australian Treaty Series No 49, Articles 1–16.

59 [1974] Australian Treaty Series 2.

as the 1992 Convention on Biological Diversity[60] and the 1992 United Nations Convention on Climate Change.[61] Nevertheless, while there is considerable evidence of conciliation as a means for dispute settlement, state practice associated with conciliation is not extensive. Merrills noted in 2011 that in the 90 years of conciliation being available as a means of dispute settlement, less than 20 cases had been heard.[62] He observed that:

> When one bears in mind the more than 200 bilateral treaties and the various multilateral instruments with similar provisions, it is clear that conciliation has failed to become the procedure that its promoters expected.[63]

In the case of the law of the sea, the procedures embedded within the LOSC make conciliation a prominent form of dispute settlement, but as has been noted above, the means for compulsory conciliation of a dispute are limited to the procedures found in Articles 297 and 298. Much more attention has been given in dispute settlement under the law of the sea to the courts and tribunals referred to in Part XV, Section 2, and more generally to the role of the International Court of Justice in the resolution of maritime boundary disputes in particular.[64] To date, there has been no recorded instance of Annex V conciliation having arisen under the LOSC.

There is, however, a prominent example of conciliation having been utilised as a method of dispute settlement in the law of the sea and this is the 1981 Report of the Conciliation Commission to the Governments of Iceland and Norway on the Continental Shelf between Iceland and Jan Mayen.[65] This conciliation arose out of negotiations between Iceland and Norway over the maritime boundaries between Iceland and the Norwegian territory of Jan Mayen. While resolution was reached with respect to a fisheries boundary, it was not possible to conclude a continental shelf boundary and by Agreement the parties elected to refer the matter to a conciliation commission. A precise mandate was given for the preparation of recommendations, with the Commission to:

> … take into account Iceland's strong economic interests in these sea areas, the existing geographical and geological factors and other special circumstances.[66]

The Commission was required to make a unanimous recommendation, which while non-binding on the parties was one in which the parties were required to

60 [1993] Australian Treaty Series 32.
61 [1994] Australian Treaty Series 2.
62 Merrills, *International Dispute Settlement*, p. 79.
63 Ibid., pp. 79–80.
64 See generally, Rothwell and Stephens, *The International Law of the Sea*, pp. 439–60.
65 (1981) 20 International Legal Materials 797.
66 (1981) 20 International Legal Materials 797, 799.

"pay reasonable regard to" in their further negotiations.[67] The Commission, which completed its work in a year, handed down nine recommendations to the parties, which included the establishment of a 'joint co-operation agreement' for the area in question.[68] This recommendation formed the basis for the resolution of the continental shelf issue between the two countries and was reflected in the terms of the 1981 Agreement on the Continental Shelf between Iceland and Jan Mayen.[69]

Conciliation and its Potential Application in the Philippines/China Dispute

On the basis of the above analysis of Article 298, and its interaction with the general Part XV procedures for dispute settlement and associated specific conciliation procedures under Annex V, the following observations can be made in the specific context of the Philippines/China dispute. The first is that if the Annex VII Arbitral Tribunal declines to exercise jurisdiction in reliance upon China's Article 298 Declaration, the Philippines has other dispute resolution options open to it under the LOSC, especially those provided for under Article 298 (1) with respect to compulsory conciliation. If the subject matter of the dispute between the Philippines and China is one that is considered to have arisen following the entry into force of the LOSC, does not raise issues with respect to territorial sovereignty over land or insular territory, and is one in which no negotiated agreement has been reached between the parties within a reasonable period of time, then compulsory conciliation procedures can be activated as per Article 298 and Annex V. Importantly, given the position that China has taken with respect to the Annex VII Arbitration proceedings with the Philippines, compulsory conciliation under Annex V, Section 2 can proceed in the absence of one of the parties to the dispute. Non-appearance by China before the Annex V conciliation commission would not bring about a cessation of those proceedings. If a disagreement were to arise over the competence of an Annex V conciliation commission, raised for example by China by way of formal written representations to the commission, those matters could be decided by the commission. The procedures to the applied by the Annex V conciliation commission are detailed in Annex V, with the commission to hear both parties, and to report within 12 months of its constitution. Following the report of the commission there is a clear obligation upon the parties to negotiate an agreement, and this obligation must be observed in good faith consistently with Article 300 of the LOSC.

Irrespective then of the position that China may take towards the competence of the commission under these procedures, if the commission has ruled in favour of its competence and concluded a report then China would be under a clear obligation consistent with Articles 298 and 300 of the LOSC to engage with that process in order to negotiate an agreement based on the report. If those negotiations were also to fail, then unless the parties otherwise agree, in the absence of an agreement

67 Ibid.

68 (1981) 20 International Legal Materials 797, 840, Recommendation 3.

69 (1982) 21 International Legal Materials 1222.

being reached by mutual consent, the parties shall submit the dispute to one of the courts or tribunals provided for in Section 2, Part XV of the LOSC. Those bodies include the International Court of Justice, ITLOS, or an Annex VII Arbitral Tribunal. The default court or tribunal that would be available to determine this matter would be an Annex VII Arbitral Tribunal.

Concluding Remarks

One of the defining features of the LOSC is the manner in which it provides for dispute settlement. Other than the WTO there is no other equivalent compulsory multilateral dispute settlement framework that states commit to. Not only is Part XV of the LOSC distinctive because of the obligations it imposes upon states to settlement of their disputes in a peaceful manner, but also because of the choices states have available to them in settling their disputes. A range of voluntary and compulsory procedures are available. States are encouraged to make use of a range of flexible voluntary dispute settlement mechanisms, including Annex V conciliation. Compulsory means of dispute settlement also provides states with a number of courts and tribunals to which they can refer their disputes. The exceptions imbedded within Section 3, Part XV are designed to reflect a distinction between matters of fundamental state sovereignty, such as the determination of land boundaries, and matters which while of significance for state sovereignty are also vital to the efficient conduct and mutual recognition of rights and interests on the part of all states in the maritime domain. Article 298 (1)(a) of the LOSC seeks to reflect that balance by recognising that for some states matters regarding maritime boundary delimitation, and historic bays and titles should not initially be subject to determination by a court of tribunal. In that case, states are given significant encouragement to settle their dispute by way of agreement, or in the absence of agreement by way of compulsory conciliation. Even following the issuing of the report of a conciliation commission the states are given a further opportunity to negotiate a settlement based on that report. Only, following the inability of these various mechanisms to reach a settlement of the dispute will the states be required to submit themselves to a Part XV court or tribunal, which in the absence of agreement having been reached as to the forum would be before an Annex VII Arbitration.

The Philippines/China Annex VII Arbitration is entering an important phase. If the Annex VII Arbitral Tribunal were to determine that it did not possess jurisdiction to determine the dispute as a result of China's Article 298 Declaration, then consistent with Article 298 (1)(a) an issue will arise as to whether compulsory conciliation applies. This in turn will trigger a number of additional mechanisms under Article 298, and Annex V of the LOSC. If this were to occur, this would be the first instance of compulsory conciliation under the LOSC being activated thereby setting a precedent under the Convention and also becoming the focus of attention with respect to the capacity of conciliation to settle a law of the sea dispute in the modern era.

Chapter 5

The Legal Status of Maritime Features in the Sino-Philippine South China Sea Arbitration: Admissibility and Jurisdiction

Michael Sheng-ti Gau

Introduction

On 22 January 2013, the Philippines initiated arbitration against China under Article 287 and Annex VII of the United Nations Convention on the Law of the Sea (UNCLOS).[1] As stated in the Notification and Statement of Claim (the Notification),[2] the goal is "to seek a peaceful and durable resolution of the dispute in the West Philippine Sea". The Philippines challenges against China's claims and entitlement in the eastern part of South China Sea (SCS) enclosed by the "nine-dash-line", which the Philippines requests the Tribunal to declare as its exclusive economic zone (EEZ) and continental shelf.[3]

Five groups of claims were presented by the Notification:

1. China's rights concerning the SCS maritime areas are those established by UNCLOS only and consist of the territorial sea, the contiguous zone, the EEZ and the continental shelf. China's maritime claims therein are

---

1 For the Philippines' official explanations, see online <http://www.imoa.ph/press-releases/statement-by-secretary-of-foreign-affairs-albert-del-rosario-on-the-unclos-arbitral-proceedings-against-china-to-achieve-a-peaceful-and-durable-solution-to-the-dispute-in-the-wps/>. For the text of UNCLOS, see online <http://www.un.org/depts/los/convention_agreements/texts/unclos/unclos_e.pdf>.

2 See para. 2 of p. 1 of the Notification and Statement of Claims, issued by Department of Foreign Affairs of Republic of the Philippines in Manila to the Embassy of the People's Republic of China in Manila, serial no. 13-0211, 22 January 2013, available online <https://www.dfa.gov.ph/index.php/component/docman/doc_download/56-notification-and-statement-of-claim-on-west-philippine-sea?Itemid=546>.

3 See paras. 31 (Section III: The Philippines' Claims) and 41 (Section V: Relief Sought) of the Notification, *id.*

based on the "nine-dash line (U-Shaped Line)"[4] contravene UNCLOS and are invalid.[5]

2. The Mischief, McKennan, Gaven and Subi Reefs are mere low-tide elevations (LTEs). None of them is located on China's continental shelf. The Mischief and McKennan Reefs are part of the Philippines' continental shelf. China's occupation of these four maritime features and construction activities thereon is unlawful and should be terminated.[6]
3. Scarborough Shoal and the Johnson, Cuarteron, and Fiery Cross Reefs should be considered as rocks under Article 121(3) and may only generate territorial sea. Having unlawfully claimed maritime entitlements beyond 12 nautical miles (M) from these features, China should refrain from preventing Philippine vessels from exploiting the living resources in waters adjacent to Scarborough Shoal and Johnson Reef and from undertaking other activities inconsistent with UNCLOS at or in the vicinity of these features.[7]
4. The Philippines is entitled under UNCLOS to a 12-M territorial sea, a 200-M EEZ, and a continental shelf measured from its archipelagic baselines. China has unlawfully claimed and exploited the living and non-living resources in this EEZ and continental shelf and prevented the Philippines from exploiting the living and non-living resources therein.[8]
5. China has unlawfully interfered with the Philippines' exercise of its navigational rights and other rights under UNCLOS within and beyond the Philippines' EEZ. China should desist from these unlawful activities.[9]

On 19 February 2013, China officially refused to join the litigation,[10] based on, *inter alia*, its 2006 Declaration covering the disputes brought by the Philippines

4 The term "nine-dash line" is interchangeable with "U-Shaped Line" and "eleven-dash line". For various names of this line, see K. Zou, "China's U-Shaped Line in the South China Sea Revisited", *Ocean Development and International Law* 43 (2012): 18.

5 See 1st–2nd claims under para. 31 and 1st–3rd reliefs under para. 41 of the Notification, *supra* n. 2.

6 See 3rd–5th claims under para. 31 and 4th–7th reliefs under para. 41 of the Notification, *id.*

7 See 6th–7th claims under para. 31 and 8th–9th reliefs under para. 41 of the Notification, *id.*

8 See 8th–9th claims under para. 31 and 10th–11th reliefs under para. 41 of the Notification, *id.*

9 See 10th claim under para. 31 and 12th–13th reliefs under para. 41 of the Notification, *id.*

10 See the statement made on 19 February 2013 by the spokesman of the Foreign Ministry of China (English translation): "China's position on the South China Sea issue is clear and consistent. China's sovereignty over the Nansha Islands and their adjacent waters is based on sufficient historical and jurisprudential evidence. Meanwhile, bearing in mind the larger interests of China-Philippines relations and regional peace and stability, China has always been committed to solving disputes through bilateral negotiations and has made unremitting

and depriving the Arbitral Tribunal of necessary jurisdiction to entertain the case. The default rules were applied to establish the arbitral tribunal (the Tribunal) on 25 June 2013. The first meeting of the Tribunal was held on 11 July 2013, when the Permanent Court of Arbitration (PCA) was appointed as Registry.[11] On 27 August 2013, the Tribunal adopted its own Rules of Procedure and issued the first Procedural Order to fix 30 March 2014 as the deadline for the Philippines to submit its Memorial. The Tribunal directed the Philippines to fully address all issues in the Memorial, including matters relating to the jurisdiction of the Tribunal, the admissibility of the Philippines' claims, and the merits of the dispute.[12]

As directed, the Philippines presented the Memorial[13] consisting of 15 Submissions with the same structure of the Notification. The original 4th Group of Claims[14] disappeared. However, the legal arguments and the Figures revealed that the Sino-Philippine maritime boundary has been *settled*, and used as the point of departure. For the LTE part of the arguments in the Original 2nd Group of Claims, Second Thomas Shoal has been added into the Memorial, together with the Sino-Philippine maritime confrontations occurring there since January 2013.

As the Tribunal must settle the outstanding issues of jurisdiction and admissibility before ruling on the substantive legal issues, China's default of appearance provides a room for legal scholars to contribute by providing professional advice to the Tribunal. With such assistance, the Tribunal may better fulfil the obligation under Article 9 of Annex VII to UNCLOS, which is to "satisfy itself not only that it has jurisdiction over the dispute but also that the claim is well-founded in fact and law".[15]

Due to space constraint, this chapter deals with the admissibility and jurisdiction issues of the legal status of nine maritime features, which are the 2nd–3rd Groups of Claims in the Notification.[16]

---

efforts to safeguard stability in the South China Sea and promote regional co-operation. It is also the consensus reached by ASEAN (Association of Southeast Asian Nations) countries and China in the *Declaration on the Conduct of Parties in the South China Sea* (DOC) to resolve disputes through negotiations between directly concerned sovereign states. The Philippines' note and its attached notice not only violate the consensus, but also contain serious errors in fact and law as well as false accusations against China, which we firmly oppose". Available online <http://www.fmprc.gov.cn/eng/xwfw/s2510/2511/t1015317.shtml>.

11 For the information released by the Permanent Court of Arbitration, serving as Registry of this arbitration, see online: <http://www.pca-cpa.org/showpage.asp?pag_id=1529>.

12 The Rules of Procedure can be found in the same website. *Id.*

13 The Memorial was submitted on 30 March 2014.

14 For a criticism on the original 4th Group of Philippine Claims, see Gau, n. 16 below, pp. 114–15.

15 Article 9 of Annex VII to UNCLOS.

16 For a comprehensive study and evaluation of the legal arguments in the Notification, see Michael Sheng-ti Gau, "The Sino-Philippine Arbitration of the South China Sea Nine-Dash-Line Dispute: Applying the Rule of Default of Appearance", 28 *Ocean Yearbook*, pp. 81–133 (May 2014). Also see Stefan Talmon and Bing Bing Jia (eds), *The South China Sea Arbitration: A Chinese Perspective* (Oxford: Hart Publishing, 2014);

Admissibility Issues concerning Legal Status of Maritime Features

Relevant submissions of the Philippines deal with the so-called "disputes" concerning (1) legal status of nine maritime features currently occupied by China in the Relevant Area, and (2) the legal capability of these features to generate maritime zones under UNCLOS legal regime. The Tribunal is requested "to adjudge and declare that ... "

> 3) Scarborough Shoal generates no entitlement to an EEZ or continental shelf:
>
> 4) Mischief Reef, Second Thomas Shoal and Subi Reef are LTEs that do not generate entitlements to a territorial sea, EEZ or continental shelf, and are not features that are capable of appropriation by occupation or otherwise;
>
> ...
>
> 6) Gaven Reef and McKennan Reef (including Hughes Reef) are LTEs that do not generate entitlement to a territorial sea, EEZ or continental shelf, but their low-water line may be used to determine the baseline from which the breadth of the territorial sea of Namyit and Sin Cowe, respectively, is measured;
>
> 7) Joshson Reef, Cuarteron Reef and Fiery Cross Reef generate no entitlement to an EEZ or continental shelf.[17]

The author asserts that none of these submissions should be considered admissible for the following reasons:

A. Scarborough Shoal

To begin with, the submission concerning Scarborough Shoal does not contribute to the formation of any dispute, as no maritime confrontations identified by the Philippines concerning it ever occurred in the water *beyond* the territorial sea generated by this feature.

The relevant submissions concerning Filipino traditional fishing activities deal with the legality dispute of China's prevention of Philippine fishermen from pursuing their livelihoods by interfering with Filipino traditional fishing activities at Scarborough Shoal, focus on China's possible violation of its UNCLOS obligation to protect and preserve the marine environment at Scarborough Shoal

---

Andreas Zimmermann and Jelena Baumler, "Navigating Through Narrow Jurisdictional Straits: the Philippines-PRC South China Sea Dispute and UNCLOS", 12 *Law and Practice of International Courts and Tribunals* (2013), pp. 431–61.

17 The author obtains the information concerning the Philippines' Memorial through a private interview with a scholar from the Philippines.

and address the issue of China's breach of its UNCLOS obligation by operating its law enforcement vessels in a dangerous manner causing serious risk of collision to Philippine vessels navigating in the vicinity of Scarborough Shoal.[18] The activities challenged by these submissions all occurred in the territorial waters surrounding Scarborough Shoal. Using "China's EEZ claim generated by Scarborough Shoal" to justify these disputed activities was neither invoked nor needed in the first place. Besides, no information was provided by the Philippines to prove that China opposes the Philippine position that "Scarborough Shoal generates no EEZ and continental shelf". It is hard for the relevant submission to constitute any dispute[19] for settlement.[20] Therefore, the so-called "dispute" concerning whether Scarborough Shoal may generate EEZ or continental shelf should be deemed hypothetical,[21] moot, non-justiciable,[22] and consequently, inadmissible.

---

18 Ibid.

19 In the judgment of *The Mavrommatis Palestine Concessions*, the Permanent Court of International Justice has defined a dispute as "a disagreement on a point of law or fact, a conflict of legal views or of interests between two persons". *The Mavrommatis Palestine Concessions*, [30 August 1924] PCIJ Series A, No. 2, 11, available online, <http://www.icj-cij.org/pcij/serie_A/A_02/06_Mavrommatis_en_Palestine_Arret.pdf>. Seen as an elaboration of such a definition, J.G. Merrills said that, "a dispute may be defined as a specific disagreement concerning a matter of fact, law or policy in which a claim or assertion of one party is met with refusal, counter-claim or denial by another". J.G. Merrills, *International Dispute Settlement*, 4th ed. (Cambridge: Cambridge University Press, 2005), p. 1. A.V. Lowe and J. Collier also describe the dispute as "a specific disagreement relating to a question of rights or interests in which the parties proceed by way of claims, counter-claims, denials and so on". J. Collier and A.V. Lowe, *The Settlement of Disputes in International Law: Institutions and Procedures*, 1st ed. (Oxford: Oxford University Press, 1999), p 1. Clearly, a dispute is built upon a combination of a claim and counterclaim.

20 Part XV of UNCLOS also requires the existence of a dispute as a condition for initiation of the Annex VII-Tribunal. See Arts. 279–83, 286–8, *supra* n. 1.

21 Article 283 of UNCLOS requires the existence of a dispute before the dispute settlement mechanism of Part XV of UNCLOS can operate. In Barbados v. Trinidad and Tobago, both Parties emphasized the need of the existence of a dispute according to Art. 283, while the Tribunal accepted such interpretation. See Barbados/Trinidad and Tobago, Award, UNCLOS Annex VII Tribunal (11 April 2006), paras. 74, 80, 196–200. The award is available online <http://www.pca-cpa.org/showpage.asp?pag_id=1152>.

22 J. Collier and A.V. Lowe, *supra* n. 20, pp. 10, 13, 156–7. (Under the heading Justiciability the two eminent scholars say that "It was mentioned above that not all disputes are suitable for judicial settlement. To be suitable, the dispute must be justiciable. A dispute is said to be justiciable if, first, a specific disagreement exists, and secondly, that disagreement is of a kind which can be resolved by the application of rules of law by judicial (including arbitral) processes. … Thus far we have been concerned with the task of establishing that a dispute has come into existence. In the case of most (but not all) tribunals a further aspect of this precondition of justiciability is that the dispute remains in existence up to the point that the judgment or award is given. To put it another way, most tribunals will refuse to give rulings on disputes that are hypothetical or have become moot".)

B. Five LTEs within the Spratly Islands Group

Mischief Reef, Second Thomas Shoal, Subi Reef, Gaven Reef, and McKennan Reef are considered as LTEs by the Philippines in order to deny their capability to generate territorial waters, EEZ or continental shelf. The critical questions to be asked are (1) has China ever used any of these five LTEs to claim territorial sea, EEZ, and continental shelf; (2) has China ever used *such* maritime zones to justify its law enforcement, exploration and exploitation activities condemned by the Philippines?

The Philippines raised problems concerning China's occupation of and construction activities on Mischief Reef, which violate: (1) China's UNCLOS obligations concerning artificial islands, installations, and structures; (2) China's duty to protect and preserve the marine environment under UNCLOS; and (3) China's duty under UNCLOS as China takes an action of attempted appropriation of this maritime feature.[23] The Philippines addresses China's alleged violation of its UNCLOS obligation to protect and preserve the marine environment at Second Thomas Shoal, and also the problems occurring in Second Thomas Shoal. These problems are: (1) China's interference with Philippines' rights of navigation in the water adjacent to this maritime feature; (2) China's prevention of the rotation and resupply of Philippine personnel stationed there; and (3) China's actions endangering the health and well-being of these Philippine personnel.[24]

However, the Philippines provides no information to prove that China justifies these disputed actions with claims of territorial water, EEZ, or continental shelf generated by Mischief Reef and Second Thomas Shoal. Thus, there can be no dispute concerning the legality of such non-existent Chinese maritime zones. The same applies to other three "LTEs". Hence, both the "claim" presented and the "disputes" created by Submissions 4 and 6 should be considered as moot and inadmissible respectively.

C. Three "rocks" within the Spratly Islands Group

Johnson Reef, Cuarteron Reef and Fiery Cross Reef are considered "rocks" by the Philippines. However, it fails to prove that: (1) China uses these three "rocks" to claim EEZ or continental shelf; and (2) China ever uses *such* maritime entitlements to justify its activities of law enforcement and exploration/exploitation of natural resources in the water and seabed surrounding these "rocks" and beyond. Due to the lack of a dispute, the claims and the disputes presented by the Philippines can only be considered as moot and inadmissible.

---

23 *Supra* n. 17 above.

24 Ibid.

D. Spratly Islands Group is the real basis for China's EEZ and continental shelf claims

Generally, China uses the *entire* Spratly Islands Group to claim EEZ and continental shelf in the Relevant Area of this case, as declared by its 2011 *Note verbale*.[25] Particularly, within the Spratly Islands Group there are at least 12 non-rock islands (e.g. Itu Aba, Thitu, and West York Islands) that China may use to claim EEZ and continental shelf,[26] reaching far enough to the location and adjacent waters of those five LTEs and three "rocks" mentioned by the Philippines. Therefore, all the China's activities criticised by the Philippines may be justified by China's EEZ and continental shelf sovereign rights and jurisdiction generated from those non-rock islands.

Contrary to what the Philippines aspires,[27] *the real disputes* the Tribunal must address[28] cannot be resolved by: (1) identifying those five "LTEs" and three "rocks";

---

25 " … Since 1930s, the Chinese Government has given publicity several times the geographical scope of China's Nansha Islands and the names of its components. China's Nansha Islands is therefore clearly defined. In addition, under the relevant provisions of the *1982 United Nations Convention on the Law of the Sea*, as well as the *Law of the People's Republic of China on the Territorial Sea and the Contiguous Zone (1992)* and the *Law on the Exclusive Economic Zone and the Continental Shelf of the People's Republic of China (1998)*, China's Nansha Islands is fully entitled to Territorial Sea, Exclusive Economic Zone (EEZ) and Continental Shelf". Mission of the People's Republic of China to the United Nations, NV, CML/8/2011, April 14, 2011, available online <http://www.un.org/Depts/los/clcs_new/submissions_files/mysvnm33_09/chn_2011_re_phl_e.pdf>.

26 Robert C. Beckman and Clive H. Schofield, "Defining EEZ Claims from Islands: A Potential South China Sea Change", 29 *The International Journal of Marine and Coastal Law* (2014), pp. 210–11. The 12 non-rock islands are: (1) Taiwan-occupied Itu Aba; (2) Philippines-occupied Thitu Island, West York Island, Northeast Cay, Nanshan Island, Loaita Island; and (3) Vietnam-occupied Spratly Island, Southwest Cay, Sin Cowe Island, Sandy Cay, Namyit Island, and Amboyna Cay.

27 On 22 January 2013, the Secretary of Foreign Affairs of the Philippines, Mr. Albert del Rosario, made a statement in a press conference which explained the initiation by the Philippines of an arbitral proceedings against China to achieve a peaceful and durable solution to the dispute in the West Philippine Sea (South China Sea). In the speech, he said that "The initiation of Arbitral Proceedings against China on the nine-dash line is an operationalization of President Aquino's policy for a peaceful and rule-based resolution of disputes in the WPS in accordance with international law specifically UNCLOS". The statement can be found at <http://www.gov.ph/2013/01/22/statement-the-secretary-of-foreign-affairs-on-the-unclos-arbitral-proceedings-against-china-january-22-2013/>.

28 Fisheries Jurisdiction Case (Spain v. Canada), Jurisdiction of the Court, Judgment, I.C.J. Reports 1998, pp. 447–9, paras. 29–31. "In order to identify its task in any proceedings instituted by one State against another, the Court must begin by examining the Application (see Interhandel, Preliminary Objections, Judgment, I.C.J. Reports 1959, p. 21; Right of Passage over Indian Territory, Merits, Judgment, I.C.J. Reports 1960, p. 27; Nuclear Tests (Australia v. France), Judgment, I.C.J. Reports 1974, p. 260, para. 24) … However, it may

and (2) challenging the legal capability of these eight maritime features to generate territorial water, EEZ, or continental shelf. If following the ICJ's practice in settling UK v. Norway,[29] Tunisia v. Libya,[30] El Salvador v. Honduras,[31] Romania v. Ukraine,[32]

---

happen that uncertainties or disagreements arise with regard to the real subject of the dispute with which the Court has been seized, or to the exact nature of the claims submitted to it. In such cases the Court cannot be restricted to a consideration of the terms of the Application alone nor, more generally, can it regard itself as bound by the claims of the Applicant. Even in proceedings instituted by Special Agreement, the Court has determined for itself, having examined all of the relevant instruments, what was the subject of the dispute brought before it, in circumstances where the parties could not agree on how it should be characterized (see Territorial Dispute (Libyan Arab Jamahiriyal/Chad), Judgment, I.C.J. Reports 1994, pp. 14–15, para. 19, and p. 28, para. 57). 30. It is for the Court itself, while giving particular attention to the formulation of the dispute chosen by the Applicant, to determine on an objective basis the dispute dividing the parties, by examining the position of both parties. … It will base itself not only on the Application and final submissions, but on diplomatic exchanges, public statements and other pertinent evidence (see Nuclear Tests (Australia v. France), Judgment, I.C.J. Reports 1974, pp. 262–263)".

29 Fisheries Case (UK v. Norway), Judgment, I.C.J. Reports 1951, p. 126. " … These are elements which might furnish reasons in support of the Judgment, but cannot constitute the decision. It further follows that even understood in this way, these elements may be taken into account only in so far as they would appear to be relevant for deciding the sole question in dispute … ".

30 Case concerning the Continental Shelf (Tunisia v. Libya), Judgment, I.C.J. Reports 1982, pp. 76–7, para. 105. "Since the Court thus does not find it necessary to pass on the question of historic rights as justification for the baselines, it is only if the method of delimitation which the Court finds to be appropriate is such that it will or may encroach upon the historic rights area that the Court will have to determine the validity and scope of those rights, and their opposability to Libya, in the context of a delimitation of the continental shelf. If however the method of delimitation thus arrived at, independently of the existence of those rights, is such that the delimitation line will undoubtedly leave Tunisia in the full and undisturbed exercise of those rights – whatever they may be – over the area claimed to be subject to them, so far as opposable to Libya, then a finding by the Court on the subject will be unnecessary".

31 Land, Island and Maritime Frontier Dispute (El Salvador v. Honduras: Nicaragua intervening), Judgment, I.C.J. Reports 1992, p. 555, para. 326. " … Secondly, notwithstanding the terms of the formal claim in the submission of El Salvador, the Chamber should not exercise its jurisdiction so as to make a finding in relation to any islands which are not in dispute. … the Chamber considers that prima facie the existence of a dispute over an island can, in the present proceedings, be deduced from the fact of its being the subject of specific and argued claim. The Chamber is entitled to conclude that, where there is an absence of such claims, there is no real dispute before the Chamber, since there is no 'disagreement on a point of law or fact' or 'a conflict of legal views or of interests', to use the terms of the Judgment in the case of the Mavrommatis Jerusalem Concessions (Judgment No. 5, P.C.I.J. Series A, No. 5, p. 11)".

32 Maritime Delimitation in the Black Sea (Romania v. Ukraine), Judgment, ICJ Reports 2009, pp. 122–3, para. 187.

and Nicaragua v. Colombia,[33] the Tribunal is advised to declare it *unnecessary* to determine the legal status of these eight maritime features.

Jurisdiction Issues

A. Disputes fall within Article 298(1)(a)(i) of UNCLOS

Assuming that the "disputes" concerning the legal status of the four "rocks" and the five "LTEs" as identified by the Philippines do exist, the result of such "legal status disputes" should be deemed *concerning* the application of Articles 74(1)[34] and 83(1)[35] of UNCLOS to Sino-Philippine maritime boundary delimitation disputes covered by Article 298(1)(a)(i).[36] Such "legal status disputes" then become the ones that Annex VII-Tribunal is precluded from settling due to China's non-acceptance declaration dated 25 August 2006 according to Article 298. It reads:

> The Government of the People's Republic of China does not accept any of the procedures provided for in Section 2 of Part XV of the Convention with respect to all the categories of disputes referred to in paragraph 1 (a) (b) and (c) of Article 298 of the Convention.[37]

The Philippines has made it clear since initiating this arbitration that the disputes *excluded* by the 2006 China's Declaration have not been submitted to this Tribunal.[38] Here, clarification for a preliminary issue is needed. Is there a room for Article 74(1) and 83(1) of UNCLOS to apply to the Sino-Philippine confrontations in the West Philippine Sea or the eastern part of SCS enclosed by the U-Shaped Line (the Relevant Area)? The answer from the Philippines is *no*, because China simply has

33 It is worth quoting the judgment of Nicaragua v. Colombia, that "[i]n the present case, the Court similarly concludes that it is not necessary to determine the precise status of the smaller islands, since any entitlement to maritime spaces which they might generate within the relevant area (outside the territorial sea) would entirely overlap with the entitlement to a continental shelf and EEZ generated by the [big] islands of San Andres, Providencia and Santa Catalina". See Territorial and Maritime Dispute (Nicaragua v. Colombia), Judgment, ICJ Reports, 2012, p. 68, para. 180.

34 Article 74(1) of UNCLOS.

35 Article 83(1) of UNCLOS.

36 Article 298(1)(a)(i) of UNCLOS.

37 Available online <http://www.un.org/Depts/los/convention_agreements/convention_declarations.htm#China upon ratification>.

38 See paras. 37–40 of the Notification, *supra* n. 2, pp. 15–16. It is worth quoting that in the beginning of Para. 40, the Philippines said that "It follows that the Philippines' claims do not fall within China's Declaration of 25 August 2006, because they do not: concern the interpretation or application of Articles 15, 74 and 83 relating to sea boundary delimitations; ... ".

no EEZ and continental shelf in the Relevant Area. As Sino-Philippine disputes based on overlapping EEZ and Continental Shelf claims do not exist,[39] Articles 74(1) and 83(1) become inapplicable there. However, as proved already,[40] China does claim EEZ and continental shelf there. Articles 74(1) and 83(1) may apply in settling the ensuing maritime boundary delimitation disputes.

Now we can address the issue of whether the disputes, if any, concerning the legal status of maritime features are *concerning* the application of Article 74(1) and 83(1). The question for decision is not whether the "legal status disputes" should be considered as *concerning* "EEZ or continental shelf delimitation",[41] as argued by the Philippines. The key issue is the *interpretation* of the term "concerning" as the second word in the first sentence of Article 298(1)(a)(i).[42] The ordinary meaning given to the term[43] "concern" as a verb is:[44] (1) have relation to; (2) *affect*;[45] and (3) be of importance to. Therefore, the term "concerning" should be interpreted as: (1) having relation to or *relating to*;[46] (2)affecting; and (3) being

39 The Philippines argues: " ..., the question before this Tribunal is whether China's claim to 'historic rights' survives its adherence to the Convention and can trump the Philippines' entitlements to an EEZ and continental shelf. ... ", *supra* n. 17.

40 Gau, n. 16 above, p. 113.

41 The ICJ was careful in such differentiation, see Aegean Sea Continental Shelf Case (Greece v. Turkey), Judgment, I.C.J. Reports 1978, p. 36, para. 86.

42 That is "disputes ***concerning*** the interpretation or application of articles 15, 74 and 83 relating to sea boundary delimitations, ... " [emphasis added] See Art. 198 of UNCLOS.

43 Articles 31–2 of the 1969 Vienna Convention on the Law of Treaty provide general principles for the treaty interpretation. The starting point for interpretation is finding the ordinary meaning for the term to be interpreted. The ordinary meaning for the term to be interpreted can be found in standard dictionaries.

44 *Oxford Advanced Learner's Dictionary of Current English*, A.S. Hornby (as General Editor), third edition published in 1980.

45 As confirmed by the ICJ in the Greece v. Turkey, the meaning of the term "concern" as a verb can be interpreted as "affect". See Aegean Sea Continental Shelf Case (Greece v. Turkey), Judgment, I.C.J. Reports 1978, p. 37, para. 89. "In the present case, moreover, quite apart from the question of the status of the above-mentioned Greek islands for the purpose of determining Greece's entitlement to continental shelf, the Court notes that during the hearings in 1976 the Greek Government referred to a certain straight baseline claimed by Turkey which is, however, contested by Greece. Although it recognized that the resulting discrepancy between the Greek and Turkish views of the limits of Turkey's territorial sea in the area is not great, it observed that the discrepancy 'obviously *affects* the question of the delimitation of the continental shelf'. The question of the limits of a state's territorial sea, as the Greek Government itself has recognized, is indisputably one which not only relates to, but *directly concerns* territorial status" [italics added].

46 The term "relating to" has been interpreted by the ICJ in Aegean Sea Continental Shelf Case as "emanating from" and "being an automatic adjunct of". "86. ... The question for decision is whether the present dispute is one 'relating to the territorial status of Greece', not whether the rights in dispute are legally to be considered as 'territorial' rights; and a dispute regarding entitlement to and delimitation of areas of continental shelf tends by its very

important to. It follows that *any dispute relating to, affecting, or important to the application of Article 74(1) and 83(1)* should be considered as *concerning* the application of these two articles and be caught by Article 298(1)(a)(i).

Both Articles 74(1) and 83(1) explicitly address delimitation *agreements* concluded by disputing parties. However, as ITLOS said in Bangladesh v. Myanmar, these two provisions also apply to judicial and arbitral delimitation decisions.[47] In other words, any dispute *concerning* the application of these two provisions to the maritime delimitation judicial settlement will be covered by Article 298(1)(a)(i), too.

Let us imagine, if China wins in any of the "legal status disputes", a particular "rock" may turn into an island and generate entitlements of EEZ and continental shelf. One particular "LTE" may turn into a rock and generate territorial water or even EEZ and continental shelf for China. As China wins more of the "legal status disputes", the size of overlapping EEZ and continental shelf gets bigger. The final result of an "equitable solution" as required by Articles 74(1) and 83(1) will be shifted accordingly.

If China loses in any of the "legal status disputes", China will have less territorial sea, EEZ or continental shelf generated from that particular feature. The size of total overlapping area of EEZ and continental shelf becomes smaller. The application of Articles 74(1) and 83(1) would lead to a different "equitable solution" accordingly. If China loses all disputes of this kind, then *from the Philippines' perspective*, China would have no EEZ and continental shelf in the Relevant Area.[48] Under such situation, Articles 74(1) and 83(1) will become inapplicable for the no-longer-existent delimitation dispute. It is hard to deny that such result affects the *application* of these two provisions. It simply ends the possibility for these rules to apply.

Therefore, the "legal status disputes" as brought by the Philippines should be considered as affecting and concerning the application of Article 74(1) and 83(1). The optional exception mechanism established by Article 298[49] then applies and deprives the Tribunal of its jurisdiction to deal with such "legal status disputes".

---

nature to be one relating to territorial status. ... In short, continental shelf rights are legally both an emanation from and an automatic adjunct of the territorial sovereignty of the coastal State. It follows that the territorial regime – the territorial status – of a coastal State comprises, ipso jure, the rights of exploration and exploitation over the continental shelf to which it is entitled under international law. A dispute regarding those rights would, therefore, appear to be one which may be said to 'relate' to the territorial status of the coastal State" Aegean Sea Continental Shelf Case (Greece v. Turkey), Judgment, I.C.J. Reports 1978, p. 36, para. 86.

47 See Dispute Concerning Delimitation of the Maritime Boundary between Bangladesh and Myanmar in the Bay of Bengal (Bangladesh v. Myanmar), Judgment of 14 March 2012, para. 183. The judgment is available online at <http://www.itlos.org/fileadmin/itlos/documents/cases/case_no_16/C16_Judgment_14_03_2012_rev.pdf>

48 It is the Philippines' position that China has no EEZ and continental shelf in the Relevant Area, as China only can rely on five LTEs and four "rocks" to claim maritime entitlements there. In short, there is no possibility for China to have any overlapping EEZ and continental shelf with Philippines' EEZ and continental shelf claims in the SCS.

49 Article 298(1)(a)(i) of UNCLOS.

B. Confirmation from judicial decisions

It is argued by the Philippines that the disputes brought to the Tribunal are not about maritime delimitation and the disputes of legal status of maritime features occupied by China are not concerning maritime delimitation either. However, all the judicial decisions invoked by the Philippines' Memorial are judgments and awards on maritime boundary delimitations, including: (1) Qatar v. Bahrain; (2) Nicaragua v. Colombia; (3) Libya v. Malta; (4) Eritrea v. Yemen; (5) Canada v. US; (6) Romania v. Ukraine; and (7) Bangladesh v. Myanmar. In those international judicial decisions settling maritime boundary delimitation disputes, the issues concerning legal status of maritime features (and their legal capability to generate maritime entitlements) constituted both preliminary and integral issues for the Court or Tribunal to address before coming to the delimitation issues proper.

After examining closely, *inter alia*, Tunisia v. Libya,[50] Canada v. US,[51] Libya v. Malta,[52] Eritrea v. Yemen,[53] Qatar v. Bahrain,[54] and Romania v.

---

50 Case concerning the Continental Shelf (Tunisia v. Libya), Judgment, I.C.J. Reports 1982, pp. 88–9, paras. 128–9. In this case, the Kerkennah Islands, surrounded by islets and low-tide elevations, and constituting by their size and position a circumstance relevant for the delimitation, and to which the Court must attribute some effect.

51 Delimitation of the Maritime Boundary in the Gulf of Maine Area (Canada v. US), Judgment, I.C.J. Reports 1984, p. 246, at 329, para. 201.

52 ICJ in the Libya v. Malta invoked the Judgment of North Sea Continental Shelf cases to say that when drawing a median line, the Court needs to ignore "the presence of islets, rocks and minor coastal projections". In this connection, "the islet of Filfla", "the uninhabited islet of Filfla", or "the uninhabited rock of Filfla" were repeatedly mentioned in the Judgment and was ignored as a basepoint at the first step of the delimitation when drawing the median line. See Continental Shelf (Libya v. Malta) Judgment, I.C.J. Reports 1985, p. 13 at pp. 20, 47–8, 52, 57; paras. 15, 62, 64, 72–3, 79-C.

53 The award of Eritrea v. Yemen is worth quoting that "147. Yemen employed both the small island of al-Tayr and the group of islands called al-Zubayr as controlling base points, so that the Yemen-claimed median line boundary is 'median' only in the area of sea west of these islands. These islands do not constitute a part of Yemen's mainland coast. Moreover, their barren and inhospitable nature and their position well out to sea, which have already been described in the Award on Sovereignty, mean that they should not be taken into consideration in computing the boundary line between Yemen and Eritrea. 148. For these reasons, the Tribunal has decided that both the single island of al-Tayr and the island group of al-Zubayr should have no effect upon the median line international boundary". See Award (given on 17 December 1999) of the Arbitral Tribunal in the 2nd Stage of the Proceedings (Maritime Delimitation) pursuant to an agreement to arbitrate dated 3 October 1996 between Eritrea and Yemen. The award is available online at < http://www.pca-cpa.org/showpage.asp?pag_id=1160>.

54 In the ICJ Judgment of Qatar v. Bahrain, the Court needs to determine the relevant coasts to measure territorial seas. "In order to determine what constitutes Bahrain's relevant coasts and what are the relevant baselines on the Bahraini side, the Court must first establish which islands come under Bahraini sovereignty". One of the issues is to decide whether

Ukraine,[55] it becomes clear that the issues of legal status of maritime features strongly *affect* the result of the settlement of maritime boundary disputes. This observation is even admitted by the Philippines itself, and is confirmed by leading law of the sea experts, e.g. Clive Schofield,[56] and Yann-Huei Song.[57] That is why such disputes were requested to be handled *first*, and such requests were followed by ICJ in, e.g. Nicaragua v. Honduras.[58] Most interestingly, in the judgment of Nicaragua v. Colombia, the ICJ put the sub-section of "Entitlements generated by Maritime Features" under Section V entitled "Maritime Boundary".[59] It proves that the issue concerning legal status of maritime features constitutes an integral part of maritime boundary delimitation, as also noted in Guyana v. Suriname,[60] and Greece v. Turkey.[61]

Qit'at Jaradah is an island or low tide elevation. The ICJ decided that it should be considered as an island. "195. The Court recalls that the legal definition of an island is … The Court has carefully analysed the evidence submitted by the Parties … On these bases, the Court concludes that the maritime feature of Qit'at Jaradah satisfies the above-mentioned criteria and *that it is an island which should as such be taken into consideration for the drawing of the equidistance line*" [italic added], Maritime Delimitation and Territorial Questions between Qatar and Bahrain, Merits, Judgment, ICJ Reports 2001, paras. 184–7, 195.

55 See 2009 ICJ Judgment of Romania v. Ukraine, where the ICJ needs to address the controversial legal status of certain features (Sacalin Peninsula and Sulina dyke) under UNCLOS legal regime so as to know if they may be treated as base points for constructing provisional equidistance line in the process of maritime delimitation. See Maritime Delimitation in the Black Sea (Romania v. Ukraine), Judgment, ICJ Reports 2009, pp. 105–8, paras. 129–40.

56 See Clive Schofield, "The Trouble with Islands: The Definition and Role of Islands and Rocks in Maritime Boundary Delimitation", in Seoung-Yong Hong and Jon Van Dyke (eds), *Maritime Boundary Disputes, Settlement Processes, and the Law of the Sea* (Leiden and Boston: Martinus Nijhoff Publishers, 2009), p. 33.

57 See Yann-Huei Song, "Okinotorishima: A 'Rock' or an 'Island'? Recent Maritime Boundary Controversy between Japan and Taiwan/China", *id.*, p. 168.

58 Case Concerning Territorial and Maritime Dispute between Nicaragua and Honduras in the Caribbean Sea (Nicaragua v. Honduras), Judgment of 8 October 2007, ICJ Reports 2007, p. 35, 39, paras. 114, 135.

59 See Territorial and Maritime Dispute (Nicaragua v. Colombia), Judgment, ICJ Reports, 2012, pp. 47–92, paras. 132–247.

60 See Guyana v. Suriname, Award (17 September 2007), Annex VII Tribunal, para. 376. "Turning to the question of whether there are any features in the geographical configuration of the relevant coastlines which justify an adjustment of the equidistance line, the Tribunal must mention the following observation found in the report of the independent expert appointed by Guyana: 'An important geographic reality in this case is that there are no offshore features, such as islands or low-tide elevations that influence the drawing of an equidistant line … '". The text of the award is available online <http://www.pca-cpa.org/showpage.asp?pag_id=1147>.

61 Aegean Sea Continental Shelf Case (Greece v. Turkey), Judgment, I.C.J. Reports 1978, p. 35, para. 83. "83. The contention based on the proposition that delimitation is

Having said that, it would most helpful if the Philippines could identify any international judicial decision addressing the legal status dispute of maritime features while not being a maritime boundary delimitation decision, *like* what the Philippines brings to the Tribunal now. Otherwise, the conclusion will most probably be that the legal status dispute of maritime features affects and concerns the settlement of maritime boundary delimitation dispute.

C. The Filipino attempt to have the unilaterally drawn maritime boundary endorsed

In the 4th Group of claims contained in the Notification,[62] the Philippines requested the Tribunal to "declare that the Philippines is entitled under UNCLOS to a 12 M Territorial Sea, a 200 M EEZ, and a Continental Shelf under Parts II, V, VI of UNCLOS, measured from its archipelagic baselines". This claim, seen together with other claims in the Notification, has been criticized as indirectly bringing a case of Sino-Philippine maritime boundary delimitation to the Tribunal.[63] Somehow, the Philippines has shifted this position, and it later removed such a claim from its submissions.

Has the Philippines given up this claim? The answer is most probably *no.* In fact, the Philippines jumped forward farther by transforming this claim in the Notification into a *well-settled premise.* What the Philippines presents for its updated claims are the legality disputes of China's actions and omissions on *trespassing* a *unilaterally drawn* Sino-Philippine maritime boundary in the Relevant Area. The Philippines attempts to display ample evidence to prove the existence of such a *settled* maritime boundary in the Arbitration case.

Firstly, as demonstrated by Figure 3.4 of Philippines' Memorial,[64] on the east and west sides of the Philippines, there are two continuous lines called the "Philippine 200 M EEZ limit". For the eastern part of the line, it seems justified for the Philippines to use a "continuous line" to draw such dispute-less limits, as no other states have

---

entirely extraneous to the notion of territorial status appears to the Court to encounter certain difficulties. Above all, it seems to overlook the basic character of the present dispute, clearly stated though it is in the first submission in Greece's Application. The basic question in dispute is whether or not certain islands under Greek sovereignty are entitled to a continental shelf of their own and entitle Greece to call for the boundary to be drawn between those islands and the Turkish coast. The very essence of the dispute, as formulated in the Application, is thus the entitlement of those Greek islands to a continental shelf, and the delimitation of the boundary is a secondary question to be decided after, and in the light of, the decision upon the first basic question. Moreover, it is evident from the documents before the Court that Turkey, which maintains that the islands in question are mere protuberances on the Turkish continental shelf and have no continental shelf of their own, also considers the basic question to be one of entitlement".

62 See paras. 31, 41 of the Notification, *supra* n. 2, pp. 14, 18–19.

63 See Gau, *supra* n. 16, pp. 123–5.

64 *Supra* n. 17 above.

overlapping claims. On the west side (West Philippine Sea or SCS) the use of a continuous line presupposes the same situation. Such a continuous line could not have been drawn, if China's *EEZ* and *continental shelf* claims in SCS had not been ignored or invalidated. There is a continuous line between China's Hainan Province and Vietnam to represent the already concluded maritime boundary. The same continuous line is used by the Philippines on the west side of the Philippines, which confirms the point just mentioned. Besides, in Figure 4.1 of Philippines' Memorial a circle of territorial sea exists, surrounding Scarborough Shoal.[65] The Philippines claims that the Sino-Philippine maritime boundary in the Northern Sector is already settled and asks the Tribunal to simply confirm it. In Figure 4.2 of its Memorial, the Philippines uses the same way to draw the sea boundary in the SCS and encircles territorial waters to represent "China's maximum potential entitlements under UNCLOS compared to its nine-dash line claim in the southern sector".[66] It once again demonstrates Philippines' position that Sino-Philippine maritime boundary is settled in the Southern Sector or should be settled in this fashion. More significantly, presenting these illustrative claims to the Tribunal, the Philippines is using them as a premise upon which the future Award should be based.

Secondly, the Philippines has made a giant leap in its position at its submission stage when compared to the above-mentioned Philippines' claim in its Notification, and argues that:

> Under Articles 57 and 76 of UNCLOS, respectively, the Philippines is entitled to a 200 M EEZ measured from its archipelagic baselines and a continental shelf extending to at least that distance, except only to the extent that nearby features generate maritime entitlements that overlap with those of the Philippines. As demonstrated in Chapter 5, none of the maritime features relevant to this case, whether in the Northern or Southern Sector, generates entitlements to an EEZ or continental shelf. Accordingly, the waters, seabed and subsoil of the South China Sea within 200 M of the Philippine coast, but beyond 12 M from any high tide feature within the South China Sea, constitute the EEZ and continental shelf of the Philippines. In other areas, it enjoys the sovereign rights and jurisdiction that UNCLOS affords.[67]

Thirdly, the Philippines asks the Tribunal to declare that China has no EEZ and continental shelf in the Relevant Area. What China has is no more than four circles of territorial waters with disputed ownership generated by the four "rocks". Putting such conclusion together with the above statement, there can be only one interpretation for the Philippines' position, i.e., the Sino-Philippine maritime boundary in the Relevant Area is well-settled or should be settled like this. Under a worst-case scenario where the Philippines loses the Arbitration, the

65 Ibid.
66 Ibid.
67 Ibid.

Sino-Philippine maritime boundary would still be considered settled *differently* by the Philippines as a consequence of this arbitration.

Thus, the Philippine arguments' attempt to persuade the Tribunal to vindicate the unilaterally drawn Sino-Philippine maritime boundary in the Relevant Area is clearly *prohibited* by general international law as pronounced by the ICJ in the Canada v. US case.[68] Hence, like another Annex VII Tribunal did in the Barbados v. Trinidad and Tobago case[69] as well as what ICJ did in the FRG v. Iceland case,[70] the

68 See Case concerning Delimitation of the Maritime Boundary in the Gulf of Maine Area (Canada v. US), Judgment, I.C.J. Reports 1984, p. 246, at p. 299, para. 112. "The Chamber therefore wishes to conclude this review of the rules of international law on the question to which the dispute between Canada and the United States relates by attempting a more complete and, in its opinion, more precise reformulation of the 'fundamental norm' already mentioned. For this purpose it will, *inter alia*, draw also upon the definition of the 'actual rules of law … which govern the delimitation of adjacent continental shelves – that is to say, rules binding upon States for all delimitations' which was given by the Court in its 1969 Judgment in the *North Sea Continental Shelf cases* (I.C.J. Reports 1969, pp. 46–47, para. 85). What general international law prescribes in every maritime delimitation between neighboring States could therefore be defined as follows: (1) No maritime delimitation between States with opposite or adjacent coasts may be effected unilaterally by one of those States. Such delimitation must be sought and effected by means of an agreement, following negotiations conducted in good faith and with the genuine intention of achieving a positive result. Where, however, such agreement cannot be achieved, delimitation should be effected by recourse to a third party possessing the necessary competence".

69 Annex VII Tribunal in Barbados v. Trinidad and Tobago re-characterized the scope of dispute by rejecting the Barbados' argument that the terms of notification submitted to institute the arbitration exclude the delimitation of the outer continental shelf. See Award of the Arbitral Tribunal in the Matter of Arbitration between Babados and Republic of Trinidad and Tobago, April 11, 2006 (Permanent Court of Arbitration), para. 213. Also see Gau, n. 16, pp. 123–5.

70 The ICJ redefined the scope of the disputes in FRG v. Iceland. "39. As to the compromissory clause in the 1961 Exchange of Notes, this gives the Court jurisdiction with respect to 'a dispute relating to such an extension', i.e., 'the extension of the fishery jurisdiction of Iceland'. The present dispute was occasioned by Iceland's unilateral extension of its fisheries jurisdiction. However, it would be too narrow an interpretation of the compromissory clause to conclude that the Court's jurisdiction is limited to giving an affirmative or negative answer to the question of whether the extension of fisheries jurisdiction, as enacted by Iceland on 14 July 1972, is in conformity with international law. In the light of the exchanges and negotiations between the Parties, both in 1959 and 1960 (paragraph 25 above) and in 1971–1972 (paragraphs 28–31 above), in which the questions of fishery conservation measures in the area and Iceland's preferential fishing rights were raised and discussed, and in the light of the proceedings before the Court, it seems evident that the dispute between the Parties includes disagreements as to the extent and scope of their respective rights in the fishery resources and the adequacy of measures to conserve them. It must therefore be concluded that those disagreements are an element of the 'dispute relating to the extension of the fishery jurisdiction of Iceland'" Fisheries Jurisdiction Case (FRG v. Iceland), Merits, Judgment, I.C.J. Reports 1974, p. 190, para. 39.

disputes to be formulated by the Philippines should be *re-characterized* as an indirect maritime delimitation dispute falling outside the jurisdiction of this Tribunal.

Admissibility Issues

The Philippines requests the Tribunal to adjudge and declare that Mischief Reef and Second Thomas Shoal are part of the EEZ and continental shelf of the Philippines. For the following reasons, it is submitted that such a claim should be deemed inadmissible:

A. Lack of dispute

No information is provided by the Philippines to prove China's *denial* of Mischief Reef and Second Thomas Shoal as part of the EEZ and continental shelf of the Philippines. In fact, it would be hard to prove that China ever has ever rejected the idea that the Philippines, as another coastal state, has maritime entitlements of EEZ and continental shelf extending from its archipelagic baselines, if established according to UNCLOS. Given the fact that these two maritime features are less than 200 M from Philippines' archipelagic baselines, they form part of Philippines' EEZ and continental shelf. As China does not oppose this Philippine claim, it is impossible for the Philippines to articulate a "dispute" for the Tribunal to settle. According to Part XV of UNCLOS, one of the conditions to initiate arbitration under Annex VII is the existence of *a dispute* concerning the interpretation or application of UNCLOS. Any claim impossible to constitute even a dispute should be considered hypothetical, moot and inadmissible by the Tribunal. Therefore, the Philippine submission should be deemed inadmissible by the Tribunal.

B. Article 286 ignored

As just said, the Philippine submission is not what China and the Philippines have been disputing. To build up a dispute, one needs to see what exactly the positions of both parties are, as required by the rulings of relevant judicial decisions, e.g. Barbados v. Trinidad and Tobago,[71] and Greece v. Turkey.[72] In the present case, the

---

71 Award of the Arbitral Tribunal in the Matter of Arbitration between Barbados and Trinidad and Tobago, 11 April 2006 (Permanent Court of Arbitration), para. 198. "198. The fact that the precise scope of the dispute had not been fully articulated or clearly depicted does not preclude the existence of a dispute, so long as the record indicates with reasonable clarity the scope of the legal differences between the Parties … ".

72 The issue of existence of a dispute was also addressed in the Aegean Sea Continental Shelf Case, "[i]t is clear from the submissions in the Greek Application and Memorial, as well as in the observations in the various Turkish diplomatic communications to Greece, that Greece and Turkey are in conflict as to the delimitation of the spatial extend

real Chinese position denied by the Philippines is that *Mischief Reef and Second Thomas Shoal are also part of China's EEZ and continental shelf.*[73] The Philippine submission is built on a premise that Mischief Reef is *not* part of China's EEZ and continental shelf. But it is clear that the *real* Sino-Philippine disputes concerning these two maritime features are two-fold: (1) "whether these two features are also part of China's EEZ and continental shelf"; and (2) "to which Party these two maritime features belong". However, these two component disputes are not brought to the Tribunal as required by Article 286 of UNCLOS.[74] What is demanded by Article 286 is the *identity* of: (1) the disputes left unresolved after Parties have gone through procedures listed in Section 1 of Part XV *with*; (2) the disputes requested to be brought to the chosen procedure listed in Section 2 of Part XV. Since the Philippines does not bring to the Tribunal *these real disputes* for settlement, Article 286 has not been complied with. It is thus unlawful to consider the Philippines *entitled* to initiate the Section 2-Procedure to settle the disputes. The Tribunal is advised to declare the Philippine submission inadmissible.

Conclusion

Based on the above reasons, it seems justified to conclude that none of the Philippine submissions should be considered as admissible, while the disputes to be constituted by each of these submissions should be deemed falling outside the jurisdiction of the Tribunal.

---

of their sovereign rights over the continental shelf in the Aegean Sea. Thus there are certain sovereign rights being claimed by both Greece and Turkey, one against the other, and it is manifest that legal rights lie at the root of the dispute that divides the two States. The Court therefore finds that a legal dispute exists between Greece and Turkey in respect of the continental shelf in the Aegean Sea". See Aegean Sea Continental Shelf Case (Greece v. Turkey), Judgment, I.C.J. Reports 1978, p. 13, para. 31.

73 See Table 5.1 of this chapter.

74 Article 286 (Application of procedures under this section) reads: "Subject to section 3, any dispute concerning the interpretation or application of this Convention shall, where no settlement has been reached by recourse to section 1, be submitted at the request of any party to the dispute to the court or tribunal having jurisdiction under this section". *Supra* n. 1.

Table 5.1 Distance between three biggest islands and nine maritime features in the Spratly Islands

Categorization Given by the Philippines	Names of the Maritime Features	Location Coordinates[1]	Distance[2] from Itu Aba (M) 10°23' N, 114°22' E	Distance from Thitu Island (M) 11°06' N, 114°17' E	Distance from West York Is(M) 11°05' N, 115°02' E	Position in Philippines' Submission
Low-tide elevation Under UNCLOS Article 13	Mischief Reef美濟礁	9°52'-9°56' N, 115°30'-115°35' E	**77–8**	**114**	**91–3**	4–5, 12, 14
	McKennan Reef 西門礁	9°54' N, 114°28' E	**42**	**91**	**101**	6
	Gaven Reef 南熏礁	10°10'-10°13' N, 114°13'-114°15' E	**7–9**	**56–8**	**75–7**	6
	Subi Reef 渚碧礁	10°54'-10°56' N, 114°04'-114°07' E	**21–2**	**31–2**	**63–5**	4
	Second Thomas Shoal 仁愛礁 (Ayungin Reef)	9°39'-9°48' N, 115°51'-115°54' E	**90–91**	**125–8**	**99–104**	11, 14
Rocks Under UNCLOS Article 121(3)	Johnson Reef 赤瓜礁	9°42' N, 114°17' E	**49**	**98**	**110**	7
	Cuarteron Reef 華陽礁	8°51'-8°52' N, 112°50'-112°53' E	**143–5**	**181–2**	**211–13**	7
	Fiery Cross Reef 永暑礁	9°30'-9°40' N, 112°53'-113°04' E	**86–114**	**120–43**	**153–81**	7
	Reed Bank 禮樂灘	11°06'-11°55' N, 116°22'-117°20' E	**128–93**	**121–81**	**71–132**	Paras. 6.16–6.22 of the Memorial

1 The coordinates for these maritime features are based on the List of Partial Standard Names for China's Islands in South China Sea (我國南海諸島部分標準地名). It was reproduced on the website of <http://www.unanhai.com/nhzddm.htm>.

2 The distances are calculated by the Latitude/Longitude Distance Calculator provided by the National Weather Service, National Hurricane Center of National Oceanic and Atmospheric Administration. See the website for calculation, <http://www.nhc.noaa.gov/gccalc.shtml>.

Chapter 6

Does China's Position Paper on the South China Sea Arbitration Constitute a Preliminary Objection?

Qiang Ye

Introduction

On 7 December 2014, the Ministry of Foreign Affairs of the People's Republic of China (the "MFA") was authorized to release a *Position Paper of the Government of the People's Republic of China on the Matter of Jurisdiction in the South China Sea Arbitration Initiated by the Republic of the Philippines* (the "Position Paper").[1] The Position Paper elaborated the legal basis for China's argument that the Arbitral Tribunal of the South China Sea (SCS) Arbitration lacks jurisdiction in this case, and demonstrated that China's decision not to participate in the proceedings stands on a solid ground in international law.[2] Though it was not submitted formally to the Tribunal, it is worth noting that the date of 15 December 2014 was the deadline prescribed by the Tribunal requesting China to submit its Counter-Memorial. The Tribunal responds to this circumstance as follows:

> The Arbitral Tribunal noted that as at 16 December 2014, China had not filed a Counter-Memorial and that the Chinese Government has reiterated that 'it will neither accept nor participate in the arbitration unilaterally initiated by the Philippines'. The Arbitral Tribunal further noted that although its members had been furnished with copies of the 7 December 2014 'Position Paper of the Government of the People's Republic of China on the Matter of Jurisdiction in the South China Sea Arbitration Initiated by the Republic of the Philippines', the Chinese Government had via communications to the Registry, made it 'clear

1 "Position Paper of the Government of the People's Republic of China on the Matter of Jurisdiction in the South China Sea Arbitration Initiated by the Republic of the Philippines", available at <http://www.fmprc.gov.cn/mfa_eng/zxxx_662805/t1217147.shtml>.

2 "Remarks by Mr. Xu Hong, Director-General of the Department of Treaty and Law of the Ministry of Foreign Affairs, on the Position Paper of the Government of the People's Republic of China on the Matter of Jurisdiction in the South China Sea Arbitration Initiated by the Republic of the Philippines", available at <http://www.fmprc.gov.cn/mfa_eng/zxxx_662805/t1217150.shtml>.

that the forwarding of the aforementioned Position Paper shall not be regarded as China's acceptance of or its participation in the arbitration'.[3]

At the same time, the Philippines has been invited to address, as it considers appropriate, any public statements made by the Chinese government in relation to the dispute.[4]

Since the Philippines initiated the SCS Arbitration in January 2013, the Chinese government has repeatedly declined the Tribunal's exercise of jurisdiction over this case. So far, the Position Paper is the most authoritative and comprehensive statement by the Chinese government on this matter. In addition, the Chinese government delivered this Position Paper via communications to the Registry of the Permanent Court of Arbitration. In doing so, the Chinese government made it "clear that the forwarding of the aforementioned Position Paper shall not be regarded as China's acceptance of or its participation in the arbitration".[5]

In general practice, the respondent state in international adjudication or arbitration may make a Preliminary Objection in writing, if such state objects to the jurisdiction of the Court or Tribunal or the admissibility of the application. According to the practice of the International Court of Justice (the "ICJ" or the "Court"), such objection falls within Incidental Proceedings, and on the basis of participation of that state in the judicial proceedings. Therefore, the Chinese government's stand of non-participation would seemingly depreciate the legal effect of its arguments in the Position Paper. However, in some cases the ICJ or the Tribunal will bifurcate its procedure and makes a decision on jurisdictional and admissibility matters prior to the deliberation of the merits of a case based on diplomatic documents – rather than Preliminary Objections.[6] Thus, for the SCS Arbitration case, the potential legal effects of the Position Paper should be evaluated carefully according to the jurisprudence of the international judicial practices.

Relevant Background

The core content of the Position Paper is "to elaborate on the legal basis for China's position that the Tribunal manifestly has no jurisdiction in this case and to demonstrate that China's position not to accept or participate in the proceedings stands on solid ground in international law".[7] The Position Paper emphasizes that

3 Third Press Release (English), dated 17 December 2014, available at <http://www.pca-cpa.org/showpage.asp?pag_id=1529>.

4 Ibid.

5 Ibid.

6 See the relevant discussions below.

7 "Remarks by Mr. Xu Hong, Director-General of the Department of Treaty and Law of the Ministry of Foreign Affairs, on the Position Paper of the Government of the People's Republic of China on the Matter of Jurisdiction in the South China Sea Arbitration Initiated

"the Arbitral Tribunal manifestly has no jurisdiction over the present arbitration" on the basis of the following reasons: firstly, "the essence of the subject-matter of the arbitration is the territorial sovereignty over several maritime features in the South China Sea, which is beyond the scope of the United Nations Convention on the Law of the Sea (UNCLOS) and the jurisdiction of the Arbitral Tribunal"; secondly, "China and the Philippines have agreed, through bilateral instruments and the Declaration on the Conduct of Parties in the South China Sea (DOC), to settle their relevant disputes through negotiation and that by unilaterally initiating the present arbitration, the Philippines has violated its obligation under international law"; thirdly, "the subject-matter of the arbitration constitutes an integral part of maritime delimitation between the two countries, thus falling within the scope of the declaration filed by China in 2006, which excludes, *inter alia*, disputes concerning maritime delimitation from compulsory arbitration and other compulsory dispute settlement procedures".[8]

The Chinese government has repeatedly stressed those positions since the Philippines initiated, on 22 January 2013, international arbitral proceedings regarding its dispute with China in the South China Sea, according to the Article 287 and Annex VII of the UNCLOS. On 19 February 2013, China returned the Philippines' diplomatic *Note* and its attached notice, and stated that China refuse to accept the Arbitration. The most important reason cited was the prior "consensus reached by the Association of Southeast Nations (ASEAN) countries and China in the [DOC] to resolve disputes through negotiations between directly concerned sovereign states. The Philippines' note and its attached notice […] violate the consensus".[9] Commenting on the composition of the Tribunal, the Chinese government argues that "[t]he claims for arbitration as raised by the Philippines are essentially concerned with maritime delimitation between the two countries in parts of the South China Sea, and thus inevitably involve the territorial sovereignty over certain relevant islands and reefs. However, such issues of territorial sovereignty are not the ones concerning the interpretation or application of the UNCLOS. Therefore, given the fact that the Sino-Philippine territorial disputes still remain unresolved, the compulsory dispute settlement procedures as contained in UNCLOS should not apply to the claims for arbitration as raised by the Philippines. Moreover, in 2006, the Chinese Government made a declaration in pursuance of Article 298 of UNCLOS, excluding disputes regarding

---

by the Republic of the Philippines", available at <http://www.fmprc.gov.cn/mfa_eng/zxxx_662805/t1217150.shtml>.

8 "Ministry of Foreign Affairs of the People's Republic of China Is Authorized to Release the Position Paper of the Government of the People's Republic of China on the Matter of Jurisdiction in the South China Sea Arbitration Initiated by the Republic of the Philippines", available at <http://www.fmprc.gov.cn/mfa_eng/zxxx_662805/t1217148.shtml>.

9 "Foreign Ministry Spokesperson Hong Lei's Regular Press Conference on February 19, 2013". Available at <http://www.fmprc.gov.cn/mfa_eng/xwfw_665399/s2510_665401/2511_665403/t1015317.shtml>.

such matters as those related to maritime delimitation from the compulsory dispute settlement procedures, including arbitration".[10] Therefore, the Tribunal obviously has no jurisdiction over the case.

On 30 March 2014, the Philippines, in conformity with the *Rules of Procedure*, submitted its Memorial to the Tribunal, addressing matters relating to the jurisdiction of the Arbitral Tribunal, the admissibility of the Philippines' claim, as well as the merits of the dispute. In the Memorial, the Philippines claims that the Tribunal has jurisdiction over the case, and that the Philippines' submissions are all admissible. On the same day, China responded that it "has stated time and again that it does not accept the Philippines' submission of disputes with China in the South China Sea for international arbitration. This position stays unchanged".[11] That because "[N]o matter how the Philippine memorial is packaged, [...] the heart of the matter are the disputes between the two sides on the sovereignty over islands and reefs, and delimitation of maritime boundaries. Yet disputes such as these have already been excluded from arbitration procedures through a declaration made by China in 2006 pursuant to the UNCLOS. In this context, China's rejection of the Philippines' submission for arbitration is solidly based on international law, and China's lawful rights as a party to UNCLOS should be truly respected. China urges the Philippines to comprehensively and effectively implement the consensus repeatedly reaffirmed between the two sides and the DOC, and return to the right track of settling the disputes through bilateral negotiations".[12]

It is clear that China has lodged repeated diplomatic objections to the other Party as well as the Tribunal, staking out the position, which is founded in fact and law, that the Tribunal has no jurisdiction over the case.

However, in the practice of international adjudication and arbitration, one of the Parties (generally speaking, the respondent states) may raise a Preliminary Objection to the Court or Tribunal if this party believes that the other party (generally speaking, the claimant states) submitted a claim which does not fall within the jurisdiction of the Court, or is otherwise not justiciable. Such objections, in nature, belong to the Incidental Proceedings of the judicial and arbitral procedure; and in purpose, for the balance of rights between both sides in the judicial proceedings. In the SCS Arbitration, Article 20 of the *Rules of Procedure* formulated by the Tribunal provides for initiating and ruling proceedings of the Preliminary Objections. Paragraph 2 of this Article stipulated that "[A] plea that

---

10 "Foreign Ministry Spokesperson Hua Chunying's Remarks on the Philippines' Efforts in Pushing for the Establishment of the Arbitral Tribunal in Relation to the Disputes between China and the Philippines in the South China Sea". Available at <http://www.fmprc.gov.cn/mfa_eng/xwfw_665399/s2510_665401/2535_665405/t1035577.shtml>.

11 "Remarks by Foreign Ministry Spokesperson Hong Lei on the Philippines' Submission of a Memorial to the Arbitral Tribunal in Relation to Disputes with China in the South China Sea". Available at <http://www.fmprc.gov.cn/mfa_eng/xwfw_665399/s2510_665401/2535_665405/t1142356.shtml>.

12 Ibid.

the Arbitral Tribunal does not have jurisdiction shall be raised no later than in the Counter-Memorial". Paragraph 3 stipulates that "the Arbitral Tribunal shall rule on any plea concerning its jurisdiction as a preliminary question [...]".[13] In international practice, States Parties may present jurisdictional objections either in the Memorial, or at any time before the submission of the Memorial.[14] As long as the Tribunal determines that the objection to its jurisdiction possesses "an exclusively preliminary character", it shall suspend the arbitral proceeding on merits, prior to ruling on any matters relating to jurisdiction or admissibility. However, this article does not mention any other legitimate form or legal effect of the objection through extra-procedural communications. Nevertheless, the articles of the *Rules of Procedure* cannot apply to objections to jurisdiction which take place outside the arbitral procedure, as the Rules are obviously formulated for, and legally binding on, activities which fall within the arbitral proceedings. Since China has clearly and repeatedly declared its stance of non-acceptance and non-participation in the arbitration, all Chinese activities fall outside the arbitral proceedings. Therefore, the Position Paper is neither a Counter-Memorial, nor *strictosensu* a Preliminary Objection. In nature, it is still a diplomatic objection, in the form of political document rather than a legal instrument, to the jurisdiction of the Tribunal as well as to the Philippines' initiation of the case. Firstly, at the beginning of the Position Paper, it reiterates that "[T]he Position Paper does not express any position on the substantive issues related to the subject-matter of the arbitration initiated by the Philippines. No acceptance by China is signified in this Position Paper of the views or claims advanced by the Philippines, whether or not they are referred to herein. Nor shall this Position Paper be regarded as China's acceptance of or participation in this arbitration".[15] Secondly, with regard to the form of written submissions, Article 18 of the *Rules of Procedure* prescribes that "[T]he Parties' written submissions shall be transmitted in the following manner: (a) The submitting Party shall transmit an electronic copy of its submission by e-mail, with accompanying evidence and legal authorities to the other Party, the Arbitral Tribunal, and the Registry".[16] Thus, in dealing with the potential legal implications of diplomatic objections and informal pleas to the Tribunal by the Chinese government, this chapter will analyze diplomatic and legal implications of

13 *Rules of Procedure*, available at <http://www.pca-cpa.org/showfile.asp?fil_id=2504>.

14 This kind of submission is in the form of "Preliminary Objections". See *Preliminary Objections of the United Kingdom (The Republic of Mauritius v. The United Kingdom of Great Britain and Northern Ireland)*. Available at <http://www.pca-cpa.org/showpage.asp?pag_id=1429>.

15 "Position Paper of the Government of the People's Republic of China on the Matter of Jurisdiction in the South China Sea Arbitration Initiated by the Republic of the Philippines", available at <http://www.fmprc.gov.cn/mfa_eng/zxxx_662805/t1217147.shtml>.

16 Article 18, *Rules of Procedure*, available at <http://www.pca-cpa.org/showfile.asp?fil_id=2504>.

the Position Paper based on the general jurisprudence of the international judicial practice, rather than within the narrower legal context of the *Rules of Procedure* provided by the Tribunal.

Bifurcation of Proceedings Based on Extra-Procedural Objections: International Judicial and Arbitral Practices

Similar to the *Rules of Procedure* adopted in the SCS Arbitration, Article 79 of the *Rules of Court* of the International Court of Justice (ICJ) provides for Preliminary Objections.[17] Paragraph 5 of that Article stipulates that "[u]pon receipt by the Registry of a preliminary objection, the proceedings on the merits shall be suspended […]"; paragraph 9 provides that "[a]fter hearing the parties, the Court shall give its decision in the form of a judgment, by which it shall either uphold the objection, reject it, or declare that the objection does not possess, in the circumstances of the case, an exclusively preliminary character". Therefore, it is clear that the Preliminary Objections presented by state parties have legal effects on litigation proceedings. They divide the proceeding into two stages, requiring the Court to decide questions of jurisdiction and admissibility first and then merits second. However, there have been some exceptions in international judicial practice where the Court bifurcated the proceedings on the basis of the pleas lodged as diplomatic objections outside the formal rules of the court, which require *stricto sensu* Preliminary Objections.

In the *Nottebohm Case*, a communication signed by the Minister for Foreign Affairs of Guatemala and addressed to the President of the Court was received in the Registry on 15 September 1952. In this communication, the government of Guatemala "drew attention to the fact that the Declaration by which it accepted the compulsory jurisdiction of the Court had, in accordance with what was stated therein, ceased to be in force after January 26th 1952",[18] therefore, it argued that the Court had no jurisdiction to deal with the case brought before it by Liechtenstein. The Court considered this communication a Preliminary Objection of Guatemala, and examined this objection at the first stage and made a judgment concerned with it alone.[19] After that, in the *Fisheries Jurisdiction Case*, the *Nuclear Tests Case*, the *Aegean Sea Continental Shelf Case*, the *Case concerning United States Diplomatic and Consular Staff in Tehran*, the *Case Concerning Border and Transborder Armed Actions*, and the *Case Concerning Military and Paramilitary Activities in and against Nicaragua*, respondent states challenged the jurisdiction of the Court through informal means rather than Preliminary Jurisdictions, and received

17 See Article 79, *Rules of Court* (1978), Adopted on 14 April 1978 and entered into force on 1 July 1978. Amendment of this Article entered into force on 1 February 2001. Available at <http://www.icj-cij.org/documents/index.php?p1=4&p2=3&p3=0>.

18 *Nottebohm case (Liechtenstein v. Guatemala)* (Preliminary Objection), Judgment of 18 November 1953: *I.C.J. Reports* 1953, p. 118.

19 Ibid.

decisions separate from the merits. Thus, the preliminary proceedings in these cases deviated from the provisions laid out in Article 79 of the ICJ *Rules of Court*.[20]

The proceedings of the aforementioned cases share the following common features. First, the respondent states presented objections to the jurisdiction of the Court by written instruments such as letters and notifications, all extra-procedural communications. Second, the Court deemed these objections to be Preliminary Objections and *de facto* applied the procedures detailed in Article 79 of the *Rules of Court*. Third, the Court gave its decision in the form of a judgment on jurisdiction at a separate [and earlier] stage of the proceedings.

In the *Aegean Sea Continental Shelf Case*, Turkey, the respondent state, sent a letter to the Court stating that it would be proper to invoke the reservation (b) to the *General Act* made by the Greek Government, thus denying the Court's jurisdiction over the case. The Greek Government advanced the contention at public hearings that reservation (b) should, in any event, be left out of consideration altogether by the Court because the question of its effect on the application of the *General Act* with respect to the present dispute was not raised by Turkey as a preliminary objection in conformity with Article 67 of the Rules of Court. Consequently, in its view, since Turkey did not file a preliminary objection in accordance with the conditions laid down in Article 67 of the Rules, it could not be regarded as having "enforced" the reservation in conformity with Article 39, paragraph 3, of the *General Act*[21] However, the Court denied the Greek's view and pointed out that "the Court has taken into account all the elements before it, including those supplied by extra-procedural communications from the respondent, for the purpose of satisfying itself as to whether its jurisdiction was established".[22] Finally, the Court decided that it had no jurisdiction over the dispute initiated by Greece on the basis of the informal communications of Turkey.

In the *Case Concerning Border and Transborder Armed Actions*, the Minister for External Relations of Honduras (defendant state), in a letter dated 29 August 1986, informed the Court that, in his Government's view, that Court had no jurisdiction over the matters raised by the Application of Nicaragua, and expressed the hope that the Court would first confine the written proceedings to issues of jurisdiction and admissibility. As the Parties had agreed that issues of jurisdiction and admissibility should be dealt with at a preliminary stage of the proceedings, the Court decided that the first pleading shall be a Memorial by Honduras dealing exclusively with the issues of jurisdiction and admissibility, and that Nicaragua shall in reply submit a Counter-Memorial confined to the same issues.[23]

---

20 Sugihara Takane, *The Institution of International Adjudication* (in Chinese), Translated by Wang Zhian and Yi Ping (Beijing: China University of Political Science and Law Press, 2006), p. 216.

21 *Aegean Sea Continental Shelf Case (Greece v.* Turkey), Judgment of 19 December 1978: *I.C.J. Reports* 1978, para. 41.

22 Ibid., para. 42.

23 *Case Concerning Border and Transborder Armed Actions (Nicaragua v. Honduras)*, Order of 22 October 1986: *I.C.J. Reports* 1986, pp. 551–2.

In its Judgment on the *Jurisdiction of the Court and Admissibility of the Application* of the *Case Concerning Military and Paramilitary Activities in and against Nicaragua*, the Court pointed out that: "[T]he present phase of examination of jurisdictional questions was opened by the Court itself by its Order of 10 May 1984, not by a forma l preliminary objection submitted by the United States; but it is appropriate to consider the grounds put forward by the United States for alleged lack of jurisdiction in the light of the procedural provisions for such objections. That being so, and since the procedural technique formerly available of joinder of preliminary objections to the merits has been done away with since the 1972 revision of the Rules of Court, the Court has no choice but to avail itself of Article 79, paragraph 7, of the present Rules of Court, and declare that the objection based on the multilateral treaty reservation of the United States Declaration of Acceptance does not possess, in the circumstances of the case, an exclusively preliminary character, and that consequently it does not constitute an obstacle for the Court to entertain the proceedings instituted by Nicaragua under the Application of 9 April 1984".[24] Thus in this case the respondent state raised an objection to the Court's jurisdiction, *inter alia*, be of default to appearance at the same time, the Court shall set forth the proceeding to examine its own jurisdiction, although this proceeding is of absence of provision in the *Rules of Court*. This power is rooted in the obligation of the Court to satisfy itself that it has jurisdiction over the dispute which provided specifically in Article 53 paragraph 2 of the Statute.[25]

In the *Case concerning United States Diplomatic and Consular Staff in Tehran*, the Court points out at the beginning of the Judgment that: "[i]n accordance with its settled jurisprudence, the Court, in applying Article 53 of its Statute, must first take up, *propriomotu*, any preliminary question, whether of admissibility or of jurisdiction, that appears from the information before it to arise in the case and the decision of which might constitute a bar to any further examination of the merits of the Applicant's case".[26] In the present case, the Court is faced with a fact that Iran denied its jurisdiction over the case through diplomatic objection by the letters. Therefore, the Court needs to "[f]irst address itself to the considerations put forward by the Iranian Government in its letters of 9 December 1979 and

---

24 *Case Concerning Military and Paramilitary Activities in and against Nicaragua (Nicaragua v. United States of America)*, Jurisdiction of the Court and Admissibility of the Application, Judgment of 26 November 1984: *I.C.J. Reports* 1984, para. 76.

25 Sugihara Takane, supra note 20, p. 217.

Statute of the Court, Article 53 reads:

1. Whenever one of the parties does not appear before the Court, or fails to defend its case, the other party may call upon the Court to decide in favour of its claim.
2. The Court must, before doing so, satisfy itself, not only that it has jurisdiction in accordance with Articles 36 and 37, but also that the claim is well founded in fact and law.

Available at <http://www.icj-cij.org/documents/index.php?p1=4&p2=2&p3=0>.

26 *Case concerning United States Diplomatic and Consular Staff in Tehran (United States of America v. Iran)*, Judgment of 24 May 1980: *I.C.J. Reports* 1980, p. 18, para. 33.

16 March 1980, on the basis of which it maintains that the Court ought not to take cognizance of the present case".[27] However, the Court did not bifurcate the proceeding and examine the aforementioned issue during the first stage. Instead, it discussed the jurisdictional and admissibility issues during the merits stage, and concluded in the final judgment.[28] The reason why the Court did so is that it has maintained that it possessed *manifest* jurisdiction over the case.

The Iranian Government in its letter of 9 December 1979 drew attention to what it referred to as the "[d]eep rootedness and the essential character of the Islamic Revolution of Iran, a revolution of a whole oppressed nation against its oppressors and their masters". The examination of the "numerous repercussions" of the revolution, it added, is "a matter essentially and directly within the national sovereignty of Iran". The Court, however, in its Order of 15 December 1979 (*Request for the indication of Provisional Measures*), made it clear that "[a] dispute which concerns diplomatic and consular premises and the detention of internationally protected persons, and involves the interpretation or application of multilateral conventions codifying the international law governing diplomatic and consular relations, is one which by its very nature falls within international jurisdiction",[29] and concluded that "[t]he considerations and arguments put forward in the Iranian Government's letters of 9 December 1979 and 16 March 1980 do not, in the opinion of the Court, disclose any ground on which it should conclude that it cannot or ought not to take cognizance of the present case".[30] Otherwise, if "there is no *manifest* lack of jurisdiction" which has been concluded in the order of indication of provisional measures, namely the existence of the *prima facie* jurisdiction in the case, the Court cannot waive the obligation to decide its jurisdiction prior to the proceeding onto the merits.

In the *Nuclear Tests Case*, the Court points out in the Order of 22 June 1973 (Request for the Indication of Interim Measures of Protection) that "the material submitted to the Court leads it to the conclusion, at the present stage of the proceedings, that the provisions invoked by the Applicant appear, *prima facie*, to afford a basis on which the jurisdiction of the Court might be founded";[31] in the meantime, it required the government of New Zealand to submit a Memorial addressed to the questions of the jurisdiction of the Court to entertain the dispute, and of the admissibility of the Application therein, as well as in the Order of

---

27 Ibid.

28 Ibid., pp. 18–20, paras. 33–8.

29 *Case concerning United States Diplomatic and Consular Staff in Tehran (United States of America v. Iran)*, Request for the Indication of Provisional Measures, Order of 15 December 1979: *I.C.J. Reports* 1979, p. 16, para. 25.

30 Ibid., p. 14, para. 31.See also *Case concerning United States Diplomatic and Consular Staff in Tehran (United States of America v. Iran)*, Judgment of 24 May 1980: *I.C.J. Reports* 1980, p. 20, para. 38.

31 *Nuclear Tests Case (New Zealand v. France)*, Request for the Indication of Interim Measures of Protection, Order of 22 June 1973: *I.C.J. Reports* 1973, p. 138, para. 18.

6 September 1973. After that, the Court decided on jurisdictional and admissible issues, and made a judgment on 20 December 1974.[32]

On 26 November 2014, the UNCLOS Annex VII Arbitral Tribunal for the *Arctic Sunrise Arbitration* (the "*Arctic Sunrise Arbitration* Tribunal") issued an Award on Jurisdiction (the "Award") which abides by the above-mentioned jurisprudence, and should play an important role in future arbitral practices.

During the proceedings, the Netherlands repeatedly requested that the Tribunal bifurcate the proceeding into two stages. On 27 February 2014, the Netherlands provided comments on the draft Rules of Procedure and the draft Procedural Order No. 1. The Netherlands noted, *inter alia*, that it considered the statement of Russia in its *Note Verbale* dated 22 October 2013 to be "a plea concerning the jurisdiction of the Arbitral Tribunal".[33] By this *Note Verbale* addressed to ITLOS, Russia stated its position with respect to the arbitration in the following terms:

> The investigative activities related to the vessel *Arctic Sunrise* and its crew have been and are being conducted by the Russian authorities, since under the [Convention], as the authorities of the coastal State, they have jurisdiction, including criminal jurisdiction, to enforce compliance with the legislation of the Russian Federation.
>
> Upon ratification of the Convention on 26 February 1997 the Russian Federation drew up a declaration stating *inter alia* that it did not accept 'the procedures provided for in section 2 of Part XV of the Convention, entailing binding decisions with respect to disputes […] concerning law-enforcement activities in regard to the exercise of sovereign rights or jurisdiction'.
>
> On the basis of the above, the Russian Federation does not accept the arbitration proceedings proposed by the Kingdom of the Netherlands under Annex VII [of the Convention] in the case of *Arctic Sunrise* and does not intend to participate in the hearing by the [ITLOS] of the request of the Kingdom of the Netherlands to prescribe provisional measures pursuant to article 290, paragraph 5 of the Convention.[34]

In the *Note Verbale* dated 27 February 2014, Russia referred again to its *Note verbale* of 22 October 2013 and confirmed its "refusal to take part in the arbitration".[35] On

32 *Nuclear Tests Case (New Zealand v. France)*, Judgment of 20 December 1974: *I.C.J. Reports* 1974, p. 457.

33 Award on Jurisdiction, para. 18, PCA Case No. 2014-02, Available at <http://www.pca-cpa.org/showfile.asp?fil_id=2845>.

34 Ibid., para. 9. See also: *Note Verbale* from the Russian Federation to the PCA dated 27 February 2014.Available at <http://www.pca-cpa.org/showfile.asp?fil_id=2532>.

35 Award on Jurisdiction, para. 19, PCA Case No. 2014-02. Available at <http://www.pca-cpa.org/showfile.asp?fil_id=2845>.

1 September 2014, the Netherlands submitted its Memorial. In paragraph 59, the Netherlands reiterated its request for bifurcation of the proceedings:

> The Kingdom of the Netherlands remains hopeful that the Russian Federation will reconsider its position and participate in these arbitral proceedings. For this reason, the Netherlands considers it vitally important that the Tribunal bifurcates the proceedings, considers the Russian Federation's diplomatic notes of 22 October 2013 (Annex N-17) and 27 February 2014 (Annex N-34) as a plea concerning jurisdiction, and rules on the plea as a preliminary question in accordance with article 20.3 of the Tribunal's Rules of Procedure.[36]

On 14 November 2014, the Tribunal sent to the Parties a draft Procedural Order No. 4 (Bifurcation), and requested comments thereon. The draft Procedural Order No. 4 stated, *interalia*, that the Tribunal would rule on Russia's Plea concerning Jurisdiction as a preliminary question, without holding a hearing. By a letter dated 18 November 2014, the Netherlands stated that it supported the draft Order. No comment or response was received from Russia. On 21 November 2014, the Tribunal issued Procedural Order No. 4 (Bifurcation) which stated, *inter alia,* that the Tribunal would rule on Russia's Plea concerning Jurisdiction as a preliminary question, without holding a hearing.[37] Five days later, the *Arctic Sunrise Arbitration* Tribunal issued the Award, although it has neither elaborated the legal basis nor the case law for bifurcation, but only repeatedly mentioning the Netherlands' requests.

The *Arctic Sunrise Arbitration* Tribunal stresses firstly in the Award that "[t]he purpose of the present Award is to decide on Russia's Plea Concerning Jurisdiction. Accordingly, the Tribunal will, in this Award, not decide on any question of fact which is not necessary for deciding on Russia's Plea Concerning Jurisdiction; and it will not decide on any other questions concerning jurisdiction, admissibility, or merits that may arise in the arbitration".[38] This was obviously different from what the Annex VII Arbitral Tribunal did in previous cases concerning the examination of jurisdictional and admissibility issues. In this case, the *Arctic Sunrise Arbitration* Tribunal decided one part of the jurisdictional issues prior to ruling on the merits, a procedure undertaken on the sole basis of the *Note verbale* from the Russian Federation. Although the *Arctic Sunrise Arbitration* Tribunal finally dismissed Russia's view and decided that its jurisdiction over the case cannot be impaired by Russia's *Note verbale*, the decision on bifurcation should itself be of great significance for future arbitral practice.

Based on the above analysis, the following conclusions can be drawn: Firstly, informal pleas through extra-procedural communications are diplomatic objections to jurisdiction and admissibility of the Court and Tribunal, and shall be deemed as having equal effect to formal preliminary objections in the judicial proceedings.

36 Ibid., para. 41.
37 Ibid., paras. 44–7.
38 Ibid., para. 59.

Secondly, under such circumstance of diplomatic objection, the Court and Tribunal shall bifurcate the proceedings, and shall duly decide on its jurisdictional and admissibility issues prior to ruling on the merits, *unless the existence of jurisdiction is manifest.*

Although the Arbitral Tribunal established in accordance with Annex VII of the UNCLOS has followed the jurisprudence of the ICJ in dealing with the objections to the jurisdiction of the Court put forward by state parties, it has yet to elaborate the case law in an Award or Order. Over the last several decades, the ICJ has tended to interpret its power to examine and decide its own jurisdiction on the basis of respondent Parties' extra-procedural objections as a responsibility under Article 53 Paragraph 2 of the Statute of the ICJ. As noted in Article 9 of Annex VII of the UNCLOS,[39] and Article 25 Paragraph 1 of the *Rules of Procedure* of the SCS Arbitration,[40] the Tribunal must elaborate its power and responsibility according to the above legal stipulations during the proceedings of the SCS Arbitration.

The Legal Effect of the Position Paper

On 17 December 2014, the Philippine government was invited to address, as it considers appropriate, any public statements (including the Position Paper) made by the Chinese government in relation to the dispute. As of the writing of this chapter, there was yet an official response from the Philippines to the Position Paper, with only a brief statement from the Philippine Foreign Affairs Spokesman Charles Jose that his government had "taken note" of the Position Paper. According to him, "the arguments raised by China are not new anymore. We know them

39 Annex VII Article 9 Default of appearance:

If one of the parties to the dispute does not appear before the arbitral tribunal or fails to defend its case, the other party may request the tribunal to continue the proceedings and to make its award. Absence of a party or failure of a party to defend its case shall not constitute a bar to the proceedings. Before making its award, the arbitral tribunal must satisfy itself not only that it has jurisdiction over the dispute but also that the claim is well founded in fact and law.

Available at <http://www.un.org/Depts/los/convention_agreements/texts/unclos/closindx.htm>.

40 *Rulesof Procedure*, Article 25:

1. Pursuant to Article 9 of Annex VII to the Convention, if one of the Parties to the dispute doesnot appear before the Arbitral Tribunal or fails to defend its case, the other Party may requestthe Arbitral Tribunal to continue the proceedings and to make its award. Absence of a Party orfailure of a Party to defend its case shall not constitute a bar to the proceedings. Before makingits award, the Arbitral Tribunal must satisfy itself not only that it has jurisdiction over thedispute but also that the claim is well founded in fact and law.

Available at <http://www.pca-cpa.org/showfile.asp?fil_id=2504>.

and we have answered those arguments in the memorial we submitted".[41] The differences between China and the Philippines concerning the jurisdiction of the Tribunal are not a surprise in question, but the Tribunal has an obligation to deem China's consistent objections to its jurisdiction as Preliminary Objections during the arbitral proceedings, and therefore to bifurcate the proceedings and decide the issue of jurisdiction and admissibility prior to the deliberation of the merits.

In the *Arctic Sunrise Arbitration*, the Netherlands repeatedly requested bifurcation of the proceedings based on the statement of Russia in its *Note verbale* dated 22 October 2013. As the Tribunal of that case did not elaborate existing jurisprudence on bifurcation during the proceedings, nor did it announce whether or not bifurcation is based on the Netherlands' request, it is possible for the Philippines to argue that the decision to bifurcate the *Arctic Sunrise Arbitration* was not based on the requests of the Netherlands. If so, it might argue that the Position Paper as well as previous diplomatic objections by China cannot be seen as the Preliminary Objections, and therefore suggest that the Tribunal examine the jurisdictional and admissibility issues in the final Award together with the merits. Thus the Position Paper might pose no legal effect on the arbitral proceedings. However, those arguments and suggestions of the Philippines may not prejudice the lawful power and obligations of the Tribunal for the following reasons.

Firstly, in the Award on Jurisdiction of the *Arctic Sunrise Arbitration*, the Netherlands' requests were all listed in "Part II Procedural History" rather than "Part IV The Tribunal's Analysis". The arbitral tribunal never discussed the jurisprudence of bifurcation in Part IV. Actually, the Russian Federation neither participated in the formulation of the *Rules of Procedure*, nor put forward any suggestion. That means the establishment of any procedures in the arbitration was done on the basis of the power of the arbitral tribunal, since the unilateral request of one Party cannot lead to the alteration of the *Rules of Procedure,* which must be based on the consensus of the two Parties or on the power of the tribunal itself. Therefore, the list of the requests of the Netherlands only means that the arbitral tribunal has safeguarded the lawful rights of the Parties.

Secondly, bifurcation depends on the power of the Tribunal, and is therefore in accordance with the jurisprudence of the ICJ as discussed above. It is also potentially a responsibility derived from Article 9 of Annex VII of the UNCLOS, and Article 25 Paragraph 1 of the *Rules of Procedure* of the SCS Arbitration.

In addition, compared with Russia's *Note verbale*, the Position Paper put forward more complex and comprehensive arguments in relation to jurisdiction and admissibility. In the case of the bifurcation of proceedings in the *Arctic Sunrise Arbitration* Tribunal, there is no reason why the SCS Arbitration Tribunal would decide that the existence of jurisdiction is manifest and that there is no need to divide the proceeding into two stages. Therefore, the Position Paper of China should play an important role in the arbitral proceedings. Although the SCS

41 "Challenges Mount to Beijing's South China Sea Claims", VOA News, 15 December 2014. Available at <http://www.vietnamtribune.com/index.php/sid/228539561>.

Arbitration Tribunal has not, as of the writing of this chapter, issued any order concerning the bifurcation of the proceedings, it is reasonable to believe that the Tribunal would deem the Position Paper as a Preliminary Objection. It would therefore have legal effects on the proceedings, effectively deterring a ruling on merits before a ruling on jurisdiction and admissibility of the Tribunal itself has been completed.

Conclusion

The Chinese government is deemed to have accepted the Annex VII Arbitration as a compulsory dispute settlement procedure when it ratified the UNCLOS. Although China filed the Article 298 exception in 2006, which excludes, *inter alia*, disputes concerning maritime delimitation from compulsory arbitration and other compulsory dispute settlement procedures, it would be, in view of the complex situations in the South China Sea, inevitable for China to be the respondent state due to the initiation of arbitration by other states. However, under international law, the foundation for international litigation or arbitration is the *consent of the States Parties* – no matter whether it is achieved by *compromis* or by jurisdictional clause, In order to prevent any abuse, the procedures for receiving objections to jurisdiction of a court and tribunal have evolved in favor of the respondent state, maintaining the balance of rights between the claimant state and the respondent. Also, international jurisprudence has developed in the past decades indicates that international courts and tribunals attach great importance to objections to jurisdiction by extra-procedural communications by the party who is also in default of appearance.

The Position Paper released by the Chinese government has clarified the reasons why China neither accepts nor participates in the SCS Arbitration. Furthermore, it has elaborated the argument that the Tribunal does not have jurisdiction over this case, arguing that the Philippines abuses its rights. In terms of its legal effect, the Position Paper should be deemed as China's Preliminary Objection in the SCS Arbitration.

Chapter 7

The *Arctic Sunrise* Case and Its Implications for China

Jun Zhao and Jiang Li

On 18 September 2013, several Greenpeace activists attempted to board Gazprom's oil platform, the Prirazlomnaya, in the Russian exclusive economic zone (EEZ). They did it in an inflatable craft launched from the *MV Arctic Sunrise* (a Netherlands flagged vessel). They were arrested by the Russian authorities. On 19 September 2013, the vessel *Arctic Sunrise* was boarded by Russian authorities who detained the vessel and 30 persons on board.[1] As the flag state of the *Arctic Sunrise*, the Netherlands criticized the Russian government for violating the freedom of navigation of the flag state and its right to exercise its jurisdiction over the vessel, and violated the right to freedom and safety of the 30 individuals arrested.[2] As the conditions of the *Arctic Sunrise* and the members detained deteriorated, the Netherlands requested the International Tribunal for the Law of the Sea (ITLOS) for the prescription of provisional measures under Article 290, paragraph 5, of the United Nations Convention on the Law of the Sea (UNCLOS).[3] Russia did not participate in the proceedings, as it declared that the Tribunal did not have jurisdiction over the case.[4]

The ITLOS analyzed the jurisdiction of a coastal state within its EEZ with respect to the Convention. In the view of the Tribunal, the declaration made by the Russian Federation with respect to law enforcement does not apply to the *Arctic Sunrise* case. Because the Russian Federation refused to attend the proceedings, the ITLOS was forced to discuss the effects of a default of appearance, and came

---

1 ITLOS Press 205: Tribunal orders the release of the *Arctic Sunrise* and the detained persons upon the posting of a bond, p. 1. On the facts of the *Arctic Sunrise* Case, See Request for prescription of provisional measures under Article 290, para. 5, of the United Nations Convention on the Law of the Sea, Chapter 2, Statement of Fact, p. 2. Available at: <http://www.itlos.org/fileadmin/itlos/documents/cases/case_no.22/Request_provisional_measures_en_withtranslations.pdf>.

2 See Request for prescription of provisional measures under Article 290, para. 5, of the United Nations Convention on the Law of the Sea, Chapter 2, Statement of Fact, paras. 19–20, 25–7, 32, pp. 4, 6, and 7.

3 ITLOS Press 201: Request for provisional measures submitted today to the Tribunal in the *Arctic Sunrise* Case, pp. 1–2.

4 See Note verbale of the Embassy of the Russian Federation in Berlin, dated 22 October 2013.

to the conclusion that the absence of the Russian Federation does not prevent the proceedings of the case. On this basis, the Tribunal analyzed the rules for provisional measures within the Convention, and made the decision of the order for provisional measures by majority votes.

The Tribunal's *Arctic Sunrise* decision will have significant implications for China, where China has so far refused to participate in an UNCLOS challenge brought by the Philippines over maritime claims in the South China Sea. This chapter offers an analysis of the arguments and reasoning in the *Arctic Sunrise* case. Furthermore, this chapter draws attention to a parallel between Russian's behavior in the *Arctic Sunrise* case and the Chinese attitude in the arbitration initiated by the Philippines. After that, in light of the *Arctic Sunrise* case, this chapter probes into China's potential strategy towards the arbitration initiated by the Philippines.

Jurisdiction of the Tribunal and Jurisdiction of the State

The *Arctic Sunrise* case involves the relationship of the jurisdiction between the coastal state, the flag state, and the ITLOS. Specifically in this case, there is a need to clarify the exception of the jurisdiction of the flag state. The EEZ is a sui generis zone where the rights of the coastal state and the third states have to be harmonized.[5] This concerns the legality of the acts initiated by the Russian Federation. Also, there is a need to clarify the relationship between the jurisdiction of the ITLOS and the domestic jurisdiction of the Russian Federation. To put it simply, it is a question of whether the declaration made by the Russian Federation in signing the UNCLOS can exclude the jurisdiction of the Tribunal in this case.

The Extent of the Jurisdiction of Coastal States in Exclusive Economic Zones

The jurisdiction of the flag state and the coastal state of vessels within the EEZ is the first question that arises in this case. The legality of the action of the Russian Federation to detain the vessel and its crew is based on whether the Russian Federation has jurisdiction within the EEZ on the *Arctic Sunrise*. As part of customary international law, the Convention states that the coastal state must not interfere with the freedom of navigation and overflight of other Member States. For

5 In certain situations, the Convention states that in the case of exclusive economic zones, the jurisdiction of the coastal state is superior to that of the flag state. However, that is not for all purposes. For example, the duties of the flag state and the coastal state to prevent vessel source pollution in the EEZ are equal, and may yet be more weighted to the flag state. Moreover, if coastal state jurisdiction can be said to trump the jurisdiction of other states in areas where they have received special competence, in areas like navigation, the rights of third states trump those of the coastal state.

vessels that are exercising the freedom of navigation, the flag state has exclusive jurisdiction. However, under special circumstances, the coastal state can acquire jurisdiction over that of the flag state. First, the Convention gave the coastal state sovereign rights over certain aspects of the EEZ. The Convention granted the coastal state preferential rights to explore and exploit the economic rights of the EEZ.[6] The coastal state possesses jurisdiction over almost all economic activities within the EEZ,[7] but it cannot extend its rights unilaterally and arbitrarily, and must respect the rights given to other states by the Convention within the zone.[8] Secondly, the UNCLOS directly prescribes the exclusive rights of the coastal state in the EEZ. The Convention stipulates that the coastal state has jurisdiction over the establishment and use of artificial islands, installations and structures, marine scientific research, and the conservation of the marine environment within the EEZ.[9] In the areas of customs, finance, health, safety, and immigration, the coastal state also retains jurisdiction over artificial installations and structures in the EEZ.[10] Third, in respect to the jurisdiction granted to the coastal state by other international treaties or rules stipulating universal jurisdiction on related activities, the coastal state can apply its laws and regulations in accordance with the provisions of the Convention and other rules of international law.[11] Fourth, for vessels violating domestic laws, even though it is within the EEZ, the coastal state can exercise the right of hot pursuit[12] and the right of visit,[13] and in proof of "reasonable ground for suspecting" or "good reasons to believe", the right to exercise its jurisdiction.[14] Lastly, the coastal state may create (i.e. designate) a safety zone of 500 meters around oil rig platforms.[15] Even though the safety zone is, in essence, a part of the

6 The coastal state enjoys preferential rights, rather than exclusive rights, to explore and exploit the economic rights of the exclusive economic zone. Even with respect to fisheries, a careful analysis of Art. 62–3 reveals that, at least on paper, the rights of the coastal state are preferential rather than exclusive. See also Art. 56, para 2.

7 See UNCLOS Article 56.1 (a).

8 The *Arctic Sunrise* Case (Kingdom of the Netherlands v. Russian Federation), Verbatim Record of Public sitting, ITLOS/PV.13/C22/1, 06/11/2013, pp. 18–19. Also see UNCLOS Article 56.2, 58, 60.3, 7.

9 See UNCLOS Article 56.1 (b), (c).

10 See UNCLOS Article 60.2.

11 The Russian Federation initially tried to prosecute the crew of the *Arctic Sunrise* with "Piracy". See Note verbale of the Embassy of the Russian Federation in Berlin, dated 22 October 2013. Also the *Arctic Sunrise* Case (Kingdom of the Netherlands v. Russian Federation), Verbatim Record of Public sitting, ITLOS/PV.13/C22/1, 06/11/2013, p. 20.

12 As far as hot pursuit is concerned, only in areas where the coastal state has received sovereign rights or jurisdiction does this right of hot pursuit apply.

13 As far as the right of visit is concerned, the limited areas enumerated in Art. 110 do not seem to give the domestic legislation of the coastal state much leeway to expand its jurisdiction.

14 See UNCLOS Article 110, 111.1–4.

15 See UNCLOS Article 60.4–7.

EEZ, but once the coastal state has enacted special laws and regulations for this zone, the violation of these laws and regulations will invoke jurisdiction of the coastal state over the intruding vessel.[16]

The *Arctic Sunrise* steered near the Russian oil rig in the Barents Sea with the intent of peaceful protest. The intentions are obviously not economical, which eliminates it from the domain of fishery, scientific research, and piracy.[17] Although Russia tried to prosecute the crew on account of piracy,[18] the only reasonable justification for its jurisdiction seems to be the fact that the *Arctic Sunrise* violated Russian regulations in respect to the safety zone of the oil rig. According to the Netherlands, the detention and arrest of the vessel and crew happened 3 nautical miles off the oil rig in the EEZ, which can only be justified by the right of visit and the right of hot pursuit. Of course, the Netherlands and the Greenpeace organization denied that the crew's actions produced any damage to the safety and normal production of the oil rig platform,[19] while also denying the legality of the actions of the right of visit and hot pursuit.[20] Due to the refusal of the Russian Federation to participate in the case, the full facts cannot be presented here, and the right of jurisdiction between the flag state and the coastal state remains unclear. We will see the case now actually go to arbitration on the merits, including this issue.

The Compulsory Jurisdiction of the Tribunal and the Exclusion Declaration of the Acceding State

The compulsory jurisdiction of the ITLOS and the Article 298 Declaration by a state party regarding compulsory jurisdiction is another issue that we must take

16 In this case, the Greenpeace organization had doubts as to whether the crew of the *Arctic Sunrise* entered the safety zone, and whether they affected normal production. Indeed, it is accepted that the Greenpeace ship itself did not enter the safety zone, but two or more small inflated speedboats did the day prior to the arrest of the ship. The Dutch stated that the *Arctic Sunrise* did not violate the Russian regulations on safety zones. See Reply to questions to the Tribunal, *Arctic Sunrise* Case, by Ministry of Foreign Affairs of Kingdom of Netherland, pp. 1–2, 4. The Dutch stated that the installation and regulations of the safety zone violated international law, see the *Arctic Sunrise* Case (Kingdom of the Netherlands v. Russian Federation), Public sitting, ITLOS/PV.13/C22/1, 06/11/2013, p. 23.

17 Although violence for political aims might constitute piracy. See Institute of Cetacean Research v Sea Shepherd Conservation Society, 725 F.3d 940 (Ninth Circuit) (2013) at p. 942 (reversing 708 F.3d 1099).

18 On the piracy charges part, Russia said or did initially bring piracy charges, but it withdrew then about 30 to 45 days after the arrest of the ship and the "Arctic 30".

19 As to whether the Dutch vessel violated Russian regulations on safety zones, and the appropriateness of the Tribunal's Order, Judge Golitsyn provided a dissenting opinion. See Dissenting Opinion of Judge Golitsyn, pp. 6–10, paras. 23–34.

20 Judge Golitsyn made a dissenting opinion on the right of visit and hotpursuit, See Dissenting Opinion of Judge Golitsyn, pp. 10–11, paras. 35–37.

into consideration. The Netherlands asked the ITLOS for an order of provisional measures in the event of the unlawful detainment of the vessel and crew by the Russian Federation, but Russia had refused to attend the proceedings on the grounds of its declaration clause in the ratification of the Convention. The UNCLOS created a compulsory dispute settlement procedure, but as an exception, it allows states to eliminate the usage of the dispute settlement mechanism in certain types or categories of disputes. According to Article 298 of the Convention, Russia exercised that right on the compulsory procedures[21] under Part XV, section 2 upon ratifying the Convention.[22] Russia's original Article 298 declaration permissibly exempted from compulsory jurisdiction boundary disputes, military activities and matters over which the UN Security Council was seized. However, its 12 March 1997 Declaration pushed the exemption further, to include "disputes concerning law enforcement activities in regard to the exercise of sovereign rights or jurisdiction".[23] This turns the focal point of the jurisdiction arguments in the *Arctic Sunrise* case to the extent of the declaration made by Russia in respect to the compulsory procedures – mainly, the analysis of the exercise of sovereign rights and the jurisdiction of law enforcement activities. The Netherlands is of the opinion that the Convention, as a package solution, should be given full and strict compliance of the rules, and the reservation of the Russian Federation in respect to law enforcement activities should be limited to section 2 and 3 of Article 297 of the Convention.[24] From the declarations made by Russia,[25] it asserts that the

21 Section 2 of Part XV of the Convention stipulated the compulsory jurisdiction of the Tribunal in maritime disputes, and Article 298 is an exception for the states on the compulsory proceedings.

22 See Note verbale of the Embassy of the Russian Federation in Berlin, dated 22 October 2013. Available at <http://www.itlos.org/fileadmin/itlos/documents/cases/case_no.22/Note_verbale_Russian_Federation_eng.pdf>.

23 See the *Arctic Sunrise* Case (Kingdom of The Netherlands v. Russian Federation) (List of Cases No. 22), Order 2013/3 (22 November 2013), (1 April 2014), <www.itlos.org>.

24 Concerning the exceptions to the compulsory proceedings, Article 298, paragraph 1(b) states: "disputes concerning military activities ... and disputes concerning law enforcement activities in regard to the exercise of sovereign rights or jurisdiction excluded from the jurisdiction of a court or tribunal under article 297, paragraph 2 or 3". We can see that, in regards to the sovereign rights and law enforcement activities, the Convention only allowed exceptions within the limits of paragraphs 2 and 3 of Article 297. See The United Nations Convention on the Law of the Sea, Article 297, 298(1)(b). For the opinion of the Netherlands, see the *Arctic Sunrise* Case (Kingdom of the Netherlands v. Russian Federation), Verbatim Record of Public Sitting, ITLOS/PV.13/C22/1, 06/11/2013, p. 12. It should be noted that only the Belarus declaration under article 298(1)(b) also did not include the words "excluded from the jurisdiction of a court or tribunal under article 297, paragraph 2 or 3".

25 The Russian Federation declares that, in accordance with article 298 of the UNCLOS, it does not accept the procedures, provided for in section 2 of Part XV of the Convention, entailing binding decisions with respect to disputes concerning the

reservation was made in respect to law enforcement activities as a whole, thereby apparently ousting the jurisdiction of the Tribunal.[26]

Following such an analysis of the extent of the declaration is the interpretation of the facts of the case. Due to the absence of Russia in the provisional measures hearing, the details and nature of the activities on board the *Arctic Sunrise* can only be gleaned from the statements of the Netherlands. The question whether Russia, as a coastal state, could acceptably trump jurisdiction of the flag state due to the conduct of the vessel remains unclear. But, from the Tribunal's view, regardless of how the activities in the case are to be interpreted, the fact remains that the Tribunal is within its rights to exercise jurisdiction with respect to the interpretation of the Russian reservation. According to *pacta sunt servanda*, the law enforcement activities within the Russian reservation should be interpreted strictly in accordance with the Convention. If the *Arctic Sunrise* did not engage in scientific research and fishery activities, then the actions by Russia, *prima facie*, would fall outside of the scope of the reservation. And as the *Arctic Sunrise* did not engage in scientific research and fishery activities, Russia cannot exclude the compulsory jurisdiction of the Tribunal in this case.[27] From an interpretive approach of the Convention, Russia may not deny the Tribunal of jurisdiction, and in any case, the differences between the parties in interpreting the rules of the Convention are enough for the Tribunal to exercise jurisdiction on this case.[28] In summary, the jurisdiction of the Tribunal in the *Arctic Sunrise* case is justified under international law.

---

interpretation or application of articles 15, 74 and 83 of the Convention, relating to sea boundary delimitations, or those involving historic bays or titles; disputes concerning military activities, including military activities by government vessels and aircraft, and disputes concerning law-enforcement activities in regard to the exercise of sovereign rights or jurisdiction; and disputes in respect of which the Security Council of the United Nations is exercising the functions assigned to it by the Charter of the United Nations.

The Russian Federation, bearing in mind articles 309 and 310 of the Convention, declares that it objects to any declarations and statements made in the past or which may be made in future when signing, ratifying or acceding to the Convention, or made for any other reason in connection with the Convention, that are not in keeping with the provisions of article 310 of the Convention. The Russian Federation believes that such declarations and statements, however phrased or named, cannot exclude or modify the legal effect of the provisions of the Convention in their application to the party to the Convention that made such declarations or statements, and for this reason they shall not be taken into account by the Russian Federation in its relations with that party to the Convention. Available at: <http://www.un.org/depts/los/convention_agreements/convention_declarations.htm#Russian Federation Upon signature>.

26 For the Russian viewpoint on the declaration, See Note verbale of the Embassy of the Russian Federation in Berlin, dated 22 October 2013.

27 See ITLOS Order, Request for the prescription of provisional measures, the *Arctic Sunrise* Case, p. 12, para. 43.

28 See ITLOS Order, Request for the prescription of provisional measures, the *Arctic Sunrise* Case, pp. 15–17, paras. 60–69.

Legality of the Default of Appearance

The *Arctic Sunrise* case presented a situation to the Tribunal that involves the absence of a party, and the application of Article 28 of the Statute of the ITLOS[29] by the Tribunal became a core issue in this case. Article 28 stipulates the consequences where a party is absent, the balance of rights between the parties, and the conditions for the application of default ruling. Because the Tribunal had never before applied Article 28 in cases prior to the *Arctic Sunrise*, it lacked the necessary guidance and reference needed to understand the meaning of the Article, and therefore turned to the ICJ, and by referring to Article 53 of the ICJ Statute,[30] was able to apply the default ruling of Article 28.[31]

Obligation to Exchange Views before Starting Formal Legal Proceedings in the ITLOS

From the order for provisional measures in this case, the Tribunal concluded that, when parties cannot hope to reach a settlement, they do not require continuous consultation before taking the case to the Tribunal.[32] There is a strong obligation – a duty – to exchange views, if not an outright one, even if the substance of the exchange is limited. Some consultation and discussion is needed. In the *Case Concerning the Land and Maritime Boundary Between Cameroon and Nigeria*, the ICJ was of the opinion that, although an exchange of views isn't a precondition for the matter to be referred to the Court, such negotiations should still take place.[33] As Judge Golitsyn wrote in his dissenting opinion, the Netherlands had never tried to undertake an exchange of views with the Russian authorities, except for the note verbale to inform the Russian authorities of its decision to refer to the Tribunal. In the judge's view, the Dutch behavior was clearly in conflict with

29 Article 28 of the Statute: "When one of the parties does not appear before the Tribunal or fails to defend its case, the other party may request the Tribunal to continue the proceedings and make its decision. Absence of a party or failure of a party to defend its case shall not constitute a bar to the proceedings. Before making its decision, the Tribunal must satisfy itself not only that it has jurisdiction over the dispute, but also that the claim is well founded in fact and law".

30 Statute of the ICJ Article 53: "Whenever one of the parties does not appear before the Court, or fails to defend its case, the other party may call upon the Court to decide in favour of its claim. The Court must, before doing so, satisfy itself, not only that it has jurisdiction in accordance with Articles 36 and 37, but also that the claim is well founded in fact and law".

31 <http://www.un.org/depts/los/convention_agreements/texts/unclos/annex6.htm>.

32 See ITLOS Order, Request for the prescription of provisional measures, the *Arctic Sunrise* Case, pp. 18, paras. 60–69.

33 See Dissenting Opinion of Judge Golitsyn, p. 3. Preliminary Objections, Judgment, I.C.J. Reports 1998, p. 275, at p. 303, para. 56.

Article 283, paragraph 1, of the Convention,[34] and therefore, the request for provisional measures should not be accepted.[35] In reality, the use of international judicial mechanisms is not to promote litigation, but serves as a last resort for the protection of justice. Before referring to international judicial mechanisms, the parties need not exhaust all negotiations, but there must be actual attempts at negotiations, as already proven by international dispute settlement in practice. In this case, the Tribunal recognized the importance of prior negotiations, but accepted that the Netherlands had already fulfilled its obligations by diplomatic means.[36] In the *Arctic Sunrise*, whether the parties have sufficiently negotiated in substance can be further questioned, the lack of negotiations lead to the logical question about the legality of the initiation of the judicial procedure.

Whether Absence of a Party will Result in the Bar of the Proceedings

The Tribunal, in acknowledging that both parties have been given ample opportunities to express their views on the matter, was of the opinion that an absent party may not constitute a bar of the proceedings in respect to the decision of provisional measures.[37] For the same reason, in the *Fisheries Jurisdiction* case, the ICJ pointed out that, according to the jurisprudence of the Court and the Permanent Court of International Justice, the non-appearance of one of the parties cannot itself constitute an obstacle to the indication of provisional measures.[38] As such, the absent party remains a party to the case, and is bound by the judgment according to Article 33.[39] In the present case, the Russian government chose to deliver a note verbale explaining that Russia had no intention of attending the proceeding for the provisional measures.[40] In the note verbale, Russia, *prima facie*, excluded the jurisdiction of the Tribunal according to Annex VII, but this does not provide legal basis for its absence, and may not deter the Tribunal from determining, for itself, whether it has jurisdiction on the matter at hand. After careful analysis, the Tribunal found that the Russian Federation only excluded the jurisdiction of the Tribunal

34 See The United Nations Convention on the Law of the Sea, Article 283.1.

35 See Dissenting Opinion of Judge Golitsyn, pp. 3–5, paras. 9–14.

36 See ITLOS Order, Request for the prescription of provisional measures, the *Arctic Sunrise* Case, pp. 17–18, paras. 72–6.

37 See ITLOS Order, Request for the prescription of provisional measures, the *Arctic Sunrise* Case, p. 13, para. 48.

38 See the *Arctic Sunrise* Case (Kingdom of the Netherlands v. Russian Federation), Verbatim Record of Public sitting, ITLOS/PV.13/C22/1, 06/11/2013, pp. 6–7.

39 Annex VI of the Convention, as in the Statute of the International Tribunal for the Law of the Sea Article 33: "1. The decision of the Tribunal is final and shall be complied with by all the parties to the dispute. 2. The decision shall have no binding force except between the parties in respect of that particular dispute".

40 See Note verbale of the Embassy of the Russian Federation in Berlin, dated 22 October 2013.

on disputes that are within the scope of section 2 and 3 of Article 293, and thus established the *prima facie* jurisdiction of the Tribunal in the *Arctic Sunrise* case. Jurisdiction is the precondition for the continuation of judicial procedures. As we can see, Russia did not exclude the Tribunal from exercising its jurisdiction by choosing not to appear, and the judicial procedure goes on.

Conditions for Default Ruling

According to Article 28 of the ITLOS Statute, before making its decision, the Tribunal must satisfy itself not only that it has jurisdiction over the dispute, but also that the claim is well founded in fact and law.[41] The Article was drafted consistent with Article 53(2) of the Statute of the International Court of Justice. When one party is absent, the Court must fulfill two conditions in order to continue the judicial procedure, namely, that is has jurisdiction over the dispute, and that the claim is well founded in fact and law.[42] First, in regards to jurisdiction, in the case concerning *Corfu Channel*,[43] the ICJ pointed out that the Court does not need to examine the accuracy in all the details of the submissions. It is sufficient for the Court to convince itself by such methods as it considers suitable that the submissions are well founded.[44] In other words, in order to make a default ruling, the Court only needs to establish preliminary jurisdiction on the matter. In this case, the Tribunal believed that in the detention of the *Arctic Sunrise*, the parties of the dispute had different views of the interpretation and application of the Convention, thereby establishing preliminary jurisdiction. Secondly, in the question of the claim of the Netherlands under fact and law, the Tribunal provided insight into the matter in its Order.[45] Notably, in the *Fisheries Jurisdiction* case, the ICJ pointed out that the legal basis of the claim needs the parties to consider all rules of international law which may be relevant to the settlement of the dispute. But it is the duty of the Court to ascertain and apply the relevant law. We should keep in mind, however, that because the Court, in ascertaining the legal basis of a party's claims, does not simply proceed on the basis of proof offered by the one participating party: a court or tribunal will address the legal basis of the claims.[46] In this case, the Netherlands

41 See the *Arctic Sunrise* Case (Kingdom of the Netherlands v. Russian Federation), Verbatim Record of Public sitting, ITLOS/PV.13/C22/1, 06/11/2013, pp. 6–7.

42 See <http://www.un.org/depts/los/convention_agreements/texts/unclos/annex6.htm; http://www.icj-cij.org/documents/?p1=4&p2=2&p3=0#CHAPTER_III>. There is another implicit requirement that the responding state has been properly informed of the case.

43 <http://www.icj-cij.org/docket/index.php?p1=3&p2=3&case=1&p3=4>.

44 The *Arctic Sunrise* Case (Kingdom of the Netherlands v. Russian Federation), Verbatim Record of Public sitting, ITLOS/PV.13/C22/1, 06/11/2013, p. 6.

45 ITLOS Order, Request for the prescription of provisional measures, the "Arctic Sunrise" case, p. 14–17, paras. 60–70.

46 The *Arctic Sunrise* Case (Kingdom of the Netherlands v. Russian Federation), Verbatim Record of Public sitting, ITLOS/PV.13/C22/1, 06/11/2013, pp. 7–8.

quoted the rights of free navigation, the rights of the coastal state in the exclusive economic zone, the compulsory jurisdiction of the Tribunal, and relevant provisions under the Universal Declaration of Human Rights.[47] The Russian Federation quoted the exceptions to compulsory jurisdiction in its note verbale. Finally, in regards to the factual basis of this case, the ICJ in *Military and Paramilitary Activities in and against Nicaragua*[48] pointed out that, while it was not bound to confine its consideration to the material formally submitted to it by the parties, it cannot, by its own enquiries, make up for the absence of one of the parties.[49] In the *Arctic Sunrise* case, even though one of the parties, Russia, refused to attend the proceedings, but the Tribunal, in having preliminary jurisdiction to examine the establishment of the factual and legal bases of the claims, was satisfied that all the conditions had been fulfilled for a default ruling.

How the Tribunal Balances the Rights of the Parties

In the event of default ruling due to absence of a party, how to protect the parties involved, especially the one not attending the proceedings, is an important question for the Tribunal to consider. Judge *ad hoc* Anderson pointed out in his declaration that the non-appearance of the Russian Federation made the factual examinations of the case and the materials on the stance of the parties extremely difficult to ascertain, and does not serve the efficient application of Part XV[50] of the Convention, or the rule of law in international relations.[51] The ICJ, in *Military and Paramilitary Activities in and against Nicaragua,* also noted the question of the equality of the parties. The Court stated that, the equality of the parties must remain the basic principle for the Court, and in the event of absence, the party which declines to appear cannot be permitted to profit from its absence, since this would amount to placing the party appearing at a disadvantage.[52] The absence of a party would leave only a shell of a dispute settlement mechanism, and not its core. Therefore, Article 28 of the Statute cannot be seen as providing a right of absence to the parties.[53] The Tribunal made a default ruling based on the principle of the equality of the parties. The Tribunal believed that Russia had been given ample opportunities to attend the proceedings, and the absence of Russia should

---

47 <http://www.un.org/en/documents/udhr/>.

48 Military and Paramilitary Activities in and against Nicaragua (Nicaragua v. United States of America), Merits, Judgment, I.C.J. Reports 1986.

49 The *Arctic Sunrise* Case (Kingdom of the Netherlands v. Russian Federation), Verbatim Record of Public sitting, ITLOS/PV.13/C22/1, 06/11/2013, p. 8.

50 Part XV of the Convention is "Settlement of Disputes".

51 See Declaration of Judge ad hoc Anderson, p. 1.

52 See the *Arctic Sunrise* Case (Kingdom of the Netherlands v. Russian Federation), Verbatim Record of Public sitting, ITLOS/PV.13/C22/1, 06/11/2013, p. 8.

53 See Joint Separate Opinion of Judge Wolfrum and Judge Kelly, p. 3.

not put the Netherlands at a disadvantage.[54] Notably, when a party is absent, even though a default ruling is applied to protect the interests of the appearing party, but protecting the interests of the non-appearing party is also a part of the equality principle. In the process of default ruling, the Tribunal must establish jurisdiction on the case, and make rulings that are within its jurisdiction. Also, it has the obligation to notify the absent party according to procedural provisions, and these procedures are all necessary to ensure procedural fairness and so equality between the parties.

Legality of the Exercise of Judicial Power by the ITLOS

Except for the jurisdiction of the Tribunal and the legality of the default ruling, another important procedural question presented by this case was: Did the Tribunal exercise its judicial powers according to the regulations of the Convention and the Statute? Was the Tribunal in accordance with the regulations of the Convention in respect to the reasons for its default ruling? In sum, in the process of the default ruling, the powers exercised by the Tribunal should be within the scope of the Convention. In the *Arctic Sunrise* case, the validity of the facts that needed to be examined are: The legal effects of the Tribunal citing an ICJ case to explain the absence of a party, the factual basis for the provisional measures, and the legal basis for the application of "bond and other financial security".

The Citing of ICJ Cases

In regards to the ruling for the provisional measures, the Tribunal did not spend much time on Article 28 of the ITLOS Statute. However, Article 28 is the only rule in the Statute stipulating the legal effects of absence, and so the application of this rule became a critical question.[55] Although the Dutch believed that Article 28 of the Statute should simply be applied consistent with Article 53 of the Statute of the International Court of Justice, there remain a few questions regarding the application of ICJ decisions by the Tribunal:

1. The Tribunal and the ICJ are dispute settlement forums established based on different legal bases, the similarities in procedural rules is just a normative aspect to it, but whether or not they can cite each other is an important aspect to the issue. Although within the realm of scientific research, we often cite ICJ cases for explanations, but when a Tribunal, in the case of having an applicable provision at hand, decides to ignore the provision, and

54 See ITLOS Order, Request for the prescription of provisional measures, the *Arctic Sunrise* Case, p. 14, paras. 54, 56.

55 See Separate Opinion of Judge Paik, p. 1.

instead turns to the rules and cases of the ICJ, this is bound to have negative impacts on its own rules.

2. Even if there are no problems with applying Article 53 of the ICJ Statute, the Court has never applied Article 53 specifically to provisional measures.[56] However, the core issue of this case is provisional measures, and there are several differences between the ICJ cases and the case at hand. Neglecting these differences can impair the arguments provided by the Tribunal.
3. Although they both apply to the absence of a party in dispute, Article 28 of the Statute and Article 53 of the statute of ICJ still have their differences. In theory, Article 28 focuses more on the procedure of the equality of rights of the appearing and non-appearing states. Article 28 did not incorporate the phrase "other party may call upon the Court to decide in favor of its claim" from Article 53 of the ICJ Statute, and instead only stipulates that "other party may request the Tribunal to continue the proceedings and make its decision"; Article 28 also added "absence of a party or failure of a party to defend its case shall not constitute a bar to the proceedings". In addition, because the claims of the parties and the jurisdiction of the Tribunal are all subject to broad interpretation, Article 28 can fully serve as the basis for provisional measures when a party is absent.[57]
4. The default ruling of the Tribunal should be within the limits of the claims made by the parties, and should not overstep or abandon the requests of the parties in search of a new path. Unquestionably, in the preliminary hearings, the Netherlands cited Article 28 as a basis for the effects of Russia's absence,[58] and as such, this should also be the basis of the argument provided by the Tribunal in assessing the effects of the absence of Russia. However, in the Order for provisional measures, the Tribunal did not base its arguments on Article 28,[59] but instead chose to find legal basis within ICJ rules and cases. The validity of this procedure is obviously questionable.
5. The Tribunal has the obligation to apply, elaborate, and interpret the rules. The Statute, which serves as a guidance for the Tribunal in the process of adjudicating cases, should be readily applied within the adjudication process unless the meaning of the rules are extremely ambiguous and unclear. As noted above, this was the first instance that the Tribunal was faced with a default ruling case. The Tribunal should have clarified the meaning of the related rules by interpretations, and thus create precedence and guidance for future cases. Regretfully, the Tribunal in this case did not serve this purpose.[60] Lacking an independent interpretation mechanism,

56 Ibid.

57 Ibid., pp. 2–6.

58 The *Arctic Sunrise* Case (Kingdom of the Netherlands v. Russian Federation), Verbatim Record of Public sitting, ITLOS/PV.13/C22/1, 06/11/2013, p. 5.

59 See Separate Opinion of Judge Paik, pp. 6–7.

60 Ibid., pp. 7–8.

the Tribunal, as a judicial mechanism, should keep in mind that when interpreting related regulations, the interpretation should not just be seen as a right, but an obligation.

The Application of Provisional Measures

As described above, the Tribunal was only requested to exercise preliminary jurisdiction in regards to the request for provisional measures by the Netherlands. As the Netherlands had requested, the Tribunal stated in its Order that Russia must release the detained vessel and crew, allow them to leave Russian territory and maritime areas under the jurisdiction of the Russian Federation, and asked both parties to submit the initial report and relevant information.[61] In addition, there was also the requirement that the Netherlands post a bond for the ship and the release of the Arctic 30. What is worth noting here is whether the Tribunal was in accordance to the rules of the Convention related to provisional measures. Article 290(5) of the Convention states that the Tribunal may prescribe, modify or revoke provisional measures if the applying party can fulfill two conditions: preliminary jurisdiction and the urgency of the situation.[62] Although the Tribunal has, without doubt, preliminary jurisdiction, but according to the cases of ICJ, what qualifies as "urgency of the situation" remains unclear. From international case law, "urgency of the situation" can be interpreted as: when a party's actions can cause irreparable and irreversible damage to the other party. Even from the literal meaning of Article 290 of the Convention, the term "damage" can only be qualified as "serious", since paragraph 1 provides for "serious harm to the marine environment".[63] The ITLOS is more and more willing to accept continuing detention of people – here the Greenpeace Arctic 30 activists – as being a substantial basis or reason to make out urgency.

In this case, the reason provided by the Netherlands to the Tribunal requesting provisional measures were that Russia, in detaining the *Arctic Sunrise*, arresting and initiating a prosecution of its crew, was in continuous violation of international law, and was allowing the general condition of the vessel to deteriorate. The Netherlands has also stressed the irreversibility of Russian actions.[64] In the ruling, the Tribunal believed that the urgency of the situation called for an order for provisional measures.[65] Obviously, in assessing whether the situation was in

---

61 ITLOS Order, Request for the prescription of provisional measures, the *Arctic Sunrise* Case, p. 23.

62 See United Nations Convention on the Law of the Sea, Article 290.

63 See Dissenting Opinion of Judge Kulyk, pp. 2–3.

64 See the *Arctic Sunrise* Case (Kingdom of the Netherlands v. Russian Federation), Verbatim Record of Public sitting, ITLOS/PV.13/C22/1, 06/11/2013, pp. 24–6.

65 See ITLOS Order, Request for the prescription of provisional measures, the *Arctic Sunrise* Case, p. 23, para. 89.

accordance with the relevant rules for provisional measures under the Convention, the Tribunal did not give significant assessment of the two conditions, "irreversible" and "irreparable", albeit the ITLOS did consider that every day the Arctic 30 people were detained – imprisoned – was a day they could never recover. As for the application of provisional measures, the two conditions above, combined with "appropriateness", constitutes a restriction on the discretion of the Tribunal by the Convention, and may not be dismissed lightly.[66] Judge Kulyk stated in his dissenting opinion that the reasons provided by the Netherlands have not reached the standard of "irreversible", and in any event, the Russian Federation has already made promises to assume responsibility for any damages incurred during the detention.[67] As a result, this case is flawed in light of the conditions set forth for the application of the provisional measures.

The Requirement for the Netherlands to Post a Bond

Judge Kulyk also pointed out in his dissenting opinion that, according to the rules of the Convention, the provisional measures are for the preservation of the respective rights of the parties, and not for the prompt release of the vessel and its crew.[68] In the Order, the Tribunal required a "bond or other financial security" as precondition for the provisional measures.[69] The question here is what is the relationship between the bond and the provisional measures? Is the decision of the Tribunal legal or valid? The application of the bond was not only to protect respective rights, but also, the specific function of the "bond" was to acknowledge the legality of the jurisdiction of the contested party, in the event of jurisdiction disputes on the international law level. Judge Kulyk is of the opinion that requiring security (here, in the form of a bond) as a condition for the provisional measures confuses the objective of swift release of the vessel and crew to the assurance of smooth compliance of the decision. But he also pointed out that, with reasonable interpretations, the two may coexist.[70] Judge Jesus wrote in his separate opinion that in the case where, under the applicable domestic law, the detainment of the vessel and crew may not be converted into a monetary penalty, a bond imposed as a condition of provisional measures may not "preserve the rights" of the detaining state. In his view, the release of the vessel and crew should be based on the freedom of navigation which the flag state enjoys.[71] Due to the special circumstances of this case, the usage of "bond" should be elaborated in detail to prevent unnecessary doubts.

66 Dissenting Opinion of Judge Kulyk, pp. 2–3.

67 Ibid., pp. 2–3, paras. 9–10.

68 Ibid., pp. 2–3, para. 12.

69 ITLOS Order, Request for the prescription of provisional measures, the *Arctic Sunrise* Case, p. 23.

70 Dissenting Opinion of Judge Kulyk, p. 7, para. 15.

71 See Separate Opinion of Judge Jesus, p. 7, paras. 11–12.

IV. From the *Arctic Sunrise* to the Philippines-China South China Sea Disputes

Along with the increasing exploitation of marine resources, maritime disputes are also growing in volume. As a leading maritime power, China wishes to exploit marine resources as a means of economic development, but also faces maritime disputes with neighboring states. Recently, the Philippines notified China that it had instituted arbitral proceedings against China under the Convention,[72] even though China had explicitly expressed its refusal to participate in such proceedings.[73] With regard to the Philippines' unilateral initiating of arbitral proceedings, many comparable points can be gleaned from the *Arctic Sunrise* case.

Exclusion of the Jurisdiction of the Tribunal in *South China Sea Arbitration* Case

In the *Arctic Sunrise* case, the Russian government chose not to attend the proceedings. Similarly, in the Philippines-China South China Sea disputes, the Chinese government chose not to participate in the proceedings. Both China and Russia relied on the declarations that they have made under Article 298 of the Convention. The Convention allows the contracting states to preclude the use of the compulsory dispute settlement mechanism by declaration. In *Arctic Sunrise* case, Russia's Article 298 declaration precluded the Tribunal from performing jurisdiction over boundary disputes, military activities and matters over which the Charter assigns powers to the UN Security Council. Also included in its 1997 declaration were, "disputes concerning law enforcement activities in regard to the exercise of sovereign rights or jurisdiction".[74] However, according to the Netherlands, Article 298 of the Convention did not attempt to exclude all law enforcement activities, just those disputes concerning scientific research and fishery activities. The Netherlands argued that the 1997 declaration should be interpreted strictly. If not, it would be in conflict with Articles 309 and 310 of the Convention. This limited interpretation received some scholarly support. According to Natalie Klein, from the appearance of Article 298 section 1, the only law enforcement activities that could be precluded by the declaration from the compulsory dispute settlement mechanism in Part XV, section 2 of the Convention are those regarding scientific research and fisheries within the exclusive economic

72 See Notification and Statement of Claim on West Philippine Sea, Department of Foreign Affairs of Philippine, Manila, 2013. 1. 22.

73 The PRC Ministry of Foreign Affairs has stated China's refusal to participate in the international arbitral proceedings brought by the Philippines in the China-Philippines dispute, 8 July 2013. Available at: <http://www.fmprc.gov.cn/mfa_chn/wjdt_611265/fyrbt_611275/t1057006.shtml>, last accessed 17 December 2013.

74 See the *Arctic Sunrise* Case (Kingdom of The Netherlands v. Russian Federation) (List of Cases No. 22), Order 2013/3 (22 November 2013), (1 April 2014) <www.itlos.org>.

zone. Also, from the establishment history of the Convention, except for the above two law enforcement activities, all other law enforcement activities fall under the jurisdiction of the Convention's compulsory dispute settlement mechanism.[75] In this case, if the *Arctic Sunrise* was not involved in scientific research or fishery activities, then Russia could not apply the reservation. In other words, Russia could not exclude the Tribunal's jurisdiction in this case.

Compared with Russia's position in the *Arctic Sunrise* case, China's arguments in the Philippines-China South China Sea disputes are stronger. On 25 August 2006, China made a declaration withdrawing from jurisdiction under paragraphs (a), (b), and (c) of Article 298(1).[76] That meant it precluded all the matters that relate to sovereignty over continental or insular land territory, sea boundary delimitations, law enforcement activities in the exclusive economic zone (scientific research and fishery) and so on. From this perspective, the Tribunal has no jurisdiction over the South China Sea disputes.

In the *South China Sea Arbitration* Case, the Philippines disguised itself as a victim and took it for granted that there were no disputes regarding sovereign rights over territory and sea boundary delimitations within the area, and that therefore the Tribunal's jurisdiction is indisputable.[77] However, in order to interpret and apply the Convention (assuming such application is necessary) requires touching on the sovereignty rights and sea boundary delimitations issues. Any reasonable person, never mind an expert or scholar, with elementary knowledge of the South Sea dispute[78] could see that the Philippines' arbitration claim lacks jurisdiction and is inadmissible. According to China's Position Document on the *South China Sea Arbitration* Case, the arbitration claims submitted by the Philippines – particularly the illegality of the U-shaped Line which China has consistently maintained,[79] and the legal status of low tide elevations under the Convention[80] – were all issues

---

75 Natalie Klein, *Dispute Settlement in the UN Convention on the Law of the Sea* (Cambridge: Cambridge University Press, 2005), p. 313.

76 The Government of the People's Republic of China does not accept any of the procedures provided for in Section 2 of Part XV of the Convention with respect to all the categories of disputes referred to in paragraph 1 (a), (b) and (c) of Article 298 of the Convention. Available at: <http://www.un.org/depts/los/convention_agreements/convention_declarations.htm#China upon ratification>.

77 See Note Verbale (No. 000223) of Philippine Mission to the United Nations.

78 Zhiguo Gao and Binbing Jia, "The Nine-Dash Line in the South China Sea: History, Status, and Implications", *American Journal of International Law*, Vol. 107, (2013), pp. 98–124.

79 See Peter A. Dutton, *The Sino-Philippine Maritime Row: International Arbitration and the South China Sea, Center for a New American Security, East and South China Seas Bulletin No. 10* (15 March 2013), p. 4. Available at: <http://www.cnas.org/files/documents/publications/CNAS_Bulletin_Dutton_TheSinoPhilippin eMaritimeRow_0.pdf>.

80 See Thang Nguyen-Dang and Hong Thao Nguyen, *China's Nine-Dotted Lines in the South China Sea: The 2011 Exchange of Diplomatic Notes*, 2011, p. 13. Electronic copy available at: <http://ssrn.com/abstract=1905502>.

related to or based on sovereignty or sovereign rights of relevant sea zones in the South China Sea. In other words, sovereign rights emanating from islands, the EEZ, and the continental shelf, etc. Through the above analysis, we do not hold that the arbitration matters submitted by the Philippines were inexorably related to the interpretation and application of the Convention and therefore grant prima facie jurisdiction to the Tribunal. The 2006 Declaration of China has already excluded the sea boundary delimitations from the compulsory dispute settlement procedure. So the Tribunal had no jurisdiction over the claims that the Philippines submitted.

Legality of the Initiation of the Arbitral Proceedings

In the *Arctic Sunrise* case, although the Tribunal had preliminary jurisdiction and published provisional measures, the Tribunal's reasoning around jurisdiction and admissibility is too simple. Although the Tribunal confirmed that the 1997 Russian Declaration was not enough to exclude jurisdiction, it also pointed out that the other matters relating to the jurisdiction and admissibility problem needed further consideration. That is to say, the jurisdiction and admissibility problem of the *Arctic Sunrise* case still leaves room for discussion. However, the *South China Sea Arbitration* Case is a rather different and clearer situation for determining admissibility and jurisdiction.

With regard to admissibility, firstly, according to Article 281 of the Convention, a peaceful solution chosen by the parties through negotiation takes precedence over the Convention's dispute settlement mechanism. In The Declaration on the Conduct of Parties in the South China Sea (the Declaration), all countries promised clearly that, "to resolve their territorial and jurisdictional disputes by peaceful means, without resorting to the threat or use of force, through friendly consultations and negotiations by sovereign states directly concerned, in accordance with universally recognized principles of international law, including the 1982 UN Convention on the Law of the Sea".[81] The Declaration also stipulated that the parties must "exercise self-restraint in the conduct of activities that would complicate or escalate disputes and affect peace and stability".[82] In the *South China Sea Arbitration* Case, the Philippines asserted that this precondition has already been fulfilled, suggesting that it made the effort of exchanging views and negotiating with China.[83] However, China did not agree with this viewpoint.[84]

81 See Article 4 of The Declaration on the Conduct of Parties in the South China Sea.

82 See paragraph 1 of Article 5 in the Declaration of Conduct of the Parties in the South China Sea.

83 See Notification and Statement of Claim on West Philippine Sea, Department of Foreign Affairs of Philippine, Manila, 2013. 1. 22, p. 3, para. 8, pp. 10–12, paras. 25–30.

84 See the website of the Ministry of Foreign Affairs of PRC: <http://www.fmprc.gov.cn/mfa_chn/wjdt_611265/fyrbt_611275/t1059312.shtml>. Last accessed 17 December 2013.

Actually, the Philippines submitted the arbitration unilaterally, which undoubtedly violated the commitments enumerated in the Declaration, and to some extent complicated the dispute.

Secondly, according to Article 283(1) of the Convention, parties to a dispute must exchange views as soon as possible, a rule confirmed by the *Arctic Sunrise* Case.[85] The requirement to exchange views is not an empty formality and the relevant parties shall try to solve the dispute without recourse to the arbitration or litigation mechanisms set out in the Convention.[86] Article 283 of the Convention stipulates that an exchange of views must be "by negotiation or other peaceful means". The Philippines invoked the claims, declarations, expressions and protests as evidence for fulfillment of the obligation to exchange views.[87] It is clear that the aforementioned actions of Philippines does not qualify as an exchange of views, nor do they qualify as "other peaceful means" which should carry the same weight as "negotiations". Therefore, the Philippines did not comply with this obligation before its arbitration submission.

Thirdly, the South China Sea disputes involve a few countries, including Vietnam, which also has disputes with the Philippines over maritime rights and interests. In order to avoid affecting the interests of third parties, the Tribunal should announce that the arbitration is inadmissible, as confirmed by the *East Timor* Case. [88] The *South China Sea Arbitration* Case shall follow the "Monetary Gold" principle and so requires China to be present and to participate. Without such participation the Court must reject the case.[89] To make a proper prediction: the *South China Sea Arbitration* Case, lacking the consent of China and relevant interested parties, will be rejected by the Tribunal on jurisdictional grounds. Furthermore, the behavior of the Philippines, which submitted the arbitration unilaterally, was in conflict with Article 294 of the Convention, which stipulates that countries must not "abuse the legal proceedings".

---

85 The *Arctic Sunrise* Case (Netherlands v. Russia), Provisional Measures, ITLOS No. 22, paras. 72–6.

86 See Separate Opinion of ad hoc Judge Sreenivasa Rao, Case Concerning Sovereignty over Pedra Branca/ Pulau Batu Puteh, Middle Rocks and South Ledge, Malaysia v. Singapore, 2008.

87 See Notification and Statement of Claim on West Philippine Sea, Department of Foreign Affairs of Philippine, Manila, 2013. 1. 22, pp. 10–12, paras. 25–30.

88 Consider here the Case Concerning East Timor (Portugal v. Australia), 1995. And see also Spain/Canada, 1998 in the ICJ, a case in which jurisdiction was declined because of Canada's Article 36(2) ICJ Statute reservation on high seas fisheries.

89 Consider here the Case Concerning the Monetary Gold Removed from Rome in 1943 (Italy v. France, the UK, the US), Judgment of ICJ, 15 June 1954. In the judgment, the Court concluded that it was a well-established principle that the court could only exercise jurisdiction over state with its consent and it shall refrain from the exercising of jurisdiction the case was unavoidable to touch the interests of a third state.

Maintenance of the Justice of Default Procedures

It is not uncommon for us to pick out situations in international arbitration practice where a party refused to participate, especially in the 1970s or 1980s.[90] The party being absent in arbitration usually chooses non-appearance out of political considerations or rejection of compulsory jurisdiction,[91] rather than merely the anxiety over possibly losing the lawsuit. As Shabtai Rosenne put it, the parties to the disputes have the right to choose litigation strategy under certain circumstances, and deciding not to attend the proceedings is one such strategy. This is not a fanciful illusion, but a political consideration.[92]

Comparing the non-appearance reasons of the Russian Federation in the *Arctic Sunrise* case, China's reasons for absence in the South China Sea proceedings seem to be stronger and more tenable. On the one hand, under the circumstances the jurisdiction of the Tribunal and admissibility of the case are under severe challenge. When the relevant parties choose a non-appearance strategy, the Tribunal shall exercise judicial restraint and avoid frustrating the reasonable expectation of the parties when the reservations were made. In other words, the Tribunal should reject the case due to lack of jurisdiction or terminate the procedure on a proper point.[93]

To maintain the justice of the arbitral procedures and the legitimacy of the institution itself,[94] the Tribunal must adopt a more cautious approach to tackling factual and legal issues and achieving an ideal balance between parties. To prevent the Philippines' potential abuse of arbitral rights, the Tribunal should try to guarantee China's procedural rights. In so doing, the Tribunal must strive to establish its rationale on a solid factual and legal footing, with due consideration for China's position.

Concretely speaking, to maintain the equality of the contesting parties, the Tribunal must provide necessary protections for China's rights when considering whether to a default ruling. In the scope of its jurisdictional powers, the Court may only rule in the areas that China did not exclude, and may not exceed that scope. In the judicial proceedings, even if China refuses to participate in the relevant procedures, China is still entitled to be notified and informed. According to Article

90 See Andreas Zimmermann, et al., *The Statute of International Court of Justice: A Commentary* (2nd ed.), (Oxford: Oxford University Press, 2012), p. 1353.

91 Non-appearance has its roots in the nature of jurisdiction to some extent. See Jerome Belkind, *Non-appearance before the International Court of Justice: Functional and Comparative Analysis* (Leiden: Martinus Nijhoof Publishers, 1984), p. 187.

92 See Shabtai Rosenne, *The Law and Practice of the International Court (1920–2005)* (Leiden: Martinus Nijhoof Publishers, 2005), p. 1360.

93 See Hersch Lauterpacht, *The Development of International Law by the International Court* (Cambridge: Cambridge University Press, 1982), pp. 95–6.

94 See Yuval Shany, *Assessing the Effectiveness of International Law* (Oxford: Oxford University Press, 2014), p. 139.

298 of the Convention, the claims that fall within the declaration made by China must be "excluded from the submission". Therefore, in the outcomes of the arbitral proceedings, China has a right to refuse any decisions made by the Court that are outside of its jurisdictional powers. Furthermore, China may refuse to accept any content in the decisions relating to the reservations made by China or any related *obiter dicta* made in the ruling.

The Importance of International Capacity to Action

China should increase and strengthen its research in the international law area, perfect and master the rules of the operation of international judicial mechanisms, and prepare enough materials to support its arguments in related maritime disputes. China must become familiar with the usage of relevant rules, develop a team of highly-trained professionals, continue to improve upon its capacity to use international law mechanisms, and enhance its ability to provide reasonable, valid, and thorough reasoning, and consequently advisable strategy in international disputes.

PART IV
The U-shaped Line and Geographic Features

Chapter 8

The U-Shaped Line and Historic Rights in the Philippines v. China Arbitration Case

Keyuan Zou and Xinchang Liu[1]

Introduction

On 22 January 2013, the Philippines, by a *Note Verbale* with the Notification and Statement of Claim on West Philippine Sea (i.e. South China Sea), instituted the compulsory arbitration procedures stipulated in the 1982 United Nations Convention on the Law of the Sea (UNCLOS) against the People's Republic of China (PRC), asking the Arbitral Tribunal to: (1) declare that China's rights in regard to maritime areas in the South China Sea, like the rights of the Philippines, are those that are established by the UNCLOS, and consist of its rights to a Territorial Sea and Contiguous Zone under Part II of the Convention, to an Exclusive Economic Zone under Part V, and to a Continental Shelf under Part VI; and (2) declare that China's maritime claims in the South China Sea based on its so-called "nine dash line" (U-shaped line) are contrary to the UNCLOS and invalid. China is not entitled to exercise "historic rights" over the waters, seabed and subsoil beyond the limits of its entitlements under the Convention in the areas encompassed within its so-called "nine-dash line".[2] On 30 March 2014, the Philippines officially submitted its Memorial to the Arbitral Tribunal which reiterated its statements regarding the U-shaped line contained in its Statement of Claims.

While the above matter raised by the Philippines is linked to other claims made by the Philippines, China's claim of "historic rights" to maritime areas is specifically highlighted by the Philippines. Despite that the arbitration case initiated by the Philippines contains various inter-related requests for relief, for the purpose of this chapter, we will pin down our focus on the legality of the U-shaped line and the historic rights it has generated, and provide the reader with a more objective and professional assessment of the legal scenario in regard to the U-shaped line. The first part of the chapter will discuss China's rights and obligations under the UNCLOS; the second part will discuss the legal status of the U-shaped line and the

1 A slightly modified version is published in the first issue of the *Chinese Journal of International Law*, 2015, pp. 57–77.

2 The diplomatic note and Philippines' "Notification and Statement of Claim" are available at <http://www.gov.ph/downloads/2013/01jan/20130122-Notification-and-Statement-of-Claim-on-West-Philippine-Sea.pdf>.

legal implications from the line for any maritime entitlement, maritime boundary delimitation and dispute settlement in the South China Sea; and the final part is the conclusion. It is to be stated that while there are various terminologies for the U-shaped line, we have chosen to use the term "U-shaped line" as it is, in our view, more precise than the term "nine-dash line" used by the Philippines.

China and the UNCLOS

On 10 December 1982, the United Nations Convention on the Law of the Sea was open for signature in Jamaica, and China signed it immediately at that time. However, China ratified it in 1996 only after the UNCLOS came into force in November 1994. It is in fact that the Third UN Conference on the Law of the Sea (1973–1982) (UNCLOS III) was the first grand diplomatic conference that the Chinese Government sent its delegation to after the PRC replaced the Republic of China (ROC or Taiwan) for the seat of China in the United Nations in 1971. China was involved in negotiation and drafting of the UNCLOS, and China accepted most of the articles of the draft Convention through consensus. Some of the proposals submitted by China were finally reflected in the UNCLOS, in particular provisions on protection of marine environment,[3] marine scientific research,[4] and dispute resolution.[5] Despite some deficiencies, in its eye, in the UNCLOS, China upholds the principles and norms of the Convention as well as most of its clauses. China regards this international treaty as the representative of the new law of the sea as opposed to the so-called old law of the sea, represented by the four Geneva Conventions on the law of the sea adopted in 1958 when the PRC was still outside the UN system and had no chance to participate in the deliberations of the four conventions.

In order to implement the UNCLOS at the domestic level, China enacted two basic ocean laws, i.e., the 1992 Law on the Territorial Sea and the Contiguous Zone and the 1998 Law on the Exclusive Economic Zone and the Continental Shelf.[6] Based on these two basic laws, China has established maritime zones under its national jurisdiction such as the internal waters, the territorial sea of 12 nautical miles from the baselines, exclusive economic zone (EEZ) of 200 nm from the baselines and the continental shelf. According to Article 2 of the Territorial Sea Law, China's territorial sea is a belt of maritime area adjacent to the land territory

3 See Articles 192, 194, 209–10, 213–18, 220, and 235 of the UNCLOS. Text is reprinted in 1833 United Nations Treaty Series 397.

4 See Articles 143, 242, 244–5 of the UNCLOS.

5 See Articles 279–80 and 283 of the UNCLOS. For relevant discussion, see Yu Mincai, "China and the UN Convention on the Law of the Sea", *Contemporary International Relations* (in Chinese), 2012, No. 10, p. 55.

6 English texts of these two laws are appended to Zou Keyuan, *China's Marine Legal System and the Law of the Sea* (Leiden and Boston: Martinus Nijhoff, 2005), pp. 338–45.

and the internal waters of China and its land territory includes its mainland and offshore islands, Taiwan and all islands appertaining thereto including the Diaoyu Islands, the Penghu Islands, the Dongsha (Pratas) Islands, the Xisha (Paracel) Islands, the Zhongsha Islands and the Nansha (Spratly) Islands, as well as all the other islands that belong to China. In addition, the internal waters of China are those waters which lie on the landward side of the baseline of China's territorial sea. The breadth of the territorial sea is actually the reiteration of the relevant provision in China's 1958 Declaration on the Territorial Sea.[7]

After China ratified the UNCLOS, it also revised and promulgated a number of new laws and regulations governing ocean affairs. For example, China promulgated the Law on the Management of the Utilization of Marine Zones in 2001 and amended the 1982 Law on Marine Environmental Protection in 1999. A more recent law related to China's ocean affairs is the Law on the Protection of Islands, which was passed by the National People's Congress (NPC) in December 2009 and came into force on 1 March 2010.[8]

In summary, China has not only accepted the norms and rules of the UNCLOS, but also, we can say, the UNCLOS is precisely one of the international laws that conform to China's national interests. For that reason, China has reiterated on many occasions that it supports the effective implementation of the UNCLOS. For example, in its Position Paper submitted to the United Nations in 2008, China emphasized that "in order to maintain a harmonious maritime order, it is important to strengthen international rule of law with the United Nations Convention on the Law of the Sea as the legal basis. The Convention, a product of many years of international negotiation, reflects the concerns of various parties in a relatively balanced manner. It has set a legal foundation and framework for building a harmonious maritime order and for addressing new maritime problems and challenges".[9] It is clear that China has no reason to go against the UNCLOS in practice and the Philippine's accusation contained in its Notification and Memorial is clearly unfounded and unreasonable.

While it is acknowledged that the UNCLOS is a "constitution for the oceans"[10] being widely recognized and accepted in the international society, and playing an indispensable role in handling international relations concerning the oceans, we

---

7 The English text can be found in Office of Policy, Law and Regulation, State Oceanic Administration (ed.), *Collection of the Sea Laws and Regulations of the People's Republic of China* (Beijing: Ocean Press, 1998) (in Chinese and English), pp. 182–3.

8 The whole text is available at <http://202.123.110.5/flfg/2009–12/26/content_1497461.htm>.

9 "Position Paper of the People's Republic of China at the 63rd Session of the United Nations General Assembly", 16 September 2008, available at <http://xn--tlq87w5j9b.cn/eng/zxxx/t512751.htm>.

10 See Tommy Koh, "A Constitution for the Oceans", in *United Nations, The Law of the Sea: United Nations Convention on the Law of the Sea with Index and Final Act of the Third United Nations Conference on the Law of the Sea* (New York: United Nations, 1983), p. xxxiii.

should also realize that the UNCLOS is under the framework of international law, and it is one of the international treaties governing ocean affairs. In this regard, it is necessary to look at Article 38 of the Statute of the International Court of Justice (ICJ) which stipulates the sources of international law, including:

- international conventions, whether general or particular, establishing rules expressly recognized by the contesting states;
- international custom, as evidence of a general practice accepted as law;
- the general principles of law recognized by civilized nations;
- subject to the provisions of Article 59, judicial decisions and the teachings of the most highly qualified publicists of the various nations, as subsidiary means for the determination of rules of law.[11]

Based on the above, there are four sources of international law and international conventions, though the most important, is one of them. The UNCLOS is within the category of "international conventions".

It is to be realized that the functioning of the UNCLOS cannot go well without the implementation of other conventions and treaties, either bilateral of multilateral, such as the four 1958 Geneva Conventions,[12] the 1992 Convention on Biological Diversity, and the 1988 Convention for the Suppression of Unlawful Acts Against the Safety of Maritime Navigation.

The South China Sea issue is a complex and enduring conundrum in international law, not only concerning territorial sovereignty, maritime boundary delimitation, international navigation, maritime security, maritime law enforcement, but also distribution of biological marine resources, exploitation and distribution of mineral resources, so that various factors arise from geology, history, politics, strategic considerations and national interests. To solve the problem as complicated as such, it is obviously not enough to simply rely on the UNCLOS only.

In addition, when we apply international law, it is necessary to look into the applicability of customary law. As mentioned above, one of the sources of international law stated in Article 38 of the Statute of the International Court of Justice is customary international law. As sources of international law, customary international law and international conventions carry equal legally binding force with no hierarchy. In the international society, it is sometimes difficult to achieve consensus between/among states because of their different positions. Therefore, in many fields, problems are left over to be settled through other legal channels

11 Article 38 of the Statute of the International Court of Justice, available at <http://www.icj-cij.org/documents/index.php?p1=4&p2=2&p3=0>.

12 They are the Convention on the Territorial Sea and the Contiguous Zone; the Convention on the High Seas; the Convention on Fishing and Conservation of the Living Resources of the High Seas; and the Convention on the Continental Shelf. According to Article 311 of the UNCLOS, the 1958 Conventions remain valid, but the UNCLOS should prevail, as between the States Parties, over them.

than the application of international conventions. Issues such as regional fishing, and rights of navigation through international canals may not be governed by the UNCLOS. In this sense, customary international law also plays an important role in the management of ocean affairs, actually reinforcing the effectiveness of the UNCLOS. In a recent article, Ashley Roach succinctly summarizes some relevant rules of customary international law not contained in the UNCLOS that are applicable to resolving disputes involving the interpretation or application of the Convention.[13]

As international law is a live system, there is no help only being limited to a single treaty to settle various complicated issues and problems. It is not only against general principles of international law, but also against the rules and reality in the international society that the Philippines only resorts to the UNCLOS to resolve its disputes with China in the South China Sea. The legal action initiated by the Philippines may in fact create obstacles in solving disputes and further exacerbate the complicated situation in the South China Sea.

Legal Status of the U-shaped Line in International Law

It is believed that the U-shaped line constitutes part of the legal basis for China's claims in the South China Sea. The line first appeared on the map in December 1914, which was compiled by Hu Jinjie, a Chinese cartographer, but only included the Pratas and the Paracels.[14] In 1935, the Committee of Examining the Water and Land Maps of the Republic of China published the names of 132 islets and reefs of the four South China Sea archipelagos. The publication had an annexed map which marked the James Shoal at the location of about 4◦ north latitude, 112◦ east longitude, though there was no demarcation of the line on the map.[15] On 1 December 1947, the Chinese Ministry of Interior renamed the islands in the South China Sea and formally allocated them into the administration of the Chinese Hainan Special Region.[16] Meanwhile, the same ministry prepared a location map of the islands in the South China Sea, which was first released for internal use. In February 1948, the Atlas of Administrative Areas of the Republic of China was officially published, in which the above map was included. This is the first official map with the line for the South China Sea. It has two general characteristics: the southernmost end of the line was set at 4◦ north latitude, thus including the James

13 See J. Ashley Roach, "Today's Customary International Law of the Sea", *Ocean Development and International Law*, 2014, Vol. 45(3), pp. 239–59, in particular, at 241.

14 See Han Zhenhua, *A Compilation of Historical Materials on China's South China Sea Islands* (Beijing, Oriental Press, 1988) (in Chinese), p. 355.

15 See Zou Keyuan, "The Chinese Traditional Maritime Boundary Line in the South China Sea and its Legal Consequences for the Resolution of the Dispute over The Spratly Islands", *The International Journal of Marine and Coastal Law*, 1999, Vol. 14(1), p. 33.

16 See Ministry of Interior, *An Outline of the Geography of the South China Sea Islands* (National Territory Series, 1947), Figure 11, p. 861.

Shoal; and an 11-segment line was drawn instead of the previous continuous line. According to the official explanation, the basis for drawing the line was: "[t]he southernmost limit of the South China Sea territory should be at the James Shoal. This limit was followed by our governmental departments, schools and publishers before the anti-Japanese war, and it was also recorded on file in the Ministry of Interior. Accordingly it should remain unchanged".[17] The map is official and, therefore, different from those previously drawn by individual cartographers. Since 1948, maps officially published in both mainland China and Taiwan is the same regarding the line.[18]

Since there is no official explanation for the line, commentators may explain it in their own ways, thus different views and opinions have arisen among Chinese scholars both from mainland China and Taiwan on the U-shaped line as: (a) line indicating that the geographic features within are Chinese territory; or (b) line of historic waters;[19] or (c) line of historic rights; and (b) line indicating that the marine resources within belong to China. According to Shicun Wu, President of the National Institute for South China Sea Studies, the U-shaped line

> is based on the theory of 'sovereignty + UNCLOS + historic rights'. According to this theory, China enjoys sovereignty over all the features within this line, and enjoys sovereign right and jurisdiction, defined by the LOS Convention, for instance, EEZ and continental shelf when the certain features fulfill the legal definition of Island Regime under Article 121 of the LOS Convention. In addition to that, China enjoys certain historic rights within this line, such as fishing rights, navigation rights and priority rights of resource development.[20]

Evidences from China's practice may be helpful for the explanation of the line. In 1958, China promulgated the Declaration on China's Territorial Sea, in which China declared that the Dongsha Islands, the Xisha Islands, the Zhongsha Islands, and the Nansha Islands all belonged to China.[21] Although the Declaration did not mention the line in the South China Sea, it had some implications for the

---

17 Han Zhenhua, *supra* note 14, pp. 181–4.

18 Zou Keyuan, "China's U-shaped Line in the South China Sea Revisited", *Ocean Development and International Law*, 2012, Vol. 43(1), pp. 18–34.

19 According to the 1993 Guidelines of the South China Sea issued by the Government of the Republic of China on Taiwan, the waters within the line are Chinese "historic waters".

20 Observer Research Foundation, "ORF South China Sea Interview", *South China Sea Monitor*, Vol. 2(1), January 2013, 9; available at <http://www.orfonline.org/cms/sites/orfonline/modules/southchina/attachments/issue1-2013_1357907409226.pdf>. Chinese approaches are also reflected in Zhiguo Gao and Bing Bing Jia, "The Nine-Dash Line in the South China Sea: History, Status, and Implications", *American Journal of International Law*, Vol. 107, 2013, pp. 98–124.

21 See Office of Laws and Regulations, State Oceanic Administration (ed.), *Collection of the Sea Laws and Regulations of the People's Republic of China* (Beijing: Ocean Press, 1991) (in Chinese and English), p. 3.

line. First, the Declaration says that between the mainland and its coastal islands and the archipelagos in the South China Sea, there existed certain areas of the high seas. Secondly, it provides that the method measuring the Chinese territorial sea of 12 nautical miles by straight baselines for the mainland and its coastal islands is also applicable to the archipelagos in the South China Sea. The above principles are reaffirmed in China's Law on the Territorial Sea and Contiguous Zone promulgated in 1992.[22] In addition, in the 1998 Law of the People's Republic of China on the Exclusive Economic Zone and the Continental Shelf, Article 14 provides that the provisions in this Law shall not affect the historic rights enjoyed by the People's Republic of China.[23]

In practice, Chinese government, in 1992, leased oil exploration blocks in an area of the South China Sea to a foreign oil company. China claimed "indisputable sovereignty" over the Nansha and Xisha Islands and their adjacent waters. When Vietnam, in 1996, leased petroleum concessions of an area of the Nansha Islands to a foreign company, China protested to such acts as "an encroachment on China's sovereignty and its maritime rights and interests".[24] In 2008, China Marine Surveillance began to conduct regular maritime patrols in waters (including the South China Sea) under China's jurisdiction. China Maritime Law Enforcement Bulletin 2008 records that " ... sent a total of 355 (frame) maritime surveillance ships, aircraft, kept watch on 406 (frame) foreign vessels, aircraft and other targets, found 38 infringement acts and stop them in time".[25] In 2009, China submitted diplomatic notes protesting the submissions of outer continental shelf claims made by Vietnam and Malaysia to the United Nations Commission on the Limits of the Continental Shelf, attaching a map of the South China Sea to its diplomatic notes,[26] and this is the first time that China officially submitted the U-shaped line map to the United Nations.

All these legislative activities, economic activities, and maritime law enforcement activities, while not directly reflecting clear proposition of the waters within the U-shaped line, have provided evidences proving China's attitude towards its territorial and maritime claims in the South China Sea. In addition

22 See Zou Keyuan, *supra* note 15, p. 35.

23 See People's Daily (in Chinese), 30 June 1998. An unofficial English translation version by Zou Keyuan can be found in The MIMA Bulletin, Vol. 7 (1), 1999, pp. 27–9. A different English translation is available in *Law of the Sea Bulletin*, No. 38, 1998, pp. 28–31.

24 Xinhua News Agency, Beijing, 17 April 1996.

25 See China Maritime Law Enforcement Bulletin 2008, available at <http://www.soa.gov.cn/zwgk/hygb/zghyxzzfgb/2008nzghyxzzfgb/201212/t20121217_22961.html>.

26 See People's Republic of China, Letter to the U.N. Secretary General, Doc. CML/17/2009, 7 May 2009; and Letter to the U.N. Secretary General, Doc. CML/18/2009, 7 May 2009, in Response to the Malaysia-Vietnam Joint Submission to the Commission on the Limits of the Continental Shelf, Executive Summary, May 2009 and Vietnam Submission to the Commission: North Area, April 2009, available at <www.un.org/los/clcsnew/clcshome.htm>.

to sovereignty, sovereign rights and maritime jurisdiction China enjoys under general international law including the UNCLOS, it is believed that the U-shaped line can generate historic rights which are allowed in general international law too.

Historic Rights

While there is no specific definition of historic rights in international law, the term historic rights is different from that of historic waters. According to Bouchez, "Historic waters are waters over which the coastal state, contrary to the generally applicable rules of international law, clearly, effectively, continuously, and over a substantial period of time, exercises sovereign rights with the acquiescence of the community of States".[27] Once recognized as historic waters, the waters became the internal waters or territorial sea of the coastal state. As it is acknowledged, the term historic waters "is still generally viewed as an established part of the international law of the sea".[28] Referring to the South China Sea, the People's Republic of China has never claimed that the waters within the U-shaped line are Chinese historic waters.

In the case of Tunisia v. Libyan Arab Jamahiriya, the International Court of Justice (ICJ) in its judgment made such a statement about historic rights that "general international law ... does not provide for a single 'regime' for 'historic waters' or 'historic bays', but only for a particular regime for each of the concrete, recognized cases of 'historic waters' or 'historic bays'".[29] The jurisprudence of the ICJ concerning historic rights is well summarized by Ted McDorman: "historic claims to waters (historic waters and historic rights) exist in international law; there is a difference between historic waters, which evolves exclusivity of rights, and historic rights, which are not exclusive; UNCLOS is not exhaustive of the rights and jurisdiction that a State may have respecting waters and resources; and there is flexibility in the rights exercisable by a State that successfully maintains a claim to historic waters".[30]

There is no express provision on historic rights or historic waters in the UNCLOS, but the Convention does mention related concepts in a couple of provisions such as Article 10(6) which provides that "[t]he foregoing provisions do not apply to so-called 'historic' bays, or in any case where the system of

27 Leo J. Bouchez, *The Regime of Bays in International Law* (Leyden: A.W. Sythoff, 1964), p. 281.

28 Clive R. Symmons, *Historic Waters in the Law of the Sea: A Modern Re-appraisal* (Leiden: Martinus Nijhoff, 2008), p. 296.

29 I.C.J. Reports 1982, p. 74.

30 See Ted L McDorman, "Rights and Jurisdiction over Resources in the South China Sea: UNCLOS and the Nine-Dash Line", in S. Jayakumar, Tommy Koh and Robert Beckman (eds), *The South China Sea Disputes and Law of the Sea* (Cheltenham: Edward Elgar, 2014), pp. 152–3.

straight baselines provided for in article 7 is applied", and Article 15 which provides that "Where the coasts of two States are opposite or adjacent to each other, neither of the two States is entitled, failing agreement between them to the contrary, to extend its territorial sea beyond the median line every point of which is equidistant from the nearest points on the baselines from which the breadth of the territorial seas of each of the two States is measured. The above provision does not apply, however, where it is necessary by reason of historic title or other special circumstances to delimit the territorial seas of the two States in a way which is at variance therewith". According to Article 298, issues of historic bays and historic titles fall within the scope of optional exceptions to compulsory dispute settlement mechanism. It can be inferred that concepts of historic rights and historic waters are very much left over to be continuously governed by general international law including customary law. It is rightly pointed out that "whether historic rights exist is not a matter regulated by UNCLOS" though some parts of the UNCLOS are relevant when it comes to the use of marine resources.[31]

In customary international law, we can see, from a series of state practices including international jurisprudence, the development of the concept of historic rights which has met the requirements of the formation of customary international law – state practice and *opinio juris*. The concept of historic rights is evolved from historic waters, which are usually defined as historic bays and historic straits. In the case of the United Kingdom v. Norway on fisheries, the ICJ formally accepted the assertion of Norway relating to historic rights. In this case, Norway's declaration of its territorial waters is not consistent with general international law, but is still determined to be valid. The ICJ examined the former practices of Norway, and found that the Norwegian maritime delineation method had been applied continuously without interruption for about 60 years, and had never been opposed by other countries. The Court thus assumed that this demarcation action was consistent with international law, and so recognized Norway's historic rights.[32] Since then, in the case of the Gulf of Fonseca in 1992, the ICJ determined such rules – the historic rights of specific waters can be shared by more than one country.[33]

There are other cases in state practice such as the historic claim of the former Soviet Union for the Peter the Great Bay,[34] and Libya's claim for the Gulf of

31 See Ted L. McDorman, ibid., p. 152.

32 See the fisheries case United Kingdom v. Norway, Judgment of 18 December 1951, available at <http://www.icj-cij.org/docket/files/5/1809.pdf>.

33 See the case of Land, Island and Maritime Frontier Dispute (El Salvador/Honduras: Nicaragua intervening), Judgment is available at <http://www.icj-cij.org/docket/files/75/6671.pdf>.

34 See J. Ashley Roach, "The Maritime Claims Reference Manual and the Law of Baselines", International Law Studies, 1998, Vol. 72, p. 181, available at <https://www.usnwc.edu/Research---Gaming/International-Law/New-International-Law-Studies-(Blue-Book)-Series/International-Law-Blue-Book-Articles.aspx?Volume=72>.

Sidra. Among the relevant cases, the most related one is the claim of historic rights by Tunisia.[35] Tunisia claimed historic rights beyond its territorial sea, particularly historic fishing rights, arguing that this historic right may influence the delimitation of exclusive economic zones (EEZ) in the future. In the view of the ICJ, historic rights or historic waters and the continental shelf belong to two completely different legal regimes under customary international law; the former is based on the acquisition and occupation, while the latter is based on the existence of rights "*ipso facto* and *ab initio*".[36] As it can be seen from the judgment, the Court recognized the existence of historic rights, and also recognized that the historic rights to certain extent would affect the delimitation of the EEZs of coastal states.

In the case of Eritrea and Yemen in 1998, the two states both claimed historic rights in the Red Sea. Eritrea claimed its rights of islands in the Red Sea based on a chain of title extending back over more than 100 years. Yemen based its claim to the disputed islands on original, historic, or traditional title. The Tribunal confirmed that

> the conditions that prevailed during many centuries with regard to the traditional openness of southern Red Sea marine resources for fishing, its role as means for unrestricted traffic from one side to the other, together with the common use of the islands by the populations of both coasts, are all important elements capable of creating certain "historic rights" which accrued in favour of both parties through a process of historical consolidation as a sort of "*servitude internationale*" falling short of territorial sovereignty. Such historic rights provide a sufficient legal basis for maintaining certain aspects of a *res communis* that has existed for centuries for the benefit of populations on both sides of the Red Sea.[37]

Finally, the Tribunal held that "neither Party has been able to persuade the tribunal that the history of the matter reveals the juridical existence of an historic title, or of historic titles, of such long-established, continuous and definitive lineage to these particular islands, islets and rocks as would be a sufficient basis for the Tribunal's decision".[38]

---

35 See the case concerning the Continental Shelf, Tunisia v. Libyan Arab Jamahiriya, Judgment of 24 February 1982, available at <http://www.icj-cij.org/docket/files/63/6267.pdf>.

36 Ibid., para. 100.

37 For details of the case, see W. Michael Reisman, "Eritrea-Yemen Arbitration (Award, Phase II: Maritime Delimitation", 94 *American Journal of International Law*, 2000, pp. 721–36.

38 See the award of the Arbitral Tribunal in the First Stage – Territorial Sovereignty and Scope of the Dispute of 9 October 1998, available at <http://www.pca-cpa.org/showpage.asp?pag_id=1160>.

On 11 May 2009, the Kingdom of Tonga submitted to the Commission on the Limits of the Continental Shelf, in accordance with Article 76, paragraph 8, of the LOS Convention, information on the limits of the continental shelf beyond 200 nautical miles from the baselines from which the breadth of the territorial sea is measured. It stated that,

> The Kingdom of Tonga is proud to have the longest continuous legal claim of historic title to maritime domain in the world. The Royal Proclamation issued by His Majesty George Tubou, King of Tonga, on 24 August 1887 claims national jurisdiction by the Kingdom of Tonga over "all islands, rocks, reefs, foreshores and waters lying between the fifteenth and twenty-third and a half degrees of south latitude and between the one hundred and seventy-third and the one hundred and seventy-seventh degrees of west longitude from the Meridian of Greenwich".[39]

In the submission, Tonga further expressed that

> Historic title is recognized in international law and in the United Nations Convention on the Law of the Sea (International Law Commission, 1962). Historic title is recognized in the Convention in the context of several other provisions, such as article 15 on the delimitation of the territorial sea between States with opposite or adjacent coasts in Part II on the Territorial Sea and Contiguous Zone, and article 46 use of terms in Part IV on Archipelagic States. The Kingdom of Tonga asserts in this Submission consistency between its claim of historic title made by means of the Royal Proclamation of 24 August 1887 and its maritime jurisdiction as established in the United Nations Convention on the Law of the Sea (the Convention).[40]

For further clarification, the Kingdom of Tonga applies the concept of historic title in international law to all those maritime spaces established under its national jurisdiction in agreement with the Convention that can be included within the geographical limits defined in the Royal Proclamation of 24 August 1887. The breadth of the maritime spaces under the national jurisdiction of the Kingdom of Tonga within and beyond the geographical limits established by the Royal Proclamation of 24 August 1887 are defined in accordance with the relevant provisions of the Convention relating to internal and archipelagic waters, the territorial sea, the contiguous zone, the exclusive economic zone and the continental shelf. Thus the implementation of the Convention is consistent with

39 A partial submission of data and information on the outer limits of the continental shelf of the Kingdom of Tonga pursuant to part VI of and annex II to the United Nations convention on the law of the sea. Available at <http://www.un.org/depts/los/clcs_new/submissions_files/ton46_09/ton2009executive_summary.pdf>.

40 Ibid.

the decision of the Kingdom of Tonga to maintain its claim of historic title over the land and maritime spaces established within the geographical limits included in the Royal Proclamation of 24 August 1887.[41]

Summarizing its claims, Tonga believes that historic rights have been acknowledged by various international conventions including the LOS Convention (for example, article 15, article 46), and the historic rights of waters claimed by Tonga, are consistent with international law, which should be recognized and protected.

Again, in the case of maritime disputes between Bangladesh and Myanmar, the two parties have agreed that Article 15 of the Convention should be applied to the delimitation of the territorial sea in this case. Therefore, in accordance with this provision, the International Tribunal for the Law of the Sea (ITLOS) needs to consider whether there are historic rights or other special circumstances causing the inapplicability of the equidistance line. In this case, the ITLOS mainly considered the issue that whether St. Martin Island of Bangladesh constitutes *other special circumstances* that should exclude the application of equidistance line principle. The tribunal observed that St. Martin Island is an area of about 8 square kilometers, permanent residents of the island are about 7,000 people, and the island is also an important operation base of Bangladesh Navy and Coast Guard. As St. Martin Island is within 12 nautical miles from Bangladesh territorial sea, and it is almost the same distance (6.5 nautical miles) to Bangladesh and to Myanmar.[42]

The Tribunal concludes that, in the circumstances of this case, there are no compelling reasons that justify treating St. Martin Island as a special circumstance for the purposes of article 15 of the Convention or that prevent the Tribunal from giving the island full effect in drawing the delimitation line of the territorial sea between the Parties.[43]

From the various international practices, we can conclude that historic rights have been asserted by many countries, and some of the international dispute settlement bodies have considered the existence of historic rights in making their judgments or awards, and admitted that the concept of historic rights is fully valid in accordance with international law. Although there are disagreements among different states in some cases, such differences are not about the concept itself, but only about the degree to recognize historic rights in detail. Moreover, such differences, in fact, will not affect the international recognition of historic rights.

Therefore, the Chinese government can prove that, within the remit of the U-shaped line, China enjoys historic rights, and such assertions are in accordance

41 Ibid.

42 See dispute concerning the delimitation of the maritime boundary between Bangladesh and Myanmar in the Bay of Bengal (Bangladesh/Myanmar), Judgment is available at <https://www.itlos.org/fileadmin/itlos/documents/cases/case_no_16/C16_Judgment_14_03_2012_rev.pdf>.

43 Dispute concerning the Delimitation of the Maritime Boundary between Bangladesh and Myanmar in the Bay of Bengal, Judgment of 14 March 2012, pp. 50–51.

with international law. The exercise of such historic rights should not be interfered by other coastal states using only the UNCLOS.

Historic rights is an abstract concept itself, but in specific international practice, it can be implemented in various formations, for example, in the consideration of the delimitation of exclusive economic zone, the delimitation of continental shelf, the distribution of fishing resources, international maritime communications, the management of marine environmental protection, the use of mineral resources, etc. Under the existing framework of international law, the factors generating historic rights should be included in the process of dispute settlement.

It is worth noting that historic rights do not conflict with the provisions of the UNCLOS, but are fully established under general international law. The Philippine allegation that all historic rights have been superseded by the UNCLOS is not true. On the contrary, the UNCLOS recognizes historic claims at least within the context of the territorial sea. It is recalled when the UN International Law Commission discussed the issues of historic waters and historic rights in the 1960s, it realized that the "concept of 'historic waters' has its root in the historic fact that States through the ages claimed and maintained sovereignty over maritime areas which they considered vital to them without paying much attention to divergent and changing opinions about what general international law might prescribe",[44] and the historic waters concept was seen as "necessary in order to maintain a State's title to some areas of water which might escape the codification formula".[45] It is clear and logical that when a coastal state extends its maritime zones outwards from the coast, such state should respect the existence of any historic rights and waters which have already existed on the high seas. When historic claims can well exist vis-à-vis territorial sea, such claims should be more justified vis-à-vis EEZ as the latter is a weaker maritime zone than a territorial sea in terms of sovereignty and national jurisdiction.

It is strongly believed that the Philippines itself has recognized the existence of historic rights in international law and used renowned international cases including the Anglo-Norwegian Fisheries Case (1951), Fisheries Jurisdiction Cases (United Kingdom v. Iceland; Federal Republic of Germany v. Iceland) (1971), Gulf of Main Case (Canada v. United States) (1984), and the Eritrea/Yemen case. Interestingly, most of them are maritime boundary delimitation cases not directly relevant to the Arbitration case as the Philippines does not ask the Arbitral Tribunal to deliberate any boundary issues. Such use of boundary delimitation cases by the Philippines would diminish the effect of its arguments for maritime entitlement in the South China Sea without a clear maritime boundary line between China and the Philippines.

---

44 See UN Secretariat, "Judicial Regime of Historic Waters, Including Historic Bays", UN Doc A/CN.4/143, 9 March 1962, reprinted in *Yearbook of the International Law Commission*, Vol. II, 1962, p. 7.

45 Ibid.; cited in Ted L. McDorman, *supra* note 30, p. 150.

China's Historic Rights in the South China Sea

China's historically formulated U-shaped line in South China Sea has given China historic entitlement to the land as well as maritime areas within the line. As clearly indicated above, China's historic entitlement is consistent with general international law and has been recognized, at least implicitly, by the international community. It is well perceived that such entitlement will play an important role in the future maritime delimitation in the South China Sea. However, on the other hand, the burden of proof lies on the Chinese side that China has the responsibility to demonstrate the existence of such historic rights and entitlement so as to convince the international society that its rights and entitlement are fully established in international law.

For the burden of proof, China may be able to argue that since ancient times, China has been continuously exercising its legitimate rights in the South China Sea, in particular in the use of marine resources, construction of artificial structures and installations, marine scientific research, maritime law enforcement, navigation, and military use.

a. Use of marine resources

In the case between Barbados and the Republic of Trinidad and Tobago of 2006, the International Court of Justice recognized the historic fishing rights as were previously recorded in the negotiations between the two countries.[46] Historical evidence from archaeological discovery proves that Chinese fishermen were active in the waters near the South China Sea islands no later than the Southern Dynasty (AD 402–589).[47] A thousand years since then, Chinese fishermen have been operating in the waters very frequently, and also created a sailing guide – "the Sea Road Book" to record the course and distance, and the names of each reef along the way of fishing, which has been in use ever since.[48] Long-term use by fishermen has established the historic fishing rights of China in the waters. While Chinese operations and utilization of biological marine resources of the waters are the most throughout the history, very few neighboring states did frequent fishing in this water area except for Vietnam that also enjoys historic fishing rights in the South China Sea. In addition to fishing, Chinese also extracted salt from the sea waters in the South China Sea. It is reasonably assumed that if technology would allow in history, the Chinese would extract other mineral resources from the sea too.

46 Case between Barbados and the Republic of Trinidad and Tobago, Arbitration Awards of 11 April 2006, p. 94.

47 Fu Kuen-chen, *Study on the Legal Status of the South China Sea* (Taipei: 123 Information Publishing, 1995) (in Chinese), p. 58.

48 Han Zhenhua, *supra* note 14, pp. 5–6.

b. Construction of artificial islands and installations

Only China has established artificial facilities in waters within the U-shaped line over history, that is, in 1925 the Chinese Government began planning the construction of observatories, radio stations and lighthouses. But due to political unrest, it was not fully completed until 1935.[49] In 1936 the Chinese Government set up observatories, radio stations and lighthouses in the Paracel Islands.[50]

c. Marine scientific research

Since ancient times there have been many records on the study of the South China Sea, and since Guo Shou Jing of the Yuan Dynasty (AD 1279), astronomical measurements have been made in the South China Sea.[51] Also in 1883, China protested the German marine investigation and surveys in the waters, and forced the Germans to stop their investigations. Since the twentieth century, the Chinese scientific investigations of the waters have never stopped.

d. Maritime law enforcement

No later than the beginning of the eighteenth century, China began to exercise law enforcement authorities including the right of hot pursuit in the South China Sea. In the *Historical Records of the Qing Dynasty* ("Qing Shi Lu"), there is a lot of information about China arresting pirates and sea robbers in the South China Sea. For example, arrests took place in October 1791, and in December 1844.[52]

e. Navigational rights

From the beginning of the third century AD, China began navigating in the South China Sea, and the Chinese people first created the names of the reefs on a chart. In the *Sea Road Book* ("geng lu bu"), there are records of the Xisha and Nansha Islands and the ranges of the big reefs, which even in today's perspective are still accurate, and there are also many other China's ancient history books recording this sea route.[53] It was the Chinese people who opened up the route. In the Song dynasty, China had opened up the maritime routes to the Philippines, starting from Quanzhou, crossing the South China Sea, passing Champa, bypassing Borneo (now

49 Ibid., p. 289.
50 Ibid., p. 227.
51 Ibid., p. 9.
52 See Yunnan Institute of History (ed.), *Records of the Qing Dynasty: Selected Historic Materials of Vietnam, Myanmar, Thailand and Laos* (Yunnan: Yunnan People's Publishing, 1985) (in Chinese), pp. 254 and 324.
53 Han Zhenhua, *supra* note 14, pp. 42–80.

western Kalimantan), and then to Ma Yi (now the Philippine Mindoro Island), San Yu (now Philippine Luzon Island in the West Bank area), and other places.[54]

f. Military use

From the historical point of view, within the U-shaped line, only China and Vietnam have historical evidence of naval operations in these waters. For example, in the Northern Song Dynasty, China had in fact visited Paracel Islands (then known as the Jiu Ru Luo Zhou "九乳螺洲").[55] And also, since the Han, Song, Yuan dynasties, there have been naval battles with the Vietnamese.[56]

The above historical evidences could be used to support China's claims to historic rights in the South China Sea, in particular in the context of exploration and use of marine resources and can constitute a convincing reply against the Philippine possible allegation that China may not demonstrate that it ever acquired 'historic rights' in maritime areas beyond its present-day UNCLOS entitlements.

In the Notification and the Statement of Claim, the Philippines repeatedly mentions that China's claims on the South China Sea are based on the U-shaped line, using the specific wording expressed as "based on", "within", "encompassed by".[57] These descriptions are seriously deviating from the true meaning of the U-shaped line. In fact, China does not claim everything within the U-shaped line, but sovereignty and maritime entitlement allowed by general international law including the UNCLOS plus historic rights acquired in accordance with general international law. It is recorded that in the 2011 diplomatic note to the Philippines, China clearly stated that

> China has indisputable sovereignty over the islands in the South China Sea and the adjacent waters, and enjoys sovereign rights and jurisdiction over the relevant waters as well as the seabed and subsoil thereof. China's sovereignty and related rights and jurisdiction in the South China Sea are supported by abundant historical and legal evidence. ... Since 1930s, the Chinese Government has given publicity several times the geographical scope of China's Nansha Islands and the names of its components. China's Nansha Islands is therefore clearly defined. In addition, under the relevant provisions of the 1982 United Nations Convention on the Law of the Sea, as well as the Law of the People's Republic of China on the Territorial Sea and the Contiguous Zone (1992) and the Law of the Exclusive Economic Zone and the Continental Shelf of the People's Republic of China (1998), China's Nansha

54 Li Yongcai (ed.), *A Brief History of Hegemony Struggling in Ocean Exploration* (Florida: Ocean Publisher, 1990) (in Chinese), p. 106.

55 Han Zhenhua, *supra* note 14, p. 7.

56 Fu Kuen-chen, *supra* note 47, pp. 165–70.

57 Notification and Statement of Claim on West Philippine Sea.

> Islands is fully entitled to Territorial Sea, Exclusive Economic Zone (EEZ) and Continental Shelf.[58]

Obviously, China's claims on the South China Sea are basically based on the provisions concerning the territorial sea, the exclusive economic zone and continental shelf under the UNCLOS, rather than historic rights deriving from the U-shaped line. The Philippines mistakenly attributed all the Chinese claims to the U-shaped line, and distorted the legal nature and status of the line, and such distortion is contrary to historical and legal facts. China, together with other States Parties to the UNCLOS in the world even including the Philippines, holds the view that the UNCLOS is the basis of the maritime claims of territorial sea, EEZ and continental shelf.

A possible distortion also lies with the Philippine allegation that China's historic rights claim only began in 1998.[59] Without mentioning the state practice of the Republic of China founded in 1911, the relevant practice of the People's Republic of China can be traced back to the 1950s when the PRC declared that the Bohai Gulf and the Chiungchow Strait were China's inland waters by historical reasons.[60] China recognized the Soviet historic bay claim to the Peter the Great Bay in 1957.[61] On the other hand, when we look at Article 14 of China's 1998 Law on the Exclusive Economic Zone and Continental Shelf, it actually does not specify that historic rights must be within the U-shaped line in the South China Sea and there is no official explanation to that effect, though in our understanding, historic rights do exist within the U-shaped line. Second, the historic rights reserved in the 1998 Law are related to the EEZ and continental shelf as it is indicated, without reference to the territorial sea. Thus the scope of these historic rights is limited.

As we all understand, the rule of historic rights is a rule of exception to general rules of international law including the UNCLOS. It is illogical, and completely incorrect, to assume that the Chinese territorial and maritime claims in the South China Sea are only historic rights. In fact, the Chinese claim to historic rights is a supplement to China's above general claims under the UNCLOS. Although China's 2009 diplomatic note is attached with a map which contains the U-shaped line, we cannot logically come to a conclusion that China's claims in the South

58 See <http://www.un.org/Depts/los/clcs_new/submissions_files/mysvnm33_09/phl_re_chn_2011.pdf>.

59 This statement may be borrowed from a hastily-researched article written by two French scholars: Florian Dupuy and Pierre-Marie Dupuy, "A Legal Analysis of China's Historic Rights Claim in the South China Sea", *American Journal of International Law*, Vol. 107, January 2013, p. 129.

60 "In several thousand years of history it has been constantly under the actual jurisdiction of our country, and not only has our country always considered it as an internal sea, but also [in fact] is internationally recognized". Fu Chu, *Concerning the Question of Our Country's Territorial Sea*, Beijing, 1959; translated in J.A. Cohen and Hungdah Chiu, *People's China and International Law* (Princeton: Princeton University Press, 1974), p. 484.

61 See *People's Daily* (in Chinese), 23 September 1957.

China Sea are all based on the U-shaped line. As the Chinese government states clearly, "China has indisputable sovereignty over the islands in the South China Sea and the adjacent waters, and enjoys sovereign rights and jurisdiction over the relevant waters as well as the seabed and subsoil thereof (see attached map). The above position is consistently held by the Chinese Government, and is widely known by the international community".[62]

By describing China's claims as historic claims, the Philippine has packed its case as a case to settle maritime entitlement disputes in the South China Sea. But in reality, without the determination of who owns the geographic features in the South China Sea, how can a court or arbitral tribunal decide on the maritime entitlement? In essence, the case initiated by the Philippines is concerned about territorial sovereignty, sovereignty-related issues, and maritime boundary delimitation which are excluded by the 2006 Chinese Declaration in accordance with Article 298 of the UNCLOS.[63] As Article 298 also mentions historic bays and titles, any disputes concerning historic rights should be exempted as well. It is opined by a leading scholar on the law of the sea that "[h]istoric title in Article 298, which is a permissible basis for a State to exempt itself from compulsory dispute settlement, must have a broader meaning than the term historic title in Article 15 where the existence of historic title merely displaces equidistance as a method of delimitation".[64]

"A dispute may be defined as a specific disagreement concerning a matter of fact, law or policy in which a claim or assertion of one party is met with refusal, counter-claim or denial by another".[65] A dispute cannot be established unilaterally, by using a claim countering against a non-existent or hypothetical claim of the other party, nor should a dispute be grounded on a premise which has no factual basis, an incorrect characterization of the legal situations between the claimant and the respondent. It is believed that the Arbitral Tribunal is able to realize this simple fact and declares no jurisdiction over the case or rebuts the Philippines' unreasonable and excessive claims.

Conclusion

Regarding the arbitration case initiated by the Philippines, China stated that it would not participate in the arbitration and accused the Philippines of complicating the

62 <www.un.org/Depts/los/clcs_new/submissions_files/vnm37_09/chn_2009re_vnm_c.pdf>.

63 On 25 August 2006, China made such a declaration. The whole text is available at <http://www.un.org/Depts/los/convention_agreements/convention_declarations.htm#China after ratification>.

64 Ted McDorman, *supra* note 30, p. 152.

65 J.G. Merrilles, *International Dispute Settlement*, 4th ed. (Cambridge: Cambridge University Press, 2005), p. 1.

issue.[66] China accused the Philippines of distorting "the basic facts underlying the disputes between China and the Philippines. In so doing, the Philippines attempts to deny China's territorial sovereignty and clothes its illegal occupation of China's islands and reefs with a cloak of 'legality'".[67] China asked the Philippines to go back to the right track of negotiation and consultation to settle the disputes so as to avoid further damages to the bilateral relations between the two countries.[68] On 7 December 2014, the Chinese Foreign Ministry was authorized to release a Position Paper of the Government of the People's Republic of China on the Matter of Jurisdiction in the South China Sea Arbitration Initiated by the Republic of the Philippines,[69] which elaborates the legal basis of China's position that the Arbitral Tribunal has no jurisdiction over the case, and the reasons why China does not participate in the proceedings.[70]

Except for the WTO disputes settlement mechanisms and economic arbitration, China does not accept the compulsory jurisdiction of the International Court of Justice nor compulsory settlement mechanisms under the UNCLOS for the disputes concerning maritime boundary delimitation, historic bays and titles or military activities.[71] As most of the reliefs to be sought by the Philippines are in fact closely related to the territorial sovereignty over the disputed islands and islets, maritime boundary delimitation, and even historic title and historic rights, China had a compelling reason to raise preliminary objections as such kind of disputes are excluded by China in accordance with Article 298 of the UNCLOS. Because of the above reasons, it seems extremely difficult for the Arbitral Tribunal to

66 See "China: No to UN arbitration on sea row", available at <http://www.abs-cbnnews.com/nation/02/01/13/china-no-un-arbitration-sea-row>.

67 "Foreign Ministry Spokesperson Hua Chunying's Remarks on the Philippines' Efforts in Pushing for the Establishment of the Arbitral Tribunal in Relation to the Disputes between China and the Philippines in the South China Sea", 26 April 2013, available at <http://www.fmprc.gov.cn/eng/xwfw/s2510/2535/t1035577.shtml>.

68 "Answers from the Foreign Ministry to the questions at a press conference on the search of the disappearing passenger airplane of the Malaysian Airlines and the issue of the South China Sea", 26 March 2014, available at <http://world.people.com.cn/n/2014/0326/c1002–24745397.html>.

69 "Position Paper of the Government of the People's Republic of China on the Matter of Jurisdiction in the South China Sea Arbitration Initiated by the Republic of the Philippines", available at <http://www.fmprc.gov.cn/mfa_eng/zxxx_662805/t1217147.shtml>.

70 "Remarks by Mr. Xu Hong, Director-General of the Department of Treaty and Law of the Ministry of Foreign Affairs, on the Position Paper of the Government of the People's Republic of China on the Matter of Jurisdiction in the South China Sea Arbitration Initiated by the Republic of the Philippines", available at <http://www.fmprc.gov.cn/mfa_eng/zxxx_662805/t1217150.shtml>. For details, see discussions in Chapter 6 of this book.

71 In August 2006, China made a declaration to exclude the categories of disputes set forth in Article 298 of the UNCLOS. China's declaration is available at <http://www.un.org/Depts/los/convention_agreements/convention_declarations.htm#China after ratification>.

establish its jurisdiction over the case.[72] But on the other hand, China's reluctance to participate in international dispute settlement mechanisms such as Annex VII Arbitration could have a negative impact on China's image in the world. It is suggested that China should participate in the arbitral proceedings to defend itself no matter how the case is disguised.[73] As the case is highly politicised with the strong support from the US Government and deep involvement of Americans,[74] there is a suspicion whether this politically backed case would have already become part of the overall rebalancing strategy of the United States in order to contain a rising China. Even if the Arbitral Tribunal would grant all the Philippine reliefs, such an award would in reality only exacerbate the tensions in the South China Sea, instead of helping settle the disputes. Nevertheless, while it is acknowledged that the Annex VII mechanism of the UNCLOS is not a proper forum for the settlement of sovereignty disputes, it is suggested that China and the Philippines could learn from their neighbors like Indonesia, Malaysia and Singapore to bring their disputes to the International Court of Justice for settlement when they could not reach agreement through bilateral talks.

72 For relevant literature, see Stefan Talmon, "The South China Sea Arbitration: Is There a Case to Answer?", in Stefan Talmon and Bing Bing Jia (eds), *The South China Sea Arbitration: A Chinese Perspective* (Oxford: Hart, 2014), pp. 15–80.

73 See Yu Mincai, "China's Response to the Compulsory Arbitration on the South China Sea Dispute: Legal Effects and Policy Options", *Ocean Development and International Law*, Vol. 45, 2014, pp. 1–16.

74 For example, the Assistant Secretary of State Daniel Russell recently gave a testimony at the U.S. Congress. According to him, "I want to reinforce the point that under international law, maritime claims in the South China Sea must be derived from land features. Any use of the 'nine dash line' by China to claim maritime rights not based on claimed land features would be inconsistent with international law". And "we fully support the right of claimants to exercise rights they may have to avail themselves of peaceful dispute settlement mechanisms. The Philippines chose to exercise such a right last year with the filing of an arbitration case under the Law of the Sea Convention". See "Maritime Disputes in East Asia", Testimony, Daniel R. Russel, Assistant Secretary, Bureau of East Asian and Pacific Affairs, Testimony Before the House Committee on Foreign Affairs Subcommittee on Asia and the Pacific Washington, DC, 5 February 2014, available at <http://www.state.gov/p/eap/rls/rm/2014/02/221293.htm>.

Chapter 9
The Law of the Sea Convention and the U-Shaped Line: Some Comments

Ted L. McDorman*

Introduction

This chapter looks at the relationship between the U-shaped line and the 1982 U.N. Convention on the Law of the Sea.[1] One of the assertions in the Philippine Statement of Claim in its case against China is that "China's maritime claims in the South China Sea based on its so-called 'nine dashed line' are contrary to UNCLOS and invalid".[2] China has made no recent public comments on the U-shaped line and has not responded directly to the Philippine assertion of the relationship between the LOS Convention and the U-shaped line. However, a spokesperson for the Chinese Ministry of Foreign Affairs on 15 September 2011 stated:

> The UN Convention on the Law of the Sea does not entitle any country to extend its exclusive economic zone or continental shelf to the territory of another, and it does not restrain or deny a country's right which is formed in history and abidingly upheld.[3]

---

* This chapter draws heavily from T.L. McDorman, "Rights and Jurisdiction Over Resources in the South China Sea: UNCLOS and the 'Nine-Dash Line'", in S. Jayakumar, Tommy Koh and Robert Beckman (eds), *The South China Sea Disputes and the Law of the Sea* (Cheltenham: Edward Elgar, 2014), pp. 144–63.

1 U.N. Convention on the Law of the Sea, 10 December 1982, entered into force 16 November 1994, 1833 *U.N.T.S.* 397.

2 Philippines, "Notification and Statement of Claim", 22 January 2013, para. 31, point 2, attached to the Statement by Secretary of Foreign Affairs Albert del Rosario on the UNCLOS Arbitral Proceedings against China to Achieve a Peaceful and Durable Solution to the Dispute in the WPS, available at <www.gov.ph/2013/01/22/statement-the-secretary-of-foreign-affairs-on-the-unclos-arbitral-proceedings-against-china-january-22-2013/> (accessed 21 May 2013).

3 China, Foreign Ministry Spokesperson Jiang Yu's Regular Press Conference, 15 September 2011, available at <www.fmprc.gov.cn/eng/xwfw/s2510/t860126.htm>.

Gao and Jia in an article in 2013 concluded that: "the nine-dash line does not contradict the obligations undertaken by China under UNCLOS; rather, it supplements what is provided for in the Convention".[4]

The discussion below is speculative since China has not articulated the legal consequences or basis of the U-shaped line. Thus, what follows is not in any way an evaluation of the U-shaped line or any legal or historical arguments that may be made for or against its legal consequences or basis. Rather, what follows hopefully provides an understanding of the legal offshore regimes within and beyond the LOS Convention with a focus on historic waters and historic rights since these terms, rightly or wrongly, have been associated with China's U-shaped line.

The LOS Convention: Offshore Rights and Jurisdiction

The LOS Convention contains two innovations respecting coastal state ocean resource rights and jurisdiction regimes:

- exclusive sovereign rights for coastal states "for the purpose of exploring and exploiting, ... the natural resources whether living or non-living, of the waters superjacent to the seabed and of the seabed and its subsoil" to a distance of 200-n. miles;[5] and
- the mineral resources of the seabed beyond national jurisdiction "are the common heritage of mankind"[6] such that no state can "claim or exercise sovereignty or sovereign rights over any part of the Area or its resources".[7]

The LOS Convention also contains detail on regimes of ocean resource rights and jurisdiction that predate the Convention:

- all states have the right to engage in fishing on the high seas, subject to treaty obligations, co-operation and conservation duties, and in certain cases the interests of adjacent coastal states;[8]
- the sovereignty of the adjacent coastal state extends to the territorial sea,[9] such that all ocean resources within the territorial sea are subject to the adjacent state's authority; and

4 Zhiguo Gao and Bing Bing Jia, "The Nine-Dash Line in the South China Sea: History, Status, and Implications" (2013), 107 *American Journal of International Law* 98, at pp. 99 and 123.

5 LOS Convention, Articles 56(1)(a) and 57.

6 *Ibid.*, Articles 136, 133 and 1.

7 *Ibid.*, Article 137(1).

8 *Ibid.*, Articles 116–19.

9 *Ibid.*, Article 2.

- a coastal state has exclusive sovereign rights over the natural resources associated with its continental shelf.[10]

What was introduced in the LOS Convention respecting these previously existing regimes are geographic limits. The high seas are the water column beyond coastal state's 200-n. mile zones. The territorial sea is between the baselines of a state and 12-n. miles. Locating the continental shelf is a bit more complicated with its inner limit being the outer limit of the territorial sea and its outer limit being either at 200-n. miles from a state's baselines or beyond that as determined by the application of the complex criteria in Article 76. The Area and its associated Common Heritage principles apply to the mineral resources of the seafloor located beyond the outer limit of a coastal state's continental shelf. The LOS Convention located the internal waters of a state, landward of baselines, but provided no detail on a state's rights within internal waters with the assumption being that, subject to several exceptions, the adjacent state has the same rights and jurisdiction over its internal waters as if it were land.

A state has an entitlement to a territorial sea and an EEZ with the regimes only applying where a state takes direct action to claim them. Internal waters exist as an operation of law as normal baselines (based on the low-water line), as opposed to straight baselines, exist for a coastal state without the necessity of the state taking direct action. As regards the legal regime of the continental shelf, LOS Convention, Article 77(3) states that: "The rights of the coastal State over the continental shelf do not depend on occupation, effective or notional, or any express proclamation". This wording tracks the approach of the International Court of Justice in the 1969 *North Sea Continental Shelf Cases* which referred to the "inherent rights" of a state to a continental shelf[11] and was referred to positively by the International Tribunal for the Law of the Sea in the 2012 *Bay of Bengal Case*.[12] As a result, the continental shelf is akin to internal waters based on normal baselines in that no direct action to assert acquisition is necessary.

Historic Waters/Historic Rights

The background and importance of historic claims to waters was explained in 1962 U.N. Secretariat Study, "Juridical Regime of Historic Waters, Including Historic Bays":

10 *Ibid.*, Articles 76–7.

11 *North Sea Continental Shelf Cases (Denmark/The Netherlands v. Germany)*, [1969] *I.C.J. Reports* 3, at para. 19.

12 *Dispute Concerning Delimitation of the Maritime Boundary between Bangladesh and Myanmar in the Bay of Bengal (Bangladesh/Myanmar)*, Judgment, 14 March 2012, para. 409, available on the website of the International Tribunal for the Law of the Sea at <www.itlos.org>.

> [T]he concept of "historic waters" has its root in the historic fact that States through the ages claimed and maintained sovereignty over maritime areas which they considered vital to them without paying much attention to divergent and changing opinions about what general international law might prescribe … .[13]

The Study noted that as international law of the sea evolved with 3-n. mile territorial seas (and then 12-n. mile territorial seas), the historic waters concept was seen as "necessary in order to maintain a State's title to some areas of water which might escape the codification formula … ".[14]

The terminology concerning historic claims to waters is often blurred. States (and others) use historic terminology interchangeable and haphazardly making it difficult to assess in the abstract what may be being claimed by a state.

Historic waters and historic rights, both of which engage historic title, have been referred to as "twin concepts".[15] A short-hand approach for the purposes here is that historic waters, where they exist, involve exclusivity of rights *ergaomnes* for the claimant state;[16] whereas historic rights usually attaches to a specific resource or activity and do not involve "zonal claims of jurisdiction or sovereignty".[17] The Tribunal in the *Eritrea/Yemen (First Stage) Arbitration* understood historic rights in the context of fishing to be something less than sovereignty (and presumably sovereignty rights).[18] Symmons comments that a possible distinction also exists in that historic waters "must necessarily be adjacent to the claimant State", while historic rights may not be so confined.[19]

While historic waters are most often associated with the rights that an adjacent coastal state has within internal waters, the International Court in the 1982 *Tunisia-Libya Continental Shelf Case* commented that:

> international law … does not provide for a single "regime" for "historic waters" or "historic bays", but only for a particular regime for each of the concrete, recognized cases of "historic waters" or "historic bays".[20]

---

13 "Juridical Regime of Historic Waters, Including Historic Bays", Study prepared by the U.N. Secretariat, U.N. Doc. A/CN.4/143, 9 March 1962, reprinted in *Yearbook of the International Law Commission*, Vol. II, 1962 (New York, 1964), at p. 7, para. 38.

14 D.P. O'Connell, *The International Law of the Sea*, Vol. I (edited by I.A. Shearer) (Oxford: Clarendon Press, 1982), at p. 425 referring to the U.N. Secretariat Study, *supra* note 13.

15 Clive R. Symmons, *Historic Waters in the Law of the Sea: A Modern Re-appraisal* (Leiden: Martinus Nijhoff, 2008), at p. 6.

16 *Ibid.*, at pp. 1 and 5.

17 *Ibid.*, at pp. 4–5.

18 *Eritrea/Yemen (First Stage) Arbitration*, 9 October 1998, reprinted at (2001), 40 *I.L.M.* 900, para. 126.

19 Symmons, *supra* note 15, at p. 6.

20 *Case Concerning the Continental Shelf (Tunisia/Libya), [1982] I.C.J. Reports* 18, at para. 100. This was cited with approval in the *Case Concerning the Land, Island and Maritime Frontier Dispute (El Salvador/Honduras: Nicaragua Intervening), [1992] I.C.J. Reports* 351, at para. 384 (*Gulf of Fonseca Case*).

In the 1992 *Gulf of Fonseca Case*, El Salvador, Honduras and Nicaragua agreed that the Gulf of Fonseca, on which all three states had coasts, was an historic bay and the Court found that a right of innocent passage existed noting that "rights of innocent passage are not inconsistent with a regime of historic waters ... ".[21] The 1962 U.N. Secretariat Study commented that "the scope of the historic title emerging from the continued exercise of sovereignty should not be wider in scope than the scope of the sovereignty actually exercised".[22]

Interaction of the LOS Convention Regimes and Historic Waters/Historic Rights

During the negotiation of the LOS Convention, draft provisions on historic waters were proposed in the context of discussions respecting the territorial sea. According to the U.S. delegation to the Conference, "There was strong opposition to a general doctrine of historic waters ... " that had been proposed, such that, ultimately, no direct wording on historic claims to waters was adopted.[23] The 1982 Convention (and before it the 1958 Convention on the Territorial Sea and Contiguous Zone[24]) notes the existence of "historic bays" (aligned with historic waters[25]), albeit in a round-about manner, where it is stated that the juridical bay provisions in the Conventions do not apply to historic bays.[26] Neither the 1982 nor 1958 Conventions provide any indication of when historic claims to waters exist, such as historic bays, or the consequence of waters being historic.[27] The same can said of "historic title" found in Article 12(1) of the 1958 Convention and 15 of the LOS Convention with one exception, where historic title exists it has the consequence that the rule of applying an equidistance line where territorial seas overlap is not applicable.

---

21 *Gulf of Fonseca Case*, *supra* note 20, at para. 393.

22 U.N. Secretariat Study, *supra* note 13, at p. 23, para. 164.

23 "U.S. Delegation Report of Third Session, 1975", in *Reports of the United States Delegation to the Third United Nations Conference on the Law of the Sea* (Honolulu: Law of the Sea Institute, 1983), at p. 94. More generally on these historic waters discussions, see: L.F.E. Goldie, "Historic Bays in International Law – An Impressionistic Overview" (1984), 11 *Syracuse Journal of International Law and Commerce* 211, at pp. 265–7. Note also: Francesco Francioni, "The Status of the Gulf of Sirte in International Law" (1984), 11 *Syracuse Journal of International Law and Commerce* 311, at p. 321 who notes the proposals were "quickly discarded".

24 Convention on the Territorial Sea and Contiguous Zone, done at Geneva on 29 April 1958, entered into force 22 September 1964, 516 *U.N.T.S.* 205.

25 See *Gulf of Fonseca Case*, *supra* note 20, at para. 383.

26 LOS Convention, *supra* note 1, Article 10(6) and Convention on the Territorial Sea and the Contiguous Zone, *supra* note 24, Article 7(6). O'Connell, *supra* note 14, at p. 419 notes: "The drafting history of paragraph (6) and the subsequent actions of the United Nations make it clear that historic claims may exist ... , which are not claims to bays". See generally: Symmons, *supra* note 15, at pp. 21–2.

27 *Libya-Tunisia Case*, *supra* note 20, at para. 100.

Article 298 of the LOS Convention indicates that states can exempt themselves from compulsory adjudication "disputes concerning the interpretation or application of articles 15, 74 and 83 relating to sea boundary delimitations, or those involving historic bays or titles".[28] While historic bays can be said to have a particular meaning, the same cannot be said for historic title. Historic title in Article 298 would appear to have a broader meaning than the term historic title in Article 15 where the existence of historic title merely displaces equidistance as a method of delimitation. In addition, given the construction of Article 298, it is arguable that historic title is not related to delimitation *per se*, but is a separate category of dispute from which a state can exempt itself from compulsory third party adjudication.

Clive Symmons, in his masterful and detailed study, takes the view that despite the modern ocean regime of rights and jurisdiction over ocean resources in the LOS Convention, historic waters are "still generally viewed as an established part of the international law of the sea".[29] The International Court in the 1982 *Libya-Tunisia Case* commented that: "Historic titles must enjoy respect and be preserved as they have always been by long usage" and that "It is clearly the case that … the notion of historic rights or waters … are governed by … customary international law" and that the LOS Convention provides no guidance.[30]

The eighth paragraph of the preamble to the LOS Convention states: " … matters not regulated by this Convention continue to be governed by the rules and principles of general international law".[31] Historic waters, not being regulated under the LOS Convention, fall within this wording even if this was not directly contemplated by the negotiators. Similarly, whether historic rights exist is not regulated by the LOS Convention, although as noted further below, when these rights involve fisheries and the resources of the continental shelf the LOS Convention may become engaged.

The LOS Convention and state practice can be said to recognize or accept that waters adjacent to a coastal state may be historic waters or subject to the historic title claimed by that state and that the criteria for elevating such claims is dealt with by customary international law and not the LOS Convention. While historic claims to waters (historic waters, historic rights) are usually understood as accruing to coastal states, there is nothing in the definition or understanding of historic waters or historic rights that precludes a non-adjacent coastal state from making such a claim, though there are no clear examples of such a claim. In this case, however, the LOS Convention (as between States Parties) is not silent.

---

28 LOS Convention, *supra* note 1, Article 298(1)(a)(i).

29 Symmons, *supra* note 15, at p. 296.

30 *Libya-Tunisia Case*, *supra* note 20, at para. 100.

31 LOS Convention, *supra* note 1, preamble, para. 8.

Fishing

The idea of states having and being able to exercise historic or traditional fishing rights in waters that would be otherwise with a state's 200-n. mile exclusive fishing zone did not fare well in the negotiation of the LOS Convention.[32] The promise of the EEZ for coastal state fishing interests effectively precluded any significant arguments that might have been made to respect or even take into account any traditional or historic fishing that arguably existed in the emerging 200-n. mile national exclusive zone. The only trace of historic or traditional fishing rights in Part V of the Convention is indirect – a factor ("the need to minimize economic dislocation in States whose nationals have habitually fished in the zone") that a coastal state "shall take into account" in the granting of access to fishery resources within their EEZ.[33]

Traditional fishing rights are mentioned in Article 51(1) of the LOS Convention where archipelagic states are to "recognize traditional fishing rights" of immediately adjacent neighbouring states within its archipelagic waters. Article 51 is expressly without prejudice to the sovereignty of the state over its archipelagic waters. The recognition of the traditional fishing rights involves an obligation to enter into a bilateral agreement regarding the exercise of such rights.[34] Items of note regarding this provision are: (a) the archipelagic state has sovereignty over its archipelagic waters; (b) the waters involved are near-shore and do not involve the EEZ; and (c) the historic right involved is not that of the adjacent coastal state but one of a neighbouring state. The latter point makes Article 51 of particular interest as one of the few direct examples of an historic right possibly accruing to a non-adjacent coastal state.

Note can be made of the 1998 *Eritrea/Yemen (First Stage) Arbitration*, which found the existence of "certain 'historic rights' which accrued in favour of both parties through a process of historical consolidation as a sort of '*servitude internationale*' falling short of territorial sovereignty … " and that: "Such historic rights provide a sufficient legal basis for maintaining certain aspects of a *res communis* that has existed for centuries for the benefit of the populations on both sides of the Red Sea".[35] The Arbitral Award indicates that an historic fishing right ascribed to foreign fishers within the waters of a coastal state does not trump coastal state sovereignty.[36]

32 See: Leonardo Bernard, "The Effect of Historic Fishing Rights in Maritime Boundaries Delimitation", a paper from the Papers from the Law of the Sea Institute-Korea Institute of Ocean Science and Technology Conference held in Seoul, Korea, May 2012, "Securing the Ocean for the Next Generation", edited by Harry N. Scheiber and Moon Sang Kwon, at p. 7, available at <www.law.berkeley.edu/files/Bernard-final.pdf>.

33 LOS Convention, *supra* note 1, Article 62(3).

34 See generally: S.N. Nandan and S. Rosenne, *United Nations Convention on the Law of the Sea, 1982: A Commentary*, Vol. II (Dordrecht: Martinus Nijhoff, 1993), pp. 448–54.

35 *Eritrea/Yemen (First Stage) Arbitration*, supra note 18, at para. 126.

36 *Ibid.*

Based on the practice of states in extending their territorial seas or fishery zones to 12-n. miles in the 1970s, D.P. O'Connell stated that: "There is no precedent for a successful claim to continued fishing rights in waters newly converted to territorial waters"; that the practice of phasing-out foreign fishing "presupposes a concession rather than a recognition of a right"; and that "most traditional fishing rights are opposable to states extending their fishery limits ... only when derived from treaty".[37] This appears to hold true as well as regards high seas areas converted to EEZs.[38] Nevertheless, as the *Eritrea/Yemen Arbitration* makes clear, historic rights in limited circumstances may exist that, while they do not undermine the sovereignty of the adjacent coastal state, require tolerance and attention to be paid by the coastal state.

Continental Shelf

As already noted, Article 77(3) of the LOS Convention, the origin of which is Article 2(3) of the 1958 Continental Shelf Convention,[39] indicates that a coastal state has an inherent or automatic right to its adjacent shelf area rather than a right that arises through territorial acquisition.[40] The 2012 *Bay of Bengal Case* stated that: "A coastal state's entitlement to the continental shelf exists by the sole fact that the basis of entitlement, namely sovereignty over the land territory, is present".[41] This inherent right aspect can be contrasted with the exclusive economic zone (EEZ) regime which, while available to states, must be positively asserted by a state.

The International Court in the *Libya/Tunisia Case* commented that:

> [T]he notion of historic rights or waters and that of the continental shelf are governed by distinct legal regimes in customary international law. The first regime is based on acquisition and occupation, while the second is based on the existence of rights "*ipso facto* and *ab initio*".[42]

The Court did not find it necessary in the *Case* to reconcile in any way the two legal regimes. Nevertheless, the establishment of the continental shelf doctrine as an autonomous legal institution, independent of other methods of territorial acquisition, implies the automatic attribution of the continental shelf to the coastal state. One of the aims behind the propagation of the doctrine was to annul any

37 O'Connell, *supra* note 14, at p. 538.
38 See: Bernard, *supra* note 32, at p. 8.
39 Convention on the Continental Shelf, done at Geneva on 29 April 1958, entered into force 10 June 1964, 499 *U.N.T.S.* 311.
40 See: O'Connell, supra note 14, at pp. 472–5.
41 *Bay of Bengal Case,supra* note 12, at para. 409.
42 *Libya-Tunisia Case, supra* note 20, at para. 100.

priority of claim in time or nature of other states over the rights of the coastal state, so that the doctrine of historic rights or acquisitive prescription would not be available.[43]

It is clear, based on the manner in which a state has its rights to a continental shelf, that historic rights or waters claims that involve or attach to resource rights contained in the continental shelf regime are not available to an asserting state where the continental shelf in question belongs to a different state on the basis of adjacency and geography.

Conclusion

Historic claims to waters, whether they be claims to historic waters and the exclusivity of rights attached thereto or claims to historic rights as regards, for example, fishing, exist in the international law of the sea and are, in part, outside the scope of the LOS Convention. While historic waters usually involves a claim to exclusive authority to treat near-shore waters as internal waters, it cannot be entirely dismissed that a claim could involve areas further away from shore and involve fishing. As historic waters involve exclusivity, the issue is more one of title than use. Such a claim beyond near-shore waters would be exceptional and inconsistent with the history on the law of the sea where, until recently, what existed were narrow bands of national waters along a coast and wide expanses of high seas within which high seas freedoms existed. This goes to the inherent difficulty of successfully making the case. And, as explained above, an historic waters claim that involves the continental shelf would be defeated if that shelf were not the shelf of the claiming state on the basis of adjacency and geography.

Historic rights, understood as not involving title *per se* are more easily and credibly asserted. However, again such rights cannot exist as regards the resources of the continental shelf of another state and, in the case of fishing rights, are severely constrained by the LOS Convention with adjudications and Article 51 of the Convention having found some room for the recognition of such rights but always subject to the overriding resource sovereignty of the adjacent coastal state.

Of final note is the question of proof of a claim of historic waters/rights. The 1962 U.N. Secretariat Study commented:

> The burden of proof of title to "historic waters" is on the State claiming such title, in the sense that, if the State is unable to prove to the satisfaction of whoever has to decide the matter that the requirements necessary for the title have been fulfilled, its claim to the title will be disallowed.[44]

43 O'Connell, *supra* note 14, at p. 482.
44 U.N. Secretariat Study, *supra* note 13, at p. 25, para. 188.

Chapter 10

The South China Sea Arbitration Case Filed by the Philippines against China: Arguments Concerning Submerged Features, Low Tide Elevations and Islands

Yann-huei Song

Introduction

On 22 January 2013, the Republic of the Philippines (the "Philippines") initiated arbitral proceedings against the People's Republic of China ("China" or the "PRC") when it presented a *Note Verbale*[1] to the Chinese Embassy in Manila, accompanying a Notification and Statement of Claim,[2] in accordance with Article 287 of the 1982 United Nations Convention on the Law of the Sea ("UNCLOS" or the "Convention") and Annex VII to the Convention.[3] The Philippines' purpose in initiating the proceedings is to seek a resolution to its disputes with China over maritime claims and entitlements in the South China Sea ("SCS").

In response, on 19 February 2013, China presented a *Note Verbale* to the Philippines rejecting and retuning the Notification and Statement of Claim.[4] Since then, despite repeated statements from Beijing, indicating that China does not accept the request, and will not participate in the arbitral proceedings, the Philippines has asked the tribunal to continue proceedings in accordance with

1 *Note verbale* from the Department of Foreign Affairs of the Republic of the Philippines to the Embassy of the People's Republic of China in Manila, No. 13-0211 (22 January 2013).

2 See Department of Foreign Affairs, the Republic of the Philippines, "SFA Statement on the UNCLOS Arbitral Proceeding against China", available at <https://www.dfa.gov.ph/index.php/2013-06-27-21-50-36/unclos>. The *Note verbale*, Notification and Statement of Claim on West Philippine Sea are available at the same address.

3 U.N. Convention on the Law of the Sea, 1833 U.N.T.S. 397, adopted in Montego Bay, Jamaica, on 10 December 1982, entry into force on 16 November 1994. For the status of the treaty, it is available at <https://treaties.un.org/Pages/ViewDetailsIII.aspx?&src=TREATY&mtdsg_no=XXI~6&chapter=21&Temp=mtdsg3&lang=en>.

4 *Note verbale* from the Embassy of the People's Republic of China in Manila to the Department of Foreign Affairs of the Republic of the Philippines, No. (13) PG-039 (19 February 2013), at 1.

Article 9 of Annex VII to UNCLOS, which states that "[i]f one of the parties to the dispute does not appear before the arbitral tribunal or fails to defend its case, the other party may request the tribunal to continue the proceedings and to make its award".

In the Notification and Statement of Claim, the Philippines argues, *inter alia*, that Mischief Reef, McKennan Reef, Gaven Reef and Subi Reef are submerged features that are not above sea level at high tide, are not islands under the Convention, and are not located on China's continental shelf. Because Mischief Reef and McKennan Reef are part of the Philippines' continental shelf, China has unlawfully occupied and engaged in unlawful construction activities on these features.[5] In addition, the Philippines claims that Scarborough Shoal, Johnson Reef, Cuarteron Reef and Fiery Cross Reef are also submerged features that are below sea level at high tide, except that each of these features has small protrusions that remain above water at high tide, which quality as "rocks" under Article 121, paragraph 3, of the Convention and therefore can generate entitlement only to a territorial sea no broader than 12 nautical miles ("nm").[6]

Based on these claims, the Philippines requests the Arbitral Tribunal to issue an award that:

1. Declares that Mischief Reef and McKennan Reef are submerged features that form part of the Continental Shelf of the Philippines under Part VI of the Convention, and that China's occupation of and construction activities on them violate the sovereign rights of the Philippines;
2. Requires that China end its occupation of and activities on Mischief Reef and McKennan Reef;
3. Declares that Gaven Reef and Subi Reef are submerged features in the SCS that are not above sea level at high tide, are not islands under the Convention, and are not located on China's continental shelf, and that China's occupation of and construction activities on these features are unlawful;
4. Requires China to terminate its occupation of and activities on Gaven Reef and Subi Reef; and
5. Declares that Scarborough Shoal, Johnson Reef, Cuarteron Reef and Fiery Cross Reef are submerged features that are below sea level at high tide except that each has small protrusions that remain above water at high tide, which are "rocks" under Article 121(3) of the Convention which therefore generate entitlements only to a Territorial Sea no broader than 12 [nautical miles]; and that China has unlawfully claimed maritime entitlements beyond 12 nm from these features.[7]

5 Notification and Statement of Claim on West Philippine Sea, *supra* note 2, para. 31, at 13.

6 *Ibid.*

7 *Ibid.*, para. 41, at 17–18.

It is argued that since all of the above-mentioned features, with the exception of Scarborough Shoal, are located within the claimed EEZ and continental shelf that are generated from Itu Aba, Thitu Island, or West York Island, the three largest land features of the Spratly archipelago in the South China Sea ("SCS"), in accordance with Articles 5, 56, 57, 76, 77 and 121, it is difficult for the Philippines' claims be accepted by the Tribunal. According to Article 9 of Annex VII to the Convention, "[b]efore making its award, the arbitral tribunal must satisfy itself not only that it has jurisdiction over the dispute but also that the claim is well founded in fact and law".[8] It is therefore argued that some claims, if not all, made by the Philippines, are not well founded in fact and law.

The purpose of this chapter is to discuss whether or not the claims made by the Philippines with regard to Scarborough Shoal and the 7 features of the Spratly archipelago, namely, Mischief Reef, Subi Reef, Gaven Reef, McKennan Reef, Johnson Reef, Cuarteron Reef, and Fiery Cross Reef, are well founded in fact and law. The main applicable provisions contained in the UNCLOS are Articles 13, 56, 57, 60, 74, 76, 83, and 121.

Case Background

On 6 May 2009, Malaysia and the Socialist Republic of Viet Nam ("Vietnam") submitted jointly to the Commission on the Limits of the Continental Shelf ("CLCS"), in accordance with Article 76, paragraph 8, of the UNCLOS, information on the limits of the continental shelf beyond 200 nm from the baselines from which the breadth of the territorial sea is measured in respect of the southern part of the SCS.[9] On the following day, Vietnam submitted independently to the CLCS information on the limits of the continental shelf beyond 200 nm from the baselines from which the breadth of the territorial sea is measured in respect of the northern part of the SCS.[10] In response to these two submissions, on 7 May 2009, China submitted a *Note verbale* to the Secretary-General of the United Nations, stating, *inter alia*, that "China has indisputable sovereignty over the islands in the SCS and the adjacent waters, and enjoys sovereign rights and jurisdiction over the relevant waters as well as the seabed and subsoil thereof".[11] A map of the U-shaped claim, with its nine-dashed line in the SCS, was attached to the two diplomatic notes (see Figure 10.1).

8 U.N. Convention on the Law of the Sea1833 U.N.T.S. 397 (n 3).

9 CLCS.33.3009.LOS (Continental Shelf Notification), 7 May 2009, available at <http://www.un.org/Depts/los/clcs_new/submissions_files/mysvnm33_09/mysvnm_clcs33_2009e.pdf>.

10 CLCS.37.2009.LOS (Continental Shelf Notification), 11 May 2009, available at <http://www.un.org/Depts/los/clcs_new/submissions_files/vnm37_09/vnm_clcs37_2009e.pdf>.

11 Permanent Mission of the People's Republic of China to the U.N., *CML/17/2009*, and *CML/18/2009*, United Nations (7 May 2009), available at <http://www.un.org/Depts/los/clcs_new/submissions_files/mysvnm33_09/chn_2009re_mys_vnm_e.pdf> and <http://www.un.org/Depts/los/clcs_new/submissions_files/vnm37_09/chn_2009re_vnm.pdf>.

In response to the Chinese diplomatic notes, the Philippines sent a *Note verbale* to the UN Secretary-General on 5 April 2011, in which the Philippines stated that it has sovereignty and jurisdiction over the geological features in the Kalayaan Island Group ("KIG"), which constitutes an integral part of the Philippines.[12] In addition, the Philippines stated that under the Roman notion of *dominium maris* and the international law principle of "*la terre domine la mer*" (the land dominates the sea), it exercises sovereignty and jurisdiction over "the waters around or adjacent to each relevant geological feature in the KIG as provided for under UNCLOS". These "adjacent" waters are defined and determined under the Convention, in particularly under the regime of islands (Article 121) of UNCLOS.[13]

Moreover, the Philippines argues that since the adjacent waters of the relevant geological features in the KIG "are definite and subject to legal and technical measurement", the Chinese claim to the "relevant waters as well as the seabed and subsoil thereof", as reflected in the nine-dash line map attached to the two *Notes verbale* sent to the UN Secretary-General on 7 May 2009, that are outside of the relevant geological features and their "adjacent waters", has no basis under international law, specifically UNCLOS. The Philippines states that these maritime areas belong to the appropriate coastal or archipelagic state, namely, the Philippines, to which these bodies of waters, the seabed, and subsoil are appurtenant, either in the 12 nm territorial sea, or 200 nm EEZ, or continental shelf in accordance with Articles 3, 4, 55, 57, and 76 of UNCLOS.[14]

On 14 April 2011, China responded to the Philippine diplomatic note by sending a *Note verbale* to the U.N. Secretary-General, asserting, among other things, that:

> [U]nder the relevant provisions of the *1982 United Nations Convention on the Law of the Sea*, as well as the *Law of the People's Republic of China on the Territorial Sea and the Contiguous Zone (1992)* and the *Law on the Exclusive Economic Zone and the Continental Shelf of the People's Republic of China (1998)*, China's Nansha Islands [Spratly Islands] [are] fully entitled to Territorial Sea, Exclusive Economic Zone (EEZ) and Continental Shelf.[15]

In addition, China accuses the Philippines of starting to invade and occupy some islands and reefs of China's Spratly Islands and of making related territorial claims

12 *Note verbale* from the Permanent Mission of the Republic of the Philippines to the United Nations to the Secretary-General of the United Nations, No. 000228, 5 April 2011, available at <http://www.un.org/Depts/los/clcs_new/submissions_files/vnm37_09/phl_re_chn_2011.pdf>.

13 *Ibid.*

14 *Ibid.*

15 Permanent Mission of the People's Republic of China to the U.N., *CML/8/2011*, United Nations, 14 April 2011, available at <http://www.un.org/Depts/los/clcs_new/submissions_files/vnm37_09/chn_2011_re_phl_e.pdf>.

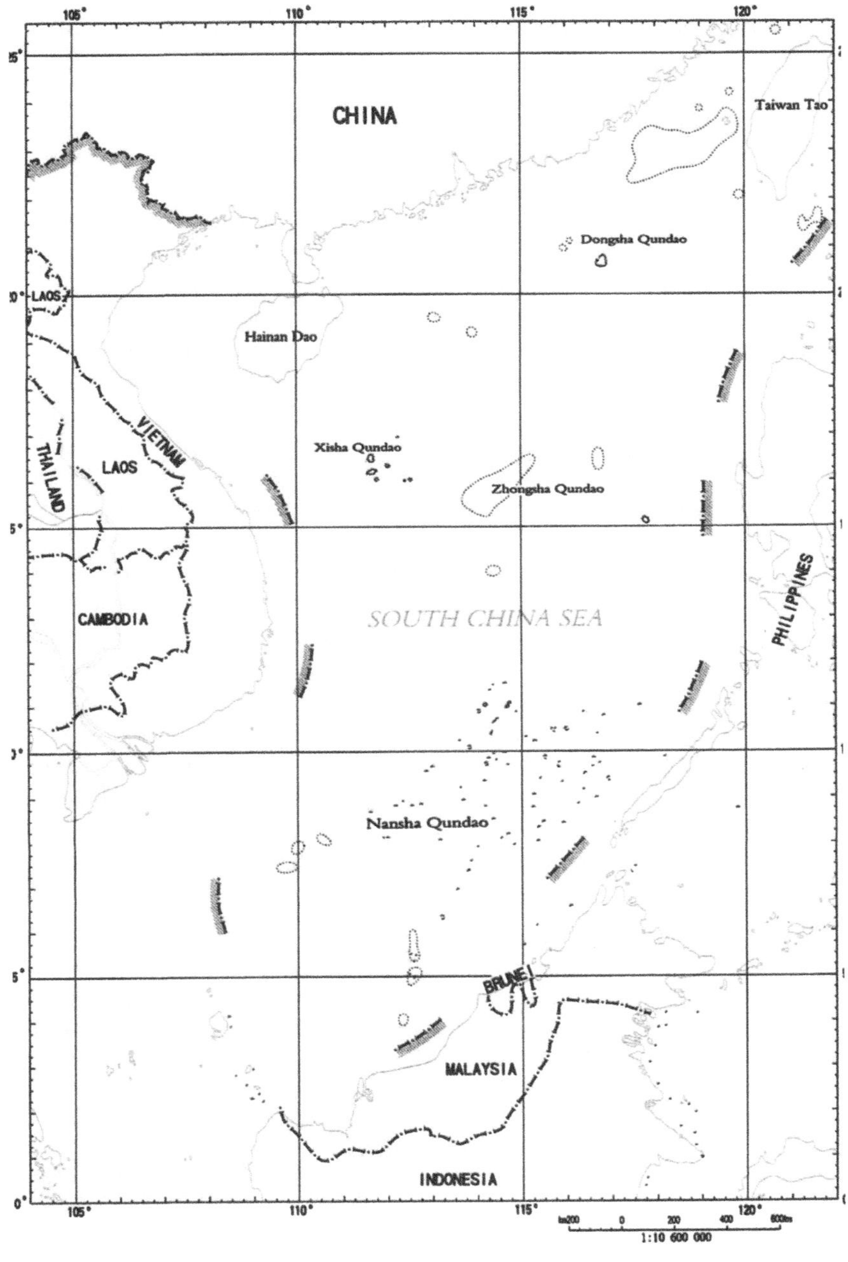

Figure 10.1 China's U-shaped Line in the South China Sea

since 1970s. China considers the Philippines' acts to constitute infringement upon its territorial sovereignty. China also states that:

> [U]nder the legal doctrine of "*ex injuria jus non oritur*", the Republic of Philippines can in no way invoke such illegal occupation to support its territorial claims. Furthermore, under the legal principle of "*la terra domine la mer*", coastal states' Exclusive Economic Zone (EEZ) and Continental Shelf claims shall not infringe upon the territorial sovereignty of other states.[16]

One month before submitting its diplomatic note to the UN Secretary-General, China dispatched two marine surveillance vessels to the maritime areas it claims in the Spratly Islands to order MV *Veritas Voyager*, a Forum Energy Plc ("FEP") survey vessel operating at the Reed Bank, to leave.[17] The survey ship had been chartered by FEP, a UK-based oil and gas company, which had been awarded a contract by the government of the Philippines to conduct seismic studies in the Sampaguita gas field. The Philippines lodged a protest against the Chinese action. In May and June 2011, Chinese vessels were spotted in the area near Bombay Shoal, Reed Bank and Amy Douglas Bank, reportedly unloading building materials, erecting posts, installing plastic buoys, and placing markers on these low tide elevations and underwater features. These are shallow waters but it was also reported that China planned to install a new advanced deep sea oil rig.[18] In response to the Chinese drilling plan, Lt. Gen. Juancho Sabban, the chief of the Philippines' Western Command, asked Filipino fishermen to be ready to use their boats to block the operation of the Chinese mega oil rig.[19] On 4 July 2011, the Chinese Embassy delivered a protest to the government of the Philippines after Manila invited foreign companies to bid for the right to explore oil and gas in 15 areas northwest of Palawan, claiming that the areas fall under China's "indisputable sovereignty".[20]

---

16 *Ibid.*

17 Ian Storey, "China and the Philippines: Implications of the Reed Bank Incident", 11(8) *China Brief*, 6 May 2011, at 6–8, available at <http://www.jamestown.org/single/?tx_ttnews%5Btt_news%5D=37902&tx_ttnews%5BbackPid%5D=517#.U3yuT84U_3>.

18 Carlyle A. Thayer, "Security Cooperation in the South China Sea: An Assessment of Recent Trends", paper presented at the First Manila Conference on the South China Sea: "The South China Sea: Toward a Regional of Peace, Cooperation, and Progress", 5–6 July 2011, Dusit Thani Hotel, Makati City, the Philippines, at 16–17. See also Michaela P. del Callar and Mario J. Mallari, "RP gov't protests China's planned oil rig, constructions in Reeds, Spratlys", *The Daily Tribune*, 2 June 2011, available at <http://www.tribuneonline.org/headlines/20110602hed4.html>.

19 Andrew Higgins, "In South China Sea, a dispute over energy", *The Washington Post*, 18 September 2011, available at <http://www.washingtonpost.com/world/asia-pacific/in-south-china-sea-a-dispute-over-energy/2011/09/07/gIQA0PrQaK_story.html>.

20 "Manila rejects new Chinese claim to territory just 50 nm away from Philippine province", *The Washington Post*, 14 November 2011, available at <http://www.

It is against this background that the Philippines began to consider the idea of submitting its dispute with China over entitlements in the SCS to adjudication in July 2011.[21] Assumingly this idea was further floated in April 2012 when tensions in the SCS flared up after the Philippines dispatched a warship to detain fishing vessels from China in the waters near the disputed Scarborough Shoal.[22] In a *Note verbale*, sent by the Department of Foreign Affairs of the Philippines to the Chinese Embassy in Manila on 26 April 2012, the Philippines formally invited China to submit their dispute to the International Tribunal for the Law of the Sea ("ITLOS") or another dispute settlement mechanism under UNCLOS.[23] China responded to the Philippines' invitation on the same day, stating that the Scarborough Shoal is the inherent territory of China and it is not a problem for international arbitration.[24] On 27 April 2012, the Chinese Foreign Ministry Spokesperson reiterated Beijing's position, adding: "Just imagine what kind of world it will be if one country can refer other countries' territory to international arbitration at will".[25] The next day, on 28 April 2012, the Director-General of the Department of Boundary and Ocean Affairs of the Chinese Foreign Ministry summoned the Philippine *charge d'affaires* "to lodge solemn representations on the intention of the Philippines to bring the dispute over the territorial sovereignty of Huangyan Island [Scarborough Shoal] to international arbitration".[26]

---

washingtonpost.com/world/asia-pacific/manila-rejects-new-chinese-claim-to-territory-just-50-miles-away-from-philippine-province/2011/11/14/gIQAv3lmJN_print.html>.

21 See Stefan Talmon, "The South China Sea Arbitration: Is There a Case to Answer?" in Stefan Talmon and Bing Bing Jia (eds), *The South China Sea Arbitration: A Chinese Perspective* (Oxford: Hart Publishing, 2014), p. 71.

22 Philippine Warship, "Chinese Boats in Standoff Near Shoal", *Taipei Times*, 12 April 2012, available at <http://www.taipeitimes.com/News/front/archives/2012/04/12/2003530121>.

23 *Note Verbale* from the Department of Foreign Affairs of the Philippines to the Embassy of the People's Republic of China in Manila, No. 12-1137 (26 April 2012).

24 Ministry of Foreign Affairs of the People's Republic of China, "Foreign Ministry Spokesperson Liu Weimin's Regular Press Conference on April 26, 2012", available at <http://www.fmprc.gov.cn/mfa_eng/xwfw_665399/s2510_665401/2511_665403/t928343.shtml>.

25 Ministry of Foreign Affairs of the People's Republic of China, "Foreign Ministry Spokesperson Liu Weimin's Regular Press Conference on April 27, 2012", available at <http://www.fmprc.gov.cn/mfa_eng/xwfw_665399/s2510_665401/2511_665403/t928330.shtml> and *Foreign Ministry Spokesperson Hong Lei's Regular Press Conference on May 8, 2012*, available at <http://www.fmprc.gov.cn/mfa_eng/xwfw_665399/s2510_665401/2511_665403/t930782.shtml>.

26 Consulate-General of the People's Republic of China in San Francisco, "The MFA Department of Boundary and Ocean Affairs Lodges Representations to the Philippines on the Intention of the Philippines to Bring the Dispute over Huangyan Island Territorial Sovereignty to International Arbitration", 29 April 2012 <http://www.chinaconsulatesf.org/eng/zgxw/t928669.htm>.

Commencement of Proceedings

On 22 January 2013, the government of the Philippines invoked its rights under Section 2 of Part XV of UNCLOS to seek a resolution of the disputes with China over maritime claims and entitlements in the SCS by initiating arbitral proceedings in accordance with Article 287 and Annex VII to the Convention.[27] A Notification and Statement of Claim were attached to a *Note verbale* that was handed to the Chinese Ambassador in Manila on the same day.[28]

In the Statement of Claim, the Philippines argues that China's nine-dash line claim is contrary to UNCLOS and thus unlawful. In addition, the Philippines states that within the maritime area encompassed by the nine-dash line, China has also laid claim to, occupied and built structures on certain submerged banks, reefs and LTEs that do not qualify as islands under UNCLOS, but are parts of the Philippine continental shelf, or the international seabed. Moreover, China has occupied certain small, uninhabitable coral projections that are barely above water at high tide, and which are "rocks" under Article 121(3) of UNCLOS. Furthermore, as argued by the Philippines, China has interfered with the lawful exercise by the Philippines of its rights within its legitimate maritime zones, as well as to the geological features and their surrounding waters. At the same time, taking note of China's Declaration made on 25 August 2006 in accordance with Articles 298 and Article 310 of UNCLOS regarding optional exceptions to the compulsory proceedings that are provided for in the Convention, the Philippines avoided raising subjects or making claims that China has, by virtue of that Declaration, excluded from arbitral proceedings, in particular those issues relating to territorial sovereignty, maritime boundary delimitation, military, and law enforcement activities.[29]

---

27 Both China and the Philippines are parties to the Convention. China ratified UNCLOS on 7 June 1996 and the Philippines on 8 May 1984. Since the two countries have not accepted the same procedure for the settlement of their disputes, under Article 287, paragraph 5, the disputes "may be submitted only to arbitration in accordance with Annex VII", unless they otherwise agree. Arbitration is one of the four procedures provided for in Article 287 for the settlement of disputes concerning the interpretation or application of the Convention. The other three procedures are: (1) the International Tribunal for the Law of the Sea established in accordance with Annex VI of the Convention; (2) the International Court of Justice; and (3) a special arbitral tribunal constituted in accordance with Annex VIII for one of more of the categories of disputes specified therein. An arbitral tribunal is constituted by the parties to the dispute in accordance with Annex VII (Arbitration) to the Convention.

28 See Department of Foreign Affairs, the Republic of the Philippines, "SFA Statement on the UNCLOS Arbitral Proceeding against China", available at <https://www.dfa.gov.ph/index.php/2013-06-27-21-50-36/unclos>. The *Note Verbale*, Notification and Statement of Claim on West Philippine Sea are available at the same address.

29 Department of Foreign Affairs, the Republic of the Philippines, "SFA Statement on the UNCLOS Arbitral Proceedings against China" (22 January 2013), available at <https://www.dfa.gov.ph/index.php/2013-06-27-21-50-36/unclos>.

In the Statement, the Philippines asks the Arbitral Tribunal to issue an Award that, among other thing, "Declares that China's maritime claims in the SCS based on its so-called nine-dash line are contrary to UNCLOS and invalid".[30] The Philippines also asserts that the Arbitral Tribunal has jurisdiction to hear and make an award based on its Notification and Statement of Claim because the dispute is about the interpretation and application by States Parties of their obligations under the UNCLOS. Article 287(1) of UNCLOS provides that "settlement of disputes concerning the interpretation and application of this Convention" may be referred by the Parties for resolution under Part XV of UNCLOS. The Philippines further asserts that the claim is well founded in fact and law based on the Notification and Statement of Claims and supplementary documents that will be submitted in the course of the arbitral proceedings.[31]

According to Article 3(a) of Annex VII to the Convention, the arbitral tribunal should, unless the parties agree otherwise, consist of five members. In its Notification and Statement of Claim, the Philippines, pursuant to Article 3(b) of Annex VII, appointed ITLOS Judge Rüdiger Wolfrum (Germany) as arbitrator on behalf of the Philippines. On 22 March 2013, acting in accordance with Article 3(c) of Annex VII, Shunji Yanai (Japan), the ITLOS President, appointed ITLOS Judge Stanislaw Pawlak (Poland) as arbitrator on behalf of China. This was followed by appointment of the remaining three members of the Tribunal by President Yanai on 23 April 2013, namely, ITLOS Judge Jean-Pierre Cot (France) and Professor Alfred Soons (of the Netherland) as arbitrators, and Ambassador Christopher Pinto (Sri Lanka) as arbitrator and President of the Tribunal. In May 2013, Ambassador Pinto withdrew from the Tribunal. As a result, President Yanai appointed former ITLOS Judge Thomas Mensah (Ghana) to replace Pinto as arbitrator and President of the Tribunal on 21 June 2013.[32]

The first meeting of the Members of the Arbitral Tribunal was held on 11 July 2013 at the Peace Palace in The Hague. It was decided that the Permanent Court of Arbitration (hereinafter "PCA") will serve as the Registry for the arbitral proceedings. On 27 August 2013, in its first Procedural Order, the Arbitral Tribunal adopted the Rules of Procedure and fixed 30 March 2014 as the date on which the Philippines should submit its Memorial. The Tribunal instructed the Philippines to address fully all issues, including matters relating to the Tribunal's jurisdiction, the admissibility of the Philippines' claims, as well as the merits of the dispute.[33] On 30 March 2014, the Philippines submitted its Memorial to the Arbitral Tribunal. On 3

30 Notification and Statement of Claim, *supra* note 2, para. 41, at 17–18.

31 *Ibid.*

32 For the history of the appointment, visit the web site of the Permanent Court of Arbitration, available at <http://www.pca-cpa.org/showpage.asp?pag_id=1532>.

33 See PCA Press Release, Arbitration between the Republic of the Philippines and the People's Republic of China: Arbitral Tribunal Establishes Rules of Procedure and Initial Timetable, The Hague, 27 August 2013, available at <http://www.pca-cpa.org/shownews.asp?ac=view&pag_id=1261&nws_id=384>.

June 2014, the Arbitral Tribunal adopted Procedural Order No. 2, in which it set 15 December 2014 as the date for China to submit its Counter-Memorial responding to the Philippines' Memorial.[34] As China had not filed its Counter-Memorial, on 16 December 2014, the Arbitral Tribunal issued its Procedural Order No. 3, in which it requests the Philippines to submit further written argument pursuant to Article 25(2) of the Rules of Procedure to address specific issues relating to both the jurisdiction of the Arbitral Tribunal and to the merits of the Parties' dispute.[35] The Tribunal set 15 March 2015 as the deadline for the Philippines to file a supplemental written submission addressing the Arbitral Tribunal's request. It also set 16 June 2015 as the deadline for China to provide any comments in response to the supplemental written submission of the Philippines.[36]

Despite of China's absence, under Article 9 of Annex VII to the Convention and Article 25 of "Rules of Procedure" in this case, the five members of the Arbitral Tribunal, including President of the Tribunal, are required to satisfy themselves that the Philippines' claims are well-grounded in fact and law. In that regard, the arbitrators have many means at their disposal to meet the requirements: (1) they can access publicly available maps and charts, and scholarly studies of the insular features included in the Memorial submitted by the Philippines; (2) they can hire technical experts to advise them; and (3) they can review China's laws, decrees, statements, and explanations about its maritime claims in the SCS.[37]

The Chinese Response to the Philippines' Request for Arbitration

In response to the Philippines' request for arbitration, on 19 February 2013, Chinese Ambassador to the Philippines presented a *Note verbale* to the Philippine Department of Foreign Affairs, in which China returned the notification and accompanying statement of claim. In addition, China made it clear that it would not accept international proceedings over the SCS dispute.[38] On the same day, Chinese Foreign Ministry spokesman Hong Lei stated that Manila's action had violated the consensus that was reached in the Declaration on the Conduct

---

34 Press Release, Arbitration between the Republic of the Philippines and the People's Republic of China, The Hague, 3 June 2014, available at <http://www.pca-cpa.org/showpage.asp?pag_id=1529>.

35 Arbitration between the Republic of the Philippines and the People's Republic of China, Permanent Court of Arbitration, Third Press Release, 17 December 2014, available at <http://www.pca-cpa.org/showpage.asp?pag_id=1529>.

36 *Ibid.*

37 *Ibid.*

38 See *Note verbale* from the Embassy of the People's Republic of China in Manila to the Department of Foreign Affairs of the Republic of the Philippines, No. (13) PG-039 (19 February 2013), at 1 and Pia Lee-Brago, "China rejects UN arbitration on West Phl Sea", *The Philippine Star*, 20 February 2013, available at <http://www.philstar.com/headlines/2013/02/20/910910/china-rejects-un-arbitration-west-phl-sea>.

of Parties in the South China Sea (hereinafter "DOC"),[39] adding that there are factual and legal mistakes and baseless accusations against China in the statement and related notice.[40] Hong pointed out that China is committed to addressing the dispute through bilateral talks. He also mentioned the consensus that was reached by China and ASEAN member states when they signed the DOC in November 2002, that is, disputes should be solved through talks between the nations directly involved.[41] In a *Note verbale* addressed to the PCA on 1 August 2013, China reiterated its position that it does not accept the arbitration filed by the Philippines and stated that it was not participating in the arbitral proceedings.[42]

On 30 March 2014, in response to the submission of the Memorial by the Philippines to the Arbitral Tribunal, Chinese Foreign Ministry spokesman Hong Lei stated at a regular press briefing:

> China has stated time and again that it does not accept the Philippines' submission of disputes with China in the South China Sea for international arbitration. This position stays unchanged. On issues concerning disputes over sovereignty of islands and reefs and delimitation of maritime boundaries, China has all along adhered to settling disputes through direct negotiations with countries concerned. This position is clearly stated in the Declaration on the Conduct of Parties in the South China Sea (DOC) jointly signed by China and ASEAN countries. It is also agreed between China and the Philippines in a series of bilateral documents. The Philippines is obliged to honor its own commitment.
>
> No matter how the Philippine memorial is packaged, the direct cause of the dispute between China and the Philippines is the latter's illegal occupation of some of China's islands and reefs in the South China Sea. At the heart of the matter are the disputes between the two sides on the sovereignty over islands and reefs, and delimitation of maritime boundaries. Yet disputes such as these have already been excluded from arbitration procedures through a declaration made by China in 2006 pursuant to the UN Convention on the Law of the Sea (UNCLOS). In this context, China's rejection of the Philippines' submission for arbitration is solidly based on international law, and China's lawful rights as a party to UNCLOS should be truly respected.

39 The text of the Declaration is available in the web site of ASEAN, available at <http://www.asean.org/asean/external-relations/china/item/declaration-on-the-conduct-of-parties-in-the-south-china-sea>.

40 "Chinese Spokesperson Hong Lei's remarks on China returned the Philippines' Notification on the submission of South China Sea issue to international Arbitration", in the web site of Embassy of the People's Republic of China in the Republic of the Philippines, 19 February 2013, available at <http://ph.china-embassy.org/eng/zt/nhwt/t1014903.htm>.

41 *Ibid.*

42 See PCA Press Release, *Arbitration between the Republic of the Philippines and the People's Republic of China: Arbitral Tribunal Establishes Rules of Procedure and Initial Timetable*, The Hague, 27 August 2013, available at <http://www.pca-cpa.org/shownews.asp?ac=view&pag_id=1261&nws_id=384>.

> China urges the Philippines to comprehensively and effectively implement the consensus repeatedly reaffirmed between the two sides and the DOC, and return to the right track of settling the disputes through bilateral negotiations.[43]

Following the submission of its Memorial to the Tribunal, the Chinese Foreign Ministry has continuously made its position on the arbitration case clear, that is, non-acceptance and non-participation. On 1 April 2014, Hong Lei, the Chinese Foreign Ministry Spokesperson, stated that China's position on non-acceptance of and non-participation in the arbitration filed by the Philippines is "clear-cut and fully supported by international law".[44] On the same day, Mr. Sun Xiangyang, *Charge d'Affaires a.i.* of the Chinese Embassy in Manila held a press conference and briefed the media on the Chinese position on the Philippines' submission of the Memorial. He gave the following reasons to explain why China does not accept the arbitration: (1) China is committed to resolving its disputes with the Philippines through bilateral negotiations; (2) China's refusal to accept the arbitration is an exercise of its right under international law; and (3) a resort to arbitration does not meet people's expectations for friendship in both China and the Philippines.[45]

On 3 April 2014, the Chinese Embassy in Manila issued a lengthy document that reiterated the three reasons for China's non-acceptance of and non-participation in the Philippines-initiated arbitration and elaborated on China's basic position on the SCS issue. He said that the Philippines' initiation of and push for international arbitration has undermined China-Philippines relations. In addition, he said, it is China's sincere wish that the disputes between China and the Philippines will be settled through bilateral negotiations. Moreover, he addressed in detail the nature of China-Philippines disputes in the SCS and the consensus reached between the two countries on the approach to deal with the SCS issue. Furthermore, he discussed the issue of Scarborough Shoal, Second Thomas Shoal, freedom and safety of navigation, and China's commitment to make the SCS a sea of peace, friendship and co-operation.[46]

---

43 Remarks by Foreign Ministry Spokesperson Hong Lei on the Philippines' Submission of a Memorial to the Arbitral Tribunal in Relation to Disputes with China in the South China Sea, Foreign Affairs, 31 March 2014, available at <http://www.fmprc.gov.cn/mfa_eng/xwfw_665399/s2510_665401/2535_665405/t1142356.shtml>.

44 Ministry of Foreign Affairs of the People's Republic of China, "Foreign Ministry Spokesperson Hong Lei's Regular Press Conference on March 31, 2014", available at <http://www.fmprc.gov.cn/mfa_eng/xwfw_665399/s2510_665401/2511_665403/t1142811.shtml>.

45 Embassy of the People's Republic of China in the Republic of the Philippines, *Press Conference By Chinese Embassy On Philippines' Submission of a Memorial to the Arbitral Tribunal on disputes of the South China Sea with China*, 1 April 2014, available at <http://ph.china-embassy.org/eng/xwfb/t1143166.htm>.

46 Embassy of the People's Republic of China in the Republic of the Philippines, Zhang Hua, Spokesperson, *China's Position on the Territorial Disputes in the South China Sea between China and the Philippines*, 3 April 2014, available at <http://ph.china-embassy.org/eng/xwfb/t1143881.htm>.

On 21 May 2014, China sent a *Note verbale* to the Permanent Court of Arbitration, in which it reiterated China's position that it "does not accept the arbitration initiated by the Philippines" and this *Note verbale* "shall not be regarded as China's acceptance of or participation in the proceedings".[47] On 7 December 2014, the Chinese Government reiterated that "it will neither accept nor participate in the arbitration unilaterally initiated by the Philippines" in its "Position Paper of the Government of the People's Republic of China on the Matter of Jurisdiction in the South China Sea Arbitration Initiated by the Republic of the Philippines".[48] Via communications to the Registry, the Chinese government sent copies of the Position Paper to members of the arbitral tribunal, arguing that the arbitral tribunal established at the request of the Philippines does not have jurisdiction over the arbitration case. At the same time, the Chinese government made it clear that the forwarding of the aforementioned Position Paper to the tribunal shall not be regarded as China's acceptance of or its participation in this arbitration case.[49]

Geographical Facts about the Features Mentioned in the Philippines' Statement of Claim

There are eight geographical features mentioned in the Philippines' Statement of Claim, namely: (A) Scarborough Shoal; (B) Mischief Reef; (C) McKennan Reef; (D) Gaven Reef; (E) Subi Reef; (F) Johnson Reef; (G) Cuarteron Reef; and (H) Fiery Cross Reef (see Table 10.1). Geographical information about these features is provided below.

A. Scarborough Shoal[50]

This geographical feature (*Huangyan Dao* or *Minzhu Jiao* in Chinese, Scarborough Shoal or Scarborough Reef in English, and known as Panatag Shoal or Bajo de Masinloc in the Philippines) lies between Macclesfield Bank and Luzon of the Philippines. The shoal is approximately 198 km from west of Subic Bay, Philippines. The nearest landmass is Palauig, Zambales, on Luzon Islands in the

47 *Arbitration between the Republic of the Philippines and the People's Republic of China,* PRESS RELEASE, PCA, The Hague, 3 June 2014, available at <http://www.pca-cpa.org/showpage.asp?pag_id=1529>.

48 Position Paper of the Government of the People's Republic of China on the Matter of Jurisdiction in the South China Sea Arbitration Initiated by the Republic of the Philippines, Ministry of Foreign Affairs of the People's Republic of China, 7 December 2014, available at <http://www.fmprc.gov.cn/mfa_eng/zxxx_662805/t1217147.shtml>, para. 1.

49 *Ibid.*, para. 2.

50 See WIKIPEDIA, available at <http://en.wikipedia.org/wiki/Scarborough_Shoal> accessed 2 June 2014.

Philippines, 220 km due east. It is a 55 km chain of reefs and rocks with an area of 150 km^2 and a lagoon.[51] All, except for six rocks, are submerged at high tide. In February 1999, Taiwan used the normal baseline method to draw baselines surrounding Scarborough Shoal.[52] In March 2009, the Philippines enacted An Act to Amend Certain Provisions of Republic Act No. 3046, as Amended by Republic Act of 5446, to Define the Archipelagic Baseline of the Philippines and For Other Purposes, in which, under Section 2, among others, the baseline in Scarborough Shoal should be determined according to "Regime of Islands" and as belong to the Republic of the Philippines consistent with UNCLOS.[53] China, the Philippines and Taiwan claim sovereignty over Scarborough. Tensions between Beijing and Manila escalated in April 2012 when the government of the Philippines dispatched a warship to detain fishing vessels from China in the waters near Scarborough Shoal.[54] Since then, Scarborough Shoal has been under the effective control of China.

B. Mischief Reef[55]

Mischief Reef, also known as Meiji Jiao in China and Panganiban Reef in the Philippines, is a coral reef in the Spratly Islands in the SCS, located 250 kilometers west of the coast of Palawan. This feature, occupied and controlled by China, but also claimed by Philippines and Vietnam, is a LTE. China began building structures on Mischief Reef in 1995. Since 1998, China has constructed more facilities on top of the reef, which include a number of buildings built on concrete platforms, quays, a greenhouse, and weather and telecommunications equipment.

---

51 The lagoon has an area of 130 km^2 and a depth of 15 m.

52 The First Part of the Baselines of the Territorial Sea of the Republic of China, Decree No. Tai 88 Nei Tze #06161, 5 EXECUTIVE YUAN GAZETTE, no. 6 (10 February 1999), at 36–7, available at <http://www.land.moi.gov.tw/pda/content.asp?cid=91&mcid=1284> (in Chinese) See also LIMITS IN THE SEA No. 127, Taiwan's Maritime Claims, U.S. Department of State, Bureau of Oceans and International Environmental and Scientific Affairs, available at <http://www.state.gov/documents/organization/57674.pdf>, at 25–6 .

53 Republic Act No. 9522, 10 March 2009, An Act to Amend Certain Provisions of Republic Act No. 3046, As Amended by Republic Act No. 5446, To Define the Archipelagic Baseline of the Philippines and for Other Purposes, available at <http://www.chanrobles.com/republicacts/republicactno9522.php#.U4wcg84U_3g>.

54 "Philippine Warship, Chinese Boats in Standoff Near Shoal", *Taipei Times* (12 April 2014), available at <http://www.taipeitimes.com/News/front/archives/2012/04/12/2003530121>.

55 For more information, visit WIKIPEDIA, available at <http://en.wikipedia.org/wiki/Mischief_Reef>.

Table 10.1 The Features located in the SCS and mentioned by the Philippines in the Notification and Statement of Claim 22 January 2013

	Location	Size	**Distance from coast of mainland or island**	**Geological nature**	**Occupation or effective control**	**Jurisdictional issue**
Scarborough Shoal	15°11′N 117°46′E	Total area, including an inner lagoon, is 150 km^2	325 nm from Woody Island of the Paracel Islands	Rocks or Islands? (At high tide, six features are above water)	China	Possible overlapping EEZ and continental shelf
Mischief Reef	09°55′00"N 115°32′00"E	Total area including an inner lagoon is 46 km^2	250 Km west of Palawan	LTE	China	Possible overlapping EEZ and continental shelf
McKennan Reef	09°55′00"N 114°29′00"E	Total area is 2.5 km^2	182 nm from Palawan	LTE	China	Possible overlapping EEZ and continental shelf
Gaven Reef	10°12′30"N 114°13′00"E	Total area is 2 km^2	200 nm from Palawan	LTE	China	Possible overlapping EEZ and continental shelf
Subi Reef	10°55′30"N 114°05′00"E	Total area is 16.1 km^2	232 nm from Palawan	LTE	China	Possible overlapping EEZ and continental shelf
Johnson Reef	09°42′40"N 114°16′45"E	n/a	188 nm from Palawan	Rocks or Islands?	China	Possible overlapping EEZ and continental shelf
Cuarteron Reef	08°51′30"N 112°50′00"E	Total area is 7.6 km^2	248 nm from Palawan	Rocks or Islands?	China	Possible overlapping EEZ and continental shelf
Fiery Cross Reef	09°38′00"N 112°57′00"E	Submerged at high tide, but one rock at its southwest end about the size of a table	257 nm from Palawan	Rocks or Islands?	China	Possible overlapping EEZ and continental shelf

Source: Based on the information provided for in Wikipedia and Baidu.

C. McKennan Reef[56]

This reef, known in the Philippines as Chigua Reef and in China as Ximen Jiao, lies 182 nm from the nearest point on Palawan and 567 nm from the nearest point on Hainan. McKennan Reef is seven nm from Sin Cowe Island, which is the seventh largest of islands in the Spratly archipelago. China gained effective control of this reef in 1988. According to David Hancox and Victor Prescott, McKennan Reef has an area of about 2.5km^2.[57] It is located to the west of Dongmen Jiao (Hughes Reef) and considered as a LTE. In 1988, China also gained control of Hughes Reef.[58]

D. Gaven Reef[59]

Gaven Reef, known in China as Nanxun Jiao and Burgos in the Philippines, is one of the reefs in the Tizard Bank of the Spratly Islands in the SCS. It is located 544 nm from the nearest point in China and 200 nm from the nearest point on Palawan. China gained control this feature in 1988.[60] Gaven Reef is approximately six nm from Namyit (Hongxiu Dao), the eleventh largest island of the Spratly archipelago occupied by Vietnam.

E. Subi Reef[61]

Subi Reef, known in the Philippines as Zamora Reef and in China as Zhubi Jiao, is a reef in the Spratly Islands of the SCS located 232 nm from the nearest point on Palawan and 502 nm from the nearest point in mainland China. It is about 16 nm southwest of Philippine-occupied Thitu Island. The reef dries at low-tide, but is covered by water at high tide. In 1988, China gained control of Subi Reef.[62] It currently falls under the jurisdiction of Sansha city, Hainan province, China.

---

56 For more information, visit WIKIMAPIA, available at <http://wikimapia.org/9641420/McKennan-Reef> and <http://www.baike.com/wiki/%E8%A5%BF%E9%97%A8%E7%A4%81> (in Chinese)

57 David Hancox and Victor Prescott, "A Geographical Description of the Spratly Islands and an Account of Hydrographic Surveys Amongst Those Islands", (1995) 1(6) *IBRU Maritime Briefing*1–88 at p. 11.

58 Pan Shiying, "The Nansha Islands: A Chinese Point of View", *Window* (3 September 1993), at 29.

59 For more information, visit WIKIPEDIA, available at <http://en.wikipedia.org/wiki/Gaven_Reefs>.

60 Pan Shiying, supra note 58.

61 For more information, visit WIKIPEDIA, available at <http://en.wikipedia.org/wiki/Subi_Reef>.

62 Pan Shiying, *supra* note 58.

F. Johnson Reef[63]

Johnson Reef, also known as Chigua Jiao in China and Mabini reef in the Philippines, is a reef in the Spratly Islands in the SCS controlled by China. It was the site of the Johnson Reef Skirmish in 1988, fought by China and Vietnam which resulted in more than 70 Vietnamese deaths, two Vietnamese boats being sunk and the Chinese conquering the reef. This reef lies 188 nm from the nearest point on Palawan and 567 nm from the nearest point on Hainan Island of China. Johnson Reef is located approximately 92 nm due west of Second Thomas Shoal and 25 nm due south of Gaven Reef. The reef is submerged at high tide, but according to the U.S. gazetteer, it is visible at high tide.[64]

G. Cuarteron Reef[65]

Cuarteron Reef, known in China as Huayang Jiao and Calderon Reef in the Philippines, is a reef at the east end of the London Reefs in the Spratly Islands of the SCS. It is located 248 nm from the nearest point on Palawan and 585 nm from the nearest point on Hainan Island of China. China gained control of the reef in 1988. It has a supply platform and a reef fortress. The supply platform has anti-aircraft guns, naval guns, search radars and radio communications equipment. At least one rock is approximately 1 to 2 meters above sea level at high tide.

H. Fiery Cross Reef[66]

Fiery Cross Reef, also known as Yongshu Jiao in China and Kagitingan Reef in the Philippines, is a group of three reefs in the Spratly Islands in the SCS. It is located approximately 40 nm due north of Cuarteron Reef and 257 nm from the nearest point on Palawan and 547 nm from Hainan Island. China gained control of the reef in 1988 when a "marine observation station" was built in accordance with a resolution adopted by the International Oceanographic Commission under UNESCO in 1987. Currently the reef has three two-story buildings and one three-story building. Two lighthouses, a helipad and a pier were also built.

---

63 For more information, visit WIKIPEDIA, available at <http://en.wikipedia.org/wiki/Johnson_South_Reef>.

64 South China Sea, Map and Gazetteer, U.S. Government, 803425AI (G02257) 1–10, January 2010. The map and gazetteer are available online at the website of the Centre for International Law, National University of Singapore, available at <http://cil.nus.edu.sg/wp/wp-content/uploads/2011/06/75967_South-China-Sea-1.pdf> and <http://cil.nus.edu.sg/wp/wp-content/uploads/2011/06/75967_gazetteer.pdf>.

65 For more information, visit WIKIPEDIA, available at <http://en.wikipedia.org/wiki/Cuarteron_Reef>.

66 For more information, visit WIKIPEDIA, available at <http://en.wikipedia.org/wiki/Fiery_Cross_Reef>.

Although Itu Aba Island, Thitu Island and West York Island are not mentioned in the Philippines' Statement of Claim, geographical facts about these three land features should also be included for the purpose of discussion (See Table 10.2).

I. Itu Aba Island[67]

Itu Aba, known in China as Taiping Dao and Ligao in the Philippines, is the largest of the Spratly Islands in the SCS, with a total land area of 41.3 hectares. Itu Aba, disputed by China, Taiwan, Vietnam, and the Philippines, is controlled by Taiwan. Administratively it is under the jurisdiction of Kaohsiung City. The distance from Taiwan to the island is about 1,600 km. There is a 1,198 meter-long runway that was completed in late 2007. In February 2008, Taiwan's president landed on the island in an air force C-130 cargo plane to inaugurate the airstrip. At present, more than 200 Coast Guard personnel and a number of soldiers from Taiwan's Navy and Air Force are stationed on the island. Taiwan's Navy and Coast Guard send vessels regularly to the islands. Cargo vessels of private shipping companies also sail to Itu Aba once or two times a month to supply the island's daily needs. In 2007, the City Government of Kaohsiung, in accordance with Article 45 of Taiwan's Fisheries Law, promulgated the establishment of a sea turtle protected area in Itu Aba. In March 2008, then presidential candidate Ma Ying-jeou proposed in his ocean policy to establish a marine peace park in Itu Aba. Itu Aba is the largest island and the only island with fresh water in the Spratly archipelago, and has the capacity to sustain human habitation and economic life of its own. Accordingly, it can be established that it is an island and thus can generate a 200 nm EEZ and a continental shelf.

J. Thitu Island[68]

Thitu Island, known as Zongye Dao in China and Pagasa in the Philippines, is the second largest island in the Spratly archipelago and is one of the nine islands occupied by the Philippines in the SCS. Its covers approximately 37.2 hectares and located about 480 km west of Palawan. It has a 1.4 km unpaved airstrip (named Rancudo Airstrip) which serves both military and commercial air transportation needs. The Philippine Air Force regularly sends fighter jets from Palawan to make reconnaissance missions in Philippine-controlled regions in the Spratly archipelago. The presence of the airstrip on Thitu Island makes such reconnaissance missions easier. There is also a port, called Loneliness Bay. Around 30–50 Filipino soldiers are stationed on the island, together with about 300 civilian people at its height, and nowadays about 55. The Philippine navy vessel sails to Thitu Island once a

---

67 For more information, visit WIKIPEDIA, available at <http://en.wikipedia.org/wiki/Taiping_Island>.

68 For more information, visit WIKIPEDIA, available at <http://en.wikipedia.org/wiki/Thitu_Island>.

Table 10.2 The Three Largest Land Features of the Spratly Archipelago in the SCS

	Location	Size	**Distance from coast of mainland or island**	**Geological nature**	**Occupation or effective control**	**Jurisdictional issue**
Itu Aba Island	10°23′00″N 114°21′30″E	Total land area 0.49 km^2	201 nm from Palawan	Island	Taiwan	Possible overlapping EEZ and continental shelf
Thitu Island	11°03′15″N 114°17′00″E	Total land area 0.33 km^2	480 km from Palawan	Island	Philippines	Possible overlapping EEZ and continental shelf
West York Island	11°05′30″N 115°01′30″E	Total land area 0.21 km^2	196 nm from Palawan	Island	Philippines	Possible overlapping EEZ and continental shelf

Source: Based on the information provided for in Wikipedia and Baidu.

month to supply the island's daily needs. The island has 20 houses, a community center, a clinic, an eight floor watch tower, desalination plant, several electricity generators, a weather station, and a mobile launch tower.

The island is claimed by China, Vietnam, Taiwan, and the Philippines. In response to the visit of Taiwan's President Chen Shui Bian to the disputed Taipin Dao (Itu Aba) in the Spratly Islands by C-130 cargo plane in February 2008, the Philippines began to renovate Pagasa airstrip in March 2008 which was followed by the visit of Philippine Air Force Chief Lt Gen Pedrito S. Cadungog in May 2008. He and his staff conducted a visual inspection of the repairs and improvements to the Rancudo Airstrip and other minor facilities on the island. In addition, it was reported that the Philippines intended to develop Thitu Island as a tourist destination. Based on available information, it appears that Thitu Island can sustain human habitation and an economic life of its own and therefore pass the tests contained in Article 121(3) of UNCLOS. Accordingly whichever country establishes sovereignty over the island can use it as a base point from which a 200 nm EEZ and a continental shelf are claimed.

K. West York Island[69]

West York Island, known in the Philippines as Likas and in China Xiyue Dao, is the third largest island of the Spratly Islands chain in the SCS, with an area of 18.6 hectares. It is the second largest island among the Philippine-occupied Spratly Islands. It is located 47 nm northeast of Thitu Island. Several Filipino soldiers are stationed here. This island is also claimed by China, Taiwan and Vietnam.

The Philippines' Arguments Concerning the Features in Question

The Philippines argues that Mischief Reef, McKennan Reef, Gaven Reef and Subi Reef are not islands under Article 121 of the Convention. These features, far remote from China's territorial sea, EEZ and continental shelf, are all at best LTEs that are part of another state's continental shelf, or the international seabed. The Philippines claims that Mischief Reef, located approximately 130 nm west of the Philippine island of Palawan, is a submerged bank and is part of the Philippines' continental shelf. McKennan Reef, located approximately 180 nm from Palawan, is a LTE and is also part of its continental shelf. In addition, the surrounding waters of Mischief Reef and McKennan Reef are within the Philippines' EEZ. Moreover, Gaven Reef, located approximately 205 nm northwest of Palawan and Subi Reef, located approximately 230 nm west of Palawan, are also LTEs.[70]

69 For more information, visit WIKIPEDIA, available at <http://en.wikipedia.org/wiki/West_York_Island>.

70 Notification and Statement of Claim, *supra* note 2, para. 14–19, at 6–8.

The Philippines argues that Scarborough Shoal, Johnson Reef, Cuarteron Reef and Fiery Cross Reef are "rocks" within the meaning of Article 121(3) of the Convention. The six small rocks, collectively known as Scarborough Shoal, are located approximately 120 nm west of the Philippine island of Luzon, and protrude above sea level within the Philippines' EEZ. None of them is more than 3 meters above level at high tide and none measures more than a few meters in width. None of these "rocks", which lie in close proximity to one another, generates entitlement to more than a 12 nm territorial sea.[71]

The Philippines also argues that Johnson Reef, Cuarteron Reef and Fiery Cross Reef are submerged reefs with no more than a few rocks protruding above sea level at high tide. Johnson Reef has a few rocky protrusions rising above water at high tide. Cuarteron Reef is a collection of coral rocks reaching no higher than 1.5 meters. Fiery Cross Reef consists of a submerged bank with protruding rocks no more than a meter above sea level high tide. The Philippines considers these insular features "rocks" under Article 121(3) of UNCLOS and therefore cannot generate 200 nm EEZ or continental shelf.[72]

The Philippines' claims with regard to the legal nature and rights of the eight features located in the northern and southern sectors of the SCS raise an important question that is closely related to the Tribunal's jurisdiction over the case and admissibility of the claims made by the Philippines. In particular, it raises the question of whether or not the Philippines' claims are well founded in fact and law.

Applicable Law, Specifically UNCLOS

The Philippines' arguments with regard to legal status and rights of the features should be examined in accordance with the relevant provisions contained in the UNCLOS, in particular, Article 13 (LTEs), Article 60 (Artificial islands, installations and structures in the exclusive economic zone), and Article 121 (Regime of islands). In addition, other relevant provisions of the Convention include: Article 56 (Rights, jurisdiction and duties of the coastal state in the exclusive economic zone); Article 74 (Delimitation of the exclusive economic zone between states with opposite or adjacent coasts); Article 77 (Rights of the coastal state over the continental shelf); and Article 83 (Delimitation of the continental shelf between states with opposite or adjacent coasts). The interpretation and application of these provisions should be based on the geographical facts of the features as described previously.

If the six protruding features of Scarborough Shoal, as argued by the Philippines, are "rocks" within the meaning of Article 121(3) of UNCLOS because they "cannot sustain human habitation or economic life of their own", these features and Scarborough Shoal as a whole can generate entitlement to no more than a 12 nm territorial sea. In other words, they should have no EEZ or continental

71 *Ibid.*, para. 20, at 8.

72 *Ibid.*, para. 22–4, at 9–10.

shelf. If this claim is established, due to the fact that Scarborough Shoal is located within the EEZ that is established by the Philippines in accordance with Article 47 (Archipelagic baselines), Article 56 (Specific legal regime of the exclusive economic zone) and Article 57 (Rights, jurisdiction and duties of the coastal state in the exclusive economic zone), fishermen from the Philippines are allowed to fish in the water beyond 12 nm mile territorial sea that is measured from the baseline of Scarborough Shoal. However, as explained later, this claim has both factual and legal problems.

If Mischief Reef, Mckennan Reef, Gaven Reef and Subi Reef, as the Philippines argues, are LTEs and they are situated at a distance exceeding the breadth of the territorial sea that is measured from baseline of any land features in the Spratly archipelago, in accordance with Article 13 of UNCLOS, they should have no territorial sea of their own. Certainly they cannot generate an EEZ and a continental shelf. However, Article 60(1) of the Convention provides that in its EEZ, the coastal state "shall have the exclusive right to construct and to authorize and regulate the construction, operation and use of: (a) artificial islands; (b) installations and structures for the purposes provided for in Article 56 and other economic purposes; (c) installations and structures which may interfere with the exercise of the rights of the coastal State in the zone". In addition, under Article 60(2), the coastal state "shall have exclusive jurisdiction over such artificial islands, installations and structures, including jurisdiction with regard to customs, fiscal, health, safety and immigration laws and regulations". If Mischief Reef, McKennan Reef, Gaven Reef and Subi Reef are located within the EEZ claimed legally under UNCLOS by China or Taiwan, the construction, operation and use of artificial islands, installations and structures for the purposes provided for in Article 56 of the Convention and other economic purposes are allowed. This is also applicable to Johnson Reef, Cuarteron Reef and Fiery Cross Reef.

The interpretation or application of Articles 56, 57 and 60 of the UNCLOS to the eight features, namely Scarborough Shoal, Mischief Reef, Subi Reef, McKennan Reef, Gaven Reef, Johnson Reef, Cuarteron Reef and Fiery Cross Reef, are closely related to the interpretation or application of Article 121 of the Convention to Itu Aba Island, Thitu Island, and West York Island, the three largest land features in the Spratly archipelago. If these three features, as argued by the Philippines, "cannot sustain human habitation or economic life of their own", in accordance with Article 121(3), they cannot generate an EEZ or continental shelf, which, as a result, gives rise to the questions concerning legality of China's appropriation, occupation, and construction/operation/use of installations and structures on the eight features that are specified in the Philippines' Statement of Claim. If it is established that these three features can sustain human habitation or have economic life of their own, the Philippines' claims with regard to these features should be rejected.

Although the legal status of the three land features, namely, Itu Aba Island, Thitu Island, and West York Island, is the key for the Tribunal to consider if Chinese actions and activities that are conducted on the eight features and/or in the maritime zones that are allowed to generate, in particular with regard to a 200 nm EEZ, in accordance with relevant provisions of UNCLOS, the Philippines does not ask the Tribunal to consider the legal status and rights of these three land features in its Statement of Claim. But, according to a report by *Philippine Daily Inquirer*, there are 14 paragraphs discussing the legal status of Itu Aba Island in the Memorial submitted by the Philippines to the Tribunal on 30 March 2014.[73] In addition, on 16 March 2015, the Philippines submitted detailed responses and extensive additional information to the Tribunal. The submission consists of 12 volumes totaling over 3,000 pages. Volume I consists of 200 pages of written argument. Volume II consists of a 200-page Atlas containing detailed information about 49 islands, reefs and other features in the SCS.[74] Although the supplemental information, just like the Memorial submitted by the Philippines to the Tribunal on 30 March 2014, is kept confidential, it is believed that Itu Aba Island, Thitu Island and West York Island are included in the list of the 49 islands that are included in Volume II of the Philippines' supplemental Memorial. Accordingly it is likely that the Tribunal would touch upon the issues concerning legal status of Itu Aba Island and its right to generate a 200 nm EEZ or continental shelf.

Arguments against the Philippines' Claims

The claims made by the Philippines in its Statement of Claim with regard to the eight features – namely Scarborough Shoal, Mischief Reef, Subi Reef, McKennan Reef, Gaven Reef, Johnson Reef, Cuarteron Reef and Fiery Cross Reef – are not well founded in fact and law.

The Philippines requests the Tribunal to adjudge and declare that Scarborough Shoal collectively is a "rock" that generates entitlement only to a territorial sea no broader than 12 nm, and that China has unlawfully claimed maritime entitlement beyond 12 nm from this feature. However, it is suggested that Scarborough Shoal " ... has attracted fishermen for many years and it is reasonable to assume that the rocks and the drying reefs can sustain economic life of their own in the context of Article 121 (3) of LOS Convention".[75] Indeed fishing is the main economic activity in the lagoon of Scarborough Shoal and its surrounding waters. Although it is

73 Nikko Dizon, "'Integrity issue' vs SolGen: Legal strategy or disloyalty to country?" *Philippine Daily Inquirer* (20 August 2014), available at <http://globalnation.inquirer.net/109598/sol-gen-jardeleza-questioned-by-jbc-on-handling-of-phs-spratlys-claim/>.

74 Statement on the Philippines' Supplemental Submission to the Arbitral Tribunal, Department of Foreign Affairs, Republic of the Philippines, 17 March 2015, available at <http://www.dfa.gov.ph/index.php/newsroom/dfa-releases/5667-statement-on-the-philippines-supplemental-submission-to-the-arbitral-tribunal>.

75 Clive Schofield, "Maritime Boundary Delimitation in East Asian Seas: Overcoming an Obstacle to Cooperation", at 24, paper presented at CSCAP Maritime Cooperation Working Group Meeting, Hanoi, 26–7 May 2014.

difficult to establish that the six protruding features can sustain human habitation, they do have an economic life of their own. It should be noted that there are two requirements mentioned in Article 121(3), namely (a) sustain human habitation and (b) sustain economic life of its own, for a feature that is above water at high tide not to be treated as a "rock" and therefore capable of generating an EEZ and a continental shelf. Since Scarborough Shoal has an economic life of its own, it can be established that it is an Article 121(2) island and therefore is entitled the right to generate an EEZ or a continental shelf.

The Philippines requests the Tribunal to adjudge and declare that Mischief Reef and McKennan Reef are submerged features that form part of the Philippines' continental shelf under the Convention, and that China's occupation of and construction activities on them violate the sovereign rights of the Philippines.[76] However, it should be pointed out that no baselines have been announced by China in the Spratly Islands in accordance with its 1992 Territorial Sea Law and UNCLOS. In addition, although China claims in its *Note verbale* sent to the UN Secretary-General on 14 April 2011 that under the relevant provisions of the UNCLOS, as well as its 1992 Territorial Sea Law and the 1998 EEZ and Continental Shelf Law, China's Spratly archipelago, considered a group of islands, is fully entitled to territorial sea, EEZ and continental shelf, and it is yet to be determined which features are entitled to a 12 nm territorial sea, 200 nm EEZ, and 200 nm continental shelf. Accordingly, the Philippines claims with regard to maritime zones generated from Mischief Reef and McKennan Reef are not well founded in fact and law.

The Philippines' claim that China's occupation of and construction activities on Mischief Reef and McKennan Reef violate its sovereign rights should also be rejected because these features are located within the EEZ and continental shelf that are generated under Article 56 of UNLCOS for Itu Aba Island which is claimed by China as its territory. Due to the fact that Itu Aba is an island within the meaning of Article 121(2) of UCNLOS, and that Mischief Reef is located 74.7 nm from Itu Aba Island, China is entitled not only the right of appropriation by occupation, but also the exclusive right to construct and to authorize and regulate the construction, operation and use of artificial islands, installations and structures under Article 60 of the Convention for the purposes provided for in Article 56 and other economic purposes in the EEZ of Itu Aba Island. The Philippines' claim that Mischief Reef and McKennan Reef are part of its EEZ and continental shelf is inadmissible because it gives rise to a dispute over maritime boundary delimitation between China and the Philippines as both Mischief Reef and McKennan Reef are located within the EEZ that is generated from Itu Aba Island.

It is likely that the Philippines' claims that Gaven Reef and Subi Reef are LTEs and therefore cannot generate entitlement to a territorial sea, EEZ or continental shelf will be accepted by the Tribunal. It is also possible that the Tribunal will accept its claim that Johnson Reef, Cuartron Reef and Fiery Cross Reef generate no entitlement to a 200 nm EEZ or continental shelf.

76 Notification and Statement of Claim, *supra* note 2, para. 41, at 17.

Taking note of the declaration made by China on 25 August 2006 under Article 298 of UNCLOS,[77] the Philippines deliberately evades reference to the disputes over territorial sovereignty and maritime boundary delimitation in its Statement of Claim. These disputes are excluded from the Tribunal's jurisdiction.[78] With regard to sovereignty disputes over islands, UNCLOS does not contain any provisions in any of its articles for resolution of these disputes. However, once the ownership of the disputed islands is settled, the states that own the islands are entitled to the right to establish a territorial sea of up to 12 nm measured from the baseline in conformity to the provisions of the Convention. In addition, such states are allowed to claim exclusive sovereign rights and jurisdiction over maritime resources in the area up to 200 nm that is measured seaward from the baseline of a small island, but not from a "rock" as defined by Article 121(3). Similarly, such a state could claim the continental shelf surrounding an island. The nature and maritime entitlements of the features mentioned in the Philippines' Statement of Claim cannot be considered in isolation from the issue of sovereignty.

It is unlikely that the Tribunal will not to touch upon the legal status and rights of Itu Aba Island, Thitu Island and West York Island when it considers the request made by the Philippines. As pointed out by Robert Beckman, it is estimated that "less than forty of the features in the Spratly Islands meet UNCLOS's definition of an island". This geographical situation raises several questions that are related to the interpretation and application of Article 121 of the Convention. Beckman asks:

> First, how many of the features are islands because they are naturally formed areas of land surrounded by and above water at high tide? Second, how many of the islands are entitled only to a territorial sea and contiguous zone because they are rocks that cannot sustain human habitation or economic life of their own? Third, how many of the islands are in principle also entitled to an EEZ and continental shelf because they can sustain human habitation or economic life?[79]

The Philippines' claims are closely related to the legal status of Itu Aba Island, Thitu Island and West York, which are the three largest land features in the Spratly island group. It is difficult for the Tribunal to accept the Philippines arguments that these three features are "rocks" within the meaning of Article 121(3). Although

---

77 The Government of the People's Republic of China does not accept any of the procedures provided for in Section 2 of Part XV of the Convention with respect to all the categories of disputes referred to in paragraph 1(a), (b) and (c) of Article 298 of the Convention. For the Declaration, visit the UN web site, available at <http://www.un.org/Depts/los/convention_agreements/convention_declarations.htm>.

78 See para. 7 of the Statement of Claim (n 2).

79 Robert Beckman, "The UN Convention on the Law of the Sea and the Maritime Disputes in the South China Sea" (2013) 107(1) *The American Journal of International Law* 142–63 at p. 142.

the number of features that are located in the Spratly archipelago and qualify as islands in accordance with Article 121 of the UNCLOS varies, Mark J. Valencia, Jon M. Van Dyke, and Noel A. Ludwig suggest that between 25 and 35 of the 80–90 distinct features in the Spratly area are above water at high tide, and therefore they qualify as "islands" under Article 121 of the Convention.[80] If the three largest land features, namely, Itu Aba Island, Thitu Island and West York, are not islands, there will be no island at all in the Spratly archipelago.

Based on a number of writings on the Spratly Islands, Gregory B. Poling suggests that there are 30 features in the Spratly archipelago that are classified as "islands" which include Cuarteron Reef, Fiery Cross Reef, Gaven Reef, Itu Aba Island, Johnson South Reef, Thitu Island, and West York Island.[81] Robert Beckman and Clive H. Schofield suggest that because they all have vegetation, and in some cases roads and structures have been built on them, the following features, from largest to smallest in estimated area, are "islands" and therefore entitled in principle to EEZ and continental shelf under UNCLOS: Itu Aba; Thitu Island; West York Island; Northeast Cay; Southwest Cay; Spratly Island; Namyit Island; Nansha(n) Island; Sand Cay; Loaita Island; Sin Cowe Island; and Amboyna Cay.[82] In January 2010, the U.S. Government released a South China Sea Map and Gazetteer, in which Cuarteron Reef, Fiery Cross Reef, Gaven Reef, and Johnson Reef are specified as geographical features that are visible at high tide. In addition, Itu Aba, Sin Cowe, Thitu, and West York are labeled as "Island" in the Map.[83]

80 Mark J. Valencia, Jon M. Van Dyke, and Noel A. Ludwig, *Sharing the Resources of the South China Sea* (Honolulu: University of Hawaii Press, 1999), pp. 41–2.

81 This determination is based on Monique Chemillier-Gendreau, *Sovereignty over the Paracel and Spratly Islands* (The Hague: Kluwer Law International, 2000), pp. 17–18; David Hancox and Victor Prescott, "A Geographical Description of the Spratly Islands and an Account of Hydrographic Surveys amongst Those Islands" (1995) 1(6)*IBRU Maritime Briefing* 3–30; and Cire Sarr, 'Digital Gazetteer of the Spratly Islands', August 2011, available at <http://www.southchinasea.org/2011/08/19/digital-gazetteer-of-the-spratly-islands/> accessed 31 May 2014. See Gregory B. Poling, "The South China Sea in Focus: Clarifying the Limits of Maritime Disputes", A report of the CSIS Sumitro Chair for Southeast Asia Studies, Center for Strategic & International Studies, July 2013, available at <http://csis.org/files/publication/130717_Poling_SouthChinaSea_Web.pdf>.

82 Robert C. Beckman and Clive H. Schofield, "The South China Sea Disputes: Formula for a Paradigm Shift?" *RSIS COMMENTARIES* (19 February 2014), at 1–2, available at <http://www.eurasiareview.com/19022014-south-china-sea-disputes-formula-paradigm-shift-analysis/>.

83 South China Sea, Map and Gazetteer, U.S. Government, 803425AI (G02257) 1–10, January 2010. The map and gazetteer are available online at the website of the Centre for International Law, National University of Singapore, available at <http://cil.nus.edu.sg/wp/wp-content/uploads/2011/06/75967_South-China-Sea-1.pdf> and <http://cil.nus.edu.sg/wp/wp-content/uploads/2011/06/75967_gazetteer.pdf>.

Concluding Remarks

Because Mischief Reef, McKennan Reef, Grven Reef and Subi Reef, treated as LTEs by the Philippines, are located within the 200 nm EEZ and continental shelf of Itu Aba Island, Thitu Island, and West York Island, the three largest islands in the Spratly archipelago, Article 60 should be applied. Under this provision, it is legal for China to build artificial islands, construct installations and structures within the zone. The Philippines is entitled to claim a 200 nm EEZ and continental shelf drawn from its archipelagic straight baselines, but the disputed and overlapping maritime zones generated by the islands in the Spratly archipelago should be excluded from the Arbitral Tribunal's jurisdiction because of China's 2006 Declaration. In addition, because China's activities are conducted in accordance with the relevant provisions contained in UNCLOS, in particular Articles 56, 60 and 121, the Philippines' claims in relation to the legal status and right, as well as Chinese occupation of and construction activities on the features, namely, Mischief Reef, Subi Reef, Gaven Reef, McKennan Reef, Johnson Reef, Cuarteron Reef, and Fiery Cross Reef, are ill-founded and inconsistent with the applicable law. Finally, the nature and maritime entitlements of the eight features mentioned in the Philippines' Statement of Claim cannot be considered by the Tribunal in isolation from the issue of sovereignty. The holder of the entitlements to an EEZ and a continental shelf under the Convention is the coastal state with sovereignty over these land features in the SCS. Accordingly, it would be difficult for the Arbitral Tribunal to rule in the Philippines' favor on claims related to the submerged features, LTEs and islands.

Chapter 11
The Significance of Offshore Geographic Features to Maritime Claims

Robert Beckman and Leonardo Bernard

Introduction

Disputes over the sovereignty of offshore geographic features and the maritime zones surrounding them have long been a source of tension and conflict in many parts of the world. Although the issues of sovereignty and the determination of maritime boundaries are two distinct matters with each governed by different rules of international law, they are often confused and conflated into one.

The 1982 United Nations Convention on the Law of the Sea (UNCLOS)[1] does not prescribe procedures for the determination of sovereignty. Instead, UNCLOS sets out what maritime zones may be claimed from land territory (including offshore geographic features), as well as the rights and jurisdiction of states in such maritime zones. A dispute over which state has the better claim to territorial sovereignty over offshore geographic features can only be resolved if the claimants, after assessing the merits of their claims internally with their own governments, either agree to settle the dispute through direct negotiations or agree to refer the dispute to an international court or international arbitral tribunal. What often complicates the dispute is the lack of clarity of the status of the offshore features, which is important in determining sovereignty claims and the maritime zones generated from such features.

This chapter aims to shed light on the types of offshore geographic features that can be subjected to claims of sovereignty by states. It will then discuss the different entitlements of maritime zones generated by different types of offshore geographic features. Finally, this chapter will analyze the obligations of claimants in the disputed maritime zones.

1 "United Nations Convention on the Law of the Sea", 10 December 1982, UNTS 1833, 3 (entered into force 16 November 1994). As of 1 October 2014, UNCLOS has 166 parties (including the European Union), with Niger being the latest party to have acceded to the Convention on 7 August 2013.

Status of Islands, Rocks and Low-Tide Elevations

Under international law, islands are subject to the rules and principles of territorial acquisition.[2] International law, however, "do[es] not justify a general assumption that low-tide elevations are territory in the same sense as islands", since there is a significant difference in the attributes that UNCLOS ascribes to islands and low-tide elevations.[3] The ICJ further explained that low-tide elevations are not akin to islands or other land territory.[4] Thus, it is clear that the only offshore features subject to appropriation and entitled to maritime claims of their own are "islands", including the sub-category of islands knows as "rocks".[5] Despite this, low-tide elevations can be of significance in drawing baselines from which the territorial sea is measured,[6] and special rules on baselines apply to islands situated on reefs.[7]

What confuses the situation is that offshore geographic features are often described as reefs, shoals, cays, atolls or banks. Although these terms are not legal terms of art, it is helpful to have some idea of their meaning. They were described in the 2012 decision in the *Nicaragua v. Columbia* case as follows:[8]

> In the western part of the Caribbean Sea there are numerous reefs, some of which reach above the water surface in the form of cays. *Cays are small, low islands composed largely of sand derived from the physical breakdown of coral reefs by wave action and subsequent reworking by wind.* Larger cays can accumulate enough sediment to allow for colonization and fixation by vegetation. Atolls and banks are also common in this area. *An atoll is a coral reef enclosing a lagoon. A bank is a rocky or sandy submerged elevation of the sea floor with a summit less than 200 metres below the surface.* Banks whose tops rise close enough to the sea surface (conventionally taken to be less than 10 metres below water level at low tide) are called shoals. Maritime features which qualify as islands or low-tide elevations may be located on a bank or shoal.

It is clear from the above paragraph that reefs, atolls, banks and shoals are submerged features incapable of being subjected to claims of sovereignty. However, there are offshore geographic features that may qualify as islands (including rocks and

2 *Maritime Delimitation and Territorial Questions between Qatar and Bahrain (Qatar v.Bahrain)*, [2001] ICJ Rep. 40, paras. 205–6; *Sovereignty over PedraBranca/ PulauBatuPuteh,Middle Rocks and South Ledge (Malaysia/Singapore)*, [2008] ICJ Rep. 12, paras. 295–6.

3 *Qatar v.Bahrain*, para. 206.

4 Ibid.

5 UNCLOS, Art. 121(3).

6 UNCLOS, Art. 13(1).

7 UNCLOS, Art. 6.

8 *Territorial and Maritime Dispute (Nicaragua v. Colombia)*, [2012] ICJ Rep. 50 (*Nicaragua v. Colombia)*, para. 20 (emphasis added).

cays) or as low-tide elevations, comprised from reefs and/or located on an atoll, bank or shoal. In such situations, only those parts of such atoll, bank or shoal that are above water at high tide can be subjected to claims of sovereignty, and not the whole atoll, bank or shoal.

Definition of Islands and Low-Tide Elevations in UNCLOS

An island is defined in Article 121(1) of UNCLOS as a naturally formed area of land, surrounded by and above water at high tide. A low-tide elevation is defined in Article 13 of UNCLOS as a naturally formed area of land, which is surrounded by and above water at low tide but submerged at high tide. In short, an island must be above water at high tide and a low-tide elevation must be above water at low tide. These legal terms of art apply to all offshore geographic features, notwithstanding the fact that they be described on maps or in government gazettes as islands, rocks, reefs, shoals, cays or banks.[9]

Both an island and a low-tide elevation are defined in UNCLOS as a "naturally formed area of land".[10] A question that arises is what constitutes "land". UNCLOS does not address this issue. It would appear from writers that the physical composition of the land (whether it is a mainland coast, an island, an elevation or other feature) does not affect its status, so long as it is comprised of "natural" material. Dipla writes that "land" normally means "an elevation of the seabed created through natural phenomena and consisting of soil or other types of earth material (sand, mud, gravel deposits, limestone mixed with coral debris, etc.) but not ice".[11] Other commentators have noted that low-tide elevations can be mud flats or sand bars.[12]

Reefs and coral formations by nature do not fit into the normal category of what we mean as land territory. Most coral reefs are constructed from polyps (tiny living creatures) and the calcium carbonate secreted by the polyps. Coral reefs are therefore living organisms rather than rock or mineral-based inorganic material. Nevertheless, despite the fact that coral is an organic material, reefs are treated in the same manner as inorganic material where the law of the sea is concerned. The ICJ confirmed the above analysis in its 2012 decision in the *Nicaragua v. Columbia* case. It stated that neither the composition nor the size of a feature is relevant in determining whether it meets the definition of an island:[13]

---

9 See Barbara Kwiatkowska and Alfred H.A. Soons, "Entitlement to Maritime Areas of Rocks Which Cannot Sustain Human Habitation or Economic Life of Their Own", (1990) 21 *Netherlands Yearbook of International Law* 139, pp. 151–2.

10 UNCLOS, Arts. 13 and 121(1).

11 Haritini Dipla, "Islands", in *The Max Planck Encyclopedia of Public International Law, Volume VI*, ed. R. Wolfrum (Oxford: Oxford University Press, 2006), p. 406.

12 J. Ashley Roach and Robert Smith, *United States Responses to Excessive Maritime Claims*, 2nd ed. (Leiden: Martinus Nijohoff Publishers, 1996), p. 67.

13 *Nicaragua v. Colombia*, para. 37 (emphasis added).

> No matter which tidal model is used, it is evident that QS 32 is above water at high tide. Nicaragua's contention that QS 32 cannot be regarded as an island within the definition established in customary international law, because it is composed of coral debris, is without merit. *International law defines an island by reference to whether it is "naturally formed" and whether it is above water at high tide, not by reference to its geological composition.* The photographic evidence shows that QS 32 is composed of solid material, attached to the substrate, and not of loose debris. *The fact that the feature is composed of coral is irrelevant.* Even using Nicaragua's preferred tidal model, QS 32 is above water at high tide by some 0.7 metres. The Court recalls that in the case concerning *Maritime Delimitation and Territorial Questions between Qatar and Bahrain (Qatar* v. *Bahrain)* (*Merits, Judgment, I.C.J. Reports 2001*, p. 99, para. 197), it found that Qit'at Jaradah was an island, notwithstanding that it was only 0.4 metres above water at high tide. The fact that QS 32 is very small does not make any difference, since international law does not prescribe any minimum size which a feature must possess in order to be considered an island. Accordingly, the Court concludes that the feature referred to as QS 32 is capable of appropriation.

From the above excerpt, it is evident that geological composition is irrelevant to the determination of whether a feature is an island. Rather, the relevant factor is whether a feature is naturally formed. The ICJ also made clear that the size of a feature is irrelevant in determining whether it is an island, so long as the feature is above water at high tide.

Entitlement of Islands and Rocks to Maritime Zones

The distinction between islands, rocks and low-tide elevations is important because it will affect the maritime zones that can be generated from each feature. One of the longstanding principles in the law of the sea is the principle of "land dominates the sea" or "*la terredomine la mer*", which means that it is "the terrestrial territorial situation that must be taken as starting point for the determination of the maritime rights of a coastal State".[14] This principle has been affirmed by the ICJ in numerous cases as a principle of customary international law.[15]

Article 121(2) of UNCLOS provides that as a general rule an island is entitled to the same maritime zones as land territory. However, Article 121(3) of UNCLOS creates an exception by stating that "rocks which cannot sustain human habitation or economic life of their own shall have no exclusive economic zone

14 *Territorial and Maritime Dispute between Nicaragua and Honduras in the Caribbean Sea (Nicaragua v. Honduras)*, [2007] ICJ Rep. 659, para. 113.

15 See *Nicaragua v. Honduras; North Sea Continental Shelf (Federal Republic of Germany/Denmark; Federal Republic of Germany/Netherlands),* [1969] ICJ Rep. 51, para. 96; *Aegean Sea Continental Shelf (Greece v Turkey)*, [1978] ICJ Rep.36, para. 86; *Qatar v. Bahrain*, para. 185.

or continental shelf". In other words, the significance of Article 121(2) and (3) is one of "entitlement". Islands are entitled to the same maritime zones as other land territory, that is, a territorial sea, a contiguous zone, a continental shelf and an exclusive economic zone (EEZ). Rocks, on the other hand, are not entitled to an EEZ or continental shelf of their own. They are only entitled to a territorial sea and a contiguous zone.

In its 2012 judgement in the *Nicaragua v. Columbia* case, the ICJ agreed with this reading of Article 121 with respect to the entitlement to maritime rights from islands and rocks, and declared that the article was part of customary international law:[16]

> The Court observes, however, that *the entitlement to maritime rights accorded to an island by the provisions of paragraph 2 is expressly limited by reference to the provisions of paragraph 3.* By denying an exclusive economic zone and a continental shelf to rocks which cannot sustain human habitation or economic life of their own, paragraph 3 provides an essential link between the long-established principle that "islands, regardless of their size, enjoy the same status, and therefore generate the same maritime rights, as other land territory" *(ibid.)* and the more extensive maritime entitlements recognized in UNCLOS and which the Court has found to have become part of customary international law. *The Court therefore considers that the legal régime of islands set out in UNCLOS Article 121 forms an indivisible régime, all of which (as Colombia and Nicaragua recognize) has the status of customary international law.*

Scholars are not in agreement on the object and purpose of Article 121(3). Kwiatkowska and Soons have argued that its objective is to limit the category of islands able to generate an EEZ extending to 200 nautical miles (nm) and a continental shelf extending to the outer edge of the continental margin, thus preventing what would otherwise be a substantial limitation on areas subject to the regimes of high seas and the common heritage of mankind.[17] Oxman argued the contrary, stating that the purpose of the Convention is to expand coastal states' jurisdiction over natural resources, and that Article 121(3) has the opposite effect.[18]

An examination of the legislative history of Article 121(3) demonstrates that it was controversial from the outset. It was debated most extensively during the 1974 session of UNCLOS III in Caracas.[19] The present text was inserted in 1975 by the Chairman of Committee II in the draft text known as the Informal Single Negotiating

16 *Nicaragua v. Colombia*, para. 139 (emphasis added).

17 Kwiatkowska and Soons, *supra* note 9, p. 144.

18 Bernard H. Oxman, "On Rocks and Maritime Delimitation" in *Looking into the Future: Essays on International Law in Honor of W. Michael Reisman*, eds. Mahnoush H. Arjasani, Jacob Katz Cogan, Robert D. Sloane and Siegfried Wiessner (Leiden: Martinus Nijhoff Publishers, 2011), p. 897.

19 Kwiatkowska and Soons, *supra* note 9, p. 141.

Text.[20] In the subsequent negotiations from 1975 to 1982, various attempts were made to amend the paragraph or to delete it completely. The states which were in favor of deleting paragraph 3 include the United States, the United Kingdom, France and Japan.[21] This is understandable because as former colonial powers, they would be able to claim a full 200 nm EEZ from small uninhabited offshore islands under their sovereignty. In the end, all attempts to reach a compromise on amending Article 121 failed. This is because the delegations at the negotiations were divided according to whether they would benefit from the provision because they possessed small uninhabited offshore islands, or whether they felt that paragraph 3 was necessary to ensure that tiny uninhabitable islands did not become the legal basis for vast claims to resources of the oceans.[22] The 1975 provision remained in the final text without amendments despite its obvious ambiguities because the delegates could not reach a compromise on clearer wording.

The ambiguity in Article 121(3) has generated much debate, in part because no minimum size is provided to distinguish between a rock and an island, and no objective test is set out for examining the ability of an island to sustain human habitation or economic life. For example, does "sustain" human habitation mean that a small community of people must be able to live on the island without outside assistance? Would this require the island to have a natural source of water and sufficient land to plant crops for food? And what is meant by "sustain economic life"? A major problem in analyzing the literature on these issues is that many of the writers are putting forth arguments in support of the position of their country.

With respect to state practice, the most famous instant of a "pull-back" was by the United Kingdom, with respect to the island of Rockall following the protests of Ireland, Denmark (Faroe Islands), and Iceland on the establishment by the United Kingdom of a continental shelf and 200 nm fishery zone around Rockall.[23] One of the most controversial cases in Asia on the issue of rocks versus islands is the Japanese claim to an EEZ and extended continental shelf from Okinotorishima. When Japan submitted their claim to an extended continental shelf to the Commission on the Limits of the Continental Shelf (CLCS), both China and Korea submitted Notes Verbale to the UN Secretary-General, stating that Okinotorishima is a rock within the meaning of Article 121(3) of UNCLOS and is not entitled to an EEZ and continental self of its own.[24] Due to these objections, the CLCS is withholding its recommendation with regards to area surrounding Okinotorishima.

20 Ibid.

21 *The Law of the Sea, Regime of Islands – Legislative History of Part VIII (Article 121) of the United Nations Convention on the Law of the Sea,* UN Sales No. E.87.V.11, (UN Office for Ocean Affairs and the Law of the Sea, 1998).

22 Kwiatkowska and Soons, *supra* note 9, pp. 141–2.

23 David H. Anderson, "Report No 9–5" in *International Maritime Boundaries*, Vol. II, ed. Jonathan L.Charney and Lewis M. Alexander (Leiden: Martinus Nijhoff Publishers, 1993), p. 1767.

24 Chinese Note Verbale to the United Nations Secretary-General, No. CML/2/2009, February 6, 2009, accessed 14 November 2012 <http://www.un.org/Depts/los/clcs_new/

Maritime Zones from Islands Situated on Atolls and Islands Having Fringing Reefs

Article 6 of UNCLOS provides that the seaward low-water line of the reef is the baseline for measuring the territorial sea from such islands. This article is not free from ambiguity and has been the subject of some literature by technical experts.[25] Article 6 of UNCLOS reads as follows:

> Article 6 Reefs
> In the case of islands situated on atolls or of islands having fringing reefs, the baseline for measuring the breadth of the territorial sea is the seaward low-water line of the reef, as shown by the appropriate symbol on charts officially recognized by the coastal State.

The key to understanding Article 6 on reefs is that it is not applicable to all reefs. It is only applicable to "islands" situated on reefs or atolls or to islands which have fringing reefs. It creates an exception to the general rule that the normal baseline is the low-water line along the coast of the island. It is important to understand that these reefs and atolls are not, by themselves, entitled to any maritime zones. Their existence around or in the immediate vicinity of an island allows these reefs or atolls to be used as basepoints to measure the limit of maritime zones generated by the island. Thus, it is the island that is entitled to generate maritime zones – not the reefs or atolls.

Low-Tide Elevations and Maritime Zones

Because low-tide elevations are not islands, they are not entitled to maritime zones of their own. However, in certain circumstances they can be used as basepoints in measuring the breadth of the territorial sea. Article 13 of UNCLOS provides that if a low-tide elevation is situated within 12 nm of either the mainland or an island, the low-water line on that elevation may be used as the baseline for measuring the breadth of the territorial sea. However, if a state employs the use of straight baselines, such baselines cannot be drawn from low-tide elevations except in particular circumstances. Article 7(4) provides that straight baselines shall not be drawn to and from low-tide elevations, unless lighthouses or similar installations, which are permanently above sea level, have been built on them or in instances where the drawing of straight baselines to and from such elevations has received general international recognition.

---

submissions_files/jpn08/chn_6feb09_e.pdf>; Korean Note Verbale to the United Nations Secretary-General, No. MUN/046/09 27 February 2009, accessed 14 November 2012 <http://www.un.org/Depts/los/clcs_new/submissions_files/jpn08/kor_27feb09.pdf>.

25 Hiran Jayewardene, *The Regime of Islands* (Leiden: Martinus Nijhoff Publishers, 1990), p. 98.

Although UNCLOS provides that only islands are entitled to maritime zones of their own, it does not expressly state that low-tide elevations are not subject to appropriation or to a claim of sovereignty. The ICJ considered this issue in several cases, but its decisions were not entirely clear.[26] However, in its 2012 judgement in the *Nicaragua v. Columbia* case, the ICJ finally clarified the issue by declaring that low-tide elevations were not capable of appropriation:[27]

> It is well established in international law that islands, however small, are capable of appropriation (see, e.g., *Maritime Delimitation and Territorial Questions between Qatar and Bahrain (Qatar* v. *Bahrain), Merits, Judgment, I.C.J. Reports 2001*, p. 102, para. 206). By contrast, *low-tide elevations cannot be appropriated,* although "a coastal State has sovereignty over low-tide elevations which are situated within its territorial sea, since it has sovereignty over the territorial sea itself" (*ibid.*, p. 101, para. 204) and low-tide elevations within the territorial sea may be taken into account for the purpose of measuring the breadth of the territorial sea … .

The ICJ thus has clarified that only islands, as defined by Article 121, are capable of appropriation.

Islands in Areas of Overlapping Maritime Claims

When the EEZ or continental shelf claims from the mainland territory of two states overlap, they have obligations under Articles 74 and 83 of UNCLOS with respect to the areas of overlapping claims. The areas of overlapping claims become more complicated if there are islands belonging to one or both of the claimants in the areas of overlapping claims. Several general comments can be made about the treatment of tiny offshore islands by international courts and arbitral tribunals in maritime boundary delimitation cases.

First, the cases usually arise because there are overlapping continental shelf and/or EEZ claims from the mainland territories of two opposite or adjacent states and the court or tribunal is tasked with drawing the maritime boundary between them. One of the issues before the court or tribunal would be what effect should be given to offshore islands belonging to one of them when delimiting the maritime boundary between the two states.

Second, although it is sometimes argued that one or more of the islands should have no EEZ or continental shelf of its own because it is a rock within Article 121(3), the courts and tribunals have decided in maritime delimitation cases that they can delimit the maritime boundary without deciding the issue of whether a

26 *Qatar v. Bahrain,* para. 206.

27 *Nicaragua v. Colombia*, para. 26 (emphasis added).

given feature is a rock within Article 121(3). The ICJ in the *Nicaragua v. Colombia* decision, for example, stated that:[28]

> The Court cannot, therefore, accept Nicaragua's submission that an equitable solution can be achieved by drawing a 3-nautical-mile enclave around each of these islands. It concludes that *Roncador, Serrana, the Alburquerque Cays and East-Southeast Cays are each entitled to a territorial sea of 12 nautical miles, irrespective of whether they fall within the exception stated in Article 121, paragraph 3, of UNCLOS. Whether or not any of these islands falls within the scope of that exception is therefore relevant only to the extent that it is necessary to determine if they are entitled to a continental shelf and exclusive economic zone.* In that context, the Court notes that the whole of the relevant area lies within 200 nautical miles of one or more of the islands of San Andrés, Providencia or Santa Catalina, each of which – the Parties agree – is entitled to a continental shelf and exclusive economic zone. The Court recalls that, faced with a similar situation in respect of Serpents' Island in the *Maritime Delimitation in the Black Sea* case, it considered it unnecessary to determine whether that island fell within paragraph 2 or paragraph 3 of Article 121 of UNCLOS (*Maritime Delimitation in the Black Sea (Romania* v. *Ukraine), Judgment, I.C.J. Reports 2009*, pp. 122–123, para. 187). In the present case, *the Court similarly concludes that it is not necessary to determine the precise status of the smaller islands, since any entitlement to maritime spaces which they might generate within the relevant area (outside the territorial sea) would entirely overlap with the entitlement to a continental shelf and exclusive economic zone generated by the islands of San Andrés, Providencia and Santa Catalina.*

Third, in such cases the court or tribunal usually gives tiny offshore islands partial or no effect in delimiting the maritime boundary between the two states. The courts and tribunals do this by taking into account the characteristics of the offshore island in the delimitation process. They sometimes decide that the small islands should not be used as basepoints when constructing the provisional median line between the two states. For example, in the *Nicaragua v. Colombia* case, the ICJ did not use three Columbian islands as basepoints in determining the provisional median line. It explained its position as follows:[29]

> So far as the Colombian coast is concerned, the Court considers that Quitasueño should not contribute to the construction of the provisional median line. The part of Quitasueño which is undoubtedly above water at high tide is a minuscule feature, barely 1 square m in dimension. *When placing base points on very small maritime features would distort the relevant geography, it is appropriate to disregard them in the construction of a provisional median line.* In the *Maritime Delimitation*

28 *Nicaragua v. Colombia*, para. 180 (emphasis added).
29 *Nicaragua v. Colombia*, para. 202 (emphasis added).

> *in the Black Sea* case, for example, the Court held that it was inappropriate to select any base point on Serpents' Island (which, at 0.17 square km was very much larger than the part of Quitasueño which is above water at high tide), because it lay alone and at a distance of some 20 nautical miles from the mainland coast of Ukraine, and its use as a part of the relevant coast "would amount to grafting an extraneous element onto Ukraine's coastline; the consequence would be a judicial refashioning of geography, which neither the law nor practice of maritime delimitation authorizes" (*Maritime Delimitation in the Black Sea (Romania v. Ukraine), Judgment, I.C.J. Reports 2009*, p. 110, para. 149). These considerations apply with even greater force to Quitasueño. In addition to being a tiny feature, it is 38 nautical miles from Santa Catalina and its use in the construction of the provisional median line would push that line significantly closer to Nicaragua. Colombia did not place a base point upon Serrana. The Court's decision not to place a base point upon Quitasueño means, however, that it must consider whether one should be placed upon Serrana. *Although larger than Quitasueño, Serrana is also a comparatively small feature, whose considerable distance from any of the other Colombian islands means that placing a base point upon it would have a marked effect upon the course of the provisional median line which would be out of all proportion to its size and importance. In the Court's view, no base point should be placed on Serrana.* The Court also considers that there should be no base point on Low Cay, a small uninhabited feature near Santa Catalina.

Fourth, international courts and arbitral tribunals sometimes also decide that small islands, even if they might be entitled to EEZ and continental shelf, such entitlement will be limited to follow the outer limit of territorial sea, which is 12 nm around such islands. This is because to give it more would have a disproportionate effect on the maritime boundary, given the relative size of the islands compared to the mainland and the length of the coastlines of the islands and the mainland. In its decision in the *Nicaragua v. Columbia* case, the ICJ also followed this practice:[30]

> That leaves Quitasueño and Serrana, both of which the Court has held fall on the Nicaraguan side of the boundary line described above. In the Court's view, *to take the adjusted line described in the preceding paragraphs further north, so as to encompass these islands and the surrounding waters, would allow small, isolated features, which are located at a considerable distance from the larger Colombian islands, to have a disproportionate effect upon the boundary. The Court therefore considers that the use of enclaves achieves the most equitable solution in this part of the relevant area.* Quitasueño and Serrana are each entitled to a territorial sea which, for the reasons already given by the Court (paragraphs 176–180 above), cannot be less than 12 nautical miles in breadth. Since Quitasueño is a rock incapable of sustaining human habitation or an economic life of its own and thus falls within the rule stated in Article 121, paragraph 3, of UNCLOS, it

30 *Nicaragua v. Colombia*, para. 238 (emphasis added).

> is not entitled to a continental shelf or exclusive economic zone. Accordingly, the boundary between the continental shelf and exclusive economic zone of Nicaragua and the Colombian territorial sea around Quitasueño will follow a 12-nautical-mile envelope of arcs measured from QS 32 and from the low-tide elevations located within 12 nautical miles from QS 32 (see paragraphs 181–183 above). In the case of Serrana, the Court recalls that it has already concluded that it is unnecessary to decide whether or not it falls within the rule stated in Article 121, paragraph 3, of UNCLOS (paragraph 180 above). *Its small size, remoteness and other characteristics mean that, in any event, the achievement of an equitable result requires that the boundary line follow the outer limit of the territorial sea around the island.* Theboundary will therefore follow a 12-nautical-mile envelope of arcs measured from Serrana Cay and other cays in its vicinity.

Thus, small islands may be given some effect in determining maritime boundaries, but only a partial or reduced effect.

Low-Tide Elevations in Areas of Overlapping Maritime Claims

In many cases, there are low-tide elevations in areas of overlapping territorial sea claims, EEZ claims or continental shelf claims. As the ICJ held in the *PedraBranca case*, if there is a low-tide elevation in an area of overlapping territorial sea claims, it is under the sovereignty of the state in whose territorial sea it lies.[31] Until the boundary issue is resolved, it is located in an area of overlapping claims.

If there is a low-tide elevation in an area of overlapping EEZ claims or continental shelf claims, there is no issue of territorial sovereignty. The low-tide elevation is part of the seabed and is not subject to appropriation. However, if it is within 12 nm from an island, it can be used as a basepoint in measuring the breadth of the territorial sea from the island. If it is not within 12 nm from an island, it forms part of the seabed. It has no entitlement to maritime zones of its own. If it is not within 12 nm from an island, but lies within the 200 nm EEZ of a coastal state, the coastal state would have sovereign rights to explore and exploit the resources in the area around the feature. The same reasoning would apply if the low-tide elevation is situated in an area of overlapping continental shelf claims.

The same principles would apply to a submerged feature in the EEZ or on the continental shelf. It is part of the seabed. Once the maritime boundary is resolved, the state in whose EEZ the said submerged feature lies or within whose continental shelf it lies will have the right to explore and exploit the living and non-living natural resources of the submerged feature. Until the boundary is resolved, it is an area of overlapping claims.

If such a feature is situated in an area of overlapping EEZ or continental shelf claims, the two states concerned would be under the obligations set out in

31 *Malaysia/Singapore*, paras. 295–6.

Articles 74 and 83 of UNCLOS on the delimitation of EEZ and continental shelf boundaries. The maritime boundary is to be effected by an agreement between the two states. If no agreement can be reached within a reasonable time, the two states concerned shall resort to the dispute settlement procedures set out in Part XV of UNCLOS, unless they have exercised their right to opt out of the dispute settlement procedures for disputes on the delimitation of maritime boundaries.

Pending agreement on the maritime boundary, the states concerned, in a spirit of understanding and co-operation, are under an obligation to make every effort to enter into provisional arrangements of a practical nature and, during this transitional period, not to jeopardize or hamper the reaching of the final agreement. Such arrangements shall be without prejudice to the final delimitation.[32]

The obligation not to take unilateral action to jeopardize or hamper the reaching of a final agreement means that states cannot take any unilateral actions in the area of overlapping claims which would cause permanent change or damage or which have a permanent physical impact on the environment.[33] For example, a state could not begin drilling for gas or oil in the area in dispute.

If a state has placed an installation or structure on a low-tide elevation or submerged feature in an area of overlapping EEZ or continental shelf claims, a dispute could arise as to which state has jurisdiction over the installation or structure, since both states will claim that it lies within their EEZ. The state adding the installation or structure runs the risk of the other state having jurisdiction over that feature if the maritime boundary issue is resolved in a manner that results in the feature being in the EEZ or on the continental shelf of the other state. It could also be in violation of its obligations under Articles 74 or 83 if the installation or structures cause permanent change.

Artificial Islands, Installations and Structures

Another article in UNCLOS that is important for understanding the status of low-tide elevations is Article 60 on artificial islands, installations and structures in the EEZ. This article also applies to artificial islands, installations and structures on the continental shelf.[34]

A. Legal Status of Artificial Islands, Installations and Structures

Article 60 provides that the coastal state shall have the exclusive right to construct and to authorize and regulate the construction, operation and use of: (a) artificial islands; (b) installations and structures for the purposes provided for in Article

32 UNCLOS, Art. 74(3).

33 *Guyana v. Suriname*, Arbitral Court, Award, 17 September 2007, para. 407, accessed 14 November 2012 <http://www.pca-cpa.org/showpage.asp?pag_id=1147>.

34 UNCLOS, Art. 80.

56 and other economic purposes; and (c) installations and structures that may interfere with the exercise of the rights of the coastal state in the zone. Coastal states have exclusive jurisdiction over such artificial islands, installations and structures, including jurisdiction with regard to customs, fiscal, health, safety and immigration laws and regulations.[35]

The term "artificial island" is not defined in UNCLOS. However, it generally refers to a feature that is above water at high tide because of land reclamation or other activities of man. In other words, it fails to meet the definition of an "island" under Article 121 of UNCLOS because it is not a "naturally formed" area of land, but rather is a man-made feature. Installations and structures are also not defined, but they would refer to things like buildings, lighthouses, research stations and oil platforms.

Article 60(8) of UNCLOS provides that artificial islands, installations and structures in the EEZ do not possess the status of islands. They have no territorial sea of their own and their presence does not affect the delimitation of the territorial sea, the EEZ or the continental shelf.

The coastal state may, where necessary, establish reasonable safety zones around such artificial islands, installations and structures in which it may take appropriate measures to ensure the safety both of navigation and of the artificial islands, installations and structures. The breadth of the safety zones shall be determined by the coastal state, but shall not exceed a distance of 500 meters around them.[36] Additionally, coastal states have an obligation to adopt laws and regulations to prevent, reduce and control pollution of the marine environment arising from artificial islands, installations and structures under their jurisdiction, pursuant to Articles 60 and 80.[37]

It should be noted that there is a difference between the rights and jurisdiction of the coastal state over artificial islands and the rights and jurisdiction of the coastal state over installations and structures. The coastal states have exclusive rights and jurisdiction over artificial islands, but their rights and jurisdiction over installations and structures is limited to those used for "economic purposes".[38] This presumably gives a state the right to construct an installation or structure for military purposes in the EEZ of another state, so long as the installation or structure does not interfere with the exercise of the rights of the coastal state in the zone.

Similarly, installations and structures may be constructed by states in the EEZ of another state if they are constructed for marine scientific research purposes. Such installations and structures must not be deployed so as to constitute an obstacle to established international shipping routes, and must bear identification marking indicating the state in which they are registered and have warning

35 UNCLOS, Art. 60(2).
36 UNCLOS, Art. 60(5).
37 UNCLOS, Art. 208.
38 UNCLOS, Art. 60(1)(a) and (b).

signals.[39] Similarly, these installations and structures do not possess the status of islands, although a reasonable safety zone not exceeding 500 meters may be established around them.[40]

Artificial islands, installations or structures may be constructed on low-tide elevations or submerged features. If they are constructed on a low-tide elevation, and that low-tide elevation is situated within 12 nm of the mainland or an island, that low-tide elevation can be used as a basepoint for measuring the breadth of the territorial sea. If they are constructed on a submerged feature, they cannot be used as a basepoint.

UNCLOS does not provide sufficiently for situations in which the legal status of islands is changed by natural phenomena or artificial efforts.[41] Natural occurrences, such as accretion, avulsion and erosion, and sea-level rise can result in a shift in status from island to non-island, or from submerged feature to island; a shift which in turn may affect its legal status.

Alex Oude Elferink writes that an island that is reinforced with coastal defences in principle remains an island in the sense of Article 121 and an artificial island does not become an island if there is an accretion of land that is natural in origin.[42] Islands that are newly formed by natural processes after human intervention in the natural environment will in principle fall under Article 121. The distinction between an island and an artificial island will necessarily involve an assessment of both law and fact.

Environmental Obligations Concerning Artificial Islands, Installations and Structures

The state that occupies or controls an island, rock or low-tide elevation has obligations under UNCLOS to protect and preserve the marine environment from activities on such feature, including land reclamation works or the building of installations or structures. Under Article 194(1) of UNCLOS, states have an obligation to take all measures consistent with the Convention to prevent, reduce and control pollution of the marine environment from any source. Under Article 194(2), states shall take all measures necessary to ensure that activities under their jurisdiction and control are so conducted as to not cause damage by pollution to other states and their environment.

---

39 UNCLOS, Arts. 261 and 262.

40 UNCLOS, Arts. 259 and 260.

41 Choon-Ho Park, "The Changeable Legal Status of Islands and 'Non-Islands' in the Law of the Sea: Some Instances in the Asia-Pacific Region", in *Bringing New Law to Ocean Waters*, ed. D.D. Caron and H.N. Scheiber (Leiden: Martinus Nijhoff Publishers, 2004), p. 490.

42 Alex Oude Elferink, "Artificial Islands, Installations, and Structures", in *The Max Planck Encyclopedia of Public International Law, Volume 1*, ed. R. Wolfrum (Oxford: Oxford University Press, 2012), p. 662.

In addition to these general obligations, the International Tribunal for the Law of the Sea held in the *MOX Plant* case and the *Land Reclamation* case that states have a duty to cooperate or a due regard obligation with respect to planned activities under their jurisdiction and control that may pollute the marine environment of another state.[43] The duty to cooperate set out in these cases seems to include a duty to give timely notice to the potentially affected state of the planned activities, to provide it with relevant information about the planned activities and to consult with it in good faith. It also implies an obligation to exchange information and to negotiate in good faith in order to balance the competing interests of the two states.[44] A good argument can be made that the above obligations apply to a state in control of an island or low-tide elevation that is located within the EEZ or on the continental shelf of another state.

Conclusions

The only offshore geographic features that are subject to appropriation and entitled to maritime zones of their own are islands. If an area of land is naturally formed and surrounded by and above water at high tide, it is an island, no matter how small and no matter whether it is composed of rock, sand or coral.

As a general principle, islands are entitled to the same maritime zones as other land territory. However, Article 121(3) provides that "rocks" that cannot sustain human habitation or economic life of their own shall have no EEZ or continental shelf. Although international courts and tribunals have been reluctant to interpret and apply the intentionally ambiguous language of Article 121(3) in maritime boundary cases, they have in practice given substantially reduced effect to tiny uninhabitable offshore islands when delimiting maritime boundaries.

Under UNCLOS and the decisions of international courts and tribunals, low-tide elevations and submerged features are not subject to a claim to sovereignty because sovereignty can only be claimed over land territory and islands. Low-tide elevations can be used as basepoints in measuring the breadth of territorial sea if they are situated with 12 nm of the mainland or an offshore island.

Submerged features and low-tide elevations are part of the seabed and are governed by the rules and principles of the relevant zone. If they are within the

43 *The MOX Plant Case (Ireland v. United Kingdom)*, Request for Provisional Measures, Order, 3 December 2001, para. 82 <http://www.itlos.org/fileadmin/itlos/documents/cases/case_no_10/Order.03.12.01.E.pdf>; *Case Concerning Land Reclamation by Singapore in and Around the Straits of Johor (Malaysia v. Singapore)*, Provisional Measures, Order, 8 October 2003, para. 92 <https://www.itlos.org/fileadmin/itlos/documents/cases/case_no_12/Order.08.10.03.E.pdf>.

44 Robert Beckman, "State Responsibility and Transboundary Pollution", in *Transboundary Pollution: Evolving Issues of International Law and Policy*, ed. S. Jayakumar, et al. (forthcoming, Edward Elgar Publishing, 2015).

territorial sea or archipelagic waters, they are under the sovereignty of the coastal state. If they are within the 200 nm EEZ of a state, they are governed by Part V of UNCLOS. If they are on the extended continental shelf of the coastal state, they are governed by Part VI of UNCLOS.

Low-tide elevations and submerged features can be made into artificial islands. Installations or structures can also be built on them. In such cases, the provisions of UNCLOS on artificial islands, installations and structures would be applicable with respect to jurisdiction, safety zones, etc. Also, a low-tide elevation that has an installation or a structure built on it would not lose its status as a low-tide elevation. Furthermore, it could be used as a basepoint for measuring the breadth of the territorial sea if it is situated within 12 nm from the mainland land territory or an island. If low-tide elevations or submerged features lie in areas of overlapping EEZ or continental shelf claims, there are limitations on what unilateral actions the claimant states can take with regard to them.

PART V
Law Enforcement and Regional Impact

Chapter 12

Fishery Resources Management in a Disputed Maritime Zone: A Political and Legal Analysis

Kuan-Hsiung Wang

Introduction

The South China Sea is a maritime area full of disputes on sovereignty, sovereign rights, traditional and non-traditional security issues and marine space utilization, including fisheries and environmental protection. In other words, the South China Sea is essential for the regional and international stability of food, economies, maritime transportation and so on.

Disputes emerging from the South China Sea are complicated since they include issues of island sovereignty, maritime delimitation, resource utilization (including living and non-living resources), as well as non-traditional security. To clarify the situation, South China Sea disputes could be separated into two parts: sovereignty of land features and maritime zones that could be claimed based on the occupied features.

It would make sense that the best way to solve the disputes would be delimiting boundaries so that the areas of sovereignty and jurisdiction could be decided. However, such a situation is not always possible, mainly because the negotiation and adoption of a maritime boundary between the related states has always focused on political considerations, and there are no well-established laws for creating boundaries. Although it is recognized that an "equitable solution" is one of the most important principles in creating a boundary, no definite elements have been decided. Besides geographical and geological factors, coastal length, traditional fishing activities, relative impact on livelihood and economic dependency are all considerations recognized in different cases.

Under such circumstances, joint development could be accepted as a solution to the disputes. In other words, all claimants should work out a way to solve the disputes, rather than building up more conflict through complicating the resolution. The purpose of this chapter is to clarify certain ideas about the practices of the United Nations Convention on the Law of the Sea (UNCLOS), especially since the Philippines initiated the arbitration procedure against China in January 2013, a procedure in which China insists it will not participate.

The theoretical background for this chapter is based on the application of the provisional arrangement in UNCLOS Article 74 paragraph 3. States with maritime jurisdiction disputes should seek agreements to reach an equitable solution, and maritime delimitation would be the best option. However, such a solution might not be found easily in many disputed cases, where political posturing is diametrically opposed to the spirit of the UNCLOS. In order to resolve the disputes and better utilize resources, a provisional arrangement or a modus vivendi seems most feasible in the absence of a final resolution.

Moving toward Cooperation as an Obligation

A general obligation to cooperate in the disputes has received specific attention in some international treaties and other documents, especially in the UNCLOS, as well as other related instruments. The 1982 UNCLOS and the 1995 Agreement for the Implementation of the Provisions of the United Nations Convention on the Law of the Sea of 10 December 1982 Relating to the Conservation and Management of Straddling Fish Stocks and Highly Migratory Fish Stocks (UNFSA) are two examples. Both provide certain provisions on the regulation of cooperation among states in dealing with the issues of high seas fisheries.

Before those instruments are discussed, one of the basic issues to be considered is the nature of the duty to cooperate. It is noteworthy that the duty to cooperate among states is either amicable or antagonistic. Such a concept can be traced back to certain documents made more than four decades ago, such as a United Nations General Assembly Declaration in 1970 that stated, "States have the duty to co-operate with one another, irrespective of the differences in their political, economic and social systems, in the various spheres of international relations".[1]

Such duty could be characterized into two forms: a duty to enter into negotiations and a duty to negotiate and to reach an agreement. Obviously, both duties of cooperation will require negotiations entered into good faith. Moreover, the parties concerned shall be obliged to work together in a good faith effort to reach an agreement and to carry that agreement through to a successful conclusion.[2] Under such considerations, certain provisions in UNCLOS and UNFSA embrace the spirit of cooperation.

---

1 1970 Declaration on Principles of International Law concerning Friendly Relations and Cooperation among States in accordance with the Charter of the United Nations, General Assembly Resolution 2625(XXV), U.N. Doc. A/8082 (24 October 1970). Also, Anne Peters, "International Dispute Settlement: A Network of Cooperational Duties", *European Journal of International Law*, Vol. 14, No. 1 (2003), pp. 1–34.

2 L. Guruswamy, "The Promise of the United Nations Convention on the Law of the Sea: Justice and Environmental Disputes", 25 *Ecology Law Quarterly* (1998), p. 189; quoting from Stuart M. Kaye, *International Fisheries Management*, (The Hague: Kluwer Law International, 2001), p. 111.

According to Article 118 of UNCLOS, states fishing in the same living marine resources area or in the same area of the high seas shall cooperate in the conservation of these resources. With respect to straddling fish stocks and highly migratory species in the high seas, such an obligation is supplemented with the special obligations of the relevant coastal states and states fishing for these stocks in adjacent areas of the high seas to cooperate for the conservation of these stocks.[3] Taking into consideration the practices in recent years of states and international organizations, these obligations have become a part of customary international law.[4]

Part 3 of the UNFSA includes several provisions for mechanisms for cooperation in the conservation of straddling fish stocks and highly migratory species. States fishing for stock on the high seas may choose not to join or participate but are then obligated to apply the management measures adopted by the organization or arrangement, in order to be entitled to fish the stock.[5] If the straddling fish stock or highly migratory fish stocks are not subjected to the regulatory competence of any organization or arrangement, states fishing for the stock on the high seas and the relevant coastal states are obligated to establish either an organization or other appropriate arrangements.[6]

It is a customary law that states with maritime jurisdiction disputes should seek agreements to reach an equitable solution, and maritime delimitation would be the best option, but such a solution might not be found easily in many disputed cases where political posturing is diametrically opposed to the spirit of the UNCLOS. In order to resolve the disputes and better utilise resources, a provisional arrangement or a *modus vivendi* seems most feasible in the absence of a final resolution. Articles 74 of the UNCLOS offer a working procedure toward the delimitation issues of the overlapping exclusive economic zone:

1. The delimitation of the exclusive economic zone between States with opposite or adjacent coasts shall be effected by agreement on the basis of international law, as referred to in Article 38 of the Statue of the International Court of Justice, in order to achieve an equitable solution.
2. If no agreement can be reached within a reasonable period of time, the States concerned shall resort to the procedures provided for in Part XV.
3. Pending agreement as provided for in paragraph 1, the States concerned, in a spirit of understanding and co-operation, shall make every effort to enter into provisional arrangements of a practical nature and, during this transitional period, not to jeopardise or hamper the reaching of the final agreement. Such arrangements shall be without prejudice to the final delimitation.

---

3 UNCLOS arts. 63(2) – 64(1).

4 Tore Henriksen, Geir Honneland and Are Sydnes, *Law and Politics in Ocean Governance: The UN Fish Stocks Agreement and Regional Fisheries Management Regimes* (Leiden: Martinus Nijhoff, 2006), p. 15.

5 UNFSA, Article 8(4).

6 UNFSA, Article 8(5).

4. Where there is an agreement in force between the States concerned, questions relating to the delimitation of the exclusive economic zone shall be determined in accordance with the provisions of that agreement.

During the period of provisional arrangements, not only should the arrangement itself not hamper the final resolution, but also each of the parties should control itself so that a provisional arrangement could operate between states in dispute to keep the disputes under control or – at the very least – to avoid any further aggravation of conflict. The conflict should be managed so that any incident would not hurt or help the position of either side. Furthermore, if the states in dispute agree, they could explore and exploit resources without touching upon the issues of delimitation or sovereignty, that is to say, distinguishing the issue of sovereign rights from the one of sovereignty. Therefore, for the best result, states in dispute should take the following two actions:

Article 74(3) of the UNCLOS provides that, the states concerned, in a spirit of understanding and co-operation, shall make every effort to enter into provisional arrangements of a practical nature. The phrase, "in a spirit of understanding and co-operation", indicates that the parties concerned should negotiate with a spirit of good faith (or *bona fide*). The obligation to seek agreement in good faith is defined in many well-established precedents of international juridical cases. For example, in the 1969 North Sea Continental Shelf Cases, the International Court of Justice stated that:

> [T]he parties are under an obligation to enter into negotiations with a view to arriving at an agreement and not merely to go through a formal process of negotiation as a sort of prior condition for the automatic application of a certain method of delimitation in the absence of agreement; they are under an obligation so to conduct themselves that the negotiations are meaningful.[7]

Also, in the 1984 Gulf of Maine Case, the Court said that the parties were under duty to negotiate "and to do so in good faith, with a genuine intention to achieve a positive result".[8]

Even if the parties fail to reach a final agreement, they still have to restrain themselves from taking any action that would cause the dispute to deteriorate. That is to say, mutual restraint should be exercised pending final agreement or settlement in order not to impede the completion of the final delimitation. Only under such a presumption can the arrangement correspond to the spirit of the provision, "not to jeopardize or hamper the reaching of the final agreement".

---

7 International Court of Justice, *North Sea Continental Shelf Cases (Federal Republic of Germany/Denmark; Federal Republic of Germany/Netherlands)*, Judgment of 20 February 1969, para. 85(a).

8 International Court of Justice, *Delimitation of the Maritime Boundary in the Gulf of Maine Area (Canada/United States of America)*, Judgment of 12 October 1984, para. 87.

Furthermore, the words "shall make every effort" indicate that this requirement is not just an impracticable encouragement, but a mandatory rule whose breach would imply a violation of international law. In other words, it would be a first priority for the states concerned to consider the feasibility of reaching a provisional agreement on the dispute.

Also, such provisional arrangement has two characteristics:[9]

1. Transitional nature. In the interest of regional stability, the states concerned shall enter into provisional arrangements so as not to jeopardize or hamper the reaching of the final delimitation. Thus, the obligation to seek a solution to a dispute through peaceful means is not diminished by the interim agreements. It is because they are characterized as "provisional", the arrangements are interim and they are preliminary or even preparatory to the final agreed status of the area and the utilization of its resources. The interim measures could not be interpreted as constituting a barrier to the final solution. The parties meanwhile maintain their rights and claims as well as their respective positions in the conflict.[10]
2. Practical nature. Because the provisional arrangement is of a practical nature, it focuses on practical issues, i.e. utilization of resources, and puts the maritime boundary/jurisdiction delimitation and sovereignty issues aside. Additionally, owing to its practical nature, a provisionally arranged fishing zone would have no relevance, for example, to a disputed hydrocarbon-rich area. In other words, the utilization of living resources is separate from the utilization of non-living resources.

Fishing Ban as a Management Measure

Geographically, there are three maritime areas in the East Asian region, the Sea of Japan, the East China Sea and the South China Sea. Under the UNCLOS provision, all of them could be treated as "semi-enclosed seas" in the sense that they are surrounded by two or more states and connected to another sea or the

9 Rainer Lagoni, "Interim Measures Pending Maritime Delimitation Agreements", 78 *American Journal of International Law* (1984) p. 345; Robert Beckman and Tara Davenport, "Non-living Resources in Disputed Areas in the East China Sea: Law and Policy Issues concerning Provisional Arrangements under UNCLOS", International Symposium on The East China Sea and the Law of the Sea: Defusing Tensions and Enhancing Cooperation" Organized by the Guanghua Law School, Zhejiang University, China, 21–2 August 2012, Zhejiang University, Hangzhou, China. See <http://cil.nus.edu.sg/wp/wp-content/uploads/2012/09/ProfBeckman-TaraDavenport-Provisional_Arrangements_in_the_East_China_Sea_Draft_of_18Aug2012.pdf>.

10 Interim Agreement in the Fisheries Dispute between the UK and Iceland, 13 November 1973, *ICJ Report* (1974), para. 37.

ocean by a narrow outlet.[11] The UNCLOS has provided a legal framework for the establishment of the maritime legal order in East Asia. East Asian countries, apart from Cambodia and North Korea, have acceded to the UNCLOS.[12] In order to implement the UNCLOS, countries have adopted relevant domestic laws and regulations for the management of their own maritime zones and maritime activities within their jurisdiction.[13]

Because the South China Sea is semi-enclosed, any change in the ecosystem of the semi-enclosed sea will have significant impact on the whole area. It is generally recognized that the living resources in the South China Sea area migrate from one claimant's EEZ to another, particularly those highly migratory species, such as tuna and other shared stocks. Each country may already have its own assessment of its living resources in its EEZ, assuming that the definition and delineation of each EEZ is clear. The problem is that many of those EEZ boundaries are not well defined or agreed upon by the relevant parties. Likewise, there are various conflicting claims to islands that complicate and defer the determination of the EEZ boundaries. For this reason, there is a need to co-operate on the assessment of the living resources in the South China Sea area without regard to jurisdictional boundaries. The basis for this endeavour would be Article 123 of the UNCLOS regarding enclosed and semi-enclosed seas.[14] The UNCLOS has foreseen this problem, since Article 123 provides:

> States bordering an enclosed or semi-enclosed sea should co-operate with each other in the exercise of their rights and in the performance of their duties under this Convention. To this end they shall endeavour, directly or through an appropriate regional organization:
>
> a) to co-ordinate the management, conservation, exploration and exploitation of the living resources of the sea;
>
> b) to co-ordinate the implementation of their rights and duties with respect to the protection and preservation of the marine environment;
>
> c) to co-ordinate their scientific research policies and undertake where appropriate joint programmes of scientific research in the area;

---

11 UNCLOS Article 122, "For the purposes of this Convention, 'enclosed or semi-enclosed sea' means a gulf, basin or sea surrounded by two or more States and connected to another sea or the ocean by a narrow outlet or consisting entirely or primarily of the territorial seas and exclusive economic zones of two or more coastal States".

12 Table recapitulating the status of the Convention and of the related Agreements, as at 10 October 2014 <http://www.un.org/Depts/los/reference_files/status2010.pdf>.

13 Zou Keyuan, *Law of the Sea in East Asia: Issues and Prospects* (Oxford: Routledge, 2005), p. 2.

14 Hasjim Djalal, "Issue Paper for Technical Working Group on the Resources Assessment of the South China Sea Informal Workshop", in the Second Working Group Meeting on Resources Assessment and Ways of Development in the South China Sea, Jakarta, Indonesia, 5–6 July 1993, pp. 1–2.

d) to invite, as appropriate, other interested states or international organisations to co-operate with them in furtherance of the provisions of this article.

It is also necessary for all parties concerned to be aware that fish are migratory and fishery resources are exhaustible, so that rational use of the South China Sea and the preservation of its marine environment are important to all parties.

From a geographical viewpoint, if all coastal states claim the establishment of a 200-mile EEZ, the extent of ocean area under national jurisdiction would reach approximately 31.9 million nm^2 or about 30 percent of the world's marine surface. More importantly, over 90 percent of the world commercial catch in volume terms is estimated to be taken within 200 miles of land.[15] So the establishment of the EEZ is a serious matter for any distant-water fishing nation. More seriously, in a semi-enclosed sea like the South China Sea, littoral states extending their maritime jurisdiction inevitably create overlapping claims and areas. This has led to serious fishery disputes.

The resources of the South China Sea, both living and non-living, are rapidly being exploited by the people of the region, who are heavily concentrated along the coastline.[16] Overfishing and a declining average annual fish catch now threaten the extensive fishing industry. Fishermen are forced to apply more efficient and aggressive fishing techniques, and to venture further out to new fishing grounds. For the most extreme cases, some even apply illegal methods such as blast fishing and cyanide poisoning. Fish and coral habitats are also degraded by increased sedimentation, especially from land development. Coral reefs have been ravaged to provide building materials and plundered for ornamental commodities.[17]

15 Lewis M. Alexander and Robert D. Hodgson, "The Impact of the 200-Mile Economic Zone on the Law of the Sea", 12 *San Diego Law Review* (1975), p. 586; J.E. Carroz, "The Living Resources of the Sea", in Rene-Jean Dupuy (ed.), *The Management of Humanity's Resources: The Law of the Sea* (The Hague: Martinus Nijhoff Publishers, 1982), p. 199.

16 In terms of the South China Sea LME which is bordered by China, Indonesia, Malaysia, Philippines, Taiwan and Vietnam. It covers an area of 3.2 million km^2, of which 0.31 percent is protected, and contains 7.04 percent and 0.93 percent of the world's coral reefs and sea mounts, respectively. S. Heileman, "South China Sea: LME #36", in K. Sherman and G. Hempel (eds), *The UNEP Large Marine Ecosystem Report: A Perspective on Changing Conditions in LMEs of the World's Regional Seas.* UNEP Regional Seas, Report and Studies No. 182 (2008), United Nations Environment Programme, Nairobi, Kenya.

17 <http://www.southchinasea.org/why.html>. Also Global International Waters Assessment (GIWA), Preliminary Results for the Scoping and Assessment of the South China Sea and Sulu-Celebes Seas. Draft discussion paper in the Regional GIWA Workshop, November 5–8, 2001, Bangkok, Thailand (2001), quoted from Porfirio M. Alino, "The South China Sea-Revisiting: The Large Marine Ecosystem Approach". See <http://innri.unuftp.is/pdf/South%20China%20Sea.pdf>. Also United Nations, "Oceans and the Law of the Sea: Report of the Secretary-General", UN GA Doc. A/69/71 (21 March 2014) <http://daccess-dds-ny.un.org/doc/UNDOC/GEN/N14/272/55/PDF/N1427255.pdf?OpenElement>.

Take the fishing ban[18] that the Chinese government announced in May 2012 for instance. The ban, covering areas north of the 12th parallel, including Huangyan Island but excluding most of the Nansha Islands, was a part of ongoing efforts to rehabilitate the northern part of the South China Sea's marine living resources. According to the Hainan Provincial Marine and Fishing Department, all 8,994 locally-registered fishing vessels were moored. It was emphasized that the fishing ban was adopted to promote sustainable development as well as the biological situation of the fishing industry in the South China Sea and protect the fundamental interests of fishermen, said officials from the South China Fishery Administration Bureau under the Ministry of Agriculture (MOA). Violators would face punishments including fines, license revocations, equipment confiscation and possible criminal charges, according to a statement issued by the Fishery Bureau under the MOA. The provincial fishing authority said fishing vessels with fishing permits for the Nansha Islands are required to install and activate positioning equipment so they will not accidentally enter banned areas.

The fishing ban was also applicable to foreign ships. A spokesman from the Fishery Bureau under the MOA expressed that fishing activity conducted by foreign ships in banned areas would be deemed as a "blatant encroachment on China's fishery resources".[19] According to a study on the fishery production, said production showed an increase of 40 percent after the implementation of fishing ban. This proved the fishing ban is an appropriate means toward the end of managing and conserving fishery resources. Nonetheless, such a conservation and management measure is not accepted by other claimants, for instance, the Philippines.

The Philippines' Department of Foreign Affairs responded to China's fishing ban by saying they would ignore it and that their "position is that we do not recognize China's fishing ban, as portions of the ban encompass our Exclusive Economic Zone". In addition, the Philippines decided that, "in view of the accelerated depletion of our marine resources, it would be advisable for us to issue our own fishing ban for a period of time to replenish our fish stock". This would only make the situation worse.

A Positive Way of Thinking

For a better resolution to the fishing activities disputes between China and the Philippines (both insist fishing rights are damaged by the other party), the answer might be implementing a cooperation mechanism on managing and conserving fishery resources.

---

18 "Fishing ban starts in South China Sea", Xinhuanet (17 May 2012), at <http://news.xinhuanet.com/english/china/2012–05/17/c_131592412.htm>.

19 *Ibid.*

Trawlers were introduced to the Southeast Asian countries in the 1960's. With their efficiency and higher production rate, trawlers became a popular fishing method. At the outset, there was, for these countries, neither a fishing policy nor the concept of fishery resources management to limit the occurrence of fishing efforts. With no oversight over fishing, more and more fishermen competed with each other for the same stocks in the same fishing grounds. Thus, this eventually led to overfishing in the South China Sea region.[20]

In tackling fishery disputes and promoting co-management mechanism of fishery resources in the South China Sea, the following steps should be considered:[21]

A. Defining and minimizing disputed areas

The first task for the states concerned might be to define and minimize the disputed area. Then, a joint committee could be established to manage the issues of fishing vessels, either from the relevant states or other states operating in the disputed area.

B. Definition and determination of stocks and allowable catch of living resources in the region

Based on tagging studies, changes in hooking-rates and the size of catch, bluefin tuna, yellowfin tuna, skipjack tuna and mackerels are the major highly migratory species in South China Sea region. Because some of their migration routes are through two or more countries, they are also shared stocks. Therefore, in order to get the maximum benefit from management, it is necessary to categorize those shared species into:

- Joint stocks which live partly within South China Sea waters and partly within the 200 nm fisheries zone of a country which is not within South China Sea region;
- Autonomous stocks which live entirely within South China Sea waters and which the whole of the littoral states can manage as they wish.

Then a further stock analysis can be performed.

20 Pakjuta Khemakorn, *Sustainable Management of Pelagic Fisheries in the South China Sea Region* (New York: United Nations – The Nippon Foundation Fellow, November 2006), pp. 29–38.

21 George Kent, "Harmonizing Extended Zone Legislation in Southeast Asia", *Ocean Development and International Law* (1983), pp. 247–68.

C. Data collection and surveillance

The required information or data for fisheries management may include the following:

- Biological information: such as status of stocks, trends in catches per unit of fishing effort;
- Technical information: such as numbers and kinds of fishing vessels and gear;
- Economic information: such as trends in fish prices, incomes to fishermen;
- Social information: such as trends in numbers of fishermen, mobility into and out of fisheries.

D. Determination of maintaining or restoring populations of harvested species at levels that can produce the maximum sustainable yield

This concerns the limitation of the amount of fishing efforts by setting total allowable catches (TAC), the limitation of access, the regulation of the methods, and technical aspects of fishing. Minimizing mesh size is one example.

E. Allocating quotas among littoral states

Allocating quotas is important because:

- Effective management is impossible if the TAC is not divided into quotas, because the fishing vessels of each state would otherwise compete with each other in order to maximize their share of the TAC before it is exhausted. The result would be the depletion of the resources;
- Littoral states can plan their fishing vessels development, marketing, etc., if they have guaranteed shares of the TACs.

F. Regional/extra-regional joint ventures involving technology transfers and development

Joint ventures have become increasingly important to fishery management, because they are a good approach to upgrading the host country's fishing industry through personnel training and technology transfers.

G. Harmonizing or standardizing legislations

For fishery management, standardized laws might be established for the licensing of foreign fishing vessels for access to the South China Sea waters. Distant-water fishing nations in the region could be given privileged access. In a semi-enclosed sea, it is important to have laws harmonized so that a legislation vacuum can be avoided.

Conclusion

Fishing or fishery is a vital part of the world's diet, economy, and biodiversity. In recent years, the fishing industry has been recognized as one of the more important elements influencing food security. World population is expected to grow from the present 7 billion people to about 9 billion by 2050, and Southeast Asia is one of the most populated regions. The growing need for nutritious and healthy food will increase the demand for fishery products from marine sources, from areas where productivity is already highly stressed by excessive fishing pressure, growing organic pollution, toxic contamination, coastal degradation and climate change. Looking towards 2050, the question is how fishery governance and the national and international policy and legal frameworks within which it is nested will ensure a sustainable harvest, maintain biodiversity and ecosystem functions and adapt to climate change.

During this period of focusing on economic development and trade, exploring the marine living resources and increasing their production might be the right choice. However, in a globalized world, it is hard to figure out the complicated web of influence between trade and environment. Fisheries are no less complicated. Nonetheless, since today is the time for conserving and managing fishery resources and international instruments and organizations have already embedded the concepts of sustainability and precautionary into the fishing activities, it might be the right time and right choice to adjust fisheries policy to include more environmental consideration. States bordering semi-enclosed seas, such as the South China Sea, should have the responsibility to embed the consideration of regional cooperation into every party's national ocean policy. Moreover, the goal of sustainable fisheries management in the South China Sea region is currently impeded by ill-organized management, which has originated from the disputes of maritime delimitation and territorial sovereignty issues. This could be a good opportunity for all claimants to the South China Sea islands/rocks to take the environment into serious consideration. Then the wording "provisional arrangements" in UNCLOS Article 74(3) could be a catalyst to the settlement of the South China Sea dispute.

Fish are a migratory and exhaustible resource, so the rational utilization of them and the preservation of their marine environment are necessary. Fishery cooperation can be the most feasible course of action for these littoral states because through cooperation fishery resources can be properly conserved and managed such that economic waste and over-exploitation can be avoided. Cooperation in the utilization of fishery resources is a feasible and practical way to start a regional cooperation regime. It sidesteps the issue of sovereignty and focuses upon a common interest, namely the utilization of living resources. Without effecting the jurisdictional boundaries as laid down in the UNCLOS, it is certainly possible to have regional joint fishery management in the South China Sea as the starting point for further cooperation. If all states in this region treat cooperation as a key step toward achieving mutual benefits, then the future for such a regional cooperation mechanism is assured.

Thus cooperation among the parties concerned in the region is essential. This is especially necessary for neighbouring countries, such as China and the Philippines. In order to avoid overfishing or depletion of resources as well as reduce fishery disputes between them, a co-managing measure has to be taken into consideration. Such measures are not possible without sincere cooperation and coordination. Without touching upon overlapping boundaries and territorial claims, it is certainly possible to have regional joint fishery management in the South China Sea as the starting point for further cooperation.

It is not difficult to locate opportunities for joint cooperation in the South China Sea region. Joint military exercises, joint development of hydrocarbon resources, marine scientific research, marine environmental protection and fisheries cooperation are options to this end. To date, however, disputes surrounding possible hydrocarbon resources in the area and actions in favor of conservation and management of fishery resources have been delayed. Nevertheless, conservation and management of fishery resources, as the starting point for cooperation, could have a "spill over effect" into other areas of cooperation.

In this respect, cooperating to manage and conserve fisheries resources is especially significant because fish are migratory and some of them are highly migratory. Moreover, overfishing is a serious and pressing problem in the region. In this regard, a maritime boundary cannot entirely protect a state's fishery resources from encroachment, because fishery resources can migrate beyond the state's jurisdiction, and overfishing beyond its borders could also have great impact on the fish stocks within its territorial boundaries.

Therefore, a proper management mechanism, subject to natural conditions, is necessary for the coastal states to keep stocks at sustainable levels. This is especially important for the claimants of the South China Sea. Because this region is semi-enclosed, any change in the fishery policy-making could have far-reaching effects on the fishery resources in this area.

Chapter 13

Law Enforcement in a Disputed Maritime Zone: A Political and Legal Analysis

Nong Hong

Introduction

The existing territorial and maritime dispute in the South China Sea (SCS) has been pending for decades. Despite tremendous efforts toward conflict management, the settlement of the decades-old maritime dispute in the SCS seems to be politically deadlocked and has encountered difficulties that may keep it from being settled quickly, if ever.

The Philippines, having lost patience with the ASEAN way of solving the dispute, has stepped forward with a series of provocative movements, including changing the name of the South China Sea to the West Philippine Sea[1] and, in April 2012, starting a stand-off with China around the Scarborough Shoal by engaging its naval ships.[2] Its most recent provocative action was on 22 January 2013 when it notified China that it would bring this largest claimant state to an arbitration tribunal according to Annex VII of the United Nations Convention for the Law of the Sea (UNCLOS).[3] In response, China, on 31 January, rejected this request based on its understanding, according to Articles 283 and 298, that the Tribunal has no jurisdiction.[4] On 25 June 2013, the fifth arbitrator was appointed and the Arbitral Tribunal set up according to Annex VII of UNCLOS, with the Registry of the Permanent Court of Arbitration ("PCA")serving as its registry.[5] On 31 March

1 Tarra Quismundo, "South China Sea renamed in the Philippines", *Philippine Daily Inquirer*, available at <http://news.asiaone.com/News/Latest%2BNews/Asia/Story/A1Story20110613–283772.html>.

2 "Scarborough Shoal Standoff: A Historical Timeline", *Inquirer Global Nation*, available at <http://globalnation.inquirer.net/36003/scarborough-shoal-standoff-a-historicaltimeline/>.

3 See <http://www.gov.ph/2013/01/22/dfa-notification-and-statement-claim-on-west-philippine-sea-january-22-2013/>.

4 "China Opposes Taking Sea Disputes to UN", *China.org.cn*, available at <http://www.china.org.cn/world/2013-01/31/content_27855302.htm>.

5 See <http://www.pca-cpa.org/showpage.asp?pag_id=1529>.

2014, the Philippines submitted its Memorial to the Arbitral Tribunal, which has not yet been released to the public.[6]

Based on its Notification and Statement of Claim, the Philippines seems to categorize its claims into three groups. First, it claims that China's U-shaped Line is not consistent with the provisions of the UNCLOS.[7] Second, it claims that the eight features that are occupied by China or claimed by China are either rocks, which are not entitled to generate exclusive economic zone (EEZ) and continental shelf as provided by the island regime of Article 121 of the UNCLOS, or low tide elevations (LTEs), which cannot be claimed by any country and belong to the countries on whose continental shelf they sit. Third, the Philippines claims that its rights in its EEZ have been hampered by China.

In terms of China's law enforcement at Scarborough Shoal and the Second Thomas Shoal, both China and the Philippines claim sovereignty over these two features. The Philippines argues that its claims do not involve sovereignty and maritime delimitation, thus the 2006 Declaration made by China based on Article 298 of the UNCLOS to exclude certain disputes from a third party compulsory settlement mechanism does not apply in this case. The author would argue that an observation of the history of the bilateral disputes will give the reader a deeper understanding of the legal merit of the claim and the political implications arising from it.

One of the core issues concerning the claims is actually law enforcement in the disputed maritime area. Despite the competing claims, the most important task is avoiding incidents at sea. There are abundant regulations on safety of navigation, including the 1972 International Regulations for Preventing Collisions at Sea (COLREGs), of which both China and the Philippines are States Parties. The coastal states have also adopted relevant domestic laws and regulations on the safety of navigation. What is missing is confidence-building and crisis management, on which the author will finish by offering a few recommendations. For this purpose, law enforcement co-operation on fishery resources management might be a starting point for solving the disputes, rather than a sudden jump to a third party dispute settlement procedure.

China's Law Enforcement at Scarborough Shoal

The Philippines claims that "China has operated vessels in a manner threatening to Philippine vessels in the vicinity of Scarborough Shoal (Huangyan Island in Chinese) by engaging in highly dangerous maneuvers that have caused serious risks of collision". It notes the conduct of Chinese vessels at Scarborough Shoal

---

6 "Foreign Ministry Spokesperson Hong Lei's Regular Press Conference on March 31, 2014", Chinese UN Mission <http://www.china-un.org/eng/fyrth/t1142811.htm>.

7 The Memorial submitted by the Philippines on 30 March 2014 to the Arbitral Tribunal of the *Philippines. v. China Case* in the South China Sea.

on 12 May 2012 based on the report from FRPLEU-QRT Officers, Bureau of Fisheries and Aquatic Resources, Bureau of Fisheries and Aquatic Resources, the Philippines. It accuses China of breaching the International Regulations for Preventing Collisions at Sea (*COLREGs*) and its obligations under Article 94 of the UNCLOS, which sets out the duties and obligations of flag states.

Review of the Disputes

The Philippines seems to deliberately avoid any clarification and discussion on the Scarborough Shoal standoff in April 2012 and the pre-2012 disputes between China and the Philippines. The Philippines realized the value of the Spratly Islands in 1930s, but never attempted to challenge China's claim until the late 1950s.[8] The Philippines' claims over the Spratlys started from 1956s when Tomas A. Cloma, together with his brother and 40 other fishermen, took "formal" possession of a large area of the Spratly Islands and announced to the public the establishment of a "Freedomland" (Kalaya'an).[9]

Its claim over the Scarborough Shoal, which is a part of Macclesfield Bank Group (Zhongsha Qundao in Chinese), started much later. Before 1997, no evidence shows that the Philippines ever claimed sovereignty over the Scarborough Shoal. Scarborough Shoal was not included in the map that was published by the Philippines' authority publisher.[10] The Philippine's position changed when, in May 1997, a group of researchers (two Japanese, three American and six Chinese) planned to visit the Scarborough Shoal for a broadcasting test, escorted by China State Oceanic Administration vessels. Philippine military spy planes and naval vessels tried to intervene. The Philippines deemed this activity as China using research vessels to enhance its sovereignty claims.[11] Since 2001, the Philippines has increased its patrols in the Scarborough Shoal and the surrounding maritime areas. Scholars have several explanations for the Philippines' new attention toward claiming Scarborough Shoal in 1997, one of which is the possible enlargement of maritime jurisdiction stipulated by the 1982 UNCLOS.[12]

Starting on 10 April 2012, China and the Philippines became embroiled in a standoff in disputed waters in the South China Sea. The standoff occurred when eight Chinese fishing boats, while taking refuge in a lagoon near Scarborough Shoal due to harsh weather, were harassed by the Philippines' largest warship, the

---

8 Guanghua Yu, *Roles and Law and Politics in China's Development* (Berlin: Springer, 2014), p. 135.

9 Wu Shicun, Solving Disputes for Regional Cooperation and Development in the South China Sea: A Chinese Perspective (Cambridge: Woodhead Publishing, 2013), p. 132.

10 Zou Keyuan, "Scarborough Reef: A New Flashpoint in Sino-Philippine Relation?", *IBRU Boundary and Security Bulletin* 7, no. 2 (Summer 1999), p. 74.

11 Andrew Sherry and Rigoberto Tiglao, Law of the Seize: Radio Amateurs Arouse Latest South China Sea Tension, *Far Eastern Economic Review* (June 1997), p. 17, 21.

12 Zou Keyuan, *supra* note 13, p. 71.

Gregorio del Pilar. Shortly after, two unarmed China Marine Surveillance vessels, which were conducting routine patrols in the area, appeared and interposed themselves between the fishing boats and the frigate, thus preventing any arrest of the fishermen.[13]

In order to deescalate the situation, the Philippines replaced its frigate with a smaller coast guard vessel.[14] China's fishing boats left the site on 13 April, followed by the withdrawal of two Chinese law enforcement vessels.[15] In mid-June 2012, the tensions generated by the standoff started to abate when the civilian vessels left the shoal on the pretext of the onset of the typhoon season. On 16 June, President Aquino recalled all Philippine vessels because of the onslaught of a seasonal typhoon. On 18 June, Beijing announced that Chinese fishing boats were heading back to port. A Chinese foreign ministry spokesperson stated that with the withdrawal of the civilian ships, "[w]e (China) hope (that) there will continue to be an easing in the situation and hope bilateral cooperation will recover and be safeguarded". The following day, the China Maritime Search and Rescue Center sent a rescue ship to assist Chinese fishing boats leaving the area due to rough sea conditions. The coordinated withdrawal of Philippine and Chinese civilian vessels from the shoal happened while consultations between the two states were ongoing. Despite the withdrawal of the vessels, both states persisted in their claim of sovereignty over the shoal.[16]

Some hold that the incident underscores China's current maritime strategy that "involves using civilian vessels to challenge littoral states that run the risk of exacerbating a critical situation by resorting to military means and engaging the People's Liberation Army's Navy (PLAN) ships lurking in the background".[17] This opinion could be justified, since China has on many occasions firmly reiterated the fact that the Philippine Navy was involved at the start of this standoff in the first place, when it should be the jurisdiction of coast guards to exercise law enforcement.

Some claim that China makes regular use of China's Coast Guard ships to assert and defend its maritime territorial claims, with Chinese Navy ships sometimes available over the horizon as a backup force.[18] Chinese Coast Guard ships are unarmed or lightly armed, but can be effective in asserting and defending maritime territorial claims, particularly in terms of confronting or harassing foreign vessels

---

13 Wu Shicun, "The Huangyan Island Standoff: A Review of the Claims and the Prospects for the Future" <http://www.nanhai.org.cn/en/cg_detail.asp?newsid=2282&lm=cg>.

14 R. Cruz De Castro, "China's Realpolitik Approach in the South China Sea Dispute: The Case of the 2012 Scarborough Shoal Stand-Off", paper presented at "Managing Tensions in the South China Sea", 5–6 June 2013.

15 Wu Shicun, "The Huangyan Island Standoff".

16 Cruz De Castro, "China's Realpolitik Approach in the South China Sea", 9.

17 *Ibid.*

18 Ronald O'Rourk, "Maritime Territorial and Exclusive Economic Zone (EEZ) Disputes Involving China: Issues for Congress", 3 July 2014 <http://fas.org/sgp/crs/row/R42784.pdf>.

that are similarly lightly armed or unarmed.[19] In addition to being available as backup for China's Coast Guard ships, Chinese navy ships conduct exercises that in some cases appear intended, at least in part, at reinforcing China's maritime claims.[20] Some observers believe China also uses civilian fishing ships to assert and defend its maritime claims.[21]

The Philippines claimed that the warship *Gregorio del Pilar* was deployed to protect the marine environment and resources in the shoal and assert the Philippine sovereignty over the area as a coastal state.[22] According to some security practitioners in the Philippines, the Philippine Coast Guard is so poorly equipped that the Philippine Navy has to take over some responsibilities in its maritime law enforcement.[23]

The Philippine Coast Guard is an armed and uniformed service primarily tasked with enforcing laws within Philippine waters, conducting maritime security operations, safeguarding life and property at sea, and protecting the marine environment and resources, similar to coast guards around the world. The new Philippine Coast Guard law established the guard as a distinct law enforcement entity.[24]

Geoffrey Till's analysis of the role of coast guards and navies is reflected in the Philippine's case. Apart from its traditional mandate "to organize, train, equip, maintain, develop and deploy forces for prompt and sustained naval and maritime operations in support of the Unified Commands in the accomplishment of the AFP mission",[25] it is also mandated "to assist the proper governmental

---

19 See, for example, Megha Rajagopalan and Greg Torode, "China's Civilian Fleet a Potent Force in Asia's Disputed Waters", Reuters.com, 5 March 2014. See also O'Rourk, "Maritime Territorial and Exclusive Economic Zone (EEZ) Disputes Involving China".

20 See, for example, Trefor Moss and Rob Taylor, "Chinese Naval Patrol Pompts Conflicting Regional Response", 20 February 2014, *Wall Street Journal.*

21 See James R. Holmes. A Competitive Turn: How Increased Chinese Maritime Actions Complicate U.S. Partnerships, Washington, Center for a New American Security, December 2012, East and South China Sea Bulletin 7 <http://www.cnas.org/files/documents/flashpoints/CNAS_bulletin_Holmes_ACompetitiveTurn.pdf>, 1; James R. Holmes, "China's Small Stick Diplomacy", 21 May 2012, *The Diplomat* <http://thediplomat.com/2012/05/21/chinas-small-stick-diplomacy/>; Jens Kastner, "China's Fishermen Charge Enemy Lines", *Asia Times Online*, 16 May 2012; Carlyle A. Thayer, "Paracel Island: Chinese Boats Attack Vietnamese Fishing Craft", *Thayer Consultancy Background Brief*, 28 May 2013, 1.

22 Cruz De Castro, "China's Realpolitik Approach in the South China Sea", 4.

23 A round table discussion was held between the National Institute for South China Sea Studies and the Philippine Association of China Studies in Beijing on 17 April 2013.

24 Philippine Coast Guard Law of 2009, based on the 2007 Integrity Development Review of the AFP–Philippine Navy by the EC-OMB Corruption Prevention Project.

25 "EC-OMB Corruption Prevention Project Integrity Development Review of the AFP-Philippine Navy Executive Summary" <http://www.ombudsman.gov.ph/docs/statistics/2007_afp-pn_summary.pdf>.

agencies in the enforcement of laws and regulations pertaining to navigation, immigration, customs revenue, opium, quarantine, fishing and neutrality in the territorial and contiguous waters of the Philippine Archipelago".[26] The Philippine government tried to justify the fact that the Philippine Navy was directly involved in the Huangyan Island (Scarborough Shoal) Dispute in April 2010, although its argument may not be accepted by China.

China's reaction in the Scarborough Shoal standoff signals a reassuring intention to keep the PLAN's power dry and to manage disputes with civilian ships that are, at most, only lightly armed. This is part of a new Chinese foreign policy approach of "reactive assertiveness": the idea is that China tries to avoid fights, but if someone launches a fight against China, it will offer a forceful response. It has also been called "non-confrontational assertiveness", and this perhaps is the better term because it captures the manner in which China reacts assertively while, like at Scarborough Shoal, still showing significant restraint.[27]

Legal Analysis

The Philippines claims that China has exercised illegal maritime law enforcement in the Scarborough Shoal area. However, as Michael Sheng-ti Gau points out, "One may well perceive a situation in which these so-called 'unlawful activities' turn out to be lawful enforcement measures by Chinese coastguard vessels, which enforce Chinese fisheries law and regulations in the Chinese EEZ in the South China Sea".[28] The Philippines' claim is based on the assumption that China is not a coastal state in the South China Sea and that there can only be the Philippines EEZ or high seas in that region. China thus is deemed as a flag state. This claim shows that the dispute is closely relevant to the extent of the Philippines' and Chinese maritime zones in the South China Sea and, in case of overlapping zones, delimiting those zones. The extent of maritime zones and delimitation of overlapping claims, however, depends on the question of territorial sovereignty over the islands in the South China Sea. "Those are the subject matters at the core of the disputes between the two countries and both are excluded from the Tribunal's jurisdiction".[29] Hence, the Philippines's argument that its claims in the Arbitration Case do not involve sovereignty disputes is groundless.

The Philippines' second argument is about jurisdiction. The Philippines claimed that "the military activities exception does not apply", and "the limited exception" for certain "law enforcement activities" does not apply either.

---

26 Ibid.

27 Trefor Moss, "China's Not-So-Hard Power Strategy", *The Diplomat*, 28 June 2012.

28 Michael Sheng-ti Gau, "Issues of Jurisdiction in Cases of Default of Appearance", in Stephan Talmon and Bing Bing Jia (eds), *The South China Sea Arbitration: A Chinese Perspective* (NP: Hart Publishing, 2014), 97.

29 Ibid.

Article 298(1) of the UNCLOS stipulates that,

> When signing, ratifying or acceding to this Convention or at any time thereafter, a State may, without prejudice to the obligations arising under section 1, declare in writing that it does not accept any one or more of the procedures provided for in section 2 with respect to one or more of the following categories of disputes: **(b) disputes concerning military activities, including military activities by government vessels and aircraft engaged in non-commercial service, and disputes concerning law enforcement activities** in regard to the exercise of sovereign rights or jurisdiction excluded from the jurisdiction of a court or tribunal under **article 297, paragraph 2 or 3**.

In the *Arctic Sunrise* Case, Russia stated:

> Upon the ratification of the Convention on the 26th February 1997 the Russia Federation made a statement, according to which, *inter alia*, "it does not accept procedures provided for in Section 2 of Part XV of the Convention, entailing binding decisions with respect to dispute […] concerning law enforcement activities in regard to the exercise of sovereign rights or jurisdiction".[30]

Acting on the above statement, Russia has notified the Netherlands by *note verbale* that "it does not accept the arbitration procedures under Annex VII to the Convention initiated by the Netherlands in regard to the case concerning the vessel *Arctic Sunrise* and the [it] does not intend to participate in the proceedings of the International Tribunal of the Law of the Sea in respect of the request of the Kingdom of Netherlands … ".[31]

The Netherlands contends that:

> Under Article 298, paragraph 1(b), of the Convention, the optional exception in connection with disputes concerning law enforcement activities in regard to the exercise of sovereign fights or jurisdiction to the applicability of Section 2 of Part XV of the Convention only applies with respect to "disputes […] excluded from the jurisdiction of a court or tribunal under article 297, paragraph 2 or 3". Such disputes concern marine scientific research and fisheries, respectively, neither of which is at issue in the present case".

The Philippines takes the same position as the Netherlands, arguing that the limited exception for certain "law enforcement activities" does not apply.

---

30 The Embassy of the Russia Federation in the Federal Republic of Germany's note verbale dated 22 October 2013 to the Registry of *Arctic Sunrise Case*, in the Order of the *Arctic Sunrise Case*, 4.

31 Order of the *Arctic Sunrise Case*, 4.

The Philippines asserts that its makes no claims regarding China's exercise of sovereign rights with respect to living resources in China's EEZ. Moreover, "the Philippines's claims only concern areas where China has no entitlement to an EEZ or continental shelf". Therefore, "the law enforcement activities exception is inapplicable to these proceedings". This argument is based on the assumption that Scarborough Shoal only enjoys the status of "rock", a status which only entitles it to 12 nautical miles of territorial sea. The *Guyana v Surinam* dispute (arbitration under Annex VII of the United Nations Convention on the Law of the Sea) may have an implication for the South China Sea arbitration case. This case related to the legitimacy of law enforcement acts carried out by two Surinamese naval patrol vessels, which ordered a Guyanese drilling ship and its support vessels out of disputed waters claimed by both countries. Guyana insisted that Suriname's naval vessels resorted to the use of force on 3 June 2000 by expelling its drilling ships while Suriname asserted that this was an adequate law enforcement act in its own waters. The Arbitration Tribunal concluded that the action by the Suriname was more consistent with a military action than mere law enforcement activity and violated the Charter of the United Nations chapter I article 2 (4).

Article 297(3)(a) of the UNCLOS stipulates that disputes concerning the interpretation or application of the provisions of this Convention with regard to fisheries shall be settled in accordance with section 2, except that the coastal state shall not be obliged to accept the submission to such settlement of any dispute relating to its sovereign rights with respect to the living resources in the exclusive economic zone or their exercise, including its discretionary powers for determining the allowable catch, its harvesting capacity, the allocation of surpluses to other states and the terms and conditions established in its conservation and management laws and regulations. China, from May to August every year, issues the Notice of Regulating Fishing Activities in the South China Sea, including the period when fishing activities shall be prohibited, and the location and the types of fishing that these regulations apply to. China would argue that the dispute between itself and the Philippines is associated with "its sovereign rights with respect to the living resources in the exclusive economic zone or their exercise, including its discretionary powers for determining the allowable catch, its harvesting capacity, the allocation of surpluses to other states and the terms and conditions established in its conservation and management laws". However, again, this argument would be also challenged by the Philippines saying that it only applies in a coastal states' EEZ, which will eventually relate to the maritime delimitation between two countries.

The Philippines also accused China of conducting dangerous operations contrary to Article 94(3)(4)(5) of UNCLOS. This claim denies China's status as a coastal state and defines China as merely a flag state. The claims that China's has infringed the marine environment, based on Article 194 3(b) is also groundless. Both China and the Philippines are parties to the COLREG. They are obligated to comply with its regulations. China has accordingly issued regulations including the Working Rules on the Maritime Law Enforcement by Public Security Organs adopted by the China Maritime Bureau in 2010.

China argues that when Chinese law enforcement vessels enter into the sea in question, it is for the purpose of enforcing the law as is normal within the territory and territorial waters considered to be those of China, under the power granted to the vessel by Chinese domestic law. When a Chinese vessel enforces the law in the relevant sea area, the applicable laws are international law and Chinese domestic law. The international law in question is principally the UNCLOS, to which both the Philippines and China are signatories, while the relevant domestic laws in China are those relevant to territorial waters.

That a foreign government vessel has the right to innocent passage through the sea in question is stipulated in Articles 18 and 19 of UNCLOS. However, a coastal state may take steps conforming to the spirit of UNCLOS in response to the non-innocent passage of a foreign government vessel.

At present, the Philippines and China have different opinions on the ownership of the Scarborough Shoal. As long as this difference exists and there are no effective means to resolve it or reduce tensions, the government vessels of both sides must make every effort to avoid unforeseen incidents in the relevant sea area. Moreover, each side should consider itself to be a law-abiding coastal state, and as such seek to avoid at all costs forcible action against the government vessel of the other side in order to enforce the rights of the coastal state.

What is most important is that when enforcing the law, government vessels must avoid the use of arms at all costs.

China's Law Enforcement at Second Thomas Shoal

The Philippines asserts that China has moved aggressively to challenge the long-standing presence of the Philippines at Second Thomas Shoal (Renai Jiao in Chinese). It then continues to claim that China violates the sovereign rights and jurisdiction of the Philippines. Based on its claims that "only the Philippines has sovereign rights over the continental shelf in the area where Ayungin Shoal [Second Thomas Shoal] is located", it asserts that China has no right to conduct law enforcement or any other kind of jurisdiction in the vicinity of Second Thomas Shoal, including "interfering with the Philippines's rights of navigation in the waters at, and adjacent to, Second Thomas Shoal; preventing the rotation and resupply of Philippine personnel stationed at Second Thomas Shoal; and endangering the health and well-being of Philippine personnel stationed at stationed at Second Thomas Shoal".

To analyze the Philippines' claims, it is necessary to review the chronicle of the Philippines covering the Second Thomas Shoal. In 1987, during a comprehensive multidisciplinary survey in the Nansha Islands, a team from the Chinese Academy of Sciences (CAS) landed on the Second Thomas Shoal, erecting a stone tablet and leaving other landmarks. Unreconciled to its thwarted attempts at the Mischief

Reef in February 1995 and October 1998, the Philippines cast its eyes to the Second Thomas Shoal, which was just 14 nautical miles away from the Mischief Reef and could act as a home ground for the Philippines to harass and monitor China's Mischief Reef.

A military ship ran aground near the Second Thomas Shoal in 1999 and since then Filipino troops have been stationed on the vessel at all times, on the pretext that the bilge was leaky, as a symbol of the Philippines claims to the territory. Despite Chinese protests, the Philippines has refused to withdraw its soldiers and the ship. For some time now, Chinese Coast Guard vessels have guarded the surroundings of the shoal and monitored the Philippine supply to the ship.[32]

The Scarborough Shoal incident on 10 April 2012 and the stranding of China's No.560 naval frigate on 11 July 2012 on a shore off the Half Moon Shoal imposed great pressure on the Philippines. In December 2012, the Philippines deployed more than 80 marines to several islands and reefs in the Nansha Islands, with 12 marines and several technicians on the Second Thomas Shoal. On 6 March 2013, China's official vessels conducted a patrol in the waters around the Second Thomas Shoal and did not attract any protest from the Philippines. Then China's marine affairs authorities announced that the Second Thomas Shoal had been re-controlled by China and China's fishing vessels could operate freely there. China also planned to build pilotage facilities.[33]

On 26 April 2013, China's Foreign Ministry Spokesperson Hua Chunying held a press conference and listed the eight insular features that the Philippines had taken since the 1970s, without mentioning the Second Thomas Shoal.[34] China believes that this showed that the Second Thomas Shoal was in China's effective control. On 9 May 2013, Philippine Navy dispatched the *BRP Apolinario Mabini* (PS-36), the *BRP Rizal* (PS-74) and the *BRP Mangyan* (AS71) to the waters around the Second Thomas Shoal for monitoring missions after the rumor that several Chinese vessels were present in the same waters. On 21 May 2013, Philippine Department of Foreign Affairs Spokesperson Raul Hernandez said that the Philippines had filed a diplomatic protest to complain about China's encroachment upon the Philippines' established maritime borders, "with the entry of at least three government ships around the Ayungin Shoal".[35]

---

32 Zachary Keck, "Second Thomas Shoal Tensions Intensify", 13 March 2014, *The Diplomat.*

33 "PLA Strengthens Fortifications in the South China Sea", 11 August 2013, *Want China Times* <http://www.wantchinatimes.com/news-subclass-cnt.aspx?id=20130811000010&cid=1101>.

34 "Foreign Ministry Spokesperson Hua Chunying's Remarks on the Philippines' Efforts in Pushing for the Establishment of the Arbitral Tribunal in Relation to the Disputes between China and the Philippines in the South China Sea", Chinese Embassy in Croatia website <http://hr.chineseembassy.org/eng/fyrth/t1035577.htm>.

35 "PH Protests Presence of Chinese Ships in Ayungin Shoal", *Inquirer* <http://globalnation.inquirer.net/75155/ph-protests-presence-of-chinese-ships-in-ayungin-shoal/>.

Based on the above review, it is obvious that the dispute between China and the Philippines did not begin after the proceedings of the Philippines-China Arbitration, but can be traced back to 1999 when a rusty Philippine ship grounded on the Second Thomas Shoal on the pretext that the bilge was leaky.

Conclusion: How to Avoid Incidents at Sea in Disputed Waters

Fundamentally, as seen from the above, the disputes between the Philippines and China, among others, are maritime law enforcement activities in disputed maritime zones pending maritime delimitation. Hence, the urgent issue facing both countries is how to avoid incidents at sea in line within international regulations and norms on the safety of navigation, including:

- The International Convention on Standards of Training, Certification and Watch-keeping for Seafarers, 1978;
- The International Convention for the Safety of Life at Seas (SOLAS), 1974;
- Protocol to SOLAS 1978; Protocol to SOLAS, 1988;
- The Convention on the International Regulation for Preventing Collisions at Sea (COLREG), 1972;
- The International Convention of the Suppression of Unlawful Acts at Sea (SUA 1988), 2005, Protocol to SUA Convention;
- The 14th Western Pacific Naval Symposium, 2014, Code for Unplanned Encounters at Sea (CUES).

The coastal states have also adopted relevant domestic laws and regulations on the safety of navigation. In considering safe navigation and crisis management in the disputed areas, it is first necessary that both sides clarify their own relevant domestic laws as well as their interpretations of international laws including UNCLOS. This should be followed by identifying the views of the other side on issues of concern, and examining the scope of the authority and roles of the law enforcement agencies as regards security activities in the disputed waters. Recognition and understanding of the relevant issues is an important foundation for avoiding problems arising from misjudgment about the intentions of the other party.

Secondly, both sides should discuss crisis management measures in the disputed areas. Topics should include adequate consideration for human life or vessels in law enforcement operations, rescue of collision victims, means of communications, and identifying causes of collisions. Moreover, based on the findings, they should jointly study prevention of collisions, incidents, and escalation of problems following an incident.

Thirdly, it is necessary for both sides to take part in confidence-building activities in the disputed areas, which would help to ease tensions in the region, and, in the longer term, improve bilateral relations. Furthermore, it is extremely important that the maritime law enforcement agencies of both sides, following the instructions their respective governments, engage in each other directly and improve their communication. This measure would play a highly-significant role in reducing unforeseen incidents and misinterpretations of the intentions of other countries, easing the state of crisis and preventing an escalation of the problem. It is of great importance to deepen mutual trust by promoting mutual understanding and contact between the law enforcement agencies of both sides.

Chapter 14
The Impact of the Arbitration Case on Regional Maritime Security

Sam Bateman

Introduction

In the short-term and regardless of whether a traditional or non-traditional view is taken of regional maritime security, the decision by the Philippines to take China to international arbitration over its maritime claims has had a negative impact on regional maritime security. This non-consensual move has added fuel to the "war of words" in the South China Sea, increased tensions, and inhibited progress towards a binding Code of Conduct, as well as towards the development of effective co-operation for managing the sea and its resources.

In the longer-term, should the Philippines succeed in winning some of its case, there may be positive outcomes in terms of clarifying the position with regard to some questions of international law in the South China Sea disputes, but should the Philippines not be successful, nothing will have been achieved. This chapter will discuss issues associated with the impact of the arbitration case on regional maritime security both traditional and non-traditional. It will conclude that while on balance it would have been better overall for regional maritime security if the Philippines had not launched its unilateral action, China could save the situation now by deciding to participate in the tribunal's proceedings.

The Arbitration Case

Although the stated objective of the Philippine's action in initiating compulsory arbitration procedures against China was 'to achieve a peaceful and durable solution to the dispute',[1] this may not be achieved. The case has been tacitly supported by the United States, and thus has added to tensions between Beijing and Washington. It has met with little enthusiasm among the other members of ASEAN, particularly the members that are not claimants to features in the South

1 Statement by Secretary of Foreign Affairs Albert del Rosario on the UNCLOS Arbitral Proceedings against China to Achieve a Peaceful and Durable Solution to the Dispute in the West Philippine Sea <http://www.dfa.gov.ph/index.php/component/docman/cat_view/8-other-documents?limitstart=0>.

China Sea.[2] As the International Institute for Strategic Studies (IISS) has claimed, 'Manila's strategy might actually have strengthened Beijing's hand: its move has undermined ASEAN unity and risks negatively impacting efforts to establish a Code of Conduct' and 'the chances of an amicable resolution may not have been increased'.[3]

In opting for arbitration procedures, the Philippines rejected peaceful settlement procedures involving bilateral negotiations, but China asserts that the Philippines has not adequately pursued negotiations in good faith to settle the dispute.[4] As one commentary claimed, 'despite what the Philippines argues, all good faith avenues to peaceful dispute resolution, including provisional arrangements of a practical nature (UNCLOS Articles 74 and 83) have not been exhausted'.[5] By way of adding to its adverse consequences, the arbitration is likely to be a lengthy process that may settle little or achieve nothing.[6] In the meantime, it will serve to delay progress on a binding Code of Conduct for the South China Sea and the establishment of effective regimes for managing the sea and its resources.

This chapter does not discuss the details of the Philippines' case. Rather it considers the impact of the case on both traditional and non-traditional maritime security in the region. It acknowledges that the concept of maritime security is now much wider and more diverse than the traditional one of defence against military threats and the protection of national interests and sovereignty at sea. Under the theme of comprehensive security, the concept now includes non-traditional maritime security issues, such as piracy, terrorism, natural disasters, climate change, illegal fishing, marine pollution, maritime safety and the smuggling of drugs, arms and people. Dealing with these issues can be seen as part of the obligations of countries bordering the South China Sea under Part IX of the 1982 UN Convention on the Law of the Sea (UNCLOS).

---

2 International Institute for Strategic Studies (IISS), "Philippine legal move stirs South China Sea disputes", *Strategic Comments*, Edition 13, 11 April 2013 <https://www.iiss.org/en/publications/strategic%20comments/sections/2013-a8b5/philippine-legal-move-stirs-south-china-sea-disputes-bd84>.

3 IISS, "Philippine legal move stirs South China Sea disputes".

4 Yu Mincai, "China's Response to the Compulsory Arbitration on the South China Sea Dispute: Legal Effects and Policy Options", *Ocean Development and International Law*, 45:1, p. 4.

5 Sourabh Gupta, "The whole nine dashes and why the Philippines' arbitration case against China is a bad idea", *East Asia Forum*, 28 July 2013, p. 2 <http://www.eastasiaforum.org/2013/07/28/the-whole-nine-dashes-and-why-the-philippines-arbitration-case-against-china-is-a-bad-idea/>.

6 Mark Valencia, "A political maelstrom in the South China Sea", *Japan Times*, 15 August 2013 <http://www.japantimes.co.jp/opinion/2013/08/15/commentary/world-commentary/a-political-maelstrom-in-the-south-china-sea/#.U-LIkNLlorw>.

Defining Maritime Security

Regional countries are not agreed on a definition of maritime security. Some include non-traditional security threats within their definition, but others are uncomfortable with including environmental threats and illegal fishing. Fishing is a particularly sensitive issue due to controversies over the exercise of traditional fishing rights and the number of countries in the region whose fishers have traditionally fished in waters now part of the exclusive economic zones of other countries. The lack of effective fisheries management arrangements in the South China Sea and delays in setting up these arrangements has serious implications for the future food security of the region. Each year without action means a further decline in the fish stocks of the sea.

Traditional maritime security, involving defence against military threats and the protection of national interests and sovereignty at sea, is primarily a national concern although all countries have a common interest in a stable regional maritime security environment and good order at sea. Common interests are most evident with non-traditional maritime security and are thus attract most attention at regional maritime security forums, such as the ASEAN Maritime Forum (AMF); the ARF Inter-Sessional Meeting (ISM) on Maritime Security; and the Maritime Security Expert Working Group (MSEWG) established by the ASEAN Defence Ministers' Meeting Plus (ADMM Plus). In view of the sensitivities involved and the principle of non-interference in the national affairs of other countries, these forums give little attention to traditional maritime security issues, including the sovereignty disputes in the South China Sea. These issues provide examples of the "wicked problems" of maritime security.[7] The Philippines' arbitration case may only have added to their "wickedness" in that they were already difficult enough to solve without the complication of long and uncertain arbitration proceedings.

Impact on Traditional Maritime Security

By serving to increase tensions in the South China Sea, the Philippine's case had added to regional instability, and thus added to the threat perceptions of regional countries. It has become part of the "war of words" between China on the one hand, and the Philippines, Vietnam and the United States on the other. Rather than helping to resolves the disputes in the South China Sea, the case may make their resolution more difficult, while further implicating the United States in a conflict that is primarily for the claimants themselves to settle.[8]

---

7 Sam Bateman, "Solving the 'Wicked Problems' of Maritime Security – Are Regional Forums up to the Task?", *Contemporary Southeast Asia*, Vol. 33, No. 1 (2011), pp. 1–28.

8 Gupta, "The whole nine dashes", p. 1

Competition is increasing between the key protagonists in the South China Sea. In August 2012, the U.S. State Department issued a comprehensive statement on the American position in the South China Sea. While noting that the United States takes no position on competing territorial claims over land features in the sea, the statement went on to criticize some actions by China as running counter to collaborative diplomatic efforts to resolve differences and risking further escalating tensions in the region.[9] Unsurprisingly, China responded shortly afterwards with a robust statement strongly condemning the US position claiming that the US statement showed 'total disregard for the facts' and sent 'a seriously wrong message'.[10] The same sort of "war of words" continues to the present day.

These exchanges are yet another demonstration of the game of "tit for tat" in the South China Sea – one player replies to another player's action and the other player retaliates in turn.[11] Unless the players demonstrate some common interest and mutual understanding, the game can spiral out of control, leading to a "lose-lose" outcome. "Tit for tat" responses have been very evident in the South China Sea in the last five years or so. The joint submission by Malaysia and Vietnam in May 2009 to the Commission on the Limits of the Continental Shelf (CLCS) is a leading example of an action that prompted such responses. This was a strongly nationalistic approach to resource allocation in the South China Sea.[12] It amounted to a "zero-sum" claim by these two countries to the seabed resources of the entire southern part of the China Sea to the exclusion of other interested parties, Brunei, China and the Philippines, which all protested the submission. Such protests are legitimate actions to preserve rights but they also add to the "war of words".

The "war of words" describes the shrill propaganda war that has developed between China on the one hand, and the Philippines and Vietnam on the other. The Philippines' arbitration case has promoted a similar round of global commentary mostly critical of China for rejecting it. As one American commentator has observed, this rejection provided 'a small victory for Manila', and potentially swung international public opinion towards the Philippines.[13] The irony is that while this commentator was critical of China's decision to opt out of the arbitration

9 U.S. Statement Department, *South China Sea*, Press Statement by Patrick Ventrell, Acting Deputy Spokesperson, Office of Press Relations, Washington DC, 3 August 2012 <http://www.state.gov/r/pa/prs/ps/2012/08/196022.htm>.

10 CNN Wire Staff, "China blasts U.S. for sending 'wrong message' on South China Sea disputes", *CNN*, 6 August 2012 <http://edition.cnn.com/2012/08/05/world/asia/china-us-sea-dispute/index.html>.

11 Sam Bateman, "Clash of rising powers; Tit for tat game must end", *The Straits Times*, Opinion, 25 August 2012, p. A42.

12 Sam Bateman and Clive Schofield, "Outer Shelf Claims in the South China Sea:New Dimension to Old Disputes", *RSIS Commentary No. 65*, 1 July 2009.

13 Peter A. Dutton, "The Sino-Philippine Maritime Row: International Arbitration and the South China Sea", *East and South China Seas Bulletin #10*, Center for New American Security, 15 March 2013, p. 3.

case, the United States itself would likely opt out of such categories of dispute if and when it acceded to UNCLOS.[14]

More recently, China's positioning of an offshore oil rig in the South China Sea off the Paracel Islands in May 2014 in waters claimed by Vietnam led to a storm of media comment and academic commentaries generally critical of China's actions. It caused the worst breakdown in relations between Hanoi and Beijing in many years. The "war of words" in the international media following this incident ran strongly against China. At the 2014 Shangri-La Dialogue in Singapore, Vietnam's vice-minister for defence, called for other claimant countries in the South China Sea to more strongly criticize China's behavior,[15] and U.S. Secretary of Defense Chuck Hagel condemned China for its 'destabilising, unilateral actions asserting its claims in the South China Sea', and warned that 'the United States will not look the other way when fundamental principles of the international order are being challenged'.[16] In a thinly disguised criticism of China, Japan's Prime Minister Shinzo Abe called for nations to make claims that are faithful in the light of international law and to resolve them peacefully.[17]

Most global commentary supported the Vietnamese claim that the positioning of the rig was illegal while painting the situation as another example of China's assertiveness. Vietnam and Vietnamese scholars launched a major diplomatic and public relations campaign to support the claim that China has acted illegally. In comparison, China's response was underwhelming. China can be its own worst enemy – it had a story to tell to justify its action but did not adequately tell it. As a consequence, what might be termed "the tyranny of global commentary" became a victory in the public relations "war of words" between China and Vietnam. The assertions and counter-assertions as to who is right in this dispute, even by well-informed commentators, often claiming the support of extensive historical sources, lead nowhere and have a negative impact on the situation overall. By fuelling strident nationalism in both Vietnam and China, the "war of words" has only served to make the situation worse than it might otherwise have been.

There are far-reaching implications of this "war of words" and the "tyranny of global commentary", and they are all bad. China feels increasingly isolated and contained by the United States, which has not been backward in criticizing China and appearing to support Vietnam. Bilateral relations between China and Vietnam went from bad to worse with clashes between the vessels of the two sides around the oil rig and violent nationalistic protests against China in Vietnam leaving

14 Sourabh Gupta, "Murky waters surround the rule of law in the South China Sea", *East Asia Forum*, 20 July 2014 <http://www.eastasiaforum.org/2014/07/20/murky-waters-surround-the-rule-of-law-in-the-south-china-sea/>.

15 Ridzan Rahmat, "Vietnam urges neighbours to stand up to China", *Janes' Defence Weekly*, 11 June 2014, p. 28.

16 James Hardy, "China condemns US, Japan for 'provocative' remarks, *Janes' Defence Weekly*, 11 June 2014, p. 29.

17 Gupta, "Murky waters".

people killed and hundreds of Chinese, Taiwanese and Korean factories damaged or destroyed. The confidence of foreign investors in Vietnam was shattered. Hundreds of Chinese fled the country with serious impact on investment from China, Taiwan and Singapore in particular. The international implications are also serious. Concurrently China's other main antagonist in the South China Sea, the Philippines has increased its offer to host additional American bases and forces. Japan also leapt onto the band-wagon of support for Vietnam hoping that in doing so, it will gain some moral support for its sovereignty dispute with China in the East China Sea.

The United States has become a key player in the South China Sea, and has been increasing its military presence in the region. Ithas declared a "national interest" in preserving freedoms of navigation through the South China Sea and has sought to internationalize the dispute by suggesting that China's actions threaten the security of sea lines of communication and create uncertainty and concern for oil and gas companies, including some American ones, seeking to develop the resources of the sea.[18] It has supported the Philippine case while as a non-party to UNCLOS itself, it is limited in its own ability to take action against China's claims. The continued failure of the United States to ratify UNCLOS severely undermines its ability to take the high ground on law of the sea issues in the East Asian seas.[19]

In the United States, commentators, and not just those of a right-wing persuasion, have called for Washington to show greater support for its regional friends and allies vis-à-vis China and put more military muscle behind the rebalancing to Asia.[20] Despite the expectations of some American commentators, this response may not lead to any back-down by China. The result could be just the opposite. It would fuel China's security dilemma and provide grounds for the "hawks" in Beijing to argue for even more assertive action. However, this situation might be improving as the American involvement in the Middle East and renewed focus on Europe changes the thrust of the rebalancing to the economic and political opportunities in the region rather than the security dimensions. This could lead to a more balanced perception of Washington's role in the region and a more cooperative relationship between China and the United States which would be a welcome outcome for the region.[21]

Most Western media comments on developments in the South China Sea put the blame on China for acting assertively and provoking retaliation. However, in many recent instances, it has been China that has been provoked first by actions of

---

18 Nicole Gaouette and Daniel Ten Kate, "Global Response to S. China Sea Risks Needed", *Bloomberg*, 24 July 2011.

19 Alice D. Ba, "Staking Claims and Making Waves in the South China Sea: How Troubled Are the Waters", *Contemporary Southeast Asia*, Vol. 33 No. 3 (2011), p. 282.

20 Patrick M. Cronin, "US Should Help Vietnam Counter China's Coercion", *Asia Pacific Bulletin*, No. 269, 26 Honolulu: East-West Center, June 2014

21 Barry Desker, "US pivot unravelling", *The Straits Times*, 17 September 2014 <http://www.straitstimes.com/st/print/2841050>.

another party. This was the case in recent developments between China and both Vietnam and the United States. It was also the case in 2009 when Vietnam and Malaysia lodged their joint submission for an extended continental shelf in the South China Sea, effectively claiming all mineral resources of the southern part of the sea as their own. Similarly the Philippine's declaration of a new Baselines Law in 2009 met with strong criticism from Vietnam and China prompting China to strengthen its patrols in the disputed area.[22] This led to more criticism of China for its alleged assertive action.

It is unfortunate that the South China Sea has become caught up in broader strategic tensions, both between the United States and China, and between China and India. The South China Sea has become what one observer has called the new 'Dangerous Ground' for Sino-American rivalry.[23] While the United States claims to be not taking sides in the sovereignty claims, its actions in conducting joint military exercises with the Philippines and Vietnam in disputed areas of South China Sea can be construed differently. In the streets of Beijing, Hanoi and Manila, Washington is believed to have taken sides. In this way, American engagement in the South China Sea has had the unintended consequence of boosting nationalistic fervour in all three capitals.

The United States has consistently supported the Philippines in recent years in building its maritime security presence and capabilities. This is in line with a professed common objective in a 'rule-based approach in resolving competing claims in maritime areas through peaceful, collaborative, multilateral and diplomatic processes within the framework of international law'.[24] The United States Senate has said the Philippines properly exercised its right in pushing for peaceful means in resolving the maritime disputes.[25] In July 2014, the Senate approved Resolution No. 412 entitled: 'Reaffirming the strong support of the United States Government for the freedom of navigation and other internationally lawful uses of sea and airspace in the Asia-Pacific region, and for the peaceful diplomatic resolution of outstanding territorial and maritime claims and disputes'.[26] The resolution noted that 'the Republic of the Philippines properly exercised its rights to peaceful settlement mechanisms with the filing of arbitration case under

---

22 Heda Bayron, "New Philippine Border Law Re-ignites Territorial Disputes in the South China Sea", *Voanews.com*, 2 November 2009 <http://www.voanews.com/content/a-13-2009-03-17-voa15-68812417/412905.html>.

23 Chenxin Pan, "Is the South China Sea a new 'Dangerous Ground' for US-China rivalry?" *East Asia Forum*, 24 May 2011.

24 U.S. State Department, Office of the Spokesperson, Joint Statement of the United States-Philippines Ministerial Dialogue, *Media Note*, 30 April 2014 <http://www.state.gov/r/pa/prs/ps/2012/04/188977.htm>.

25 "US Senate passes resolution supporting PH move vs China", *ABS-CBNnews.com*, 13 July 2014 <http://www.abs-cbnnews.com/nation/07/13/14/us-senate-passes-resolution-supporting-ph-move-vs-china>.

26 U.S. Senate, S. Res 412, 113th Congress (2013–2014), 2nd session, 10 July 2014, DAV14345 <www.menendez.senate.gov/download/?id=48AC88C4-0673-4FD6-8730... >.

Article 287 and Article VII of the Convention of the Law of the Sea in order to achieve a peaceful and durable solution to the dispute'.

While it may be true to say that the United States' rebalancing towards Asia has been welcomed in the region, it is equally true that most Southeast Asian countries are apprehensive about growing tensions between China and the United States. They do not like the way great power politics have intruded into the region, possibly leading to a situation where they might have to choose between China and the United States. The Philippines and Vietnam have been most welcoming as the countries which have had direct confrontations with China over the past year but while the Philippines unambiguously welcomes US support, the bilateral relationship between the United States and Vietnam is much more complex with Vietnam imposing clear limits on its defence relations with the United States.[27] Other Southeast Asian countries, notably Indonesia and Singapore, are circumspect with developments in the region with fears of an escalating situation.[28]

Washington's initiatives, such as the deployment of Littoral Combat Ships (LCS) to Singapore, increased naval exercises in the region, naval assistance to the Philippines,[29] public articulations of the aggressive AirSea Battle concept,[30] and a growing defence relationship with Vietnam inevitably provoke responses from China. They have the unfortunate consequence of being seen by China as part of a process of a "construction of threats" by the United States designed to make China the enemy.[31]

As Henry Kissinger pointed out in his book *On China*, the game of *wei qi* (or "Go") and the fear of strategic encirclement play a key role in Chinese strategic thinking.[32] The South China Sea is of great strategic importance to China. Despite US assurances to the contrary,[33] US initiatives in the South China Sea can only be seen in Beijing as part of an American plan to contain China. The entry of India

27 Carlyle A. Thayer, "Vietnam is the Real Pivot", *Thayer Consultancy Background Brief*, 12 July 2012.

28 Zakir Hussain, "Special Report; Asean Nations Welcome US Pivot", *The Straits Times* (Singapore), 27 November 2011.

29 Including a major amphibious exercise conducted in waters adjacent to the disputed Scarborough Shoal, involving the large assault ship USS Bonhomme Richard, 2,200 US marines and 1,600 Filipino troops. Alexis Romero, "Phl, US troops kick off naval exercise", *Philstar.com*, 8 October 2012 <http://www.philstar.com/article.aspx?articleid=857305&publicationsubcategoryid=200>.

30 Sam Bateman, "US AirSea Battle: Countering China's anti-access strategies" *RSIS Commentary No. 82/2011*, 19 May 2011.

31 Scott A. Snyder, "Sour Notes from China on the U.S. Rebalance to Asia", *Asia Unbound*, Council for Foreign Relations, 20 June 2014 <http://blogs.cfr.org/asia/2014/06/20/sour-notes-from-china-on-the-u-s-rebalance-to-asia/>.

32 Henry Kissinger, *On China* (New York: Penguin Books, 2012), pp. 23–5.

33 "Leon Panetta: China should not fear new US military focus", *The Guardian*, 3 June 2012 <http://www.theguardian.com/world/2012/jun/02/leon-panetta-china-asia-pacific>.

into the South China Sea, including with its hosting of Malabar naval exercises in the western Pacific,[34] adds to this appreciation, particularly when India appears to be joining the United States in expressing a national interest in the South China Sea.[35]

Impact on Non-Traditional Maritime Security

The Philippine arbitration case has had a negative impact on non-traditional maritime security in the region. It has hindered effective co-operation and contributed to delays in reaching agreement on a Code of Conduct. It has emphasized the split in ASEAN between the claimants and non-claimants. It caught ASEAN off guard and changed the tenor of the South China Sea disputes. It went against ASEAN's customary preference for a consensus and less confrontational approach to territorial disputes.[36]

As Ambassador Koh has pointed out, ASEAN has not taken a position on the merits of the disputes between China and the ASEAN claimant states.[37] Hence ASEAN as a regional grouping cannot discuss sovereignty over particular features with China. Bilateral resolution of opposing claims over South China Sea features by Vietnam, Malaysia and the Philippines would be a major step forward that would then allow subsequent bilateral negotiations with China. However, this step is unlikely while countries focus on asserting their individual claims. The Philippine arbitration case is yet another example of an individual assertion of rights.

Competition between key players makes the development of effective regimes for managing the South China Sea and its resources more difficult. Management regimes require greater recognition that cooperative measures are "building blocks" for dispute resolution and confidence-building rather than seeing the latter as the first steps. The "means" of going forward (i.e. a code of conduct and resolving the sovereignty disputes) have become the focus of attention rather than the "ends" (i.e. effective management regimes for the South China Sea and activities within it).

---

34 Three of the last six Malabar exercises involving the navies of India. Japan and the United States have been held in the western Pacific Ocean. Gurpreet S. Khurana, "'Malabar' naval exercises: trends and tribulations", *Issue Brief*, National Maritime Foundation, New Delhi, 5 August 2014 <http://www.maritimeindia.org/Archives/MALABAR-NAVAL.html>.

35 "India & Japan bond over international waters", *India Today*, 4 November 2011 <http://indiatoday.intoday.in/story/india-japan-a-k-antony-yasuo-ichikawa-south-china-sea/1/158544.html>.

36 IISS, "Philippine legal move stirs South China Sea disputes".

37 Tommy Koh, "Mapping Out Rival Claims To The South China Sea", *The Straits Times*, 13 September 2011 <http://cil.nus.edu.sg/wp/wp-content/uploads/2010/12/ProfKoh-ST13Sep2011-Mapping-out-rival-claims-to-the-South-China-Sea.pdf>.

There is a pressing need to get discussion of these regimes back on track, but the Philippine case has put that process in reverse. Cooperative regimes are becoming even more necessary as shipping traffic across the South China Sea increases with greater risks of ship-sourced marine pollution and shipping accidents; there is increased pressure on the resources of the South China Sea, living and non-living; and further destruction occurs to the sea's sensitive eco-systems and marine biodiversity.[38] There is an associated need for operational maritime confidence and security building measures to reduce the risks of a serious incident between opposing maritime forces. These risks have increased with the growing militarization of the South China Sea.

All countries bordering the South China Sea are parties to UNCLOS and thus have an obligation to cooperate in accordance with Part IX of that treaty.[39] The 2002 Declaration on Conduct of Parties in the South China Sea (DOC) also invites the littoral countries to cooperate on certain marine activities:

a. marine environmental protection;
b. marine scientific research;
c. safety of navigation and communication at sea;
d. search and rescue operations; and
e. combating national crime, including, but not limited to, trafficking in illegal drugs, piracy and armed robbery at sea, and illegal traffic in arms.[40]

The DOC committed parties to peaceful modes of dispute settlement, the application of international law, the need for building up confidence and trust, and recognition of the freedoms of navigation and overflight in the South China Sea. While it has been successful until recently in containing disputes and tensions in the South China Sea, it has not contributed to cooperative activities in the way that was hoped, or led to appropriate confidence-building measures.[41]

---

38 Yann-Huei Song, "The Study of Marine Biodiversity in the South China Sea; Joint Efforts Made in the SCS Workshop Process", Paper at the international workshop on 'The South China Sea: Cooperation for Regional Security and Development', Ho Chi Minh City, November 2010.

39 The Council for Security Cooperation in the Asia Pacific (CSCAP) has produced Guidelines for Maritime Cooperation in Enclosed and Semi-Enclosed Seas and Similar Sea Areas of the Asia Pacific, CSCAP Memorandum No. 13, June 2008 <http://www.cscap.org/index.php?page=cscap-memoranda>. The guidelines are a set of fundamental, non-binding principles to guide maritime co-operation in the enclosed and semi-enclosed seas of the region, and to help develop a common understanding and approach to maritime issues in the region.

40 ASEAN – China Declaration on the Conduct of Parties in the South China Sea (2002), Article 6.

41 Ian Storey, "Implementing CBMs in the 2002 DOC: A Roadmap to Managing the South China Sea Dispute", Paper at the international workshop on 'The South China Sea: Cooperation for Regional Security and Development', Ho Chi Minh City, November 2010.

In July 2011, China and ASEAN agreed to guidelines for developing a code of conduct between the claimant countries in the South China Sea.[42] However, the Guidelines do not refer specifically to co-operation for management of the sea but rather identify confidence building measures as the initial activities to be undertaken under the ambit of the DOC. This is yet another indication of how the focus with the South China has shifted from co-operation to one of sovereignty and dispute resolution. Confidence building is now being seen as a prerequisite of co-operation rather than co-operation being viewed as a confidence-building measure. A key question is what functional co-operation can take place without strategic trust?

At the 14th ASEAN-China Summit in November 2011, China proposed setting up the ASEAN-China Maritime Cooperation Fund of RMB3 billion (about US$470 million) to implement the practical projects under the implementation of the DOC.[43] This offer was renewed in August 2012 when Chinese Vice Foreign Minister Fu Ying said that China is ready to promote maritime connectivity with ASEAN.[44] China renewed this offer of funding at the 3rd ASEAN Maritime forum held in Manila 4–5 October 2012.[45]

Despite considerable discussion of the procedures for implementing the Fund and the importance of co-operation, ASEAN has been slow to accept the Chinese proposal and wants an agreed Code of Conduct first. This delay is due to some mistrust of China's intentions, a reluctance to concede leadership to China on the process of co-operation, and a fear among the ASEAN claimants that somehow they will be prejudicing their sovereignty claims. It has been alleged that recognition of Chinese sovereignty may be a prerequisite of going forward. The drive for a Code of Conduct has diverted attention from the very important and necessary requirement for co-operation in the sea. Thus one of the "means" of achieving co-operation (i.e. the Code of Conduct) has become an "end" in itself. More focus is required on the "ends", but the Philippine arbitration case is not helpful in this regard.

Longer Term Implications

In the longer-term and should the Philippines succeed in winning some of its case, there may be positive outcomes for maritime security. Some questions of

---

42 The guidelines are available at: <http://www.asean.org/documents/20185-DOC.pdf>.

43 ASEAN Secretariat, *ASEAN – China Dialogue Relations,* 15 April 2012 <http://www.aseansec.org/5874.htm>.

44 "China to promote maritime connectivity with ASEAN, says vice FM", 5 August, *English.news.cn,* 5 August 2012 <http://news.xinhuanet.com/english/china/2012-08/05/c_131762568.htm>.

45 "Japan urges peace as neighbors clash over islands", *Times online*, 5 October 2012 <http://www.timesonline.com/news/world/asia/china-unveils-maritime-cooperation-fund-with-asean/article_573fef3c-0a03-5bda-932d-80560d7377cc.html>.

international law in the South China Sea disputes might be clarified by judgements from the tribunal that may help clear a way ahead to the resolution of the disputes. A probable example would be a determination as to whether under UNCLOS Article 121, particular maritime features of the South China Sea are islands or rocks and which features are capable of generating maritime zones wider than the territorial sea.[46] Whether or not this will actually happen is another matter.

A key part of the Philippine claim is that none of the Spratly Islands occupied by China is capable of sustaining human habitation or economic life of its own.[47] This claim sets aside consideration of the status of the larger islands in the group: Itu Aba occupied by Taiwan, Thitu Island occupied by the Philippines, and Spratly Island itself occupied by Vietnam. By international standards, these features would appear to qualify as "full" islands under the UNCLOS regime of islands and potentially able to generate the full suite of maritime zones.[48] The Philippines may have been encouraged to take this line to question the status of features by a judgement by the International Court of Justice which refuted the idea that offshore features can generate claims to vast areas of maritime space.[49]

The Philippines case is a prime example of the interplay of politics and the law. The Philippines had political objectives in putting its case forward. It hoped to isolate China and gain international support for its position. This objective has largely been achieved but in doing so, it has put the credibility of international arbitration on the line. There are risks that the process of international arbitration will lose its credibility if for example, the panel decides that it does not have the necessary jurisdiction or it reaches unhelpful decisions that please no party.

As Mark Valencia has observed:

> In an ideal world, the outcome of the arbitration would be based solely on the law and the facts. Both sides would accept it and continue their relations. But this is not an ideal world. Indeed the outcome of this case could have significant political implications for the Law of the Sea's dispute settlement mechanism, for the Law of the Sea itself and for conduct and relations in the South China Sea and beyond.[50]

---

46 Christopher Ward, "South China Sea on the rocks: the Philippines' arbitration request", East Asia Forum, 21 April 2014 <http://www.eastasiaforum.org/2014/04/21/south-china-sea-on-the-rocks-the-philippines-arbitration-request/>.

47 Dutton, "The Sino-Philippine Maritime Row", p. 4.

48 "Sovereignty as an Obstacle to Effective Oceans Governance and Maritime Boundary Making – the Case of the South China Sea" in Clive Schofield, Seokwoo Lee and Moon-Sang Kwon (eds), *Limits of Maritime Jurisdiction* (Leiden: Brill Academic Publishers, 2013), pp. 201–24.

49 Donald R. Rothwell, "South China Sea dispute dynamics", East Asia Forum, 16 June 2013 <http://www.eastasiaforum.org/2013/06/16/south-china-sea-dispute-dynamics/>; and Gupta, "The whole nine dashes", p. 1.

50 Valencia, "A political maelstrom".

Conclusions

The longer-term implications for regional maritime security of the Philippines initiating international arbitration need to be balanced against the shorter-term implications. In the short-term, the action has increased tensions in the South China Sea and delayed both co-operation and progress towards an agreed Code of Conduct. In the longer-term, it may clarify some legal issues, but this is at the risk of undermining the international dispute settlement process. While it would have been better overall if the Philippines had not launched its case, now that it has, there is an opportunity for China to save the "lost ground" of effective co-operation and regime building by joining the action.

Consideration of the longer-term implications leads to an argument that it may be better for regional maritime security if China decided to re-participate in the arbitral proceedings. As Carl Thayer has argued, China's rejection of the Arbitration Tribunal risks undermining international law, and if it has 'indisputable sovereignty' to features in the South China Sea, then it should be prepared to argue its case.[51]. In doing so, it would help 'reassure China's increasingly anxious neighbors that it is committed to institutional rather than power-based resolution of disputes'.[52] This would assist China in gaining moral authority as the major power in East Asia and help bring international public opinion back on its side.

The basic objective of all parties to the disputes in the South China Sea should be a "win-win" outcome with the establishment of effective functional co-operation for managing the sea and activities within it. This is an obligation of all the littoral countries but the focus of discussions over the past decade has shifted from co-operation to dispute resolution and zero-sum ("win-lose") outcomes driven largely by nationalistic assertions of sovereignty. The only acceptable framework for such a regime would be a web of provisional arrangements covering co-operation for different functions and perhaps even with different areas for each function. These functions include development of oil and gas resources, fisheries management, marine safety, marine scientific research, good order at sea, and preservation and protection of the marine environment. Discussion of this functional approach must be on the regional agenda to prevent the South China Sea from simmering away as a major obstacle to maritime security and good order at sea in the region. In an ideal world, the region would jump ahead of dispute resolution and push ahead with functional co-operation.

---

51 Carlyle A. Thayer, "South China Sea: China Should Uphold International Law", *Thayer Consultancy Background Brief*, 11 May 2014.

52 Dutton, "The Sino-Philippine Maritime Row", p. 6.

Appendix 1

Notification and Statement of Claim, Government of the Republic of the Philippines, 22 January 2013

REPUBLIC OF THE PHILIPPINES
DEPARTMENT OF FOREIGN AFFAIRS
MANILA

No. **13-0211**

The Department of Foreign Affairs of the Republic of the Philippines presents its compliments to the Embassy of the People's Republic of China and, with respect to the dispute with China over the maritime jurisdiction of the Philippines in the West Philippine Sea, the Government of the Philippines has the honor to submit the attached Notification under Article 287 and Annex VII of the 1982 United Nations Convention on the Law of the Sea (UNCLOS) and the Statement of Claim on which the Notification is based, in order to initiate arbitral proceedings to clearly establish the sovereign rights and jurisdiction of the Philippines over its maritime entitlements in the West Philippine Sea.

The Government of the Philippines has initiated these arbitral proceedings in furtherance of the friendly relations with China, mindful of its obligation under Article 279 of UNCLOS to seek a peaceful and durable resolution of the dispute in the West Philippine Sea by the means indicated in Article 33 (1) of the Charter of the United Nations.

The Department of Foreign Affairs of the Republic of the Philippines avails itself of this opportunity to renew to the Embassy of the People's Republic of China the assurances of its highest consideration.

Manila, 22 January 2013

DEPARTMENT OF FOREIGN AFFAIRS
PASAY CITY

The Embassy of the People's Republic of China
Manila

Attachments: Notification and Statement of Claims

NOTIFICATION AND STATEMENT OF CLAIM

I. INTRODUCTION

1. The Republic of the Philippines brings this arbitration against the People's Republic of China to challenge China's claims to areas of the South China Sea and the underlying seabed as far as 870 nautical miles from the nearest Chinese coast, to which China has no entitlement under the 1982 United Nations Convention on the Law of the Sea ("UNCLOS", or "the Convention"), and which, under the Convention, constitute the Philippines' exclusive economic zone and continental shelf.

2. Despite China's adherence to UNCLOS iu June 1996, and the requirement of Article 300 that States Parties fulfill in good faith their obligations under the Convention, China has asserted a claim to "sovereignty" and "sovereign rights" over a vast maritime area lying within a so-called "nine dash line".that encompasses virtually the entire South China Sea. By claiming all of the waters and seabed within the "nine dash line", China has extended its self-proclaimed maritime jurisdiction to withiu 50 nautical miles ("M") off the coasts of the Philippiue islands of Luzon and Palawan, and has iuterfered with the exercise by the Philippines of its rights under the Convention, iucluding withiu its own exclusive economic zone and continental shelf, in violation of UNCLOS.

3. Further, withiu the maritime area encompassed by the "nine dash liue", China has laid claim to, occupied and built structures on certain submerged banks, reefs and low tide elevations that do not qualify as islands under the Convention, but are parts of the Philippines' continental shelf, or the international seabed; and China has interfered with the exercise by the Philippines of its rights in regard to these features, and in the waters surrounding them encompassed by China's designated security zones.

4. In addition, China has occupied certain small, uninhabitable coral projections that are barely above water at high tide, and which are "rocks" under Article 121(3) of UNCLOS. China has claimed maritime zones surrounding these features greater than 12 M, from which it has sought to exclude the Philippines, notwithstanding the encroachment of these zones on the Philippines' exclusive economic zone, or on international waters.

5. In June 2012, China fonnally created a new administrative unit, under the authority of the Province of Hainan, that included all of the maritime features and waters within the "nine dash line". In November 2012, the provincial government of Hainan Province promulgated a law calling for the inspection, expulsion or

detention of vessels "illegally" entering the waters claimed by China within this area. The new law went into effect on 1 January 2013.

6. In response to these and other unlawful acts in contravention of UNCLOS, the Philippines seeks an Award that: (1) declares that the Parties' respective rights and obligations in regard to the waters, seal;ied .and maritime features of the South China Sea are governed by UNCLOS, and that China's claims based on its "nine dash line" are inconsistent with the Convention and therefore invalid; (2) determines whether, under Article 121 of UNCLOS, certain of the maritime features claimed by both China and the Philippines are islands, low tide elevations or submerged banks, and whelher they are capable of generating entitlement to maritime zones greater than 12 M; and (3) enables the Philippines to exercise and enjoy the rights within and beyond its exclusive economic zone and continental shelf that are established in the Convention.

7. The Philippines does not seek in this arbitration a determination of which Party enjoys sovereignty over the islands claimed by both of them. Nor does it request a delimitation of any maritime boundaries. The Philippines is conscious of China's Declaration of 25 August 2006 under Article 298 of UNCLOS, and has avoided raising subjects or making claims that China has, by virtue of that Declaration, excluded from arbitral jurisdiction.

8. All of the Philippines' claims in this arbitration have been th.e subject of good faith negotiations between the Parties. There have been numerous exchanges of views. The requirements of Article 279 have been satisfied. There is, therefore, no bar to the Arbitral Tribunal's exercise of jurisdiction over the claims asserted by the Philippines.

II. FACTUAL BACKGROUND

A. Maritime Areas

9. The South China Sea, part of which is known in the Philippines as the West Philippine Sea, is a semi-enclosed sea in Southeast Asia that covers approximately 2.74 million square kilometers. The Sea is surrounded by six States and Taiwan. To the north are the southern coast of mainland China, and China's Hainan Island. To the northeast lies Taiwan. To the east and southeast is the Philippines. The southern limits of the sea are bounded by Brunei, Malaysia and Indonesia. And to the west is Vietnam.

10. There are many small insular features in the South China Sea. They are largely concentrated in three geographically distinct groups: the Paracel Islands

in the northwest; Scarborough Shoal in the east; and the Spratly Islands in the southeast. The Paracel Islands are not relevant to this arbitration. Scarborough Shoal, located approximately 120 M west of the Philippines' coast and more than 3SOM from China, is a submerged coral reef with six small protrusions of rock above sea level at high tide. The Spratly Islands are a group of approximately 150 small features, many of which are submerged reefs, banks and low tide elevations.· They lie between 50 and 350 M from the Philippine island of Palawan, and more than 550M from the Chinese island of Hainan. None of the Spratly features occupied by China is capable of sustaining human habitation or an economic life of its own.

11. Notwithstanding its adherence to UNCLOS, China claims almost the entirety of the South China Sea, and all of the maritime features, as its own. Specifically, China claims "sovereignty" or "sovereign rights" over some L94 million square kilometers, or 70% of the Sea's waters and underlying seabed within its so-called "nine dash line." China first officially depicted the "nine dash line" in a letter of 7 May 2009 to the Unitd Nations Secretary General. It is reproduced below. According to China, it is sovereign over all of the waters, all of the seabed, and all of the maritime features within this "nine dash line".

12. In the east, the "nine dash line" depicted in China's letter is less than 50 M off the Philippine island of Luzon. In the southeast, it is within 30 M from Palawan. In both respects, it cuts through – and cuts off – the Philippines' 200 M exclusive economic zone and continental shelf, in violation of UNCLOS. Within the area encompassed by the "nine dash line", China has engaged in conduct that has unlawfully interfered with the Philippines' right of navigation, notwithstanding that some of the area is in the Philippines' own exclusive economic zone, and the rest is high seas; and China has interfered with the exercise by the Philippines of its rights to the living and non-living resources in 'its exclusive economic zone and continental shelf extending west from the island of Luzon, and northwest from the island of Palawan. China has also violated the Philippines' rights by exploiting the living resources in the Philippines' exclusive economic zone.

13. China's interference with and violations of the Philippines' rights under UNCLOS have been steadily escalating. In June 2012, China placed the entire maritime area within the "nine dash line" under the authority of the Province of Hainan, which, in November 2012, in the exercise of its administrative authority, promulgated a law that requires foreign vessels to obtain China's permission before entering the waters within the "nine dash line", and provides for inspection, expulsion and detention of vessels that do not obtain such permission.The law went into effect on 1 January 2013.

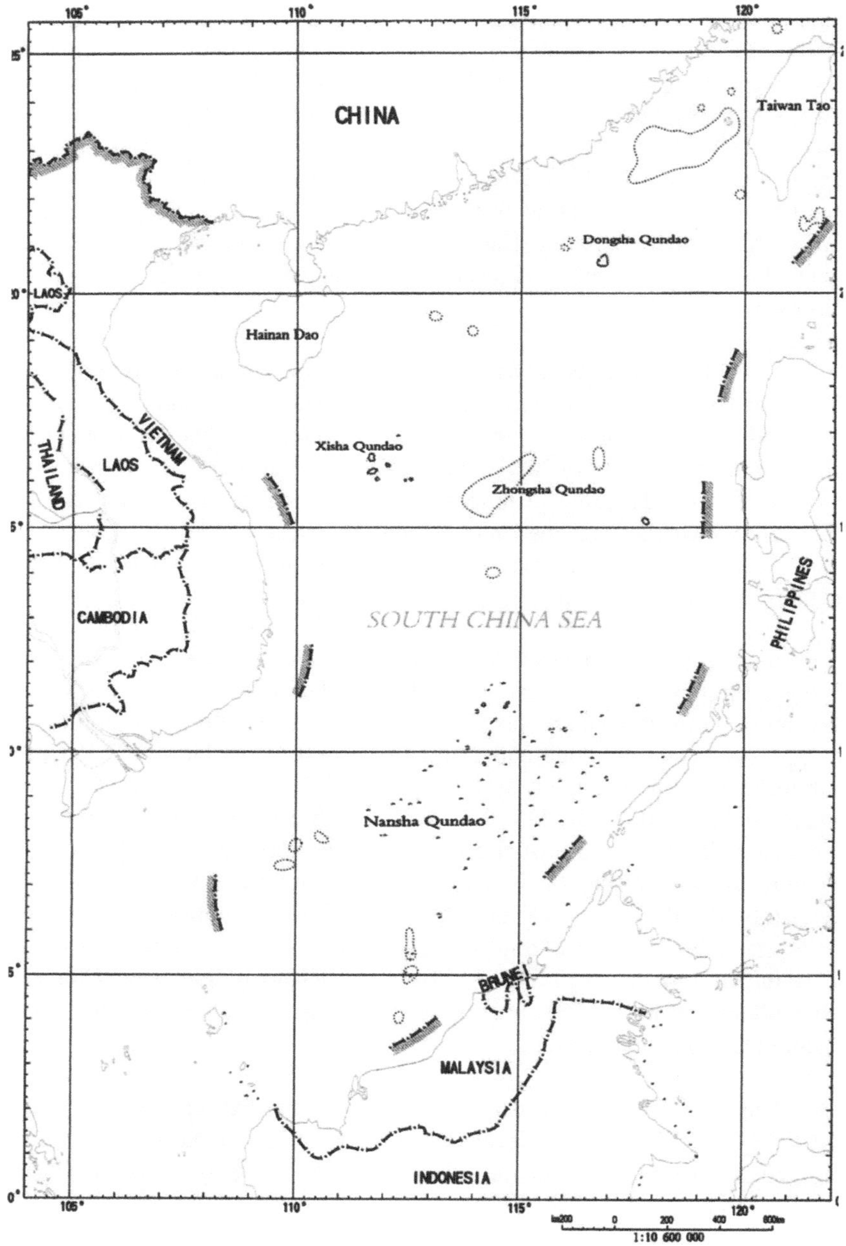

105°
110°
115°
120°
CHINA
Taiwan Tao
Dongsha Qundao
LAOS
Hainan Dao
VIETNAM
THAILAND
LAOS
Xisha Qundao
Zhongsha Qundao
CAMBODIA
SOUTH CHINA SEA
PHILIPPINES
Nansha Qundao
BRUNEI
MALAYSIA
INDONESIA
1:10 600 000

B. Submerged Features

14. Even before its first official espousal of the "nine dash line", China began to seize physical control of a number of submerged features and protruding rocks in the Spratly Islands, in the southeastern part of the Sea, and to construct artificial "islands" on top of them. Among the submerged features that China occupied and altered in this manner are: Mischief Reef, McKennan Reef, Gaven Reef and Subi Reef. None of these features is an island under Article 121 of UNCLOS. They are all at best low tide elevations, far removed from China's territorial sea, exclusive economic zone and continental shelf. Because they are not above water at high tide, they are part of another State's continental shelf, or the international seabed. Yet, China has not only acted unlawfully by seizing control of these submerged features; it has declared maritime zones around them, from which it has illegally sought to exclude the Philippines and other States.

15. Mischief Reef (Chinese name = Meiji Jiao; .known in the Philippines as Panganiban Reef) is a submerged bank that is part ofthe Philippines' continental shelf, approximately 130 M from Palawan (and more than 600 M southeast of China's Hainan Island, the nearest Chinese land territory). Mischief Reef lies at approximately 9° 54'N - 115° 32'E. Since 1995, China has constructed buildings and other facilities 011 stilts and concrete platforms at four different sites atop Mischief Reef, despite repeated protests from the Philippines.

16. McKennan Reef (Chinese name = Ximen Jiao; known in the Philippines as Chigua Reef) is a low tide elevation located at approximately 9°53'5"N - 1 l4° 28 'E. It is approximately 180 M west of the Philippine island of Palawan, and is also part of the Philippines' continental shelf. China has constructed buildings and other facilities on stilts and concrete platforms at this feature, as well, despite the Philippines' protests.

17. China has not only unlawfully seized parts of the Philippines' continental shelf, but has also wrongfully sought to prevent Philippine vessels from approaching Mischief Reef and McKennan Reef, even though the surrounding waters are within the Philippines' exclusive economic zone.

18. Gaven Reef (Chinese name = Nanxun Jiao) is a low tide elevation located at approximately 10° 13' N - 114° 13'E. It lies approximately 205M northwest of Palawan.

19. Subi Reef (Chinese name = Zhubi Jiao; known in the Philippines as Zamora Reef) is a low tide elevation located at approximately 10°55'N - 1 14° 05'E. It lies approximately 230 M west of Palawan.

C. Insular Features

20. In 2012, China seized six small rocks that protrude above sea level within the Philippines' exclusive economic zone, unlawfully claimed an exaggerated maritime zone around these features, and wrongfully prevented the Philippines from navigating, or enjoying access to the living resources within this zone, even though it forms part of the Philippines' EEZ. These half dozen protrusions, which are known collectively as Scarborough Shoal (Bajo de Masinloc in the Philippines; Huang Yan Dao in China), are located approximately 120 M west of the Philippine island of Luzon. They are rocks both literally and under Artide 121 of UNCLOS. None is more than 3meters ("m") above sea level at high tide; and none measures more than a few meters in width. None of the rocks, which lie in close proximity to one another, generates entitlement to more than a 12 M territorial sea. Yet, China, which like the Philippines asserts sovereignty over Scarborough Shoal, claims a much larger maritime zone for itself, to the limit of the "nine dash line" approximately 70M to the east.

21. Until April 2012, Philippine fishing vessels routinely fished in this area, which is within the Philippines' 200 M exclusive economic zone. Since then, China has prevented the Philippines from fishing at Scarborough 'Shoal or in its vicinity, and undertaken other activities inconsistent with the Convention. Only Chinese vessels are now allowed to fish in these waters, and have harvested, inter alia, endangered species such as sea turtles, sharks and giant clams which are protected by both international and Philippine law.

22. To the southwest of Scarborough Shoal, in the Spratly Islands, China has seized similar features. China presently occupies the following features which, though above water at high tide, are uninhabitable and incapable of supporting economic life in their natural state. They are therefore "rocks" within the meaning of Article 121(3) of UNCLOS:

- Johnson Reef (Chinese name = Chigua Jiao; known in the Philippines as Mabini Reef), located at approximately 9°42' N - 114°22' E and approximately 180 M northwest of Palawan.
- Cuarteron Reef (Chinese name Huayang Jiao; known in the Philippines as Calderon Reef), located at approximately 8°51'N - 112°50'E and approximately 245 M west of Palawan; and
- Fiery Cross Reef (Chinese name = Yongshu Jiao; known in the Philippines as Kagitingan Reef), located at approximately 9°J3'N - 112°54'E and approximately 255 M west of Palawan;

23. All of these features are submerged reefs with no more than a few rocks protrnding above sea level at high tide. Johnson Reef has a few rocky protrnsions rising above water at high tide. Cuarteron Reef is a collection of coral rocks reaching no higher than 1.5 m. Fiery Cross Reef consists of a submerged bank with protruding rocks no more than 1 m above sea level at high tide.

24. Notwithstanding that all of these insular features are "rocks" under Article 121(3) of UNCLOS, China unlawfully claims entitlements to maritime zones greater than 12 M in the waters and seabed surrounding them, and wrongfully excludes the Philippines and other States from these areas. Moreover, in the case of Scarborough Shoal and Johnson Reef, the maritime zones claimed by China unlawfully encroach upon the Philippines' 200 M exclusive economic zone and continental shelf extending from Luzon and Palawan, and prevent the Philippines from enjoying its rights under the Convention within 200 M.

D. Exchanges of Views

25. On numerous occasions, dating back at least to 1995, the Philippines and China have exchanged views regarding the settlement of their disputes concerning entitlements to maritime areas in the South China Sea, the exercise within those maritime areas of rights pertaining to navigation and the exploitation of living and non-living resources, and the status of maritime features in the Spratly Islands and at Scarborough Shoal.

26. The Parties have been exchanging views on these disputes in attempts to achieve negotiated solutions since the first "Philippines-China Bilateral Consultations on the South China Sea Issue" were held in August 1995. However, despite many bilateral meetings and exchanges of diplomatic correspondence over more than 17 years since those first consultations were held, no settlements have been reached on any of these disputed matters.

27. In regard to entitlements to maritime areas in the South China Sea, the Philippines has consistently expressed the view to China in bilateral meetings and diplomatic correspondence that it is entitled to an exclusive economic zone and continental shelf of 200 M from its archipelagic baselines, and to the exclusive enjoyment of the living and non-living resources in these zones, as well as to the right to navigate without interference by China within and beyond its 200 M limit. In response, China has repeatedly expressed the conflicting view that it is entitled to all the maritime space encompassed by its "nine dash line", to all the living and non-living resources within this limit, and to control navigation within this area. By its diplomatic note dated 21 November 2012, the Philippines declared, as it did on numerous prior occasions, that it caimot accept the validity of the "nine dash line" or China's claims based thereon. Over the past 17 years of such exchanges of views, all possibilities of a negotiated settlement have been explored and exhausted.

28. With respect to the status of maritime features in the Spratly Islands and adjacent waters, and rights to navigate and exploit the 'living resources in these waters, the Parties have exchanged views since at least August 1995, and as recently as July 2012. The Philippines has repeatedly protested Chinese activities on and adjacent to Subi Reef and Mischief Reef, which form part of the Philippines"

continental shelf, as well as China's claims and activities in regard to the other maritime features in the Spratly group occupied or claimed by China. China has consistently rejected the Philippines' protests and maintained its occupation of and activities on these features. Each Party has protested interference by the other with its claimed navigational lights, and with its claimed rights to the living resources, in the waters adjacent to these features. None of the protests, or ensuing meetings or diplomatic correspondence in which views were exchanged, resulted in the settlement of these disputes.

29. With respect to the status of the maritime features at Scarborough Shoal and adjacent waters, and rights to navigate and exploit the living resources in these waters, the Parties have been exchanging views regarding the settlement of their dispute since at least May 1997. Most recently, during a series of meetings in Manila in April 2012, the Parties once again exchanged views on these matters without arriving at a negotiated solution. As a result of the failure of negotiations, the Philippines later that month sent China a diplomatic note in which it invited China to agree to bring the dispute before an appropriate adjudicatory body. China declined the invitation.

30. The diplomatic record leaves no doubt that the requirement in Article 283 that the "parties to the dispute shall proceed expeditiously to an exchange of views regarding its settlement by negotiation or other peaceful means" has been satisfied.

III. THE PHILIPPINES' CLAIMS

31. Based on the foregoing and the evidence to be submitted in the course of this arbitration, the Philippines asserts the following claims:

- China's rights in regard to maritime areas in the South China Sea, like the rights of the Philippines, are those that are established by UNCLOS, and consist of its rights to a Territorial Sea and Contiguous Zone under Pait II of the Convention, to an Exclusive Economic Zone under Part V, and to a Continental Shelf under Part VI;
- Accordingly, China's maritime claims in the South China Sea based on its so-called "nine dash line" are contrary to UNCLOS and invalid;
- Submerged features in the South China Sea that are not above sea level at high tide, and are not located in a coastal State's tenitorial sea, are part of the seabed and cannot be acquired by a State, or subjected to its sovereignty, unless they form part of that State's Continental Shelf under Part VI of the Convention;
- Mischief Reef, McKennan Reef, Gaven Reef and Subi Reef are submerged features that are not above sea level at high tide, are not islands under the Convention, are not located on China's Continental

Shelf; and China has unlawfully occupied and engaged in unlawful construction activities on these features;

- Mischief Reef and McKennan Reef are part of the Philippines' Continental Shelf under Part VI of the Convention.
- Scarborough Shoal, Johnson Reef, Cuarteron Reef and Fiery Cross Reef are submerged features that are below sea level at high tide, except that each has small protrusions that remain above water at high tide, which qualify as "rocks" under Article 121(3) of the Convention, and generate an entitlement only to a Tenitorial Sea no broader than 12 M; and China has unlawfully claimed maritime entitlements beyond 12 M from these features;
- Chiria has unlawfully prevented Philippine vessels from exploiting the living resources in the waters adjacent to Scarborough Shoal and Johnson Reef;
- The Philippines is entitled under UNCLOS to a 12 M Territorial Sea, a 200 M Exclusive Economic Zone, and a Continental Shelf under Parts II, V and VI of UNCLOS, measured from its archipelagic baselines;
- China has unlawfully claimed rights to, and has unlawfully exploited, the living and non-living resources in the Philippines' Exclusive Economic Zone and Continental Shelf, and has unlawfully prevented the Philippines from exploiting the living and non-living resources within its Exclusive Economic Zone and Continental Shelf; and
- China has unlawfully interfered with the exercise by the Philippines of its rights to navigation under the Convention.

IV. JURISDICTION OF THE TRIBUNAL

32. The Philippines and China are both parties to UNCLOS, having ratified the Convention on 8 May 1984 and 7 June 1996, respectively. It follows that both Parties have given their advance consent to the regime of settlement of disputes concerning the interpretation and application of the Convention established in Part XII.

33. Article 279 of the Convention requires States Paiiies to seek a solution by peaceful means in accordance with the UN Charter. Article 283(1) further requires that when a dispute arises between States Parties, they should proceed expeditiously to an exchange of views regarding a settlement by negotiation or other peaceful means. The Philippines has complied with the requirements of Article 279 and Article 283(1) fully and in good faith, and has exhausted possibilities of settlement by negotiation.

34. As the Philippines and China have failed to settle the dispute between them by peaceful means of their own choice, Article 281(1) allows recourse to the

procedures provided for in Part XV, including compulsory procedures entailing binding decisions under Section 2 of Part XV. Article 286 allows these compulsory procedures to be initiated by any State Party in the court or tribunal having jurisdiction under Section 2.

35. The choice of compulsory procedures is governed by Article 287, the first paragraph of which allows a State Party, by means of a written declaration, to choose one or more of the means for settlement of disputes listed therein, including recourse to an arbitral tribunal under Annex VII of the Convention. States Parties to a dispute which have not made declarations pursuant to Article 287(1) are deemed by operation of Article 287(3) to have accepted arbitration in accordance with Annex VII.

36. Since neither the Philippines nor China has made a declaration pursuant to Article 287(1), and since no agreement to the contrary cmrently exists, it follows that, in accordance with Article 287(5), this dispute may be submitted to arbitration under Annex VII of the Convention.

37. The jurisdiction of an Annex VII tribunal extends to any dispute concerning the interpretation or application of the Convention, subject to the provisions of Section 3 of Part XV.

38. Section 3 of Part XV contains optional exceptions from jurisdiction in Article 98. Such exceptions have been invoked by China in a formal declaration dated 25 August 2006.

39. None of these exceptions is applicable to the Philippines' claims in this arbitration. The present dispute concerns (a) whether, in light of China's repeated assertions of alleged "sovereign rights and jurisdiction" within the so-called "nine dash line", the Parties' respective rights and obligations in regard to the waters, seabed and maritime features of the South China Sea are governed by the provisions of UNCLOS, including but not limited to Articles 3-14 of Part II, Articles 55 and 57 of Part V, Article 76 of Part VI, Artile 121 of Part VIII d Article 300 of Part XVI; (b) whether China.'s Claims based on the "nine dash line" are inconsistent with those provisions; (c) whether, under Article 121 of UNCLOS, certain of the maritime features in the South China Sea are islands, low tide elevations or submerged banks, and whether they are capable of generating entitlements to maritime zones greater than 12 M; and (d) whether China has violated the right of navigation of the Philippines in the waters of the South China Sea, and the rights of the Philippines in regard to the living and non-living resources within its exclusive economic zone and continental shelf.

40. It follows that the Philippines' claims do not fall within China's Declaration of 25 August 2006, because they do not: concern the interpretation or application of

Articles 15, 74 and 83 relating to sea boundary delimitations; involve historic bays or titles within the meaning of the relevant provisions of the Convention; concern military activities or law enforcement activities; or concern matters over which the Security Council is exercising functions assigned to it by the UN Charter.

V. RELIEF SOUGHT

41. In light of the above, and the evidence to be submitted in the course of this arbitration, the Philippines respectfully requests that the Arbitral Tribunal issue an Award that:

- Declares that China's rights in regard to maritime areas in the South China Sea, like the rights of the Philippines, are those that are established by UNCLOS, and consist of its rights to a Territorial Sea and Contiguous Zone under Part II of the Convention, to an Exclusive Economic Zone under Part V, andto a Continental Shelf under Part VI;
- Declares that China's maritime claims in the South China Sea based on its so-called "nine dash line" are contrary to UNCLOS and invalid;
- Requires China to bring its domestic legislation into conformity with its obligations under UNCLOS;
- Declares that Mischief Reef and McKennan Reef are submerged features that form part of the Continental Shelf of the Philippines under Part VI of the Convention, and that China's occupation of and construction activities on them violate the sovereign rights of the Philippines;
- Requires that China end its occupation of and activities on Mischief Reef and McKennan Reef;
- Declares that Gaven Reef and Subi Reef are submerged features in the South China Sea that are not above sea level at high tide, are not islands under the Convention, and are not located on China's Continental Shelf, and that China's occupation of and construction activities on these features are unlawful;
- Requires China to terminate its occupation of and activities on Gaven Reef and Subi Reef;
- Declares that Scarborough Shoal, Johnson Reef, Cuarteron Reef and Fiery Cross Reef are submerged features that are below sea level at high tide, except that each has small protrusions that remain abQve water at high tide, which are "rocks" under Article 121(3) of the Convention and which therefore generate entitlements only to a Territorial Sea no broader than 12 M; and that China has unlawfully claimed maritime entitlements beyond 12 M from these features;

- Requires that China refrain from preventing Philippine vessels from exploiting in a sustainable manner the living resources in the waters adjacent to Scarborough Shoal and Johnson Reef, and from undertaking other activities inconsistent with the Convention at or in the vicinity of these features;
- Declares that the Philippines is entitled under UNCLOS to a 12 M Territorial Sea, a 200 M Exclusive Economic Zone, and a Continental Shelf under Parts II, V and VI of UNCLOS, measured from its archipelagic baselines;
- Declares that China has unlawfully claimed, and has unlawfully exploited, the living and non-living resources in the Philippines' Exclusive Economic Zone and Continental Shelf, and has unlawfully prevented the Philippines 'from exploiting living and non-living resources within its Exclusive Economic Zone and Continental Shelf;
- Declares that China has unlawfully interfered with the exercise by the Philippines of its rights to navigation and other rights under the Convention III areas within and beyond 200 M of the Philippines' archipelagic baselines; and
- Requires that China desist from these unlawful activities.

VI. APPOINTMENT OF ARBITRATOR

42. In accordance with the requirements of UNCLOS Annex VII, Article 3(b), the Philippines hereby appoints Judge Rudiger Wolfrum as a member of the Arbitral Tribunal.

VII. RESERVATION OF RIGHTS

43. The Philippines reserves the right to supplement and/or amend its claims and the relief sought as necessary, and to make such other requests of the Arbitral Tribunal as may be required, to preserve its rights under UNCLOS, including a request for provisional measures.

Respectfully submitted,

Francis H. Jardeleza
Solicitor General
Republic of the Philippines Agent

22 January 2013

Appendix 2

Position Paper of the Government of the People's Republic of China on the Matter of Jurisdiction in the South China Sea Arbitration Initiated by the Republic of the Philippines, 7 December 2014

POSITION PAPER OF THE GOVERNMENT OF THE PEOPLE'S REPUBLIC OF CHINA ON THE MATTER OF JURISDICTION IN THE SOUTH CHINA SEA ARBITRATION INITIATED BY THE REPUBLIC OF THE PHILIPPINES

7 December 2014

I. Introduction

1. On 22 January 2013, the Department of Foreign Affairs of the Republic of the Philippines presented a note verbale to the Embassy of the People's Republic of China in the Philippines, stating that the Philippines submitted a Notification and Statement of Claim in order to initiate compulsory arbitration proceedings under Article 287 and Annex VII of the United Nations Convention on the Law of the Sea ("Convention") with respect to the dispute with China over "maritime jurisdiction" in the South China Sea. On 19 February 2013, the Chinese Government rejected and returned the Philippines' note verbale together with the attached Notification and Statement of Claim. The Chinese Government has subsequently reiterated that it will neither accept nor participate in the arbitration thus initiated by the Philippines.

2. This Position Paper is intended to demonstrate that the arbitral tribunal established at the request of the Philippines for the present arbitration ("Arbitral Tribunal") does not have jurisdiction over this case. It does not express any position on the substantive issues related to the subject-matter of the arbitration initiated by the Philippines. No acceptance by China is signified in this Position Paper of the views or claims advanced by the Philippines, whether or not they are referred to herein. Nor shall this Position Paper be regarded as China's acceptance of or participation in this arbitration.

3. This Position Paper will elaborate on the following positions:

- The essence of the subject-matter of the arbitration is the territorial sovereignty over several maritime features in the South China Sea, which is beyond the scope of the Convention and does not concern the interpretation or application of the Convention;
- China and the Philippines have agreed, through bilateral instruments and the Declaration on the Conduct of Parties in the South China Sea, to settle their relevant disputes through negotiations. By unilaterally initiating the present arbitration, the Philippines has breached its obligation under international law;
- Even assuming, *arguendo*, that the subject-matter of the arbitration were concerned with the interpretation or application of the Convention, that subject-matter would constitute an integral part of maritime delimitation

between the two countries, thus falling within the scope of the declaration filed by China in 2006 in accordance with the Convention, which excludes, *inter alia*, disputes concerning maritime delimitation from compulsory arbitration and other compulsory dispute settlement procedures;

- Consequently, the Arbitral Tribunal manifestly has no jurisdiction over the present arbitration. Based on the foregoing positions and by virtue of the freedom of every State to choose the means of dispute settlement, China's rejection of and non-participation in the present arbitration stand on solid ground in international law.

II. The essence of the subject-matter of the arbitration is the territorial sovereignty over several maritime features in the South China Sea, which does not concern the interpretation or application of the Convention

4. China has indisputable sovereignty over the South China Sea Islands (the Dongsha Islands, the Xisha Islands, the Zhongsha Islands and the Nansha Islands) and the adjacent waters. Chinese activities in the South China Sea date back to over 2,000 years ago. China was the first country to discover, name, explore and exploit the resources of the South China Sea Islands and the first to continuously exercise sovereign powers over them. From the 1930s to 1940s, Japan illegally seized some parts of the South China Sea Islands during its war of aggression against China. At the end of the Second World War, the Chinese Government resumed exercise of sovereignty over the South China Sea Islands. Military personnel and government officials were sent via naval vessels to hold resumption of authority ceremonies. Commemorative stone markers were erected, garrisons stationed, and geographical surveys conducted. In 1947, China renamed the maritime features of the South China Sea Islands and, in 1948, published an official map which displayed a dotted line in the South China Sea. Since the founding of the People's Republic of China on 1 October 1949, the Chinese Government has been consistently and actively maintaining its sovereignty over the South China Sea Islands. Both the Declaration of the Government of the People's Republic of China on the Territorial Sea of 1958 and the Law of the People's Republic of China on the Territorial Sea and the Contiguous Zone of 1992 expressly provide that the territory of the People's Republic of China includes, among others, the Dongsha Islands, the Xisha Islands, the Zhongsha Islands and the Nansha Islands. All those acts affirm China's territorial sovereignty and relevant maritime rights and interests in the South China Sea.

5. Prior to the 1970s, Philippine law had set clear limits for the territory of the Philippines, which did not involve any of China's maritime features in the South China Sea. Article 1 of the 1935 Constitution of the Republic of the Philippines, entitled "The National Territory", provided that "The Philippines comprises all the territory ceded to the United States by the Treaty of Paris concluded between

the United States and Spain on the tenth day of December, eighteen hundred and ninety-eight, the limits which are set forth in Article III of said treaty, together with all the islands embraced in the treaty concluded at Washington between the United States and Spain on the seventh day of November, nineteen hundred, and the treaty concluded between the United States and Great Britain on the second day of January, nineteen hundred and thirty, and all territory over which the present Government of the Philippine Islands exercises jurisdiction." Under this provision, the territory of the Philippines was confined to the Philippine Islands, having nothing to do with any of China's maritime features in the South China Sea. Philippine Republic Act No. 3046, entitled "An Act to Define the Baselines of the Territorial Sea of the Philippines", which was promulgated in 1961, reaffirmed the territorial scope of the country as laid down in the 1935 Constitution.

6. Since the 1970s, the Philippines has illegally occupied a number of maritime features of China's Nansha Islands, including Mahuan Dao, Feixin Dao, Zhongye Dao, Nanyao Dao, Beizi Dao, Xiyue Dao, Shuanghuang Shazhou and Siling Jiao. Furthermore, it unlawfully designated a so-called "Kalayaan Island Group" to encompass some of the maritime features of China's Nansha Islands and claimed sovereignty over them, together with adjacent but vast maritime areas. Subsequently, it laid unlawful claim to sovereignty over Huangyan Dao of China's Zhongsha Islands. In addition, the Philippines has also illegally explored and exploited the resources on those maritime features and in the adjacent maritime areas.

7. The Philippines' activities mentioned above have violated the Charter of the United Nations and international law, and seriously encroached upon China's territorial sovereignty and maritime rights and interests. They are null and void in law. The Chinese Government has always been firmly opposed to these actions of the Philippines, and consistently and continuously made solemn representations and protests to the Philippines.

8. The Philippines has summarized its claims for arbitration in three categories:

First, China's assertion of the "historic rights" to the waters, sea-bed and subsoil within the "nine-dash line" (i.e., China's dotted line in the South China Sea) beyond the limits of its entitlements under the Convention is inconsistent with the Convention.

Second, China's claim to entitlements of 200 nautical miles and more, based on certain rocks, low-tide elevations and submerged features in the South China Sea, is inconsistent with the Convention.

Third, China's assertion and exercise of rights in the South China Sea have unlawfully interfered with the sovereign rights, jurisdiction and rights and freedom of navigation that the Philippines enjoys and exercises under the Convention.

9. The subject-matter of the Philippines' claims is in essence one of territorial sovereignty over several maritime features in the South China Sea, which is beyond the scope of the Convention and does not concern the interpretation or application of the Convention. Consequently, the Arbitral Tribunal has no jurisdiction over the claims of the Philippines for arbitration.

10. With regard to the first category of claims presented by the Philippines for arbitration, it is obvious that the core of those claims is that China's maritime claims in the South China Sea have exceeded the extent allowed under the Convention. However, whatever logic is to be followed, only after the extent of China's territorial sovereignty in the South China Sea is determined can a decision be made on whether China's maritime claims in the South China Sea have exceeded the extent allowed under the Convention.

11. It is a general principle of international law that sovereignty over land territory is the basis for the determination of maritime rights. As the International Court of Justice ("ICJ") stated, "maritime rights derive from the coastal State's sovereignty over the land, a principle which can be summarized as 'the land dominates the sea'" *(Maritime Delimitation and Territorial Questions between Qatar and Bahrain (Qatar v. Bahrain),* Merits, Judgment of 16 March 2001, I.C.J. Reports 2001, p. 97, para. 185; cf. also *North Sea Continental Shelf (Federal Republic of Germany/Denmark; Federal Republic of Germany/Netherlands)*, Judgment of 20 February 1969, I.C.J. Reports 1969, p. 51, para. 96; *Aegean Sea Continental Shelf (Greece v. Turkey),* Jurisdiction of the Court, Judgment of 19 December 1978, I.C.J. Reports 1978, p. 36, para. 86). And, "[i]t is thus the terrestrial territorial situation that must be taken as starting point for the determination of the maritime rights of a coastal State" (*Qatar v. Bahrain,* I.C.J. Reports 2001, para. 185; *Territorial and Maritime Dispute between Nicaragua and Honduras in the Caribbean Sea (Nicaragua v. Honduras),* Judgment of 8 October 2007, I.C.J. Reports 2007, p. 696, para. 113). Recently the ICJ again emphasized that "[t]he title of a State to the continental shelf and to the exclusive economic zone is based on the principle that the land dominates the sea", and that "the land is the legal source of the power which a State may exercise over territorial extensions to seaward" *(Territorial and Maritime Dispute (Nicaragua v. Colombia),* Judgment of 19 November 2012, I.C.J. Reports 2012, p. 51, para. 140).

12. The preamble of the Convention proclaims "the desirability of establishing through this Convention, with due regard for the sovereignty of all States, a legal order for the seas and oceans". It is apparent that "due regard for the sovereignty of all States" is the prerequisite for the application of the Convention to determine maritime rights of the States Parties.

13. As far as the present arbitration is concerned, without first having determined China's territorial sovereignty over the maritime features in the South China

Sea, the Arbitral Tribunal will not be in a position to determine the extent to which China may claim maritime rights in the South China Sea pursuant to the Convention, not to mention whether China's claims exceed the extent allowed under the Convention. But the issue of territorial sovereignty falls beyond the purview of the Convention.

14. The Philippines is well aware that a tribunal established under Article 287 and Annex VII of the Convention has no jurisdiction over territorial sovereignty disputes. In an attempt to circumvent this jurisdictional hurdle and fabricate a basis for institution of arbitral proceedings, the Philippines has cunningly packaged its case in the present form. It has repeatedly professed that it does not seek from the Arbitral Tribunal a determination of territorial sovereignty over certain maritime features claimed by both countries, but rather a ruling on the compatibility of China's maritime claims with the provisions of the Convention, so that its claims for arbitration would appear to be concerned with the interpretation or application of the Convention, not with the sovereignty over those maritime features. This contrived packaging, however, fails to conceal the very essence of the subject-matter of the arbitration, namely, the territorial sovereignty over certain maritime features in the South China Sea.

15. With regard to the second category of claims by the Philippines, China believes that the nature and maritime entitlements of certain maritime features in the South China Sea cannot be considered in isolation from the issue of sovereignty.

16. In the first place, without determining the sovereignty over a maritime feature, it is impossible to decide whether maritime claims based on that feature are consistent with the Convention.

17. The holder of the entitlements to an exclusive economic zone ("EEZ") and a continental shelf under the Convention is the coastal State with sovereignty over relevant land territory. When not subject to State sovereignty, a maritime feature per se possesses no maritime rights or entitlements whatsoever. In other words, only the State having sovereignty over a maritime feature is entitled under the Convention to claim any maritime rights based on that feature. Only after a State's sovereignty over a maritime feature has been determined and the State has made maritime claims in respect thereof, could there arise a dispute concerning the interpretation or application of the Convention, if another State questions the compatibility of those claims with the Convention or makes overlapping claims. If the sovereignty over a maritime feature is undecided, there cannot be a concrete and real dispute for arbitration as to whether or not the maritime claims of a State based on such a feature are compatible with the Convention.

18. In the present case, the Philippines denies China's sovereignty over the maritime features in question, with a view to completely disqualifying China

from making any maritime claims in respect of those features. In light of this, the Philippines is putting the cart before the horse by requesting the Arbitral Tribunal to determine, even before the matter of sovereignty is dealt with, the issue of compatibility of China's maritime claims with the Convention. In relevant cases, no international judicial or arbitral body has ever applied the Convention to determine the maritime rights derived from a maritime feature before sovereignty over that feature is decided.

19. Secondly, in respect of the Nansha Islands, the Philippines selects only a few features and requests the Arbitral Tribunal to decide on their maritime entitlements. This is in essence an attempt at denying China's sovereignty over the Nansha Islands as a whole.

20. The Nansha Islands comprises many maritime features. China has always enjoyed sovereignty over the Nansha Islands in its entirety, not just over some features thereof. In 1935, the Commission of the Chinese Government for the Review of Maps of Land and Waters published the Map of Islands in the South China Sea. In 1948, the Chinese Government published the Map of the Location of the South China Sea Islands. Both maps placed under China's sovereignty what are now known as the Nansha Islands as well as the Dongsha Islands, the Xisha Islands and the Zhongsha Islands. The Declaration of the Government of the People's Republic of China on the Territorial Sea of 1958 declared that the territory of the People's Republic of China includes, *inter alia*, the Nansha Islands. In 1983, the National Toponymy Commission of China published standard names for some of the South China Sea Islands, including those of the Nansha Islands. The Law of the People's Republic of China on the Territorial Sea and the Contiguous Zone of 1992 again expressly provides that the Nansha Islands constitutes a part of the land territory of the People's Republic of China.

21. In Note Verbale No. CML/8/2011 of 14 April 2011 addressed to Secretary-General of the United Nations, the Permanent Mission of China to the United Nations stated that "under the relevant provisions of the *1982 United Nations Convention on the Law of the Sea*, as well as the *Law of the People's Republic of China on the Territorial Sea and the Contiguous Zone (1992)* and the *Law on the Exclusive Economic Zone and the Continental Shelf of the People's Republic of China (1998)*, China's Nansha Islands is fully entitled to Territorial Sea, Exclusive Economic Zone (EEZ) and Continental Shelf." It is plain that, in order to determine China's maritime entitlements based on the Nansha Islands under the Convention, all maritime features comprising the Nansha Islands must be taken into account.

22. The Philippines, by requesting the Arbitral Tribunal to determine the maritime entitlements of only what it describes as the maritime features "occupied or controlled by China", has in effect dissected the Nansha Islands. It deliberately makes no mention of the rest of the Nansha Islands, including those illegally seized

or claimed by the Philippines. Its real intention is to gainsay China's sovereignty over the whole of the Nansha Islands, deny the fact of its illegal seizure of or claim on several maritime features of the Nansha Islands, and distort the nature and scope of the China-Philippines disputes in the South China Sea. In addition, the Philippines has deliberately excluded from the category of the maritime features "occupied or controlled by China" the largest island in the Nansha Islands, Taiping Dao, which is currently controlled by the Taiwan authorities of China. This is a grave violation of the One-China Principle and an infringement of China's sovereignty and territorial integrity. This further shows that the second category of claims brought by the Philippines essentially pertains to the territorial sovereignty dispute between the two countries.

23. Finally, whether or not low-tide elevations can be appropriated is plainly a question of territorial sovereignty.

24. The Philippines asserts that some of the maritime features, about which it has submitted claims for arbitration, are low-tide elevations, thus being incapable of appropriation as territory. As to whether those features are indeed low-tide elevations, this Position Paper will not comment. It should, however, be pointed out that, whatever nature those features possess, the Philippines itself has persisted in claiming sovereignty over them since the 1970s. By Presidential Decree No. 1596, promulgated on 11 June 1978, the Philippines made known its unlawful claim to sovereignty over some maritime features in the Nansha Islands including the aforementioned features, together with the adjacent but vast areas of waters, sea-bed, subsoil, continental margin and superjacent airspace, and constituted the vast area as a new municipality of the province of Palawan, entitled "Kalayaan". Notwithstanding that Philippine Republic Act No. 9522 of 10 March 2009 stipulates that the maritime zones for the so-called "Kalayaan Island Group" (i.e., some maritime features of China's Nansha Islands) and "Scarborough Shoal" (i.e., China's Huangyan Dao) be determined in a way consistent with Article 121 of the Convention (i.e., the regime of islands), this provision was designed to adjust the Philippines' maritime claims based on those features within the aforementioned area. The Act did not vary the territorial claim of the Philippines to the relevant maritime features, including those it alleged in this arbitration as low-tide elevations. In Note Verbale No. 000228, addressed to Secretary-General of the United Nations on 5 April 2011, the Philippine Permanent Mission to the United Nations stated that, "the Kalayaan Island Group (KIG) constitutes an integral part of the Philippines. The Republic of the Philippines has sovereignty and jurisdiction over the geological features in the KIG." The Philippines has maintained, to date, its claim to sovereignty over 40 maritime features in the Nansha Islands, among which are the very features it now labels as low-tide elevations. It is thus obvious that the only motive behind the Philippines' assertion that low-tide elevations cannot be appropriated is to deny China's sovereignty over these features so as to place them under Philippine sovereignty.

25. Whether low-tide elevations can be appropriated as territory is in itself a question of territorial sovereignty, not a matter concerning the interpretation or application of the Convention. The Convention is silent on this issue of appropriation. In its 2001 Judgment in *Qatar v. Bahrain*, the ICJ explicitly stated that, "International treaty law is silent on the question whether low-tide elevations can be considered to be 'territory'. Nor is the Court aware of a uniform and widespread State practice which might have given rise to a customary rule which unequivocally permits or excludes appropriation of low-tide elevations" (*Qatar v. Bahrain*, I.C.J. Reports 2001, pp. 101–102, para. 205). "International treaty law" plainly includes the Convention, which entered into force in 1994. In its 2012 Judgment in *Nicaragua v. Colombia*, while the ICJ stated that "low-tide elevations cannot be appropriated" (*Nicaragua v. Colombia*, I.C.J. Reports 2012, p. 641, para. 26), it did not point to any legal basis for this conclusory statement. Nor did it touch upon the legal status of low-tide elevations as components of an archipelago, or sovereignty or claims of sovereignty that may have long existed over such features in a particular maritime area. On all accounts, the ICJ did not apply the Convention in that case. Whether or not low-tide elevations can be appropriated is not a question concerning the interpretation or application of the Convention.

26. As to the third category of the Philippines' claims, China maintains that the legality of China's actions in the waters of the Nansha Islands and Huangyan Dao rests on both its sovereignty over relevant maritime features and the maritime rights derived therefrom.

27. The Philippines alleges that China's claim to and exercise of maritime rights in the South China Sea have unlawfully interfered with the sovereign rights, jurisdiction and rights and freedom of navigation, which the Philippines is entitled to enjoy and exercise under the Convention. The premise for this claim must be that the spatial extent of the Philippines' maritime jurisdiction is defined and undisputed, and that China's actions have encroached upon such defined areas. The fact is, however, to the contrary. China and the Philippines have not delimited the maritime space between them. Until and unless the sovereignty over the relevant maritime features is ascertained and maritime delimitation completed, this category of claims of the Philippines cannot be decided upon.

28. It should be particularly emphasized that China always respects the freedom of navigation and overflight enjoyed by all States in the South China Sea in accordance with international law.

29. To sum up, by requesting the Arbitral Tribunal to apply the Convention to determine the extent of China's maritime rights in the South China Sea, without first having ascertained sovereignty over the relevant maritime features, and by formulating a series of claims for arbitration to that effect, the Philippines contravenes the general principles of international law and international

jurisprudence on the settlement of international maritime disputes. To decide upon any of the Philippines' claims, the Arbitral Tribunal would inevitably have to determine, directly or indirectly, the sovereignty over both the maritime features in question and other maritime features in the South China Sea. Besides, such a decision would unavoidably produce, in practical terms, the effect of a maritime delimitation, which will be further discussed below in Part IV of this Position Paper. Therefore, China maintains that the Arbitral Tribunal manifestly has no jurisdiction over the present case.

III. There exists an agreement between China and the Philippines to settle their disputes in the South China Sea through negotiations, and the Philippines is debarred from unilaterally initiating compulsory arbitration

30. With regard to disputes concerning territorial sovereignty and maritime rights, China has always maintained that they should be peacefully resolved through negotiations between the countries directly concerned. In the present case, there has been a long-standing agreement between China and the Philippines on resolving their disputes in the South China Sea through friendly consultations and negotiations.

31. Under the Joint Statement between the People's Republic of China and the Republic of the Philippines concerning Consultations on the South China Sea and on Other Areas of Cooperation, issued on 10 August 1995, both sides "agreed to abide by" the principles that "[d]isputes shall be settled in a peaceful and friendly manner through consultations on the basis of equality and mutual respect" (Point 1); that "a gradual and progressive process of cooperation shall be adopted with a view to eventually negotiating a settlement of the bilateral disputes" (Point 3); and that "[d]isputes shall be settled by the countries directly concerned without prejudice to the freedom of navigation in the South China Sea" (Point 8).

32. The Joint Statement of the China-Philippines Experts Group Meeting on Confidence-Building Measures, issued on 23 March 1999, states that the two sides reiterated their commitment to "[t]he understanding to continue to work for a settlement of their difference through friendly consultations" (para. 5), and that "the two sides believe that the channels of consultations between China and the Philippines are unobstructed. They have agreed that the dispute should be peacefully settled through consultation" (para. 12).

33. The Joint Statement between the Government of the People's Republic of China and the Government of the Republic of the Philippines on the Framework of Bilateral Cooperation in the Twenty-First Century, issued on 16 May 2000, states in Point 9 that, "The two sides commit themselves to the maintenance of peace and stability in the South China Sea. They agree to promote a peaceful settlement

of disputes through bilateral friendly consultations and negotiations in accordance with universally-recognized principles of international law, including the 1982 United Nations Convention on the Law of the Sea. They reaffirm their adherence to the 1995 joint statement between the two countries on the South China Sea ...".

34. The Joint Press Statement of the Third China-Philippines Experts' Group Meeting on Confidence-Building Measures, dated 4 April 2001, states in Point 4 that, "The two sides noted that the bilateral consultation mechanism to explore ways of cooperation in the South China Sea has been effective. The series of understanding and consensus reached by the two sides have played a constructive role in the maintenance of the sound development of China-Philippines relations and peace and stability of the South China Sea area."

35. The mutual understanding between China and the Philippines to settle relevant disputes through negotiations has been reaffirmed in a multilateral instrument. On 4 November 2002, Mr. Wang Yi, the then Vice Foreign Minister and representative of the Chinese Government, together with the representatives of the governments of the member States of the Association of Southeast Asian Nations ("ASEAN"), including the Philippines, jointly signed the Declaration on the Conduct of Parties in the South China Sea ("DOC"). Paragraph 4 of the DOC explicitly states that, "The Parties concerned undertake to resolve their territorial and jurisdictional disputes by peaceful means ... through friendly consultations and negotiations by sovereign states directly concerned, in accordance with universally recognized principles of international law, including the 1982 UN Convention on the Law of the Sea."

36. Following the signing of the DOC, the leaders of China and the Philippines have repeatedly reiterated their commitment to the settlement of disputes by way of dialogue. Thus, a Joint Press Statement between the Government of the People's Republic of China and the Government of the Republic of the Philippines was issued on 3 September 2004 during the State visit to China by the then Philippine President Gloria Macapagal-Arroyo, which states in paragraph 16 that, "They agreed that the early and vigorous implementation of the 2002 ASEAN-China Declaration on the Conduct of Parties in the South China Sea will pave the way for the transformation of the South China Sea into an area of cooperation."

37. Between 30 August and 3 September 2011, President Benigno S. Aquino III of the Philippines paid a State visit to China. On 1 September 2011, the two sides issued a Joint Statement between the People's Republic of China and the Republic of the Philippines, which, in paragraph 15, "reiterated their commitment to addressing the disputes through peaceful dialogue" and "reaffirmed their commitments to respect and abide by the Declaration on the Conduct of Parties in the South China Sea signed by China and the ASEAN member countries in 2002". The Joint Statement, consequently, reaffirmed Paragraph 4 of the DOC relating to settlement of relevant disputes by negotiations.

38. The bilateral instruments between China and the Philippines repeatedly employ the term "agree" when referring to settlement of their disputes through negotiations. This evinces a clear intention to establish an obligation between the two countries in this regard. Paragraph 4 of the DOC employs the term "undertake", which is also frequently used in international agreements to commit the parties to their obligations. As the ICJ observed in its Judgment in *Bosnia and Herzegovina v. Serbia and Montenegro*, "[t]he ordinary meaning of the word 'undertake' is to give a formal promise, to bind or engage oneself, to give a pledge or promise, to agree, to accept an obligation. It is a word regularly used in treaties setting out the obligations of the Contracting Parties ... It is not merely hortatory or purposive" *(Application of the Convention on the Prevention and Punishment of the Crime of Genocide (Bosnia and Herzegovina v. Serbia and Montenegro)*, Judgment of 26 February 2007, I.C.J. Reports 2007, p. 111, para. 162). Furthermore, under international law, regardless of the designation or form the above-mentioned instruments employ, as long as they intend to create rights and obligations for the parties, these rights and obligations are binding between the parties (*Cf. Maritime Delimitation and Territorial Questions between Qatar and Bahrain (Qatar v. Bahrain)*, Jurisdiction and Admissibility, Judgment of 1 July 1994, I.C.J. Reports 1994, pp. 120–121, paras. 22–26; *Land and Maritime Boundary between Cameroon and Nigeria (Cameroon v. Nigeria: Equitorial Guinea intervening),* Judgment of 10 October 2002, I.C.J. Reports 2002, pp. 427, 429, paras. 258, 262–263).

39. The relevant provisions in the aforementioned bilateral instruments and the DOC are mutually reinforcing and form an agreement between China and the Philippines. On that basis, they have undertaken a mutual obligation to settle their relevant disputes through negotiations.

40. By repeatedly reaffirming negotiations as the means for settling relevant disputes, and by emphasizing that negotiations be conducted by sovereign States directly concerned, the above-quoted provisions of the bilateral instruments and Paragraph 4 of the DOC obviously have produced the effect of excluding any means of third-party settlement. In particular, the above-mentioned Joint Statement between the People's Republic of China and the Republic of the Philippines concerning Consultations on the South China Sea and on Other Areas of Cooperation of 10 August 1995 stipulates in Point 3 that "a gradual and progressive process of cooperation shall be adopted with a view to eventually negotiating a settlement of the bilateral disputes". The term "eventually" in this context clearly serves to emphasize that "negotiations" is the only means the parties have chosen for dispute settlement, to the exclusion of any other means including third-party settlement procedures. Although the above-mentioned bilateral instruments and Paragraph 4 of the DOC do not use such an express phrase as "exclude other procedures of dispute settlement", as the arbitral tribunal in the *Southern Bluefin Tuna Case* stated in its Award, "the absence of an express exclusion of any procedure ... is

not decisive" (*Australia and New Zealand v. Japan*, Award on Jurisdiction and Admissibility, 4 August 2000, p. 97, para. 57). As discussed earlier, in respect of disputes relating to territorial sovereignty and maritime rights, China always insists on peaceful settlement of disputes by means of negotiations between the countries directly concerned. China's position on negotiations was made clear and well known to the Philippines and other relevant parties during the drafting and adoption of the aforementioned bilateral instruments and the DOC.

41. Consequently, with regard to all the disputes between China and the Philippines in the South China Sea, including the Philippines' claims in this arbitration, the only means of settlement as agreed by the two sides is negotiations, to the exclusion of any other means.

42. Even supposing that the Philippines' claims were concerned with the interpretation or application of the Convention, the compulsory procedures laid down in section 2 of Part XV of the Convention still could not be applied, given the agreement between China and the Philippines on settling their relevant disputes through negotiations.

43. Article 280 of the Convention states that, "Nothing in this Part impairs the right of any States Parties to agree at any time to settle a dispute between them concerning the interpretation or application of this Convention by any peaceful means of their own choice." Article 281 (1) provides that, "If the States Parties which are parties to a dispute concerning the interpretation or application of this Convention have agreed to seek settlement of the dispute by a peaceful means of their own choice, the procedures provided for in this Part apply only where no settlement has been reached by recourse to such means and the agreement between the parties does not exclude any further procedure."

44. As analysed above, through bilateral and multilateral instruments, China and the Philippines have agreed to settle their relevant disputes by negotiations, without setting any time limit for the negotiations, and have excluded any other means of settlement. In these circumstances, it is evident that, under the above-quoted provisions of the Convention, the relevant disputes between the two States shall be resolved through negotiations and there shall be no recourse to arbitration or other compulsory procedures.

45. The Philippines claims that, the two countries have been involved in exchanges of views since 1995 with regard to the subject-matter of the Philippines' claims for arbitration, without however reaching settlement, and that in its view, the Philippines is justified in believing that it is meaningless to continue the negotiations, and therefore the Philippines has the right to initiate arbitration. But the truth is that the two countries have never engaged in negotiations with regard to the subject-matter of the arbitration.

46. Under international law, general exchanges of views, without having the purpose of settling a given dispute, do not constitute negotiations. In *Georgia v. Russian Federation*, the ICJ held that, "Negotiations entail more than the plain opposition of legal views or interests between two parties, or the existence of a series of accusations and rebuttals, or even the exchange of claims and directly opposed counter-claims. As such, the concept of 'negotiations' ... requires – at the very least – a genuine attempt by one of the disputing parties to engage in discussions with the other disputing party, with a view to resolving the dispute" *(Application of the International Convention on the Elimination of All Forms of Racial Discrimination (Georgia v. Russian Federation)*, Preliminary Objections, Judgment of 1 April 2011, I.C.J. Reports 2011, p. 132, para. 157). In addition, the ICJ considered that "the subject-matter of the negotiations must relate to the subject-matter of the dispute which, in turn, must concern the substantive obligations contained in the treaty in question" (Ibid., p. 133, para. 161).

47. The South China Sea issue involves a number of countries, and it is no easy task to solve it. Up to the present, the countries concerned are still working together to create conditions conducive to its final settlement by negotiations. Against this background, the exchanges of views between China and the Philippines in relation to their disputes have so far pertained to responding to incidents at sea in the disputed areas and promoting measures to prevent conflicts, reduce frictions, maintain stability in the region, and promote measures of cooperation. They are far from constituting negotiations even on the evidence presented by the Philippines.

48. In recent years, China has on a number of occasions proposed to the Philippines the establishment of a China-Philippines regular consultation mechanism on maritime issues. To date, there has never been any response from the Philippines. On 1 September 2011, the two countries issued a Joint Statement between the People's Republic of China and the Republic of Philippines, reiterating the commitment to settling their disputes in the South China Sea through negotiations. But, before negotiations could formally begin, the Philippines sent on 10 April 2012 a naval vessel to the waters of China's Huangyan Dao to seize Chinese fishing boats together with the Chinese fishermen on board. In the face of such provocations, China was forced to take response measures to safeguard its sovereignty. Thereafter, China once again proposed to the Philippine Government that the two sides restart the China-Philippines consultation mechanism for confidence-building measures. That proposal again fell on deaf ears. On 26 April 2012, the Philippine Department of Foreign Affairs delivered a note verbale to the Chinese Embassy in the Philippines, proposing that the issue of Huangyan Dao be referred to a third-party adjudication body for resolution and indicating no willingness to negotiate. On 22 January 2013, the Philippines unilaterally initiated the present compulsory arbitration proceedings.

49. The previous exchanges of views regarding the South China Sea issue between the two countries did not concern the subject-matter of the Philippines' claims for

arbitration. For instance, the Philippines cited a statement released by the Chinese Foreign Ministry on 22 May 1997 regarding Huangyan Dao, in order to show that there exists between the two countries a dispute concerning the maritime rights of Huangyan Dao and that the two countries had exchanged views with regard to that dispute. However, the Philippines deliberately omitted a passage from that statement, which reads: "The issue of Huangyandao is an issue of territorial sovereignty; the development and exploitation of the EEZ is a question of maritime jurisdiction, the nature of the two issues are different and hence the laws and regulations governing them are also different, and they should not be discussed together. The attempt of the Philippine side to use maritime jurisdictional rights to violate the territorial sovereignty of China is untenable." This passage makes clear the thrust of the statement: the Philippines shall not negate China's sovereignty over Huangyan Dao on the pretext that it is situated within the EEZ of the Philippines. This shows that the exchange of views in question was centred on the issue of sovereignty.

50. It should be further noted that, the Philippines has attempted to show that the subject-matter of the exchanges of views between China and the Philippines since 1995 concerns the interpretation or application of the Convention, but nothing could be farther from the truth than this. Historically, the Philippines, by Republic Act No. 3046 of 17 June 1961, proclaimed as part of its territorial sea the vast areas of sea between the most outlying islands in the Philippine archipelago and the treaty limits established in the Treaty of Paris concluded between the United States and Spain in 1898, among other international treaties, thus claiming a belt of territorial sea far beyond 12 nautical miles. By Presidential Decree No. 1596 promulgated on 11 June 1978, the Philippines made its claim for sovereignty over the so-called "Kalayaan Island Group" (i.e., some maritime features of China's Nansha Islands), together with the adjacent but vast areas of waters, sea-bed, subsoil, continental margin, and superjacent airspace. As conceded by the Philippines itself, only with the adoption on 10 March 2009 of Republic Act No. 9522 did it begin the ongoing process to harmonize its domestic law with the Convention, with a view to eventually relinquishing all its maritime claims incompatible with the Convention. That Act provided, for the first time, that the maritime areas of the so-called "Kalayaan Island Group" (i.e., some maritime features of China's Nansha Islands) and "Scarborough Shoal" (i.e., China's Huangyan Dao) "shall be determined" so as to be "consistent with Article 121" of the Convention (i.e., the regime of islands). Therefore, given that the Philippines itself considers that only in 2009 did it start to abandon its former maritime claims in conflict with the Convention, how could it have started in 1995 to exchange views with China on matters concerning the interpretation or application of the Convention that are related to the present arbitration?

51. The Philippines claims that China cannot invoke Paragraph 4 of the DOC to exclude the jurisdiction of the Arbitral Tribunal, given its own grave breach of the

terms of the DOC. This is groundless. In support of its allegations against China, the Philippines claims that China has taken measures including the threat of force to drive away Philippine fishermen from the waters of Huangyan Dao in spite of their long-standing and continuous fishing activities in those waters, and that China has blocked the Philippines from resupplying a naval ship which ran and has stayed aground at Ren'ai Jiao and certain navy personnel on board. But the fact is that, regarding the situation at Huangyan Dao, it was the Philippines that first resorted to the threat of force by dispatching on 10 April 2012 a naval vessel to detain and arrest Chinese fishing boats and fishermen in the waters of Huangyan Dao. Regarding the situation at Ren'ai Jiao, which is a constituent part of China's Nansha Islands, the Philippines illegally ran a naval ship aground in May 1999 at that feature on the pretext of "technical difficulties". China has made repeated representations to the Philippines, demanding that the latter immediately tow away the vessel. The Philippines, for its part, had on numerous occasions made explicit undertaking to China to tow away the vessel grounded due to "technical difficulties". However, for over 15 years, instead of fulfilling that undertaking, the Philippines has attempted to construct permanent installations on Ren'ai Jiao. On 14 March 2014, the Philippines even openly declared that the vessel was deployed as a permanent installation on Ren'ai Jiao in 1999. China has been forced to take necessary measures in response to such provocative conduct. In light of these facts, the Philippines' accusations against China are baseless.

52. While it denies the effect of Paragraph 4 of the DOC for the purpose of supporting its institution of the present arbitration, the Philippines recently called on the parties to the DOC to comply with Paragraph 5 of the DOC and to provide "the full and effective implementation of the DOC", in a proposal made in its Department of Foreign Affairs statement dated 1 August 2014. This selective and self-contradictory tactic clearly violates the principle of good faith in international law.

53. The principle of good faith requires all States to honestly interpret agreements they enter into with others, not to misinterpret them in disregard of their authentic meaning in order to obtain an unfair advantage. This principle is of overriding importance and is incorporated in Article 2(2) of the Charter of the United Nations. It touches every aspect of international law (*Cf.* Sir Robert Jennings and Sir Arthur Watts (eds.), *Oppenheim's International Law*, 9th ed., 1992, vol. 1, p. 38). In the *Nuclear Tests Case*, the ICJ held that, "One of the basic principles governing the creation and performance of legal obligations, whatever their source, is the principle of good faith. Trust and confidence are inherent in international co-operation" *(Nuclear Tests Case (Australia v. France)*, Judgment of 20 December 1974, I.C.J. Reports 1974, p. 268, para. 46).

54. On this occasion, China wishes to emphasize that the DOC is an important instrument, adopted by China and the ASEAN member States following many years of arduous negotiations on the basis of mutual respect, mutual understanding

and mutual accommodation. Under the DOC, the parties concerned undertake to resolve their territorial and jurisdictional disputes through friendly consultations and negotiations by sovereign States directly concerned. In addition, the parties reaffirm their commitment to the purposes and principles of the Charter of the United Nations, the 1982 Convention, the Treaty of Amity and Cooperation in Southeast Asia, the Five Principles of Peaceful Coexistence, and other universally recognized principles of international law which shall serve as the basic norms governing state-to-state relations. The Parties commit themselves to exploring ways for building trust and confidence in accordance with the above-mentioned principles and on the basis of equality and mutual respect; reaffirm their respect for and commitment to the freedom of navigation in, and overflight above, the South China Sea as provided for by universally recognized principles of international law, including the 1982 Convention; and undertake to exercise self-restraint in the conduct of activities that would complicate or escalate disputes and affect peace and stability including, among others, refraining from action of inhabiting on the presently uninhabited islands, reefs, shoals, cays, and other features, and to handle their differences in a constructive manner. The DOC also lists a number of ways to build trust and areas of cooperation for the Parties concerned to seek and explore pending the peaceful settlement of territorial and jurisdictional disputes. As a follow-up to the DOC, the parties have undertaken to negotiate a "Code of Conduct in the South China Sea".

55. The DOC has played a positive role in maintaining stability in the South China Sea, and in enhancing maritime cooperation, building trust and reducing misgivings between China and the ASEAN member States. Every provision of the DOC constitutes an integral part of the document. To deny the significance of the DOC will lead to a serious retrogression from the current relationship of cooperation between China and the ASEAN member States in the South China Sea.

56. As a member of the ASEAN and having been involved throughout the consultations on the DOC, the Philippines should have fully appreciated the significance of the DOC for the peaceful settlement of the disputes in the South China Sea through negotiations. At present, in order to maintain stability in the region and create conditions for peaceful settlement of the South China Sea issue, China and the ASEAN member States have established working mechanisms to effectively implement the DOC, and have been engaged in consultations regarding the "Code of Conduct in the South China Sea". By initiating compulsory arbitration at this juncture, the Philippines is running counter to the common wish and joint efforts of China and the ASEAN member States. Its underlying goal is not, as the Philippines has proclaimed, to seek peaceful resolution of the South China Sea issue, but rather, by resorting to arbitration, to put political pressure on China, so as to deny China's lawful rights in the South China Sea through the so-called "interpretation or application" of the Convention, and to pursue a resolution of the South China Sea issue on its own terms. This is certainly unacceptable to China.

IV. Even assuming, *arguendo*, that the subject-matter of the arbitration were concerned with the interpretation or application of the Convention, that subject-matter would still be an integral part of maritime delimitation and, having been excluded by the 2006 Declaration filed by China, could not be submitted for arbitration

57. Part XV of the Convention establishes the right for the States Parties to file a written declaration to exclude specified categories of disputes from the compulsory dispute settlement procedures as laid down in section 2 of that Part. In 2006 China filed such a declaration in full compliance with the Convention.

58. On 25 August 2006, China deposited, pursuant to Article 298 of the Convention, with Secretary-General of the United Nations a written declaration, stating that, "The Government of the People's Republic of China does not accept any of the procedures provided for in section 2 of Part XV of the Convention with respect to all the categories of disputes referred to in paragraph 1 (a), (b) and (c) of Article 298 of the Convention". In other words, as regards disputes concerning maritime delimitation, historic bays or titles, military and law enforcement activities, and disputes in respect of which the Security Council of the United Nations is exercising the functions assigned to it by the Charter of the United Nations, the Chinese Government does not accept any of the compulsory dispute settlement procedures laid down in section 2 of Part XV of the Convention, including compulsory arbitration. China firmly believes that the most effective means for settlement of maritime disputes between China and its neighbouring States is that of friendly consultations and negotiations between the sovereign States directly concerned.

59. China and the Philippines are maritime neighbours and "States with opposite or adjacent coasts" in the sense of Articles 74 and 83 of the Convention. There exists an issue of maritime delimitation between the two States. Given that disputes between China and the Philippines relating to territorial sovereignty over relevant maritime features remain unresolved, the two States have yet to start negotiations on maritime delimitation. They have, however, commenced cooperation to pave the way for an eventual delimitation.

60. On 3 September 2004, the two sides issued a Joint Press Statement of the Government of the People's Republic of China and the Government of the Republic of the Philippines, stating that "[t]he two sides reaffirmed their commitment to the peace and stability in the South China Sea and their readiness to continue discussions to study cooperative activities like joint development pending the comprehensive and final settlement of territorial disputes and overlapping maritime claims in the area" (para. 16).

61. Two days before the issuance of the Joint Press Statement, upon approval by both governments and in the presence of the Heads of State of the two countries,

China National Offshore Oil Corporation and Philippine National Oil Company signed the "Agreement for Joint Marine Seismic Undertaking in Certain Areas in the South China Sea". On 14 March 2005, the agreement was expanded to a tripartite agreement, with the participation of Vietnam Oil and Gas Corporation. This is a good example of the constructive efforts made by the States concerned to enhance cooperation and create conditions for a negotiated settlement of the disputes in the South China Sea. The maritime area covered by that agreement is within that covered in the present arbitration initiated by the Philippines.

62. On 28 April 2005, during a State visit to the Philippines by the then Chinese President Hu Jintao, China and the Philippines issued a Joint Statement of the People's Republic of China and the Republic of the Philippines, in which the two sides "agreed to continue efforts to maintain peace and stability in the South China Sea and ... welcomed the signing of the Tripartite Agreement for Joint Marine Seismic Undertaking in the Agreement Area in the South China Sea by China National Offshore Oil Corporation, Vietnam Oil and Gas Corporation and Philippine National Oil Company" (para. 16).

63. On 16 January 2007, during the official visit to the Philippines by the then Chinese Premier Wen Jiabao, China and the Philippines issued a Joint Statement of the People's Republic of China and the Republic of the Philippines, which stated that "the Tripartite Joint Marine Seismic Undertaking in the South China Sea serves as a model for cooperation in the region. They agreed that possible next steps for cooperation among the three parties should be explored to bring collaboration to a higher level and increase the momentum of trust and confidence in the region" (para. 12).

64. In light of the above, it is plain that China and the Philippines have reached mutual understanding to advance final resolution of the issue of maritime delimitation through cooperation. In any event, given China's 2006 declaration, the Philippines should not and cannot unilaterally initiate compulsory arbitration on the issue of maritime delimitation.

65. To cover up the maritime delimitation nature of the China-Philippines dispute and to sidestep China's 2006 declaration, the Philippines has split up the dispute of maritime delimitation into discrete issues and selected a few of them for arbitration, requesting the Arbitral Tribunal to render the so-called "legal interpretation" on each of them.

66. It is not difficult to see that such legal issues as those presented by the Philippines in the present arbitration, including maritime claims, the legal nature of maritime features, the extent of relevant maritime rights, and law enforcement activities at sea, are all fundamental issues dealt with in past cases of maritime delimitation decided by international judicial or arbitral bodies and in State

practice concerning maritime delimitation. In short, those issues are part and parcel of maritime delimitation.

67. Maritime delimitation is an integral, systematic process. Articles 74 and 83 of the Convention stipulate that maritime delimitation between States with opposite or adjacent coasts "shall be effected by agreement on the basis of international law, as referred to in Article 38 of the Statute of the International Court of Justice, in order to achieve an equitable solution". Both international jurisprudence and State practice have recognized that all relevant factors must be taken into account to achieve an equitable solution. In this light, the international law applicable to maritime delimitation includes both the Convention and general international law. Under this body of law, maritime delimitation involves a consideration of not only entitlements, effect of maritime features, and principles and methods of delimitation, but also all relevant factors that must be taken into account, in order to attain an equitable solution.

68. The issues presented by the Philippines for arbitration constitute an integral part of maritime delimitation between China and the Philippines, and, as such, can only be considered under the overarching framework of maritime delimitation between China and the Philippines, and in conjunction with all the relevant rights and interests the parties concerned enjoy in accordance with the Convention, general international law, and historical or long-standing practice in the region for overall consideration. The Philippines' approach of splitting its maritime delimitation dispute with China and selecting some of the issues for arbitration, if permitted, will inevitably destroy the integrity and indivisibility of maritime delimitation and contravene the principle that maritime delimitation must be based on international law as referred to in Article 38 of the ICJ Statute and that "all relevant factors must be taken into account". This will adversely affect the future equitable solution of the dispute of maritime delimitation between China and the Philippines.

69. Ostensibly, the Philippines is not seeking from the Arbitral Tribunal a ruling regarding maritime delimitation, but instead a decision, *inter alia*, that certain maritime features are part of the Philippines' EEZ and continental shelf, and that China has unlawfully interfered with the enjoyment and exercise by the Philippines of sovereign rights in its EEZ and continental shelf. But that obviously is an attempt to seek a recognition by the Arbitral Tribunal that the relevant maritime areas are part of the Philippines' EEZ and continental shelf, in respect of which the Philippines is entitled to exercise sovereign rights and jurisdiction. This is actually a request for maritime delimitation by the Arbitral Tribunal in disguise. The Philippines' claims have in effect covered the main aspects and steps in maritime delimitation. Should the Arbitral Tribunal address substantively the Philippines' claims, it would amount to a *de facto* maritime delimitation.

70. The exclusionary declarations filed by the States Parties to the Convention under Article 298 of the Convention must be respected. By initiating the present compulsory arbitration as an attempt to circumvent China's 2006 declaration, the Philippines is abusing the dispute settlement procedures under the Convention.

71. China's 2006 declaration, once filed, automatically comes into effect. Its effect, as prescribed under Article 299 of the Convention, is that, without the consent of China, no State Party can unilaterally invoke any of the compulsory procedures specified in section 2 of Part XV against China in respect of the disputes covered by that declaration. In return, China simultaneously gives up the right to unilaterally initiate compulsory procedures against other States Parties in respect of the same disputes. The rights and obligations are reciprocal in this regard.

72. The Philippines claims that, having chosen none of the four compulsory dispute settlement procedures listed under Article 287 of the Convention, China as a State Party shall therefore be deemed to have accepted compulsory arbitration. This is a deliberately misleading argument. The purpose and the effect of China's 2006 declaration is such that the disputes listed therein are fully excluded from the compulsory settlement procedures under the Convention. Whether or not China has selected any of the four compulsory procedures under Article 287, as long as a dispute falls within the scope of China's 2006 declaration, China has already explicitly excluded it from the applicability of any compulsory procedures under section 2 of Part XV of the Convention, including compulsory arbitration.

73. Although the Philippines professes that the subject-matter of the arbitration does not involve any dispute covered by China's 2006 declaration, since China holds a different view in this regard, the Philippines should first take up this issue with China, before a decision can be taken on whether or not it can be submitted for arbitration. Should the Philippines' logic in its present form be followed, any State Party may unilaterally initiate compulsory arbitration against another State Party in respect of a dispute covered by the latter's declaration in force simply by asserting that the dispute is not excluded from arbitration by that declaration. This would render the provisions of Article 299 meaningless.

74. Since the entry into force of the Convention, the present arbitration is the first case in which a State Party has unilaterally initiated compulsory arbitration in respect of a dispute covered by a declaration of another State Party under Article 298. If this twisted approach of the Philippines could be accepted as fulfilling the conditions for invoking compulsory arbitration, it could be well imagined that any of the disputes listed in Article 298 may be submitted to the compulsory procedures under section 2 of Part XV simply by connecting them, using the Philippines' approach, with the question of interpretation or application of certain provisions of the Convention. Should the above approach be deemed acceptable, the question would then arise as to whether the provisions of Article 298 could still retain any

value, and whether there is any practical meaning left of the declarations so far filed by 35 States Parties under Article 298. In light of the foregoing reasons, China can only conclude that, the unilateral initiation by the Philippines of the present arbitration constitutes an abuse of the compulsory procedures provided in the Convention and a grave challenge to the solemnity of the dispute settlement mechanism under the Convention.

75. To sum up, even assuming that the subject-matter of the arbitration were concerned with the interpretation or application of the Convention, it would still be an integral part of the dispute of maritime delimitation between the two States. Having been excluded by China's 2006 declaration, it could not be submitted to compulsory arbitration under the Convention.

V. China's right to freely choose the means of dispute settlement must be fully respected, and its rejection of and non-participation in the present arbitration is solidly grounded in international law

76. Under international law, every State is free to choose the means of dispute settlement. The jurisdiction of any international judicial or arbitral body over an inter-State dispute depends on the prior consent of the parties to the dispute. This is known as the principle of consent in international law. It was on the basis of this principle that the States participating in the Third United Nations Conference on the Law of the Sea reached, after extended and arduous negotiations, a compromise on Part XV relating to dispute settlement as a package deal.

77. The compulsory dispute settlement procedures provided in Part XV of the Convention apply only to disputes concerning the interpretation or application of the Convention. States Parties are entitled to freely choose the means of settlement other than those set out in Part XV. Articles 297 and 298 of the Convention, moreover, provide for limitations on and optional exceptions to the applicability of the compulsory procedures with regard to specified categories of disputes.

78. The balance embodied in the provisions of Part XV has been a critical factor for the decision of many States to become parties to the Convention. At the second session of the Third United Nations Conference on the Law of the Sea, Ambassador Reynaldo Galindo Pohl of El Salvador, co-chair of the informal group on the settlement of disputes, on introducing the first general draft on dispute settlement, emphasized the need for exceptions from compulsory jurisdiction with respect to questions directly related to the territorial integrity of States. Otherwise, as has been noted, "a number of States might have been dissuaded from ratifying the Convention or even signing it" (Shabtai Rosenne and Louis B. Sohn (eds.), *United Nations Convention on the Law of the Sea 1982: A Commentary*, 1989, vol. v,

p. 88, para. 297.1). It follows that the provisions of Part XV must be interpreted and applied in such a manner so as to preserve the balance in and the integrity of Part XV.

79. China highly values the positive role played by the compulsory dispute settlement procedures of the Convention in upholding the international legal order for the oceans. As a State Party to the Convention, China has accepted the provisions of section 2 of Part XV on compulsory dispute settlement procedures. But that acceptance does not mean that those procedures apply to disputes of territorial sovereignty, or disputes which China has agreed with other States Parties to settle by means of their own choice, or disputes already excluded by Article 297 and China's 2006 declaration filed under Article 298. With regard to the Philippines' claims for arbitration, China has never accepted any of the compulsory procedures of section 2 of Part XV.

80. By virtue of the principle of sovereignty, parties to a dispute may choose the means of settlement of their own accord. This has been affirmed by the Convention. Article 280 provides that, "Nothing in this Part impairs the right of any States Parties to agree at any time to settle a dispute between them concerning the interpretation or application of this Convention by any peaceful means of their own choice."

81. The means thus chosen by the States Parties to the Convention takes priority over the compulsory procedures set forth in section 2 of Part XV. Article 281(1) of section 1 of Part XV provides that, "If the States Parties which are parties to a dispute concerning the interpretation or application of this Convention have agreed to seek settlement of the dispute by a peaceful means of their own choice, the procedures provided for in this Part apply only where no settlement has been reached by recourse to such means and the agreement between the parties does not exclude any further procedure." Article 286 states that, "Subject to section 3, any dispute concerning the interpretation or application of this Convention shall, where no settlement has been reached by recourse to section 1, be submitted at the request of any party to the dispute to the court or tribunal having jurisdiction under this section." Accordingly, where parties to a dispute have already chosen a means of settlement and excluded other procedures, the compulsory procedures of the Convention shall not apply to the dispute in question.

82. The priority and significance of the means of dispute settlement chosen by States Parties to the Convention have been further affirmed in the arbitral award in the *Southern Bluefin Tuna Case*. The tribunal recognized that the Convention "falls significantly short of establishing a truly comprehensive regime of compulsory jurisdiction entailing binding decisions", and that "States Parties ... are permitted by Article 281(1) to confine the applicability of compulsory procedures of section 2 of Part XV to cases where all parties to the dispute have agreed upon submission

of their dispute to such compulsory procedures" (*Australia and New Zealand v. Japan*, pp. 102–103, para. 62). Were the provisions of section 1 of Part XV not complied with faithfully, it would result in deprivation of the right of the States Parties to freely choose means of peaceful settlement based on State sovereignty. That would entail a breach of the principle of consent and upset the balance in and integrity of Part XV.

83. In exercise of its power to decide on its jurisdiction, any judicial or arbitral body should respect the right of the States Parties to the Convention to freely choose the means of settlement. Article 288(4) of the Convention provides that "[i]n the event of a dispute as to whether a court or tribunal has jurisdiction, the matter shall be settled by decision of that court or tribunal". China respects that competence of judicial or arbitral bodies under the Convention. Equally important, China would like to emphasize, the exercise of judicial or arbitral power shall not derogate from the right of the States Parties to choose the means of settlement of their own accord, or from the principle of consent which must be followed in international adjudication and arbitration. China holds that this is the constraint that the Arbitral Tribunal must abide by when considering whether or not to apply Article 288(4) in determining its jurisdiction in the present arbitration. After all, "the parties to the dispute are complete masters of the procedure to be used to settle it" (Shabtai Rosenne and Louis B. Sohn (eds.), *United Nations Convention on the Law of the Sea 1982: A Commentary*, 1989, vol. v, p. 20, para. 280.1).

84. China respects the right of all States Parties to invoke the compulsory procedures in accordance with the Convention. At the same time, it would call attention to Article 300 of the Convention, which provides that, "States Parties shall fulfil in good faith the obligations assumed under this Convention and shall exercise the rights, jurisdiction and freedoms recognized in this Convention in a manner which would not constitute an abuse of right." While being fully aware that its claims essentially deal with territorial sovereignty, that China has never accepted any compulsory procedures in respect of those claims, and that there has been an agreement existing between the two States to settle their relevant disputes by negotiations, the Philippines has nevertheless initiated, by unilateral action, the present arbitration. This surely contravenes the relevant provisions of the Convention, and does no service to the peaceful settlement of the disputes.

85. In view of what is stated above and in light of the manifest lack of jurisdiction on the part of the Arbitral Tribunal, the Chinese Government has decided not to accept or participate in the present arbitration, in order to preserve China's sovereign right to choose the means of peaceful settlement of its own free will and the effectiveness of its 2006 declaration, and to maintain the integrity of Part XV of the Convention as well as the authority and solemnity of the international legal regime for the oceans. This position of China will not change.

VI. Conclusions

86. It is the view of China that the Arbitral Tribunal manifestly has no jurisdiction over this arbitration, unilaterally initiated by the Philippines, with regard to disputes between China and the Philippines in the South China Sea.

Firstly, the essence of the subject-matter of the arbitration is the territorial sovereignty over the relevant maritime features in the South China Sea, which is beyond the scope of the Convention and is consequently not concerned with the interpretation or application of the Convention.

Secondly, there is an agreement between China and the Philippines to settle their disputes in the South China Sea by negotiations, as embodied in bilateral instruments and the DOC. Thus the unilateral initiation of the present arbitration by the Philippines has clearly violated international law.

Thirdly, even assuming that the subject-matter of the arbitration did concern the interpretation or application of the Convention, it has been excluded by the 2006 declaration filed by China under Article 298 of the Convention, due to its being an integral part of the dispute of maritime delimitation between the two States.

Fourthly, China has never accepted any compulsory procedures of the Convention with regard to the Philippines' claims for arbitration. The Arbitral Tribunal shall fully respect the right of the States Parties to the Convention to choose the means of dispute settlement of their own accord, and exercise its competence to decide on its jurisdiction within the confines of the Convention. The initiation of the present arbitration by the Philippines is an abuse of the compulsory dispute settlement procedures under the Convention. There is a solid basis in international law for China's rejection of and non-participation in the present arbitration.

87. China consistently adheres to the policy of friendly relations with its neighbouring States, and strives for fair and equitable solution in respect of disputes of territorial sovereignty and maritime delimitation by way of negotiations on the basis of equality and the Five Principles of Peaceful Co-existence. China holds that negotiations is always the most direct, effective, and universally used means for peaceful settlement of international disputes.

88. After years of diplomatic efforts and negotiations, China has successfully resolved land boundary disputes with twelve out of its fourteen neighbours, delimiting and demarcating some 20,000 kilometres in length of land boundary in the process, which accounts for over 90% of the total length of China's land boundary. On 25 December 2000, China and Vietnam concluded, following negotiations, the Agreement between the People's Republic of China and the Socialist Republic of Viet Nam on the Delimitation of the Territorial Seas, the

Exclusive Economic Zones and Continental Shelves in Beibu Bay, establishing a maritime boundary between the two States in Beibu Bay. On 11 November 1997, the Agreement on Fisheries between the People's Republic of China and Japan was signed. On 3 August 2000, the Agreement on Fisheries between the Government of the People's Republic of China and the Government of the Republic of Korea was signed. On 24 December 2005, the Agreement between the Government of the People's Republic of China and the Government of the Democratic People's Republic of Korea for Joint Development of Oil Resources at Sea was signed. All these are provisional arrangements pending the maritime delimitation between China and those States.

89. The facts show that, as long as States concerned negotiate in good faith and on the basis of equality and mutual benefit, territorial and maritime delimitation disputes can be resolved properly between them. This principle and position of China equally apply to its disputes with the Philippines in the South China Sea.

90. China does not consider submission by agreement of a dispute to arbitration as an unfriendly act. In respect of disputes of territorial sovereignty and maritime rights, unilateral resort to compulsory arbitration against another State, however, cannot be taken as a friendly act, when the initiating State is fully aware of the opposition of the other State to the action and the existing agreement between them on dispute settlement through negotiations. Furthermore, such action cannot be regarded as in conformity with the rule of law, as it runs counter to the basic rules and principles of international law. It will not in any way facilitate a proper settlement of the dispute between the two countries. Instead it will undermine mutual trust and further complicate the bilateral relations.

91. In recent years, the Philippines has repeatedly taken new provocative actions in respect of Huangyan Dao and Ren'ai Jiao. Such actions have gravely hindered mutual political trust between China and the Philippines, and undermined the amicable atmosphere for China and ASEAN member States to implement the DOC and consult on the proposed Code of Conduct in the South China Sea. In fact, in the region of Southeast Asia, it is not China that has become "increasingly assertive"; it is the Philippines that has become increasingly provocative.

92. The issue of the South China Sea involves a number of States, and is compounded by complex historical background and sensitive political factors. Its final resolution demands patience and political wisdom from all parties concerned. China always maintains that the parties concerned shall seek proper ways and means of settlement through consultations and negotiations on the basis of respect for historical facts and international law. Pending final settlement, all parties concerned should engage in dialogue and cooperation to preserve peace and stability in the South China Sea, enhance mutual trust, clear up doubts, and create conditions for the eventual resolution of the issue.

93. The unilateral initiation of the present arbitration by the Philippines will not change the history and fact of China's sovereignty over the South China Sea Islands and the adjacent waters; nor will it shake China's resolve and determination to safeguard its sovereignty and maritime rights and interests; nor will it affect the policy and position of China to resolve the relevant disputes by direct negotiations and work together with other States in the region to maintain peace and stability in the South China Sea.

Source: http://www.fmprc.gov.cn/mfa_eng/zxxx_662805/t1217147.shtml

Index

Bold page numbers indicate figures, *italic* numbers indicate tables.

For Product Safety Concerns and Information please contact our EU representative GPSR@taylorandfrancis.com Taylor & Francis Verlag GmbH, Kaufingerstraße 24, 80331 München, Germany